Iran as Imagined Nation

Iran as Imagined Nation

Second Edition

Mostafa Vaziri

gorgias press

2013

Gorgias Press LLC, 954 River Road, Piscataway, NJ, 08854, USA

www.gorgiaspress.com

Copyright © 2013 by Gorgias Press LLC

Originally published in 1993

2013 ℺

ISBN 978-1-4632-0227-9

Second Edition

Front cover: map of Iran by Ibrahim Müteferrika produced in c. 1729 (with the permission of National Széchényi Library of Hungary, Budapest. Shell number: Budapest, OSZK TR 7 656). The photographs are of a group of European Orientalists and Iranian literati.

Library of Congress Cataloging-in-Publication Data

Vaziri, Mostafa, 1956-
  Iran as imagined nation / by Mostafa Vaziri.
      pages cm
  Includes bibliographical references and index.
  ISBN 978-1-4632-0227-9
  1. Nationalism--Iran--History. 2. National characteristics, Iranian. 3. Iranians--Ethnic identity. I. Title.
  DS266.V39 2013
  320.540955--dc23

2013019279

"History is not the past;
It is what we say about the past."

Michael G. Morony

This book is dedicated to those who have chosen to break away from territorial, religious and ethnic boasting for the sake of global dialogue and harmony – such people are the true transmitters of delight in the world.

TABLE OF CONTENTS

FOREWORD TO THE SECOND EDITION

Exactly twenty years after the first release of *Iran as Imagined Nation* (1993), it gives me great pleasure to revise my book and add an epilogue. The epilogue emphasizes updated conclusions related to core arguments and the central thesis of the book, considering the latest scholarship in the field and engaging in renewed arguments on the historicism of Iranian national identity to the extent that they were not treated in the first edition, and also offers perspectives on the implications of national identity today. The revision of the first edition text involved the shortening of parts of chapter one and honing various points in consecutive chapters. The diacritic marks in transliterating some Arabic and Persian words and names have been made consistent throughout the text, although some commonly known words, such as: 'Dari', 'Farsi' and 'Sasanian' are written without diacritics.

In 1993, the seminal thesis of this short book provided an alternative paradigm: challenging the dominant nationalist historiography which had anachronistically conceptualized and traced Iranian national identity to the remote past. The goal behind writing this book was not to produce a replacement history for Iran or an encyclopedia of Iranian topics to meet the wide-ranging demands of scholars whose scholarship had been rooted in the old methodology. Instead the book was intended to open an investigation into how the indiscriminate and imprecise construction of Iranian national history and the resulting invention of a 'national' identity for the people of antiquity had transpired. Though some critics detracted from what the book offered, only focusing on what it lacked, the book's controversial arguments have triggered a number of deeper studies regarding Iranian national identity since 1993. The critics of the book believe too much emphasis has been put on Orientalism and less credit has been granted to the rise of domestic nationalism for the formation of national identity. This has been a misreading. Chapter 8 of the book in fact emphasizes how the internal nationalist doctrine boosted and promoted Iranism and Iranian identity. However, the goal of the book has been chiefly to trace and challenge the work of the Orientalists and bring to light the anachronism of their conception of continuous Iranian identity from ancient times.

Since the thesis of the book probes the authenticity of rooting Iranian identity in the remote past, readers might ask how I view this historical challenge in relation to my own personal feelings towards Iran as the country of my birth. To answer this question I must share that I have wonderful memories of growing up in Tehran — my friends, my schooling, hearing sweet anecdotes from my parents, and experiencing a bond with the community where I grew up. I have also always been grateful that Persian has been my mother tongue, giving me access to fantastic world-class Persian literature. At the same time, as a social scientist I am not reluctant to confront new and noteworthy ideas for reflection and investigation even though it may challenge the so-called established history of the country of my birth. Thus this book is not about my personal feelings towards Iran, but rather is an invitation to investigate history in a responsible fashion by using other measuring tools such as anthropology and critical analysis, taking it out of the monopoly of a few who have perpetuated their at times stultifying assumptions about the past.

History by its nature is an inexact discipline that has often been manipulated by the array of feelings, beliefs, and old-fashioned religious dogma transmitted by pre-modern historians. Historians and other social scientists of the last two hundred years reconstructed the past based on their own generational, short-lived ideological orientations without giving consideration to the fluid nature of nation-state and nationalism. Today's academia has accepted the challenge of making the discipline more intellectually rigorous, dynamic, and objective, but of course not without resistance from those whose ideas are being questioned. While controversial, the arguments in this book certainly do not stem from my personal feelings and views, but rather from a deeper intellectual reasoning.

On a different level, academic writings on national identity need eventually to become morally justifiable, non-chauvinistic, and non-anachronistic, avoiding overtly national assertions. The nationalists' narrow claim of Iran being a unique nation possessing more than its share of importance on the world stage is an improper, intellectually sluggish approach for our time and age, abhorrent to neighboring communities, and distasteful in its lack of subtlety in approaching the question of national identity. It is more desirable for our generation to deem the histories and achievements of other communities of the world just as significant and alluring as our own.

From the perspective of the new global setting, national identities solidify our external differences by emphasizing those who 'belong' to our group and those who are 'the other', but in reality all of humanity, despite national or regional differences, shares the same space on the surface of the planet. Modern transportation and communication networks have helped us transcend our parochial pre-modern perceptions of other cultures, as exotic as they still may seem to us. Many travellers as well as social scientists have been able to learn languages and enjoy what other communities of humanity have to offer.

As a result of this global mobility, means of communication, and higher levels of education and socioeconomic status, people of diverse countries and cultures have been able to connect with other like-minded individuals who share the same occupation or savor the same spiritual and emotional inclinations in life. These encounters have, to a small extent, weakened the blind prejudice of people who exclusively identify themselves in terms of the inhabitants of their own countries, whether they have anything substantive in common with them besides their shared national identity or not. Interpersonal human connection can even supersede national identity. This modern phenomenon opens up another aspect of identity, beyond national identity, and has served to remedy some of the harsh, limited views of nationalism and national identity. The human mind is in many ways flexible and infinite and can adjust to new and self-constructed circumstances, yet it can also be deceived by illusive, finite interpretations of reality. The idea of national identity is only one of such finite historical 'illusions'.

As a final comment, given the recent rise of debates on modern nationalism and the global ramifications of national identity, the appearance of this second edition is timely and I hope it contributes to ongoing dialogue and debate.

ACKNOWLEDGMENTS

The revision of this book has been possible thanks to my friend Chandra Khaki who converted the pdf version of the entire book into Word. Thanks to Gorgias Press and their recognition of the continued relevance of this book, it will finally appear in an affordable paperback. I am pleased to express my gratitude in writing to those who inspired and helped me to produce this epilogue. Above all, I am indebted to my partner, Allison, whose readings and discussions of various drafts made significant contributions to the quality of the epilogue. The quality was improved and arguments were sharpened with the help of reading and commenting by several colleagues mentioned here. My childhood friend and intellectual mentor, Dr. Asghar Feizi, insistently encouraged me to pursue the second edition of this book, whose content was debated in the hundreds of discussions we pursued in Berkeley between 1989 and 1992. He deserves my deepest appreciation for reading and commenting on the major themes of this book. Needless to say, Professor Michael G. Morony has continued to be the inspiration and a pillar in my research to find a better balance in presenting my arguments. There are no words to express my deep gratitude for his mentorship and encouragement. I am thankful to Professor Afshin Matin-Asgari for his graceful and precise recommendations, as well as for sharing with me some sources, including his own chapter on national identity. My appreciation goes to Dr. Denis Hermann for his sharp suggestions and for sharing a number of sources with me, as well as for our earlier exchanges about the themes of this book. Professor Geoffrey Nash deserves many thanks for taking an interest in this book and sending me his sound recommendations. I am thankful to Professor Parvaneh Pourshariati for sharing with me her ideas and tips of pre-modern Iranian identity.

I would like to thank my dear friend, Dr. Uta Maley, for her continuous support of my academic work. It is my pleasure to thank Dr. László Pászti, Head of the Map Department of the National Széchényi Library of Hungary in Budapest, and Tamás Sajó for facilitating the permission to reproduce the map of Iran on the cover of this book. For their correspondence and for sending me articles, I am grateful to Professors Roy Parviz Mottahedeh and Touraj Daryaee. I am indebted to my dedicated student in Innsbruck, Jonathan Jancsary, who graciously helped me with locating some sources. Finally I am grateful to Dr. Melonie Schmierer-Lee, Acquisitions Editor of Gorgias Press, for her enthusiastic support in order to provide researchers and students of Iranian and Middle Eastern Studies with an updated and affordable paperback edition of *Iran as Imagined Nation*.

Mostafa Vaziri
Innsbruck, Austria & Kathmandu, Nepal
2012–2013

PREFACE

We may often take scholarly and academic works as serious, scientific, and absolute. In their proper parameters, the terms 'serious' and 'scientific' may be appropriate, but 'absolute' runs the risk of becoming embroiled in endless dogmatic reasoning. I undertook this study to address a misconception in scholarship in a scholarly fashion for the interests of objectivity and the improvement of reasoning in the ranges of social science topics. For the past several years I have had this hypothesis in mind and have been gathering data and pursuing research and dialogues. The more I thought about it, the more I became convinced that the hypothesis and reasoning behind my paradigm is more or less valid for many modern countries. Thus, when I took a trip around the world in the fall of 1990, I became curious about the history and identity of the different people whose countries I visited.

In the course of writing this book, I began to realize that my national sentiment — as that of many people like me whether from Iran or elsewhere — has been artificially based on differences framed as racial and territorial stereotypes by historians and national governments. Obviously, there have been very significant differences among countries, as indeed there have been differences among indigenous people of the same country; but these differences among countries, at least as portrayed in relation to Iran, were being justified in such chauvinistic terms that at times the resulting anti-Arab and anti-Turkish feelings took a pathological direction.

I have also considered how one develops a national sentiment and identity based on one's attachments, memories, and personal experiences. This type of sentiment comes when a person travels abroad or is exiled or faces foreign entities. It seems that when one says "I miss [or love] my country," one means more specifically the political unit in the geographical zone of Iran. There is a sense of cultural and linguistic attraction, besides personal memories. Perhaps, simplifying this feeling or nostalgia, it is comparable to saying that the person misses his neighborhood, playmates, house, shops, and places he frequently visited; that he misses the cultural codes, symbols, and language he once used to communicate with others; and most importantly that he misses himself in those circumstances of a time now past. In sum, one presumes at most that what one really misses is a city or farm or district where one has grown up (and not even all its neighborhoods), rather than missing the entire land. An Azerbaijani person who has not been to Baluchistan, is unlikely to miss that place in any realistic way, whatever its national designation, because it has no affiliate memories. The person will obviously not miss barren lands, expanses of sand, and unbearably harsh areas either (unless one grows up in them.) Thus, there is quite an array of psychological issues involved in maintaining a national sentiment. A fair explanation for patriotic sentiment may simply be that it is altogether a subjective matter — only a state of mind.

In modern times, the assimilation of cultural codes and the spread of historical values of a people in a single language (in an electronic age) have helped provide a cultural attachment and social relationship within a geographical region under a political system. At times, this cultural and social mechanism which may be marked as a racist phenomenon has been confused with a political entity over a region; as in the case of Iran, it has been hammered into the popular and collective consciousness that the two are synonymous.

In the final comment, I must say any preconceived national biases giving way to the lack of understanding of self and the long and complex history of human beings would lead to misconception, distance, and eventually distortion of reality. In favoring national sentiment and uniting the 'chosen people' of the time whether in its religious, linguistic, or geographical context, the knowledge and the human compassion toward one another have to suffer. Perhaps Saʿdī (d. 1291) recognized the ultimate fact that the imaginary territorial lines come and go, but the real essence of a nation is estimated against how noble the men and women think in each given generation.

> "The sons of men are members in a body whole related.
> For of a single essence are they each and all created.

When a Fortune persecutes with pain one member surely.
The other members of the body cannot stand securely.
O you who from another's troubles turn aside your view
It is not fitting they bestow the name of 'Man' on you."[1]

ACKNOWLEDGMENTS

These words can hardly express the depth of my gratitude to those who helped shape the form and content of this book, but before expressing my appreciation I would like to point out the circumstances that enabled me to think of writing this book. Certain dialogues and conversations create unexpected and provoking visions that intellectually, spiritually, and emotionally change the course of one's logic and comprehension of things. I have treasured the outcome of my conversations with Professor Michael G. Morony of UCLA, who has had an immense impact on my vision, my intellect, and my reasoning over the past few years. My attempt to make a book out of this intellectual inheritance validates my sense of trying to capture only a little of the highly sophisticated culture possessed by our most profound teachers, like Morony. I must also pay tribute to Professor Morony for reading the entire manuscript and making sound criticisms and suggestions.

The generous efforts of Professor Hamid Algar of UC/Berkeley in reading and commenting on the manuscript have resulted in an addition to the overall quality of this work. I am indebted as well to Professor Martin Schwartz of UC / Berkeley for having read Chapters 2, 3, and 4 and made numerous helpful comments, particularly on pre-Islamic issues and on the usage of the term *arya*.

For developing different aspects of the manuscript, I am grateful to a wide audience of scholars and intellectuals who contributed their ideas. Among these are Drs. Ravan Farhadi, Laurance Michalak, Housain Ziai, John Hayes, Assef Bayat, Mohammad Saffouri, Ervend Abrahamian, and Hooshang Amirahmadi. I must also thank several friends whose ongoing discussions and arguments guided me to understand other aspects

---

[1] Young, "The National and International Relations of Iran," p. 204.

of my hypothesis. In particular, I wish to acknowledge Asghar Feizi, a true friend and supporter, and Raymond Rakhshani. The thoughtful counterarguments of those who opposed my hypothesis were in themselves highly constructive. This book would not have been accomplished in its present format, had it not been for the unequal support of my brother, Morteza.

Finally, I am grateful to Steve Grey for editing and to Niloofar Mohtasham-Nouri for typing the manuscript as well as for lending their patience and frequent insight. I would also like to credit Evelyn Fazio for her earlier remarks and encouragement. Mary Glenn of Paragon House deserves special mention for her support and enthusiasm.

The hypothesis of this book is an experiment to envision, expand, and sustain dialogue that I hope will challenge prevailing old and (at times) colonial paradigms. I take sole responsibility for the inadequacies of the present book.

Mostafa Vaziri
Berkeley, California
January 1992

INTRODUCTION

Identity is an expression of a human bonding with community that we see in various groupings and that goes far back into history. In part it involves simple us-versus-them thinking: Anyone who did not speak a dialect of Greek in ancient times was termed a *barbarian* — because their words sounded to Greek ears like *bar-bar-bar-bar*. In many aboriginal tribal groups, the name of the ethnic entity in a particular region means (in that group's language) "the people," meaning I suppose that anyone not belonging to that group is not, in its eyes, altogether a person (or of the people). This seems also to be at the core of any claim to be a chosen people, people with a special relationship to God — a claim made by various racial, ethnic, and religious groups.

Modern nation-states have tried very hard to tap into this religion-based fervor of "belonging" in order to gain obedient and zealous adherents. However, the European contribution to nationalism has been particularly harmful, since it makes use of pseudo-science to establish unalterable "factual" categories by which all peoples are separated, labeled, and disposed of unequally in what is in reality an entirely arbitrary, self-serving, misanthropic way. By the same token, the appropriation of true science and the scientific method by opportunists, charlatans, and clever racists has led to a widespread discrediting of science among many people who are not themselves scientists. Western social scientists of the nineteenth century developed and approved a racial theory that coincided with ongoing national prejudices in Europe. This theory may have taken advantage of pre-existing, popular notions to justify Europeans' differences from each other and from people outside Europe, but the racial theory and the nationalist methodology it supported were nonetheless adopted by the academic world as a means of conceptualizing communities based on their alleged primordial scientifically known differences. Iran

1

was one such area to fall under investigation by the European Orientalists using this racial and national perspective.

This book questions the formation of the concept of national identity, both in a theoretical and in a practical sense, in Europe and Iran. Special emphasis is placed on the rise of this concept in historiography and other fields of social science in Europe and its subsequent (and anachronistic) imposition on Oriental lands, in particular Iran. Painstaking studies have previously been done both on the subject of national consciousness in general and on the topic of Iran's national development, but no study has ever attempted to investigate the roots of the rise of Iranian identity both in scholarship and in the sociopolitical scene. The present volume examines this in three sections: first, the rise of national identity in Europe; second, the conceptualization of Iranian identity in the standard reference works of Orientalism; and third, the emergence of Iranian identity as a result of sociopolitical upheaval of the nineteenth and twentieth centuries.

The emergence of national identity and of nation-states in Europe is investigated first, not only to understand the social-historical factors that shaped that continent's nationalist and racial thinking but also to lay a foundation in argument interpreting the vision of eighteenth- through twentieth-century Western scholars in their study of the Orient and Iran. More than three centuries ago, when Europe bore the embryonic notion of modern national consciousness after having gone through the Reformation and having achieved stronger monarchical autonomy vis-à-vis the Church, it began to use vernacular languages in developing a philosophy that suited the political culture. The localization of language and its political emancipation from the Church, along with other sociopolitical upheavals, the industrial revolution, the Napoleonic wars, and various cultural transitions — all contributed to creating a historical situation in which local self-defense, autonomy, and cultural consciousness gave way to nationalism and national identity.

In its foreign encounters through colonialism, Europe experienced a growing sense of continental and racial distinction and superiority in relation to other areas. In the eighteenth and nineteenth centuries, when colonialism, racism, capitalism, and nationalism were all in historical high gear, academic studies erected the monumental edifice of Orientalism. At this stage, the

Aryan race was singled out in pseudo-scientific treatises as the unique, able, talented, and fully-evolved race among all others. The initial identification of similarities between Sanskrit and European languages by Sir William Jones in 1786 uncovered the Indo-European language family, a linguistic conception from which the Aryan racial model was conceived. The Aryan model, as developed subsequently by F. Schlegel, Franz Bopp, the Grimm brothers, Rask, Müller, and a few others, had a multilayered utility. First, it enabled the Europeans to invent an ancient proto-European civilization and antiquity for themselves along racial lines in Asia. Second, it promoted the invidious theory of the polygenesis of man. Greek ancestry was identified as the primary basis of European intellectual development, and all influences from non-Aryan sources (e.g., Africa) were rejected. Biological racism in Europe, the breakdown of the Indo-European racial family, and the progress of other social science studies led racial and national consciousness to become almost synonymous.

Thus, Europe in the past two centuries, influenced by its repudiation of theocracy, its status in the colonial setting, and its fascination with its own academic achievements, postulated a nationalist doctrine that took analogous forms in the fields of historiography, literature, linguistics, archaeology, ethnography, and art. In its conceptualization and categorization of other lands, European scholarship relied on the same vision and methodology of national and racial data-gathering as it did in studying its own territories, constructing national histories for various lands and imaginary entities such as Iran. The land of Iran and its imagined community formed one branch of Oriental Studies that produced an avalanche of reference works.

In this volume, racial and national methodologies used by the European Orientalists to study Iran are challenged and disputed, based on their own internal shortcomings and on a number of short studies that have been done in order to proceed with a non-national, non-racial, and probably with a more sophisticated approach to historical events. *Iran* as a geographical designation was taken by the European Orientalists and transformed into a 'homogeneous' historical people endowed with all kinds of national and racial characteristics, in part to serve the ends of the political and racial consciousness being championed by authoritarian European Orientalism. The resulting interest in antiquity awakened (or perhaps engendered) the pre-Islamic and ancient national consciousness of Iran. (Egypt was the subject of similar treatment.) Philological and archaeological finds were methodologically used in an Aryan context to reinterpret and vitalize a sense of Iranism, in contradistinction to the identities of neighboring Arabs, Turks, and others. The Orientalists thus forged the name of *Iran* not only to stand for a people but also for a language family, a civilization, a culture, and a tradition, without fear of contradiction that in both the ancient and the Islamic periods there could not have been a homogeneous Iranian world. This conception obviously gained considerable credence in the age of nationalism and of overwhelmingly inescapable power of Orientalism. Philology and archaeology were employed jointly to study and label the artifacts of antiquity and to connect literature with a reconstructed national tradition by means of a national method of historiography for the Islamic period all in order to separate what had been Iranian or part of the Iranian world from what had not.

This volume also engages in various philological interpretations, such as that of A. I. Silvestre de Sacy in the eighteenth century that provided the mechanism for further national investigation and the establishment of national identity and racial consciousness on the part of the inhabitants of Iran in ancient times. In general, such Orientalists have used the ethnic or linguistic differences evident in modern times to justify the stereotype of political or cultural nationalism among the communities involved, particularly in trying to forge a non-existent national identity for the people of the remote past. The nationalist and arbitrary roots by this historiographic method, which influenced all other studies, is investigated in order to demonstrate how much it rested on preconceived racial and national biases of modern times. Recognition of these obsolete grounds may encourage us to move away from this approach toward a more tangible and legitimate philosophy of history.

Traditionally in Islamic sources, *Iranshahr* and *Fars* appear to refer to areas of land, and not to ethnicity or national identity. Thus, the use of the term *Iran* or *Fars* in literature and historical writings of the Islamic era was not intended by various medieval authors or dynasties to serve purposes of political propaganda or national revivalism as perceived by the Orientalists and nationalist authors. The pre-modern dynasties which ruled various territories within the Iranian region only wished to expand their jurisdiction in every direction possible, not merely to the limits of some vaguely understood 'Aryan' or 'Iranian' homeland. The politicization of the name of the land is strictly a nineteenth but surely a twentieth-century phenomenon that cannot be applied to the past, especially to remote, complex circumstances. This explains why the dynasties from the Ṭāhirids in the ninth century all the way to the Safavids in the sixteenth century, as far as we know, did not use the term *Iran* in any political sense.

In the Safavid, Zand, and Qājār dynasties preceding the twentieth century and the rise of Reza Shah, the term *Iran* began gradually to be used for the land in an administrative context and to a small degree (toward the end of the Qājār dynasty) in a political sense. The earlier elites had no real concept of a homogeneous Iranian people, culture, or tradition until these ideas were learned from European literature by native secularist thinkers and used to enforce national identity and to support patriotic indoctrination during the reign of Reza Shah and his son from the 1920s to the 1970s.

However, the assurance with which such Orientalists as George Rawlinson, James Darmesteter, E. G. Browne, Vladimir Minorsky, W. Barthold, B. Spuler, E. C. Bosworth, R. Frye, and many others made the necessary dynastic connection, linking the literature (in Farsi language) to a national tradition and subsequently formulating an Iranian conception of history must be analyzed and challenged. The tyranny of their paradigm and method left very little room for opposing points of view or philosophies of history. Linking the Farsi language with other traditions and historical events to the Iranian plateau by suggesting that the political dynasties that arose over that land (Safavid, Qājār, and later) were the progeny of a long and continuous Iranian heritage marks a simplistically linear vision of history. Farsi, as a transnational language was recognized by the Orientalists to be exclusively the national language and historical/cultural property of Iran; and subsequently this attribution gained momentum, particularly during the nationalist period in Iran. Concomitantly, other languages in Iran were trivialized. The history of a single language (in this case, Farsi) was linked to an entire geographical zone (Iran) in order to create the necessary nationalist basis between culture and territory (as well as between language and ethnicity). This approach was the method successfully used by nationalists in Europe and thus was applied to Iran.

The hypothesis of this book disagrees with the prevailing method of Western Orientalism, which has assigned national and racial designations to the people of antiquity and to those diverse groups who subsequently inhabited the geographic zone of Iran. The current method has obviously been elucidated in modern national and racial terms. This anachronistic treatment of Iran by European historiography gave the land's twentieth-century governments and its masses grounds to be content about their forged identity. Likewise, elsewhere it made people proud of their glory and persistence in history as Iranians. Nobody ever asked who is an Iranian? What does a Kurd have in common with a Gilaki, given that their languages, traditions, and histories have been totally dissimilar? Apart from the fervent domestic nationalist rhetoric, the philological answer provided was that they both belong to an Iranian language family. But this ignored the fact that neither the Kurds nor the Gilakis ever used the term *Iranian* in their tradition. Furthermore, the classification of the Iranian language family was a recent academic undertaking; thus, the proposition that an Iranian consciousness existed among the speakers of these language families in the past is improper and anachronistic. Obviously, many of these obscure issues were swept under the rug by the Orientalists or were answered in the form of common citizenship and patriotic propaganda by the modern centralized state in the twentieth century.

However, taking into consideration that the historical Iranian national identity has been an anachronistic conceptualization by the Orientalists, the crucial question is when the present Iranian identity began to emerge. The final section of this volume analyzes the factors involved in the nationalist secular movement toward modernization in the nineteenth century, which marked the transition period into an era of nationhood. Nationalism emerged not because it was a long-dormant but now-reawakening force[1] but because the ruling elites, the intelligentsia, the state, and eventually the clerics recognized a benefit in homogenizing the population by

---

[1] Munck, *The Difficult Dialogue: Marxism and Nationalism*, p. 144.

leading them toward nationhood. Historical heterogeneity in the continuing old imperial rule of Iran was immaterial to the process at hand, since modernization required that the unity of all communities whether religious, regional, or tribal under a single state territorial banner, be preserved. Under the influence of the European notion of nationalism the state territorial unit of Iran was used by the secularists to create a common feeling and identity among all the people. Consequently, the Turkish, Arab, Turkoman, Baluchi, Gilaki, Mazandarāni, Kurdish, Luri, Armenian, Assyrian, and other religious, linguistic, and tribal communities that lay within the old administrative boundary demarcating the Iranian plateau during the transition to modernism were all termed Iranians.

Different aspects of nation-building had to be practiced both by the intelligentsia and by the state. Legal reform promising everyone equality before the law, the nationwide use of the Farsi language, and the creation of textbooks imbued with nationalistic rhetoric were all employed to link and integrate all ethnic and linguistic groups who had previously lived so disconnectedly from one another. By examining the sociopolitical circumstances, the available literature, newspapers, and the school textbooks of the Qājār period and then relating these to those of the Pahlavi period, we can observe the transition from a traditional parochial system of identity, historical interpretation, and self-conceptualization to a state-sponsored identity. Certainly the Pahlavi regime's ability to project itself as central to the national tradition of Iran allowed it to characterize any unauthorized reform or opposing philosophy that arose in a scholarly or political context as fundamentally anti-Iranian. Likewise, any effort to study and understand regional, ethnic, or religious differences among populations within modern-day Iran was interpreted as undermining the historical unity of the population as a whole. Thus, political pluralism/dissent and cultural diversity may be noted as casualties of the ruling methodology. The nationalist academia has done no less in maintaining the notion of Iranian nationhood from ancient times onward.

The practical implications of the nationalistic/secular method established by the Orientalists and maintained by the secular natives of Iran had several far-reaching results. For one, it marginalized religious history and religious perceptions of the past.

This must have contributed to the antagonism toward secularism felt by the clergy and more pious people that reached explosive proportions in recent decades. Irrespective of their popular reception, the secular Iranian identity and the Muslim identity were at times mustered in confrontational rhetoric to create a national feeling among the urban and educated inhabitants of Iran that to a certain extent depends on cultural schizophrenia.

Finally, in scrutinizing national identity and its problems, we must cast our doubts over the speculations of the Orientalists, who constructed national history without accountability, and we must question whether the selection and application of the name *Iran* to the land could support their thesis of a larger ethnicity, culture, language, and tradition within the multicultural and multiethnic region thus designated. Methodologically, the same challenge could be made in arguing about other geographical designations or names of countries that do not necessarily support the cultural elements and internal cohesion necessary for common identity. This may be particularly true of countries or modern states in the Middle East, significantly because the name of the geographical zone has been applied to the general identity of the people in those regions.

Since the scope of this volume covers the method by which the Orientalists reconstructed Iranian identity and the impact of the resulting identity on the sociopolitical scene in Iran, it is perhaps appropriate to allude briefly to several concepts here that are not emphasized elsewhere in the text.

First, we must consider the concept of continuity. Often the transmission of norms, beliefs, and practices through different historical phases to the present has been interpreted in nationalist terms as evidence for the survival of a particular culture and people in a particular geographical zone from time immemorial. But the transmission of various cultural elements and the presence or absence of continuity in other areas of a civilization cannot prove the thesis of continuity in the identity of a particular people.

In reality, the concept of continuity depends on at least three distinct areas of human activity and potential change: language, ethnicity, and culture (including religion, custom, and knowledge of tradition). The Orientalists, however, generally focused on language as dispositive of ethnicity and then set about analyzing (or constructing) features of culture that confirmed their language-based preconceptions. A sober examination of ethnicity — at least in the case of the Iranian or Islamic period — would have been fatal to these preconceptions, but it did not occur. The Farsi language remained fairly stable from the ninth century onward (although not only in Iran) and thus provided some basis for finding continuity. However, I am concerned chiefly with the element of culture, treated as a source of continuity, in this introduction.

The adoption of, let us say, the pre-Islamic cultural practices of late antiquity and their transmission during the Islamic period (although this periodization may be totally arbitrary) to the Muslims does not simply and exclusively represent an unaffected continuation of the identity of the people who lived before the Muslims. But the admixture of the old norms with the new ones expresses its own cultural and political syntheses. It becomes more confusing when a supposed continuity of these cultural elements is attributed to a specific geographical area or to a modern nation-state in order to create a historical pedigree for the people of that nation.

It is true that Iran was never emptied of one population and refilled with another, but the presence of residual practices from antiquity intermixed with new ones in each generation or associated with the settlement of new people in different eras should not lead us to conclude that the survival of selective cultural norms represents an identity of a selected people. Such a distorted, linear vision is responsible for the manifestly false image of stagnant consistency and internal cohesion among the people living in Iran throughout its history. By transcending the issue of purity of identity and the goal of linking it to the selective continuity of cultural elements, we will be inclined to take a cautious position and not be fooled by the representations of nationalist jargon.

The survival of Zoroastrian, Manichean, and Islamic (Shi‘i) tenets in the religious sphere; of various Indian, Mongol, and Turkish cultural elements; and of hundreds of other dimensions from other communities have all in different degrees influenced, changed, and institutionalized forms of cultural continuity in different parts of Iran. Without underrating the originality of synthetic borrowings and lendings of cultural traditions by people of each generation in each region or tribe, we may reasonably conclude that the sequence of cultural interactions and linkages with the past has very little to do with modern propaganda and its imposition of certain singled-out historical cultural elements retroactively imposed by a state over the vast diverse population of a nation. Likewise, the survival of certain Zoroastrian or Shi'i cultural traditions that have been disseminated nationwide by the state as part of national culture are not necessarily a part of certain regional or tribal cultural traditions. Magnifying certain historical traditions of a tribe or other group of people into nationwide observations can hardly be taken as certain proof of the historicity of a single cultural tradition or a single identity for all the people of a nation. This is true even though a single identity has been imposed in modern times by the state after having established close ties with the dominant cultural features (particularly those that represent a historical value).

The survival of bits and pieces of various cultural traditions and their mixture with new ones is a creative adaptation that transcends the modern national direction linking pre-Islamic Iran to the Islamic period and thence to the present time represents only a modern retrospection and periodization of a complex cultural history involving a heterogeneous region. The effectiveness and the density of settlements by various new tribes and populations in different regions have played more or less important roles in cultural creativity. Thus it would be crude and disjointed to frame the extent of continuity (or absence thereof) between pre-Islamic and Islamic eras as a signs of Iranianness.

With regard to the transmission of Zoroastrian cultural elements to the non-Zoroastrian population or the transmission of the Turko-Mongol artistic style to the non-Turko-Mongol population, we should not assess such transmissions or similarities of cultural practices with the idea that they will easily determine the identity question in the historical process. What survived and flourished in different corners of Iran cannot have occurred within a national framework; it can only be replicated as such through modern nationalist interpretations.[2] Thus, historically speaking, the continuity of cultural elements is not necessarily a sign of national direction or identity of a particular nation, as the European nationalists perceived it.

---

[2] See Morony, *Iraq After the Muslim Conquest*, Introduction.

Another issue that deserves mention here is the relationship between Islam as a religious institution and Islam as a nation/national identity. In general terms, Islam appears to transcend the nation/national identity and yet adapt to its existence. Although Islam historically and theoretically has promoted the unity of all Muslims, it has been greatly affected by the reality of various preexisting or newly created cultural zones, whether in terms of language, religious beliefs, or other dominant cultural traditions. Thus the persistence of cultural zones has provided a mechanism for the subsequent development by individuals of consciousness as a Muslim and consciousness as a member of a cultural entity or zone. It was the existence of these cultural zones and the diverse Muslim populations within them that ultimately erected the phenomenon arbitrarily known as Islamic civilization. This was the outcome of the cultural creativity of Muslims not of Islam as such. However, the fruits of this civilization (at least according to the modern nation-states of the Islamic world) were results of the cultural zones and entities that are now modern nations.

Iran's claims with respect to its borrowing from and lending to Islamic civilization are based on the creativity and contributions of the cultural zone within its territory in pre-modern times. The institutionalization of pre-Islamic norms during the Islamic period is viewed as a continuation of the past and the emergence of the Farsi language (not even within Iran proper) and of cultural programming within the Islamic empire was claimed to be a specifically Iranian gift to Islamic culture. Thus the attitude compounded of being a Muslim and belonging to a cultural zone has in modern times been translated into the idea of belonging to a particular nation.

The other point that deserves to be mentioned has to do with general designations and their application to pre-modern times. Symbolic designations such as *Arab*, *'Ajam*, *Turk*, and *Tajik* were used more in the context of emphasizing the chiefly linguistic differences across different groups than in order to signify internal cohesion within any of those groups. The same is true for religious communities. The addressing of Christians as one group by Muslims, or *vice versa*, had far more to do with a general distinction of the other broad faith than with any implication of the internal homogeneity of either religion. Usually this fact is ignored by modern social scientists, leading to misperceptions about the identity of communities from sociological and historical standpoints.

When the so-called Arabs addressed their neighbors and their future subjects as *'Ajams* (translated as non-Arabs and/or other derogatory meanings),[3] they were aware of and emphasized the obvious sharp differences, particularly linguistic ones. But the usage of *'Ajam*, whatever it may have meant in context, referred neither to Arabs' own cultural homogeneity in the face of a foreign-language community nor to the homogeneity of the *'Ajam* community. It seems the term *'Ajam* became definable for the Arabs in terms of broad geographical and cultural differences from them, but from the so-called *'Ajami* point of view it is questionable whether the nature of these differences was understood and agreed on by each and all of the communities involved. In other words, *'Ajam* for the non-Arabs was a foreign application to their group, and its purpose of defining a congenial and common characteristic among them may have been vague and meaningless. In its Persian or Iranian context, the term *'Ajam* could apply to various ethnic groups in Iran (Lur, Kurd, Baluchi), or to all other non-Arab groups in the region. Unfortunately, failure to understand the ambiguous nature of the term has led modern historiographers and social scientists of Iranian Studies to distort its meaning and context.

Eventually, the term *'Ajam* came to be interpreted as having meant Iranian to the Arabs. Thus this foreign-coined term was granted much the same status as *Iran,* a geographical designation that the Orientalists chose as the identity of its population, as part of a nationalist historiographical approach that disregarded the lack of internal cohesion to support such a crude designation. It would therefore be wise to scrutinize the generally stereotyped (but now established) designations for possible historical flaws that might render them inappropriate for all practical purposes.

I am convinced that the constructed version of history about Iran, in its national context, has been associated with racial, national, and political views that do not deserve to be entirely

---

[3] Khanlari, *Z aban Shenāsī va Zabān-i Farsi*, p. 50.

discredited, but should be investigated in a responsible manner. This study establishes a methodological argument focusing on an attribution of national identity to people of the remote past that is problematic and anachronistic. It is unrealistic to marshal an argument on all the historical aspects and events recorded in the existing massive reference archives. Consequently, I have taken certain highlights of historical events constructed by prominent Orientalists for systematic analysis, both thematic and chronological.

The content of this volume invites the reader to escape the web of at times dehumanized racial and national biases and introduces a means to challenge the conservative academic literature that has had an unfortunate impact on national and racial stereotyping among people of Iran and people of neighboring countries. Although this work deals primarily with national identity, it envisions a transnational or non-national approach to history and seeks to encourage exuberant and dynamic intellectual discourse without obscuring our global ideals as one human family.

CHAPTER 1
EUROPE:
THE DAWN OF NATIONAL IDENTITY

Dominant European scholars of the nineteenth-century, including those who studied the Orient, were mostly from England, France and Germany, and they could not escape the web of European nationalism and its ramifications in all areas of thought and culture. Through the discipline of Orientalism, the complex historical and cultural components of the Orient were studied and imprudently were separated, sorted out and labeled as coming from pre-existing nations, with the assumption that such nations had taken a linear and conscious direction toward modern nation-states. The primary goal of highlighting the formation of national identity in Europe is to demonstrate how this modern concept impacted the ideology of nationalism and shaped the scholarly methodology applied in the fields of archaeology, historiography, literature and other areas of academia beginning in the late eighteenth century. This chapter also serves as a brief review of the extent to which European intellectual history gave rise to nationalism and nationalist academia.

THE EMERGENCE OF NATIONALISM

Nationalism has not always existed. If nationalism and national identity emerged in two different phases (or eras) and places — one European and the other non-European — then it must be possible to see the correlation between the two scenarios. The non-European manifestation of national sentiment, as argued and analyzed by the scholars of nationalism, has resulted from the reaction to colonial influences in these lands, although many other regional and indigenous socioeconomic and geographic factors have also been influential. European methods of historiography about non-European regions had a significant impact on the national thinking of the people of those lands. But how did

European nationalist thinking, which brought along a strong sense of nationhood, statehood, national identity, and rejection of the empirical ideal, occur without non-European influences? To answer this question, we must consider the use of vernacular languages after the Reformation, the appearance of literary figures, the new discoveries and development of language classification and their relationship to racial categories, the search for roots in antiquity, and the territorialization of communities under a banner of nation-state building and democracy.

DYNASTIES, NOT NATIONS

During the era of the Holy Roman Empire, the loyalty of Europeans was primarily to the Church and to the protectors of Christian interests, but with the empire's decline, concessionary dynasties became increasingly autonomous and powerful. The consolidation of power through dynastic linkage or military defeat created powerful monarchical institutions with a degree of Church involvement. It is important not to confuse the territories of medieval dynasties with what eventually became modern nation-states. The efforts of these early dynastic institutions were not directed at achieving fixed national goals. By 1500 CE, there were about 500 different political entities in Europe,[1] during which period the political and social orders were centripetal and hierarchical rather than boundary-oriented. Thus it is reasonable to think the impetus to create nations could not have originated during the Middle Ages. R. Emerson believes "what emerged in the way of national unity was an accidental by-product rather than an intended result."[2] In other words, in the fifteenth century to be Spanish meant to be Christian, "for there were no ethnic criteria to define what 'Spanish' meant."[3]

Often, wars in the pre-modern period were between dynasties rather than between nations. Many of these dynasties maintained their rule over a linguistically and culturally heterogeneous

---

[1] La Palombara, *Politics Within Nations*, p. 42.

[2] Emerson, *From Empire to Nation*, p. 120.

[3] Raskin, *Other Governments of Europe*, pp. 45–46.

population. The dynasties and empires of Habsburgs, Romanovs, Hohenzollerns and Ottomans (non-Europeans), ruled over a number of communities that only emerged as nations and joined the League of Nations when these empires dissolved in 1922.[4]

Ethnic and linguistic attachments and identity existed within this multileveled and multilayered system, but in a form still far removed from the modern sense of national identity. Loyalty was spontaneously given to the dominant and closest mechanism of government, not to what was imaginary and unreal to them then (and real to us today). The idea of national identity in Europe would not have occurred until the rise of nation-states in the eighteenth century and more rigorously in the nineteenth century.

THE DECLINE OF LATIN
AND THE RISE OF VERNACULAR LANGUAGES:
A BASIS FOR PROTO-NATIONAL IDENTITY

In the early stages of formation of the proto-national consciousness, the popularization of vernacular languages became primary. To understand the evolution of national consciousness, the role of language must be granted high importance both as an instrument of communication and as the basis for national thought. The Protestant Reformation and the change in the character of Latin in some sense corresponded to the rearrangement of the classical communities of feudal Christendom into smaller groups under more centralizing monarchs.[5] Printed material in vernacular languages was gradually becoming popular, and of course the success of Martin Luther, the agent of the Reformation, also had an impact on the use of the vernacular.

L. Febvre and H. J. Martin estimate that 77 percent of the books printed before 1500 CE were still in Latin; after 1500 CE, books appeared more and more frequently in vernacular languages.[6] Those who considered Latin a holy and inviolable

---

[4] Anderson, *Imagined Communities*, pp. 26, 104.

[5] Anderson, pp. 42–44.

[6] L. Febvre and H. J. Martin, *The Coming of the Books,* pp. 248–249; quoted by Anderson, p. 25.

language were now learning about a new perspective of knowledge and its link to historical progress. A new awareness emerged through language, changing the social and intellectual and eventually the political dynamics of Europe. Vernacular languages were used in many different ways to win the minds of those who spoke or understood them. As Benedict Anderson puts it, "the choice of language appears as a gradual unselfconscious, pragmatic ... development."[7] It was several centuries before French, a dialectal form of Latin, became the official language of the French courts of justice in 1539.[8] For the masses, however, spoken languages did not advance as rapidly as they did in print. By the Revolution of 1789, 50% of the people of France did not speak French at all and only 12–13% spoke a 'standardized' form of the language. In the North and South of France, nobody spoke French at all.[9] Similarly, only 2.5% of the inhabitants of Italy spoke Italian in 1860.[10]

Thus print language became an instrument of culture among the educated classes, linking people of similar linguistic background together (or those who chose to be educated in that language). In general, oral knowledge was inevitably replaced with print, and books monopolized the culture. Francis Bacon believed that print had altered the state of the world.[11] The imaginary territory of communities who spoke the same language, but with different dialects, was gradually being removed; print became the standard for "correct" language structure. However, the selection of a particular dialect to serve as the official accepted written language, for example, *Hochdeutsch*, gave fixity to the language. Although this method did not solve the differences between the dialects, it narrowed the extremities, allowing a better degree of communication through print.

---

[7] Anderson, p. 45.

[8] Ibid.

[9] Ferdinand Brunot (ed.), *Histoire de La Langue Française*, quoted by Eric Hobsbawm, *Nations and Nationalism since 1780*, p. 60.

[10] Tullio de Mauro, *Storio Linguistica dell'Italia*, p. 41, quoted in Hobsbawm, *Nations and Nationalism*, p. 61.

[11] Anderson, pp. 40–41.

The organic growth of languages began to have a direct impact on philosophical development on one hand and the defeat of Latin (from the Christian point of view, the legitimate language of God) on the other. Therefore, delatinization and creation of a channel of communication besides the spoken language became a source of inspiration. Language now became the measurement of the character of the community or nation it which it was spoken. Linguistic theories and the appearance of influential individuals in their respective fields of literature and philosophy laid a more profound foundation for the proposition that language was the basis of distinction between nations, and was a way of decreasing the domination of Latin. (The same perception was developed with Farsi as the basis of Iranian character and as a means to reduce the domination of Arabic.)

The proliferation of literature in native languages carried messages, metaphors, symbols, and fanciful ideas to native readers by stretching their historical imagination about the past and themselves. This kind of proto-national literature and the creation of epics inspired individuals to think about their national origin and their glory, but at the same time, in a way darkened and obscured their common heritage with other people.[12]

The advancement and establishment of the written language in its eloquent and exact forms provided a mechanism to theorize about the concept of unity. Toward the end of the eighteenth century, German-speaking literary figures such as T. G. Herder made strong statements about language as the foundation and the vehicle for the thought of a nation. Johann Gottlieb Fichte suggested the validity of the German language, regardless of political or religious affiliations, as the source of national sentiment.[13] Following Herder, a very influential philologist appeared, Friedrich von Schlegel, who considered German language as the basis of national unity. His period and ideas coincided with the romantic perspective. Schlegel's research in the field of Indo-European, which became popular in later years, as

---

[12] Hayes, *Essays on Nationalism*, p. 34.

[13] Ibid.; Kedourie, *Nationalism*, p. 68; see also Kohn, *History of Nationalism in the East*, pp. 350–351.

well as his blind admiration for German, deepened the search for identity through language. In 1812 he expressed this emotional ideal about the importance of the language in a culture and a nation:

> Every important and independent nation has the right, if I may say so, of possessing a literature peculiar to itself; and the meanest barbarism is that which could oppress the speech of a people and a country, or exclude it from all higher education; it is mere prejudice which leads us to consider languages that have been neglected, or that are known to ourselves as incapable of being brought to a higher perfection.[14]

Here it is interesting to note that Schlegel's emphasis on the importance and independence of a nation most likely applies to England and France, since there was not a united nation of Germany with a German language as its basis. This also applied to other communities with different languages who had not yet formed a nation.

Cultural achievements also became a focal point, in some cases probably unintentionally, for praising folk wisdom in a wider context using native languages. In the last quarter of the eighteenth century, Mozart and Haydn began to write operas in German, probably to maintain the use of German in a world of opera dominated by Italian.

Language was used by Herder, and subsequently by others, as a primordial phenomenon of nationhood. According to this concept, cognate literature appeared to support and substantiate the essence of nation and national identity. Therefore, language in its print form played a role in materializing the imaginary entities previously subsumed under the Latin language of Christian "identity." Thus language consciousness laid the basis for further defining activities and opened new channels of communication within the heterogeneous populations of various dynasties and empires. Print language accomplished two things: it pushed Latin to the margins of sociopolitical life and it fixed a specific territory

---

[14] *Geschichte der alten und neuen Literatur, Vorlesungen Gehalten zu Wien im Jahre 1817, in sammtliche werke*, Vol. II (1846), p. 24; quoted by Hayes, p. 54.

to identify the language with, both giving rise to nationalist ideology.

For the consumers of nationalism, the market was occupied not only by novelists but also by the philologists, grammarians, and lexicographers who were polishing obscure and unknown languages, classifying them into language families and finding a political status for them. Between 1789 and 1794, following France's example, Russia produced a six-volume Russian dictionary; this was followed by an official grammar in 1802. Czech, a peasant language in Bohemia (as opposed to German, the language of nobility), was given enhanced stature when a Catholic priest, Josef Dobrovsky, produced the first systematic history of Czech literature and language in 1792. Ukranian grammar and language were recognized between 1789 and 1819.

In 1870, Emperor Joseph II of Hungary decided to replace Latin with German, for political reasons and administrative purposes. This move incurred the opposition of the Hungarian-speaking nobility.[15] Thus, language historically played a pivotal role in awakening the cultural and political consciousness of its speakers.

The philosophical and spiritual development of a community was gradually reflected in its expression of the language. Poets and philosophers expressed both their own inspirations and their communities' aspirations in a convincing and eloquent fashion. Pushkin, an open-minded intellectual, was the great national poet of Russia. Dostoevsky in his novels equally voiced a Russian national sentiment and implied his support for native autocracy and orthodoxy as opposed to Western influences. Dostoevsky expressed hope that Russia would dominate Asia and that from it, immense wealth, science, power, and dignity could be produced. Another writer of Russian aspirations was N. Danilevsky, whose support of Slavism under Russian leadership was another formulation of national, racial, and chauvinist ideas and whose

---

[15] All examples from Anderson, pp. 70–72. (Ali Akbar Dehkhodā was the first modern Iranian to produce a comprehensive 52-volume Farsi dictionary, in the early 1900s.)

ideas also derived from his anti-European sentiments.[16] The work of Shakespeare, a patriot whose literature is profoundly English, was an expression of national honor. Musicians and composers also contributed their own share, consciously and unconsciously, to rising national sentiment: Smetana, Dvořák, Tchaikovsky, Haydn, Mozart and Wagner.

Language was thus increasingly viewed and popularized as the basis of national identity. Connecting language to certain ethnicity and eventually to a race had both intra-European and extra-European consequences, which leads us to look into the Indo-European language classification that resulted in formation of the Aryan racial hypothesis.

THE RISE OF RACISM AND THE FALLACY OF LINKING LANGUAGE TO ETHNICITY

Racial awareness and a sense of superiority, resulting from colonization and slavery, gave Europe a sense of itself as a white continent puzzled by how all men could be a part of the same family with such wide gaps in physiognomy, behavior, tradition, and language in the world. Europe was making rapid progress in its industrial development, while the outside world, particularly Africa, was primitive and slow in producing what Europe called science and industry. This was particularly difficult to explain, since Europeans had acknowledged Egyptian and Greek civilizations as foundations of their own. With a growing racist attitude toward people with dark skin, Europeans began to be troubled with being identified as part of the same human family. By the fifteenth century, the link between dark skin color and evil or inferiority had been established, beginning with the Portuguese slave trade in 1455 and Pope Nicholas V's decree of subjugation.[17] Clear-cut racism grew rapidly after 1650, when the colonization of Africa and America had been firmly established.[18] However, extreme racial attitudes had not reduced the interest in Africa.

---

[16] See Kohn, *Prophets*, pp. 135–157.
[17] Montagu, *The Idea of Race*, p. 23.
[18] Bernal, *Black Athena*, I pp. 201–202.

On a different level, the Hebrew language was recognized as the primordial or mother language until the eighteenth century.[19] Then the reality of Egyptian civilization's influence on the formation of Greek and subsequently on European civilization came into perspective for European scholars. Ernest Renan,[20] who praised Indo-European achievements compared to those of the Semitic people, described his perplexity about the Egyptian and Babylonian civilization in an 1862 essay: "Egypt has had a considerable part in the history of the world. Egypt is neither a Semitic nor an Indo-European system. Babylonia is not either a purely Semitic phenomenon."[21] Martin Bernal, in his first controversial volume of *Black Athena* (1987), has extensively argued the motivations and traces of the European agenda in dissociating itself from Egypt and black Africa.

The gradual rejection of Egyptian influence, which preceded the Abyssinian/Ethiopian influence on Athens and Europe, reflects two important phenomena of the late eighteenth century: sheer racism toward black Africa and Egypt, and the suggestion by Sir William Jones in 1786 that Sanskrit had strong grammatical and verbal connections with Greek and Latin.[22] Thus the study of extra-European antiquity was going to be realized on this basis.[23] Asia was now the focus, not Africa. In other words, India had replaced Egypt. The Egyptian model had exercised tremendous influence on Judaism, which passed it on to Christianity, while Judeo-Christian thought, as well as that of the ancient Athenian schools, all influenced European thought collectively. This model was in a complex way gradually being removed. As Bernal puts it, the murmur was about the new model: the Aryan model.

Ethnicity and language are two distinct phenomena which anthropologically cannot be tied together as one and the same thing. People of diverse ethnic groups sometimes speak the same language. By the same token, sometimes multiple languages are

---

[19] Poliakov, *The Aryan Myth*, pp. 188–189.

[20] See Said, *Orientalism*, pp. 130–148.

[21] Renan, *Peuples Sémitiques dans l'Histoire de la Civilisation*, p. 12.

[22] Bernal, p. 229; Hayes, p. 63.

[23] Hobsbawm, *The Age of Revolution*, p. 337; quoted by Anderson, p. 68.

spoken by the same ethnic group. The erroneous assumption, that the speakers of a language belong to a specific ethnicity, was a fallacy that infiltrated the study of the Indo-European language family, and from this the idea of a unique so-called race was conceived, namely the Aryan.

The concept of relating the development of language to the idea of race probably resulted from the manner in which facilities and information were provided to European scholars, thus allowing connection of language and ethnicity and pressing for sharp distinctions between communities according to their language and race. The new materials, facilities, and kinds of information scholars required were provided with the discoveries of new lands, colonization, the Reformation, capitalism, new scientific findings, and so on. These factors inevitably provided a collective consciousness and means of self-evaluation vis-à-vis the outside world.

INDO-EUROPEAN LANGUAGE FAMILY AND ARYAN RACE

Based on Jones's Sanskrit-Greek-Latin proposition, Friedrich von Schlegel studied Sanskrit in Paris and became the first to connect the similarity of language and race. Such an idea carried a message of the polygenesis of languages and the polygenesis of man. Schlegel believed that the work of the Egyptian civilization was done by Indian missionaries.[24] In 1808 he published his *Über die Sprache und Weisheit der Indier (On the Language and Wisdom of the Indians)*, holding Sanskrit and Persian on one hand and Greek and German on the other to prove his racial hypothesis.[25] After that, India became the Mecca for the European scholars of the nineteenth century and later. Arthur Schopenhauer claimed to be the child of India by taking great interest in Vedanta of Upanishads and Buddhism. F. Nietzsche connected himself to Persian and

---

[24] Poliakov, p. 191.

[25] Said, pp. 98, 137; Schlegel, "On the Language and Wisdom of the Indians," *A Reader in Nineteenth-Century Historical Indo-European Linguistics*, Winfred P. Lehmann (ed.), pp. 21–28.

explored Zarathustra in his philosophy.[26] F. Hegel and later Max Müller believed the source of all wisdom was in India. Goethe, infatuated with the discovery of the Indo-European concept, dedicated a work to Sir William Jones, although Goethe never showed any affinity for racial concepts.[27] However, the efforts and appreciation of Goethe in studying Indian and Persian poetry and literature, even though as part of world literature, were not divorced from the ongoing European search for cultural ancestry

Egypt was now out of the picture and the concentration of scholars in Indo-European studies was to follow Schlegel's crude idea. Gerald Rendall states explicitly in *The Cradle of the Aryans* (1889) that, from the pictorial representations on Egyptian monuments, it is evident that the white man had developed the civilization, while the same white man had to defy and dominate the dark skins of India and Persia to construct a noble life style.[28] Rendall was not the first who did not fear the contradiction in mixing the concept of race with language classification and culture. Although racial theory grew on the basis of studying comparative philology, the color of skin mattered too in light of developments in Aryan sentiment. Another paradoxical situation developed when the Jews of Europe, with white skin, were refused the usual status of Caucasian[29] because their Hebrew-Semitic language could not be classified as Indo-European. Racism grew against these people while there was silence about the other communities of Europe whose languages did not fall into the Indo-European classification (including Basques, Hungarians, and Finns).

This revolution in scholarship was matched the degree and intensity of desire for a change in the socio-intellectual spectrum in Europe. Men of letters were working out a model that sounded

---

[26] Poliakov, p. 186; see also Schwab, *La Renaissance Orientale*, pp. 447, 458.

[27] Poliakov, pp. 195–196.

[28] Rendall, *The Cradle of the Aryans*, pp. 48–49. It is interesting to note that Michelangelo's Moses' head is sculptured as a white man's head rather than as a black African; it is a curious matter how consciously this may have been judged by Europeans in an anti-Semitic period.

[29] Bernal, pp. 340–341; see also Kohn, *Age of Nationalism*, p. 19.

scholarly and was yet mixed with old Christian and traditional dogmas. In language classification, the book of Genesis was used with respect to the sons of Noah: Ham, Shem, and Japheth. In the 1826 and 1837 works of A. Picard, the division is as follows: Ham or Hemites were of Egypt and Africa; Shem or Semites were of the Levant and Syro-Arabian; and Japheth or Aryans were of the land to the north.[30] However, prior to Picard's division, A. L. Schlozer had already established the Semitic language family in 1781;[31] this was subsequently given validity and taught by the giants Ernest Renan and Etienne Quatremère in France. Again, according to the Bible, the three sons of Shem were Aram, Ashur, and Eber; these were taken, respectively, to stand for Aramaic, Assyrian, and Hebrew languages and people.[32] Japheth was traditionally known as the father of Europe. In the Middle Ages, to dignify the monarchs in England, instead of Japheth being affiliated with the monarch, Japheth was connected to the eldest son of Noah, Shem. This did not mean, in a modern sense, that the English considered themselves a Semitic race but rather henceforth guaranteed a tradition in the royal family. This fed into traditional messianic fervor, making the English subsequently less anti-Semitic and pro-Zionist.[33]

As early as the 1820s, followers of the new Aryan hypothesis made it clear that those who spoke Indo-European languages were of Aryan racial descent. In 1816, Thomas Young preferred the term *Indo-European* to *Indo-Germanisch* philology, and by the 1840s Karl Müller rejected the connection between Greek and Egyptian, Semitic, or East Mediterranean (non-European) languages.[34]

---

[30] Poliakov, p. 211.

[31] Sabatino Moscati, Anton Spitaler, Edward Ullendor, Wolfram von Soden, *An Introduction to the Comparative Grammar of the Semitic Languages*, p. 3.

[32] Moscati, *Ancient Semitic Civilizations*, p. 23.

[33] Poliakov, pp. 39–43. The Balfour Declaration of 1917, a British proposal for a homeland for the Jews, may have had to do with this line of thought that Shem's descendants are close cousins of the traditional English royal family.

[34] Bernal, introduction, p. 227.

Subsequently, the theory of Aryan ships crossing from Anatolia to Greece was supported. Egyptian influences on Greece were discarded, and the Egyptian civilization itself was attributed to a stock of emigrated Aryans. An outdated work of the Australian Gordon Childe, *The Aryans* (1926), states that the Greeks were preceded by the Anatolians through the Aegean Sea.[35] Although such a concept was controversial, it was carefully investigated by the Indo-Europeanists.[36] If, as reported, we place the date of arrival of the immigrants in Greece at 1900 BCE[37] and believe they came from East Mediterranean regions, then, prior to this date, the Mesopotamian civilization must already have flourished, as must have those in East and North Africa. Indeed, Egypt is known to have maintained civilization starting from 4000 BCE. How could these primitive Greeks not have been influenced by (or borrowed from) either civilization? Both Wyatt and Bernal reveal that the Greeks borrowed and introduced key words of industry and science from Egyptian into Greek.[38] On the other hand, Moscati supports many modern scholarly views such as the Greeks' being clearly influenced by the people and civilization of Mesopotamia.[39] But the major argument of Indo-Europeanists and other supporters of the Aryan hypothesis was that the Greek language was different in structure from the so-called Semitic languages of the regions mentioned and had a close connection with Sanskrit, Latin, and other European languages. Although William Jones, apart from proposing a connection among Sanskrit, Greek, and Latin, had also detected a similarity between Indian and Semitic, namely between Sanskrit and Hebrew,[40] this similarity did not gain attention and was ruled out.

---

[35] Childe, *The Aryans*, pp. 16–17.

[36] Renfrew, *Archeology and Language: The Puzzle of Indo-European Origins*, pp. 168–177.

[37] Wyatt, "The Indo-Europeanization of Greece," *Indo-European and Indo-Europeans*, p. 89.

[38] Wyatt, p. 97; Bernal, Chapter 3.

[39] Moscati, *Ancient Semitic Civilization*, p. 57.

[40] See Bernal, p. 230; Moscati, *An Introduction to Comparative Grammar*, p. 17; Poliakov, p. 190.

Modern scholarship began to overthrow the medieval anthropology which had been based on the scriptures. Now, attempts were made to extricate Europe from Judeo-Christian elements, and to look toward India as the origin of European ancestry.[41]

Sanskrit became a basis for comparing and classifying languages, since scholars examining the relationship of phonetics and morphology supposed that German language was purer and more ancient in that language family. It was discovered that the German and Celtic languages were connected with Old Persian.[42] German-speaking savants such as J. C. Adelung, A. L. von Schlozer, Jakob Grimm, and Max Müller, along with V. Rask, J. G. Herder, and F. Bopp,[43] developed the theory of an original Aryan language, from which not only Sanskrit, Latin, Greek, and German but also Persian, Armenian, Celtic, and Slavonic tongues had been derived. This classification was strongly promoted, and Max Müller and his colleagues put a racial and biological tag on this language family. At some point, Herder believed that Germans might be related to the Persians ethnically and racially.[44] Soon it was assumed that the Aryan people were racially superior,[45] undoubtedly due to European superiority and sheer racism. The term *Aryan* itself, which Schlegel had coined from the words meaning 'honor'[46] in both Sanskrit *(ari)* and German *(Ehre)*, became the basis for the conception of a racial family hypothesized by linguists with interest

---

[41] I suspect that many attempts have been made to dissociate Christianity from Judaism, while India became the root of Aryan civilization. The book *Jesus Lived* in *India* (Dorset, England: Elements Books Ltd., 1986), by the German scholar Holger Kersten, could be among the (even subconscious) attempts to connect India to Europe and disconnect Jesus' teaching and ideas from his Semitic milieu.

[42] Krifka, "Sprach e," *Geo-Wissen,* 2 (1989), p. 88.

[43] Renan, *Peuples Sémitiques,* p. 10, emphasizes Bopp's effort to distinguish the Indo-Germanic or Indo-European languages from that of the Semitics.

[44] Poliakov, p. 186.

[45] Hayes, *Essays,* pp. 63–67; Said, p. 206.

[46] Poliakov, p. 193 ; Pictet, *Les Origines Indo-Europeénnes,* p. 38.

in race. The theory of the evolutionary process formulated by Charles Darwin involving the survival of the fittest and natural selection added more fuel to energize the theory of the formation of civilizations.

By the 1850s the Indo-European language family and the alleged Aryan race that spoke these languages had become established "facts," since philology had now become a credible academic discipline. Subsequently, a more complicated racial theory was introduced.[47] English, French, and German scholars showed greater fervor in adopting and developing the Aryan theory than did the other communities of Europe.[48] Among the many English, French, and Germans who believed this theory, it is relevant to name Arthur de Gobineau, a French diplomat and traveler who wrote his enthusiastically racist and controversial book *L'Essai sur l'inégalité des races humaines* between 1848 and 1851. Gobineau wrote this book when he was living in Bern, Hanover, and Frankfurt; upon its completion he dedicated it to the King of Hanover. Gobineau speaks passionately about the historical achievements of the Aryans, listing India and Iran as examples of Aryan civilization in Asia.[49] His resentful language against Oriental, African, and Semitic people is evident from his comparison of the "ten great civilizations of mankind" (initiated by white people), to the notion that civilization remained unknown to Africans and Orientals.[50] Gobineau also supported his predecessors' idea that Egyptian civilization was established by the arrival of Aryan stock from Asia, which encouraged anthropologists such as Elliot Smith to study and affirm it.[51]

Gobineau had given himself the right to put the integrity of the human race on trial by postulating his judgments about the unequal physical beauty, force, intelligence, and skull capacity of various ethnic people.[52] In his strong belief in biological inequality

---

[47] Bernal, pp. 330–331.

[48] Poliakov, p. 199.

[49] See Schwab, pp. 451–455.

[50] Gobineau, *L'Essai sur l'inégalité des races humaines,* pp. 371–379.

[51] Ibid., p. 379; Bernal, pp. 225–226; Kedouri, p. 72.

[52] Gobineau, pp. 371–379.

he ridiculed those liberals who spoke about the dogma of fraternity.[53] And so Gobineau's work became one of the bibles of racism — a first step toward Nazism and catastrophe. Furthermore, Gobineau's racist expositions also had the dreadful result of inciting in Indo-Iranian people a Western-inspired appetite for racial discrimination, leading to a strong racist belief in the East. His two books, *Trois ans en Asie* (1859) and *Les Religions et les Philosophies dans l'Asie Centrale* (1865), explore the mystical and recurrent Aryan people of India or Iran, those who were not conscious of their alleged racial superiority vis-à-vis their neighbors until it was recently "revealed" to them by expositors such as Gobineau.

As for the study of the genealogy of philology, which coincided with the peak of colonization in Africa and Asia by European powers, it became even more apparent that the non-white people (blacks and Orientals), lacked the power to resist the whites. This confirmed in theory and in practice the European domination of whites over non-whites. The world map began to have racial significance: only one and a half continents were from the white or Aryan race — Europe and the western half of Asia. Now the established dominations were achieved through political, economic, and (more importantly) scholarly schemes that subjugated the world and enabled the European authorities through historical reconstruction to reanimate the past and maintain control of the status quo.[54]

The work of anthropologists, archaeologists, and historians aimed, however, to work out the relationship between language, race, and culture. These investigators inquired repeatedly into the questions of if and how a physical characteristic of a particular race played any role in the traits of their given culture or the complexity of their language. In the vision of itself, European scholarship had breathlessly theorized the relationship of race with language. The introduction of the late eighteenth-century science of antiquity, *Altertumswissenschaft*, had facilitated seeing the origin and relationship of race and language.

---

[53] Ibid., p. 93.

[54] See Said, *Orientalism,* Chapter 3.

The search for artifacts, bones, antique objects, and the like in connection with a culture, and particularly with regards to the language spoken in that land in the past and in the present, somewhat judgmentally sketched the quality of the culture, which in turn was taken to speak for its race. In other words, in some fashion the more sophisticated the discovered objects, the more the objects were related to a "superior" race — in this case, the Aryan race, which only spoke Indo-European languages were known to be culturally "superior."

As a whole, this method of study in a more detailed fashion was applied to differences among European languages and cultures during the nineteenth century by using the concept of genetics. Pure blood and mixed blood became a way to emphasize the notion of identity and the concept of superiority over others. The isolation or migration of a stock of people was believed to create a genetic, social, and physical drift in a given period of time that naturally led the community to develop a language and inherited physical characteristics of its own. But this conception was directed toward differentiating among the languages and cultures in Europe that complicated the idea of pure race.[55] The pure blood of a particular linguistic community that might be partitioned into different (and larger) political and geographical units was an absurdity, but it worked in Europe. Pure blood connoted superiority over mixed blood, and this admittedly was the background in the battle for superior status. The English, for example, felt superior in the seventeenth century, the French in the eighteenth century, and the Germans during the time of Fichte and the romantics.[56]

The shortcomings of the methodology used to determine the Indo-European language classification on which the concept of race was conceived has raised questions and sparked efforts to investigate the roots of languages and the origin of humankind. Two criteria could be used to determine the similarity of languages: close pronunciation and morphology of words, and the structure of the grammar. As a result, two categories of linguists and

---

[55] See Boas, *Race, Language and Culture*, pp. 172–175.
[56] Kemiläinen, *Nationalism*, p. 154.

philologists have emerged: those who see a wide connection and inter-borrowing of languages whose roots may be difficult to trace or differentiate, and those who are convinced of the existence of sharp distinctions among languages and have kept a separate account of them. Thus, according to some, the Indo-European category has a connection with other language categories such as Ural-Altaic (Euroasiatic); this has been generally accepted,[57] although the fanatic Indo-Europeanists have refused to accept this.[58] The scholarly neglect of the theory of monogenesis of human language and the human family has set aside the possibility that a stock of people in ancient time could have spoken a proto-Americo-Afro-Asiatic-Indo-European language. Nonetheless, there are relative proofs indicating that the world's approximately 5,000 languages may have belonged to one family,[59] even though some scholars have remained firm in their position not to accept the connections among all languages. More importantly, it has been argued that language similarity does not necessarily corroborate genetic similarity, as genetically analyzed human bones prove.[60]

RACIAL DIFFERENCES AND ANTHROPOLOGY

The study of anthropology became, in a sense, a popular subject that endeavored to illustrate the theory of race and culture. In the first forty years of the appearance of *Bulletins et Memoires de la Societé d'anthropologie de Paris* (1860–1899) the most frequently addressed topics were "skull," "brain," "race," "man," "blacks," and "height."[61] Perplexity about the origin of humans led scholars to seek to discover whether men originated from a common stock (which would have meant monogenesis in language and family) or from different stocks (polygenesis). Darwin's theory of evolution in the mid-1800s brought its own complications, which were not

---

[57] Greenberg, "Languages of the World," *The New Lexicon Webster's Dictionary of the English Language*, p. xxxiii.

[58] Gobineau, *L'Essai*, p. 201.

[59] Krifka, "Sprache," pp. 92–93.

[60] Ibid., p. 91.

[61] Michalak, *An Analysis of Bulletins and Memoires of the Anthropological Society of Paris*, p. 2.

divorced from the contemporaneous consciousness of other European scholars. The idea of evolution (heritable variation) had been presented previously but with less evidence by Darwin's grandfather, Erasmus Darwin, and by J. B. Lamarck, but it became more feasible and acceptable when Charles Darwin elaborately laid out the animal kingdom and its evolution.

There were two parts in Darwin's hypothesis: first, the description of inherited variation in species leading to new species at different stages of the history of nature; second, the controversial revelation of the struggle for existence, or the survival of the fittest. His presentation of congenital differences between the members of the same species meant that these genetic characteristics became hereditary.[62] Darwin's theory gained momentum in the racial, linguistic, and cultural measurement of various ethnic groups. It also went, as Bertrand Russell put it, "in harmony with the growing power of the state; also with nationalism, which can appeal to the Darwinian doctrine of survival of the fittest applied, not to individuals but to nations."[63]

In an effort to formulate a coherent racial theory, an evolutionist anthropologist, Carleton Coon, argued that over 500,000 years ago Homo erectus evolved separately into Homo sapiens five times in different parts of the world, from which he traces racial variation and to which he adds a subspecies that crossed to Homo sapiens at an earlier period, evolved the most, and may have attained a higher level of civilization.[64] Having said that, Coon asserted that blacks were the last of the subspecies or races of Homo erectus to be transformed in Homo sapiens.[65] Such conceptions were obviously linked to the Aryan racial/linguistic model, which disliked including the blacks in one human family. The proof of civilization and progress was based on archaeological findings, and these were all attributed to the efforts of white peoples, and that included the Egyptian civilization. It was under

---

[62] Russell, *A History of Western Philosophy*, pp. 725–727.

[63] Ibid., p. 727.

[64] Michalak, *Carleton Coon: The Hemingway of Anthropology*, p. 10, quoting C. Coon, *The Origin of Races*.

[65] Montagu, *The Idea of Race*, p. 51; see also Gobineau, *L'Essai*, p. 323.

these intellectual circumstances that the peril of European supremacy began to increase and flourish.

Anti-Semitism equally grew and became a vehicle through which Indo-European purity contributed to the notion of separation and inequality. Certain scholars used biology and physical anthropology to support genetic arguments and used skull size to affirm the unequal foundation of human race. The color of skin, hair, or eyes is a reality of nature, but it began to be seen as correlated with temperament, language, customs, and culture as being put in national context, expanding and complicating the history of humans as a unique species. The genetic arguments and use of skull measurements to prove intelligence have been proved unreliable, and it has since been found that no racial characteristics exist in the brain.[66]

RACE, LANGUAGE, AND NATIONAL IDENTITY

Having discussed the background of language and racial classification in connection with the rise of racism, we will now investigate the relationship of these to the rise of nationalism and national identity. For one thing, it was now easier to jointly associate a race with a nation and a language. Interestingly, in the Brockhaus *Lexikon* the word *race* appeared to mean language, customs, common descent, etc., which automatically gave a racial label to any people who could envisage a nation.[67] The Aryan race was conceptualized on the basis of a language classification that was subdivided in Europe to reason out the limits of each subdivision. The Teutonic (Dutch, English, German, and Norse), Celtic, and Slavic races were attributed to the main divisions of the Aryan family.[68] With the simultaneous rise of national consciousness and linguistic-racial classification, each nation or people were gradually referred to as being characteristically and inherently different from others. Apart from common descent,

---

[66] Montagu, pp. 61–62; see also Joseph, *Nationality: Its Nature and Problems*, p. 43.

[67] Kemiläinen, pp. 96–97, 134.

[68] Joseph, p. 38.

differences in physiognomy, manners, customs, pureness of blood, and the like became criteria for national distinction.

The emergence of these ideas about regular physical distinction among peoples was first suggested by Aristotle's topographic and climatic determination for differences. In the sixteenth century, Jean Bodin, and in the eighteenth century, Montesquieu, Kant, and Voltaire affirmed climatic and geographical factors to be the basis of differences among people.[69] Of course, the extension of these observations went to the limit in modern times, where it seems to have been motivated by discrimination and bias rather than simply by scientific inquiry.

Friedrich Meinecke concludes in his book *Cosmopolitanism* that there is no nation with a pure race, although it is possible that groups of nations had a common ancestor or a similar race mixture.[70] Bernard Joseph, on the other hand, argues that, if one accepts the hypothesis that a nationality must be based on race, then nationality itself becomes invalid because no nationality can pass a blood test.[71] The nineteenth-century identification of a race with a nation, however, became a dogma with which its prominent promoters made tremendous impact on the sociopolitical philosophy of twentieth-century man. Linguistic racial theories convinced Heinrich von Trietschke that a nation should be conceived free of all sociocultural parasites. Economic considerations, apart from linguistic considerations, gave both Trietschke and Richard Wagner reason to look upon the Jews as Germans' misfortunes.[72] Treitschke in the nineteenth century esteemed Aryans and Germans and boldly opposed the mixture of races, so it should not have come as a surprise when the twentieth-century Nazi concept of pure race, nationhood, and Aryan supremacy blended all three into a corrupt social and political philosophy. As it was, Hitler's praise of pure German Aryanism on one hand and the Darwinian theory that the stronger would

---

[69] Montagu, p. 17, quoting Aristotle's *Politics*, Chapter VI; Kemiläinen, pp. 68, 72, 74, 134; Bernal, p. 204.

[70] Kemiläinen, p. 100.

[71] Joseph, p. 34.

[72] Kohn, *Proph ets and Peoples*, p. 124.

dominate the weaker on the other compelled him to write *Mein Kampf*[73] and actually commit himself to a real war on that basis.

It is true that in most of Europe the basis of identity, even to the present time, has been language, although political situations have still maintained diverse linguistic groups in a single political entity such as the former Yugoslavia and Czechoslovakia, Belgium, Britain, Switzerland, and a few others. The racial concept of the physical or ethnic characteristics in a white European continent has been influential but ultimately disproven, and in the modern sense the native language and the legal status of nationality have resolved the confusion. However, the hostility of Europeans toward recent émigrés from Africa or Asia whose legal status and native language (in a second or third generation) match those of white Europeans, remains a throwback to old schools of thought. The crude idea of race as a basis for national identity was gradually understood to be unreliable and theoretically was abandoned. Simultaneously, the illusion of nations as being a single stock or race gave way to other dynamic factors in a national identity.[74]

It is, however, important to direct criticism at those individuals responsible for conceiving the extreme racial, linguistic, or national models that played on the chauvinistic sentiment of people whose historical claims then led them into unnecessary battles. It was probably necessary to study comparative grammar, philology, roots of languages, and antiquity in order to accommodate further research for the empty-handed social scientists in an empty time and blank history.[75] The blank history of the ancient past then became filled with the important discovery of an Indo-European language connection, which soon took a racial and national direction. This direction obviously had considerable correlation with the European authoritarian role in academically compartmentalizing European and non-European civilizations on a racial and national basis. Another related phenomenon was the ongoing conflict in Europe to consolidate nation-states based on language and racial preference. However, the Indo-European and

---

[73] See Adolf Hitler, *Mein Kampf*, pp. 284–300.
[74] Baker, *National Character*, pp. 10–11.
[75] Anderson, p. 69.

Aryan hypotheses equally served the colonial purposes out of which Orientalism was conceived. The preeminence of national distinctions in the European scene disallowed bypassing the notions of language and race in a subtle discourse. Race, language, and blood relationship supported the concepts and sentiments of national identity; but alongside these, other complementary factors developed. In light of industrial advancement, economic expansion, political centralization, cultural refinements, and social and political revolutionary circumstances, the preeminence of the national interest in harmony with the national category of historiography and archaeology became the strong basis for national identity.

HISTORY AND HISTORIOGRAPHY
IN THE CONTEXT OF NATIONAL DOCTRINE

The discipline of history intends to provide people with some idea about past events. Human societies may have realized this art of compilation quite late in recording the various stages of their civilization in different parts of the world. It is, however, quite possible and plausible that such art and technique in recording events (in the modern sense, the discipline of history) did exist but its records were subsequently destroyed or buried. Our memories, unfortunately, are a branch and dimension of written history and do not stretch further. The starting point of our historical knowledge is therefore subject to question. In addition to this shortcoming, our historical awareness of the actual fragmentary historical record has been tremendously affected by interpretations and presuppositions of historians from various political or religious schools. It must be granted that, with scientific progress, the examination of the physical world has presented ideas, principles, facts, and hypotheses that in the modern sense reason out some of the mysteries of the past. However, by and large, critical historical thinking excels in constructing a transparent historical narrative in considering the faith and consciousness of people in different stages of history.

For several centuries (even to a certain degree until the present), Judeo-Christian historical thought was bound to believe that the history of humanity is known and clear: the world is only 6,000 years old, originating with Adam. It is presently evident that this vision of Adamic history is arbitrary and unexamined, and only served as a vehicle for men of letters and faith, with their avalanche of ideas, to promote and develop a complete Judeo-Christian scheme of history, past, present, and future. Saint Augustine, a renowned Christian theologian-philosopher of the fifth century, clearly showed his lack of interest in what we call history relating to political events. He argued that political events are evil and that no fundamental truth could be revealed from them.[76] In defiance to secular history, Saint Augustine took his time between 412 and 427 CE to write *The City of God,* a compilation of Christian suppositions about history.[77]

Christian historiography, in its primitive methods, presumed tentative hypotheses and assumptions that it claimed were accurate and permanent. Such an absolutist philosophy of history was planted in Christian dogma, where its fundamental shortcomings were to be detected by scientific and methodical research. The emergence of so-called liberal or secular historiography replaced and transformed the Judeo-Christian historical outlook with the arrival of the Renaissance. But the liberal categories of historiography showed no superior methodology or insightful construct of historical events either because the prevailing historical dogma was now gradually being transformed from its Judeo-Christian nature to its dynastic, nationalistic, and chauvinistic format. In studying Western civilization, one must "recognize the penetration of racism and continental chauvinism into all our historiography, or philosophy of writing history."[78]

The rapid grasp of the fruits of the Renaissance certainly created a new sociopolitical atmosphere where scientific theories changed the logic and modes of comprehension of the historians of the world events. Hannah Arendt suggests that, without the rise of secular realism to a new dignity, our historical consciousness, which contains new meanings and interpretations of man's deeds, would have been impossible.[79] It is true that new meanings, as highlights of our consciousness, were to be given to our behavior. Although Marx and Vico were not historians, they certainly

---

[76] Arendt, *Between Past and Future,* p. 66.

[77] Russell, p. 355.

[78] Bernal, p. 2.

[79] Arendt, p. 75.

introduced a different perspective of history that gained momentum with the decline of the church.

History and historiography had to be given a sophisticated dimension it previously lacked. History was no longer the plain record that Aristotle said it was;[80] perhaps, in a wiser sense, history is what historians do. In other words, history and historians aim at answering those who wish to be told what they are told. Transmitting the memories of the past was the real task, but the difficulty continued to be to free those memories from the religious or political consciousness of both the writers and the readers of history. Reasoning power and objective methods were becoming criteria for the great historians to use in bypassing the long historical naiveté of Christian Europe and to establish a sound account of historical details. Both the new reasoning and the concept of objectivity created new frustrations. 'Objective' began to mean, in a modern sense, unchangeable,[81] free from all biases, which inherently gave a new fixity to historical knowledge. Descartes, rightfully suspicious, proceeded to deny that history had any claim to be a serious study.[82] Not basing our view on Descartes, we could see post-Renaissance historical writings as the unbroken consciousness of the human mind being affected with the ongoing realities in his surroundings. In this regard, it is worthwhile to quote Hegel's idea: "Historical knowledge is not mere knowledge of the past events, but only of events so far as they enter into human activity, and are an element in the biography of an individual or group."[83]

As a result of the shift to dynastic and nationalist historiography in Europe, the Christian sources of historical knowledge were respectfully ignored, since Christians largely in transition were becoming aware and loyal as national entities in the realm of politics. This emerging consciousness, as reflected in

---

[80] Aristotle said that history is an account of what individuals have done and suffered. See Berlin, *Concepts and Categories*, p. 103.

[81] See Arendt, p. 53.

[82] Berlin, p. 103.

[83] This is derived from Hegel's distinction of *an sich und für sich*, quoted in Berlin, *Vico and Herder*, p. 29.

historical writings, may go back to the sixteenth century, although there are sporadic dynastic national histories before this date, such as that of Spain. In any event, the serious attempts came in the seventeenth and eighteenth centuries, peaking in the nineteenth century. The complex emergence of national consciousness was now being extravagantly expressed in all kinds of literatures other than history as a way to cherish the new constitution of the truth under the new sociopolitical mechanism. The basic self-misunderstanding was that this collective commitment was to reshape and explain the emergence of that age, and not necessarily a blessed and unique historical truth about humanity at large. Despite the inner light of reason or any other model for the truth, these endeavors were accompanied by illusions and error[84] that could bring about the collision of facts with their interpretations. The laying out of basic categories and raw presuppositions such as society, history, development, growth, behaviorism, and civilization could be considered grotesque generalizations used to simplify and construct our whole thinking about the world. These generalizations indeed may turn out to be false and misleading.[85]

Under the new conditions in Europe, attractive writings expressed national pride, as selections and judgments were juxtaposed in portraying historical moment. The eighteenth century was the most fertile period, particularly after the French Revolution, in synchronizing a new historical thinking that began to shake and prepare Europe for the next century, when it would bring under control its polity and its history. The histories of Europe were written out of a historiographical consciousness that in the nineteenth century was all becoming nationally defined.[86] The territorialization of the European communities brought history to a brief halt, so to speak, allowing historians to select chronicles, events, memoirs, or even individuals to add fuel to the burning nationalist passion and doctrine of European communities. This historical blindness ran the risk of misinterpreting and isolating the mini-histories from the mainstream of historical development in

---

[84] See Arendt, p. 55.

[85] Berlin, *Concepts,* pp. 108–109, 115–116.

[86] Anderson, p. 108.

human life throughout the world. Rabindranath Tagore's statement somewhat addresses this problem: "There is only one history — the history of man. All national histories are merely chapters in the larger one."[87] Furthermore, lack of respect for time and change was a complication of such a method of historiography. This heedless, anachronistic method amounted to taking the complex events of the past, while ignoring the concrete historical conditions under which the actors and events had formed a valid behavioral mechanism, to describe them in a narrow national aggregation. Another problem in developing a national history was found in the sources of antiquity and mythology (which held no national dimension in a modern sense), as Vico would say. In linking important events of the past, many gaps had to be filled; this required crucial evidence, but memories had often faded away, making a coherent and convincing narrative of history more difficult. Archaeology and anthropology made efforts to link our knowledge of one period or event to another by reconstructing what may have occurred. However, not only were the intermediate phases unknown and missed (in itself a crooked understanding of the past),[88] but the nationalist categories of historiography used also misinterpreted what archaeology and anthropology intended to achieve.

Another problem (and a classic example of the nationalist category of historiography) arose when people and selected individuals of past periods are assigned a nationality in a historical description. It is rather peculiar that some modern writers portray Moses as the first Israeli, and the founder of the nation of Israel, even though he was born in Egypt. In the same way, for many Cyrus the Great has become known as Iranian or Persian, although his ancestral background and language had nothing to do with modern Iran in the modern sense of nation or nationality. Another example is Charlemagne, emperor of the Holy Roman Empire in the ninth century. He was given German nationality and considered the founder of the First German Reich, followed by Bismarck in 1870 and Hitler in the 1930s, creating the Second and Third

---

[87] Tagore, *Nationalism*, p. 119.
[88] Berlin, *Concepts, p.*111; Kedourie, *Nationalism,* p. 75.

Reichs. There was no Germany in the ninth century, and it is highly anachronistic to consider Charlemagne as German.

Ernest Renan was right when he said: "The idea of nationality as it exists today is a new conception unknown to antiquity."[89] People of historical knowledge and ability have periodically criticized the fitting of past into present or of present into past, which is unrealistic in either case. Perhaps it is appropriate to believe that entering into the mind of another society and age through the work of a historian is a rather far-fetched idea, since scientific studies lie between the outlooks of the external observer and of the actor.[90] Berlin expresses sarcasm towards certain historians who hand-pick materials, add fact to fact with transitional and conclusive words (like *therefore, hence,* etc.) and use their extravagant imaginations to rescue an event;[91] these may not fill the factual gaps, but they are warning signals to the careful reader.

The compilation of historical records has yielded vast knowledge about the past, but in interpreting these records of various political cultures of different eras, we should keep the school of the historian under scrutiny in its anachronistic approach as well as arbitrary periodization. Ultimately, there could be as many pasts constructed as there are political thoughts.[92]

SUMMARY

The formation of national identity in the European continent has been discussed in this brief chapter in order to trace the general progress of events and knowledge in Europe that ultimately entailed grave consequences both within that continent and further afield. These grave consequences were all laid on an ideological foundation that led to prejudice, racism, nationalism, and open war.

---

[89] Renan, *Qu' est-ce qu' une nation;* quoted by Joseph, *Nationality: Its Problems and Nature,* p. 164.

[90] Berlin, *Concepts,* p. 137.

[91] Ibid., p. 110.

[92] See Pocock, "England," *National Consciousness, History, and Political Culture in Early-Modern Europe,* pp. 98–99, 116.

Moreover, they sprang out of a false conception of the ancient origins in Europe of the national idea. In fact, no such idea animated the ancient Greeks and Romans — and far less the hypothetical Indo-Europeans.

True, there has always been a fine line between nationalism and racism, but the reality of the European situation has made it at times impossible to separate the two, particularly during the nineteenth century. It is unrealistic to conceive of the sociopolitical revolutions of the time as taking place (and resulting in the formation of modern nation-states) in a theoretical vacuum. Rather, it is essential to consider the profound influence exercised by the institutions of Western academia and of colonialism.

The interchange between colonialism and academic findings had encouraged a growing arrogance among European elites vis-à-vis the outside world and created an ongoing competition among them for pieces of the economic and political pie, both on the European continent and elsewhere. The formation of nation-states led by the elites and the intelligentsia was prefigured in an ideological consciousness that resisted monolithic European domination. In some sense, the escape of the secular world from the Church's authority and subsequently from the Napoleonic ambition for conquest set the historical limits for forming a nation-state alongside the economic motivation to preserve the capitalist interests of the leading aristocracies.

National identities were inevitably formed on the basis of the state's interests, even though linguistic, cultural, and geographical zones and other criteria determined the limits of a particular nation. The dominant ideological dynamic of the new societies of Europe were characterized by their competition to dominate (or not to be dominated by) others and by their preoccupation with the search for identity. This impelled Europeans to draw boundaries wherever they could and to create even the tiniest of countries in the world.

Throughout the nineteenth and twentieth centuries, the alarming discourse with regard to national identity was focused on language classification, which was in turn connected to the notion of race. Such racial and national consciousness used the old dogmatic parochial stereotypes of the past as a springboard into the invigorated and virulent overt racism and chauvinism of modern times. Connecting language to race had two immediate results. First, the language that was proposed by the intelligentsia as the basis of national identity now began to carry all kinds of racial (and at times, pathological) emotions that brought different European groups into competition for superiority among themselves. Second, the association of the Indo-European language family with a purported proto-race (notably, the Aryan race) gave Europeans a sense of unique historical identity vis-à-vis the other ancient civilizations outside Europe.

By putting forward the Aryan hypothesis, which had primarily been extracted from philological knowledge, European scholars attempted in the field of social sciences to disconnect the so-called Aryan civilizations (whether in Central Asia or in Mediterranean regions) from all others and from any outside influences, particularly of non-white regions. The development of the Indo-European language family soon ceased to be an innocent academic hypothesis (as many perceived it then and subsequently) but instead became the basis for reconstructing historical events both in Europe and elsewhere along racial, cultural, and linguistic lines based on a nationalistic interpretation of history.

Having hypothesized the Indo-European language family in the early nineteenth century during the peak of European hegemony over non-European lands, Western scholars found it necessary to fabricate a European identity on the basis of Aryanism and Greek ancestry to confirm Europeans' superior culture and people over non-Europeans, both in antiquity and in the modern period. During this period the conceptualization of European and non-European peoples on the basis of language, ethnicity, and geographical zone gave rise to racial and national historiography.

The methodologies introduced for empirical research went unchallenged in the West as a result of their racial and national tendencies, and the disciplines of archaeology and anthropology developed a sympathetic attitude toward these methodologies. Many social scientists came to express empirical observations in their particular field or subfield that were framed and concretely catalogued in accordance with preconceived national, racial, and political categories.

However, to justify its search for national identity at home and abroad, European academia filled its libraries with a deluge of books and reports elucidating that theme. Simultaneously, many Western scholars, thanks to the pioneering exploitation of colonialism, were able to infiltrate the Orient and began to construct a national identity for its people based on the familiar methodologies. Thus, the Aryan hypothesis was first used to distinguish Aryan whites from Semitic whites, in keeping with a peculiar historiographical and philological method, and then was used in conjunction with geographical zones to conceptualize supposed national distinctions among the culturally complex and intermingled people of the Orient. The predominance of these methodologies prepared the West to undertake the task of imposing the Indo-European model both on itself and the East. In light of the emerging linguistic and racial model we now examine how Europe subsequently approached, analyzed and influenced the Orient and Iran in particular.

CHAPTER 2
EUROPE APPROACHES THE ORIENT

In the preceding chapter, the scope of national identity in Europe and the strong nationalistic mood there were examined in order to demonstrate not only how these experiences eventually gave rise to modern nations of Europe but also how the embryonic notion of nationalism affected the emerging scientific attitude on the Continent. The new humanistic outlook toward the world was now being filtered through racial and national (not necessarily cosmopolitan or inclusive) channels. Among the many regions Europe came into contact with was the Islamic world. This contact led to many decisive events which have subsequently affected outcomes in the modern period, particularly in terms of sociopolitical and economic order. Since our focus is national identity, it suffices here to refer to certain aspects of such contact between the two regions in order to demonstrate the evolution of the European approach.

Europe has had a long and historically complex relationship of contact with the Orient (Arab-Islamic peoples). Europeans probably did not set out with the specific intention of colonizing (and of studying) the Orient the way they did: the chain of events simply led to that result. To bring itself out of intellectual paralysis and scientific darkness, Europe during the late Middle Ages was taking various new directions and the Orient was viewed as being rich with accumulated knowledge. In the Muslim centers of Spain, the translation of Arabic medical books by Rhazes and 'Abbās into Latin by 1070 opened the gates to further European inquiry into the Eastern treasury of knowledge. Gerard of Cremona's translation of scientific works by Avicenna, Kindī, and Fārābī from Arabic into Latin by the mid-1100s contributed to the heightening interest in intellectual ideas that had been produced outside Europe.[1] The universities of Montpellier, Bologna, Paris, Oxford, and Salerno — seats of learning by the thirteenth and fourteenth centuries — tried to expand their curricula to share the fruits of such scientific achievements by the people of the Orient. Meanwhile, scientific and philosophical works by Galen, Hippocrates, Plato, Aristotle, and other Greeks were being translated from Arabic into Latin and used in intellectual discourse. Hellenistic thought thus found its way to Europe through, as Amin says, "the mediation of the Islamic metaphysical construct."[2] In the decades and centuries to come, Copernicus, Kepler, Galileo, and many others actually became successors to Birunī, Omar Khayyam, Tusī, and others from the Orient in the fields of astronomy and mathematics. Although the Christian and Muslim worlds maintained repressive levels of religio-political discrimination, there was an incorruptible virtue of learning that at this point synthesized the achievements of several civilizations without prejudice. The European vision of Islam at this point was provincial, based on fear and ignorance rather than on a sense of superiority.[3] However, it may be true that Europeans considered their superior enlightenment in later centuries to be due to their longstanding Christian communities (except in Lebanon and Georgia-Armenia). At any rate, the respect of scientists for each other went beyond any religious or ethnic biases. In the thirteenth century, Roger Bacon became the best-informed person in the scholarly world on the life and works of Avicenna, out of intellectual passion and guardianship for him.[4] Dante, in a metaphorical sense, exempted Avicenna from hell.[5] The Orient and the Occident were becoming one through the medium of knowledge.

---

[1] Afnan, *Avicenna: His Life and Works*, pp. 260–261; see also Rodinson, *Europe and the Mystique of Islam*, p. 16.

[2] Amin, *Eurocentrism*, p. 54.

[3] Ibid., pp. 74–75.

[4] Afnan, p. 277.

[5] Rodinson, p. 29.

There is a beauty in the examples of Adam Olearius, who in the mid-1600s taught German to his friend from Iran in exchange for learning Farsi, in order to translate the *Gulistān* of Sa'dī (a Persian poet of the thirteenth century) into German alongside Latin.[6] Goethe's infatuation with the poetry of Hafiz, quite apart from the European urge to learn all about Asia and India, expresses a human instinct for sharing the feelings of human delight. A vast store of information was constantly traveling without recognition of boundaries.

Europe and the Islamic world as a unique cultural and scientific area had gradually broken apart as Europe lifted itself to the status of conqueror from the mid-1700s on and acquired the superior consciousness of a conqueror. Until the Enlightenment of the eighteenth century, the Orient was praised but viewed as no longer having anything to teach Europe. Eurocentrism was being crystallized, and the qualitative break characterized by development of an absolute sense of superiority vis-à-vis the outside world was shaping.[7] A brief sketch of how Europeans, from simple beginnings as merchants, missionaries, and travelers, came to study and conquer the Orient follows here; it will help us trace the pathway to Orientalism, and Iranology in particular.

In the Middle Ages, religious discourse and zeal to find new converts had spurred European clergymen to look for new lands and heathen peoples. This endeavor, apart from the motivation of trade, had created missionary organizations that became unconscious means of communication, probing the force of Islamic faith and peoples as well as opening new gates. In the early Mongolian conquest of Western Asia in the mid-1200s a Franciscan missionary had come via Georgia to Azerbaijan to the court of Bāyjū, areas in which such clergymen were lucky to remain alive.[8] The subsequent Mongolian invasion by Hülagü Khan and the resulting fear of obliteration kept the Christian and Islamic camps divided and suspicious of each other's intentions, although

---

[6] Navai, *Iran va Jahān*, p. 322.

[7] Amin, pp. 72–73.

[8] Navai, pp. 14–25; see Browne, *A Literary History of Persia*, III, pp. 8–10; Dawson, *Mission to Asia*, xv–xviii, xxi–xxiii.

there were hopes to forge a Christian-Mongol alliance against Muslims. By the latter part of the thirteenth century, with the establishment of the tribal systems of the Il-Khanids in the plateau of Iran, relations with the Christian Occident were mired in minor trade and hopeless religious discourse. However, diplomatic relationships were to be developed in subsequent stages. Merchants, royal representatives, and travelers headed east (before turning their attention westwards in the fifteenth century, with the discovery of the New World).

Some of the many individuals who traveled to the Orient mirrored their perception of the Orient in their diaries and travel chronicles. At the end of the thirteenth century, Marco Polo left a heritage of Western impressions of the East. John Schiltberger, another prominent traveler, recorded accounts of Asia and Africa that are not exempt from gross errors. At the beginning of the fifteenth century, travelers and delegations from Venice and other areas of Europe visited and wrote memoirs of the East, particularly during the Timurid, Qara Qoyünlü, and Ăq Qoyünlü periods; among them were Niccolò de Conti, Bertrand Magnanelli, Baptista Padesta, and Pietro Perondeno.[9] In the sixteenth and seventeenth centuries (the Safavid period), socio-political life was also reported in travel chronicles by Pedro Teixeira (1604), Raphäel du Mans (1644–1696), Jean Baptiste Tavernier (1629–1675), Sir John Chardin (1665–1677), Pietro della Valle (1617–1624), Adam Olearius (1637–1638), Father Judasz Tadeusz Krusinski (1720–1726), and a few others. Throughout the Qājār period, many Europeans came to the East for various reasons, some leaving behind their narratives and memoirs.[10]

The coming of the Europeans to the Orient at different periods generally entailed an inferential impression of those Oriental lands that gradually filled Western libraries and minds. The horizon of European understanding of the Orient was limited by the frame of mind under which the gathered information was scrutinized. Three important events — the Industrial Revolution,

---

[9] Navai, pp. 80–141.

[10] For other contacts with the West see Lockhart, "Persia as Seen by the West," *The Legacy of Persia*, pp. 318–358; see also Navai, pp. 142–475.

the rise of capitalism, and the advent of colonialism — were directly related to each other and to the rise of academia. Even though colonialism brought Europeans into direct contact with non-European populations, it had already created a spiritual distance and dichotomy between Europe and these outside communities; and to this division the Industrial Revolution introduced the full force of its economic goals.

The knowledge acquired and exchanges made over centuries with the Orient were followed by more data from independent or colonial representatives. Academia — or Orientalism, as Edward Said has put it — created a ground in which "political knowledge" superseded "pure knowledge," with the outcome "that political imperialism governs an entire field of study, imagination, and scholarly institutions in such a way as to make its avoidance an intellectual historical impossibility."[11] European involvement with the Orient led to politico-economic gains on one hand and a scholarly combination of colonialism and Orientalism on the other. Hamid Enayat's reference to "European Orientalism whose great pioneers were long thought to be inspired by nothing less than a pure love of knowledge"[12] gives testimony to a longstanding historical naiveté; he adds, "the undeniable fact is that Orientalism was largely stimulated by, and in a sense nurtured in the bosom of colonialism."[13] European hegemony over the outside world meant colonialism and led to the exercise of asserted superiority (along with authority) in intellectualism. The English hegemony over the Indian subcontinent unavoidably produced knowledgeable colonial officers like William Jones, whose dual role as the protector of the English interest and as a scholar (pioneering Indo-European studies) was perfectly suited to the period of the eighteenth and nineteenth centuries. The invasion of Egypt by Napoleon in 1798 was in fact both a colonial and an academic exploration. French Egyptologists such as Jean Francois Champollion, the student of Antoine-Isaac Silvestre de Sacy (father of modern Orientalism), in the early nineteenth century described Egypt to the local

---

[11] Said, *Orientalism*, pp. 9, 14.

[12] Enayat, "The Politics of Iranology," p. 3.

[13] Ibid.

population by reading hieroglyphics in a fashion that had never been heard before, since the local population were unaware of their land's historical distinctiveness and its pre-Islamic glory. As it is witnessed in constructing national identity and national history, the Orientalists 'Egyptianized' every event and archaeological artifact even though the complex cultural and ethnic fabric of the region could not have easily fitted in one narrow national 'Egyptian' category.

In Paris, by the late 1700s the newly founded *École des Langues Orientales Vivantes* had appointed its first teacher, A. I. Silvestre de Sacy. De Sacy was trained in Arabic, Syriac, Chaldean, and Hebrew. Drawing on his knowledge of Muslim and Oriental peoples, he served as a fluent translator of information from the East to the West and established a career for himself as a scholar and adviser to the French foreign ministry in the early 1800s — a time when French colonial forces were assailing Muslim lands. De Sacy participated as a consultant in the French occupation of Algiers in 1830, where he translated the proclamation of the takeover to the Algerians.[14] While other universities were functioning under church auspices, Paris became the center of secular studies — in particular Oriental and Sanskrit studies. Friedrich von Schlegel, the founder of the Aryan model, studied Sanskrit in Paris in the early 1800s. Franz Bopp (also an Aryanist and the founder of German comparative linguistics) trained under de Sacy in Paris.[15] Paris and London, the capitals of the two largest colonial powers, were also the chief centers of Oriental studies. Manuscripts and ancient objects brought from the Orient poured into these cities, where scholars struggled to make sense of them. It was said that thanks to the Orientalists, the Occident discovered its face in the mirror provided by the Orient.[16]

As colonialism supported the development of Orientalism, racism and nationalism (as defined in the previous chapter) became characteristics of the elite and, to a certain extent, middle-class life

---

[14] Said, p. 124; Bernal, *Black Athena*, p. 234; see also Rodinson, pp. 54–56.

[15] Rodinson, p. 61.

[16] Boissel, *Gobineau, l'Orient et l'Iran*, p. 402.

in eighteenth- and nineteenth-century Europe. Inevitably the hegemony of Europe both in political and academic spheres affected the value judgment and authority of scholars in selecting the desired methodology to use in studying Oriental-Muslim peoples and lands in the two subsequent centuries. It was in such fashion that objective knowledge was violated by political and racial motifs. The focus of this discussion centers on how this era of nationalism, colonialism, and Orientalism also gave rise to historicism and nationalist historiography in the context of European Orientalism.

The transition of Europe from medieval to modern, from weak to powerful, from unaware to alert, and from ordinary to self-consciously superior inevitably modified its mythical history and its vision of the world order. Greece, Rome, Christendom, and the subsequent stages of national development on the Continent became the focus of European history; all other sociocultural connections with Africa or Western Asia based on Aryan hypotheses was rejected. During the period of intense racism against Africa and the Semitic peoples, European memory did not extend to recognize a period when works of Arab-Islamic or Jewish scholars were being translated and learned or to acknowledge the antecedents of the Egyptian and Mesopotamian influences on Greece. "Hellenemania," as Bernal calls it, and the love for Greek ancestry had given Europeans the courage to distinguish themselves as a superior and distinct continent with a unique identity that owed nothing to outside influences. The effect of the emergence of popularly elected governments on the development of European ideas of superiority and uniqueness vis-à-vis the despotic Oriental monarchies was another ground to identify Europeans with ancient Greeks, especially Athenians.

Not too long after its conception, however, European identity was broken into pieces by geographic racism and nationalism.[17] In revising its accounts of history, making its classifications, selections, and interpretations, Europe became too involved with itself, retaining no coherent global vision of history in the early nineteenth century, but instead undertaking a nationalist

---

[17] Amin, pp. 96–97.

historiography of its own. Historicism and empirical studies claimed to explain the basic causes of differences between people on one hand and their continuity on the other. The wisdom of such a method of study for certain territories under various empires or rulers in a given geographical location matched the existing doctrine of nationalism in Europe and provided grounds for consolidating governments and lands in the future. In fact, with the emergence of centralized modern states in the East in the twentieth century, these constructed national histories provided a justification for asserting the legitimacy of the state's rule over the land and for inaugurating modern national consciousness and identity among the people of that land.

Despite having known that the Orient possessed universal histories classified under world religions, Islamic, dynastic, and political categories, and distinct periodizations (including those of Tabarī, Ya'qubī, Mas'udī, Bayhaqī, Shahrastānī, Ibn Khaldun, and Rashid al-dīn Fazllulāh), Europeans could not resist concluding that these lands and peoples required distinct histories. Such desire without fear of distortion gave impetus to the construction of *national* histories. The problem that the people of the Orient had no role in this undertaking is correctly summarized: "They cannot represent themselves; they must be represented."[18]

European scholars came to illustrate the history and the civilization of the Orient in a way that rendered earlier Oriental history books obsolete and inconsequential. Formalized scientific fields such as philology, archaeology, and later anthropology were pursued in place of old-fashioned history. As a result of inadequacies of historical universalism and cosmopolitanism, Europeans adopted a philological explanation proposed by Sir William Jones and developed by Friedrich von Schlegel in the late 1700s and early 1800s — the Aryan hypothesis, which not only glorified the European identity in antiquity but also promoted racial and national historiographical methodology with respect to the peoples of the Orient. As a result of this hypothesis, a serious break became necessary, involving a distinction between the so-called Aryans of Asia and their neighbors and counterparts, the so-

---

[18] Said, *Orientalism*, quoting K. Marx, p. i.

called Semites (Arabs, Jews, and other categories) and the Turks. *Iran* (historically used as a geographical designation), its peoples, cultures, and languages were studied and then forced into a crude national category that has led racist Aryanism to become incorporated to an unfortunate extent in its national consciousness. In the following pages we consider attempts that have been made to study Iran as a distinct entity. In subsequent chapters we analyze the framework and shortcomings of the conceptualization of Iran as a nation.

THE OCCIDENT CONCEIVES IRAN

The beginning of formal study of Iran by Europeans can be tied to two events at the end of the eighteenth century: first, the discovery of the Indo-European language family; and second, the unavoidable competition between France and England over parts of Asia. At that time, England was holding India; and Napoleon I of France became interested in both India and the region immediately to its west — Iran. Although Iran never became a formal colony, it did become a crossroads where imperial powers established interest divisions. The European formulation of the Aryan or Indo-European hypothesis by (apart from Jones and Schlegel), J. C. Adelung, J. Grimm, M. Müller, and F. Bopp focused on working out the Indo-European language family, of which primarily Europe was the benefactor. India and Iran, part of the language laboratory, were isolated and unaware of such racial conclusions. However, on the basis of this philological outline, the Semites were identified and distinguished linguistically from the Indo-Iranian family. For various reasons, the Iranian world was also separated from the Indian one. The pretext for such a vigorous national and racial approach was to study words and to trace their similarities. In subsequent generations of Oriental studies, Avestan, Median (a few words), Old Persian (400 words),[19] Middle Persian, Soghdian, and Parthian have been among the "Iranian" languages used as sources for the Aryan hypothesis,

---

[19] Mo'in, *Farhang-i Farsi*, pp. iv–v; Browne, I, p. 7, mentions 400 words.

along with Indian and European languages. Using the study of antiquity, together with the techniques and knowledge of philology, scholars classified and codified civilizations based on their language categories. Due to this tendency, Iranian civilization was separated from antiquity onward from Mesopotamian, Egyptian, Arab, and other regional civilizations, which were by and large classified as Semitic. Philology was used as a basis for theorizing about race and for stripping the Orient's complex historical fabric into narrow national contexts. Thus, every Orientalist in Europe began his career as a philologist.[20] Linguistic considerations, dominated systematic Orientalist discourse, from which more nationalist and racist scholars emerged in the course of the nineteenth and twentieth centuries.

The Aryan race, to which it was assumed Iranians belonged, was attributed to have superior qualities vis-à-vis Semitic people, according to certain European scholars. The ancient civilizations and historical achievements of many communities in various periods, representing the outcome of a complex historical process, were conclusively reasoned to be Iranian and particularly a virtue of the Aryan (for example, by G. Rawlinson and A. de Gobineau). Ironically, such glorification of India and Iran as the historical Aryan counterparts of Europe not surprisingly came under attack by proponents of colonization, again in favor of Europe. Amin is thus right to point out in his *Eurocentrism* that the racist contrast was not between the Semitic Orient and Europe but between Europe and non-Europeans. When India was conquered, the foundation of the Indo-European language family was neglected.[21] The racial affinity of Europeans with the so-called Aryans of Asia — Indo-Iranians — was clearly incompatible with their colonial goal. The benefits of colonialism were too lucrative to be frustrated by academic restrictions. The suspicion and disillusionment of peoples of the Orient in later periods may perhaps be found in the contradiction between the West's humanistic idealism and its desire to plunder all who could not resist it. The West often failed to

---

[20] Said, p. 98.
[21] Amin, p. 96.

incorporate all elements of its civilization into a coherent and balanced application.[22]

Returning to the issue of philology as the basis of Orientalism in general and Iranology in particular, it should be recalled that the notion of language was important in the European evolution of nationalism. The Iranian languages, as the philologists classified them, became the basis of the study of Iranian history and other broad topics in a national context as well. This nationalist attempt, which went beyond the confines of philology, archaeology, and other micro-studies, had its political agenda well hidden.[23]

The nationalistic outlook of the early Orientalists influenced subsequent generations of scholars as well as the centralized state apparatus in Iran in the twentieth century and the folk-derived consciousness of the Iranian people, although none had been established in a concrete fashion. The objectives of nationalist Orientalism were in part achieved by using the name *Iran*, which has been thought to be synonymous with *Aîryana* or *Arya*,[24] as a national appellation. Here, we observe not only the deep penetration of racist convictions but also how successfully the concepts of race and nation (according to European standards) accommodated each other.

To probe the construct of national history for Iran, based on painstaking philological and archaeological studies, we must take several steps to demonstrate the shortcomings, disputability, and pretentious contempt in interpretation of the historical documents; furthermore, we must demonstrate that the term *Iran*, as the name of the land, and the notion of Iranian national consciousness are by-products of twentieth-century ideas that have no historical affiliation in the way many nationalistic Orientalists try to portray. Having said that, we must first try to establish a ground for

---

[22] Gibb, *Near Eastern Culture and Society*, T. C. Young (ed.), pp. 221–239; quoted by Banani, *The Modernization of Iran, 1921–1941*, p. 154.

[23] Enayat, p. 2.

[24] Pictet, *Les Origines Indo-Européenes*, p. 39. Subsequently, when the Aryan hypothesis was related to Iranian archaeology and history, the terms *Iran* and *Arya* were believed to have the same source; see also Browne, I, p. 4n.

investigating the evolution of the term *Iran* according both to the works of the Orientalists and to the Oriental historical documents (Arab-Persian-Islamic sources) themselves.

CHAPTER 3
THE CONCEPTUALIZATION OF IRAN IN A NATIONALISTIC CONTEXT

Iran, originally the name for a geographical region, and its descriptor, *Iranian*, gradually came to represent, both in the work of the Orientalists and nationalist thinkers, a broad category that represented one unified people, language family, a culture, and eventually an imaginary nation which had seemingly perpetuated from antiquity onward — a rather arbitrary and discrepant approach. Such approach was based on the European study of languages and cultures of antiquity and linking them together as a way to conceive a national history for Iran. Racial and linguistic theories and sharply dissonant national political philosophies bolstered by a belief in the soundness of its scholarly methodology led Europe to create asymmetry and an image of itself distinct from the rest of the world. European Orientalism chased down the residue of all historical documents in order to scrutinize them, then did so in a framework of projected racial and nationalistic ideas. The study of Iran was subjected to the same system of principles. Racism and nationalism promoted the glory of the Aryans, who constructed the Iranian nation from the Achaemenid period (550 BCE) until modern times. The pre-Islamic cultural heritage, race, and language were revitalized in the scholarship of the nineteenth century to impose a sense of Iranhood and its persistence in history. Did Iran as a nation exist during the pre-Islamic and Islamic periods? The Orientalist response, although anachronistic, has been affirmative. It is true that the name *Iran* was used for a geographical designation for an area between India and the Arab lands beginning in the third century CE, but this should not be mistaken for a proof that a homogeneous Iranian nation and people existed in that region. Such a conception was conceived primarily in a linguistic-racial sense for pre-Islamic Iran and for most of the nationalist historiography of the Islamic period. These two phases are examined in this and following chapters to demonstrate the rigid preconceptions of mainstream Orientalism about race and nation in the face of repeated inconsistencies among the Orientalists themselves, of the Arab-Persian Islamic sources, and of the complexity of the subject matter. Nevertheless, in the twentieth century, Asian/Iranian nationalism, as a by-product of European colonialism and other indigenous factors, boldly incorporated the constructed version of national history of Iran by the Orientalists into the nationalist ideology as a backbone.

Before investigating the philological and racial findings of the Orientalists with regard to the formation of the name *Iran*, we should distinguish between *Persia*, commonly used by Westerners as a synonym for Iran until early in the twentieth century, and *Iran*. In doing this we trace both the change of the term from Persia to Iran in scholarship and isolate the misleading and uncorroborated application of *Persia* or *Persian* and its conflict with *Iran* and *Iranian* for the language, people, culture, and land.

PERSIA OR IRAN

In general terms, *Persia* was used as the name for the land by the West and eventually by the entire international community until Reza Shah (1921–1941), as the monarch of Iran, demanded that *Iran* be used instead of *Persia*. In fact, Reza Shah made it clear that any mail addressed to Persia instead of Iran would be returned to the sender.[1] Europeans doubtless became familiar with the name *Persia* from the references in classical Greek sources to Persis (or Persepolis) in histories of the encounters of the Greeks with the Persians, particularly from the time of Alexander the Great. The Bible (in the books of Daniel and Esdras) also refers to *Pars* or Persia.[2] Or perhaps the vast land within Persia known to the European world as Parthia was the source of Persia.[3] We know that

---

[1] Wilber, *Iran Past and Present*, p. 127.

[2] Malcolm, *The History of Persia*, I, p. 1.

[3] Ibid., p. 536.

in the Islamic period many historical/geographical sources referred to the land as Fars (*Pars*), the term that Europeans translating Islamic books into Latin during the Middle Ages, converted into Persia[4] or Perse, although the usage of Persis by the classical Greeks may have become known in European geographical knowledge in later periods.

Modern scholarship has tried to link the present name of *Pars* to Parsa, from the period of Achaemenids.[5] Such an assertion seems to be based on the idea expressed by Mostaufi in his *Nodhat ul-Qulub* and perhaps other earlier descriptions of *Pars* as the base of the ancient kings.[6] However, using Parsa or *Pars* as the source of Western usage of the word *Persia* leaves unexplained how *Fars* was etymologically derived from the *Parsa* of ancient times. The evolution of the name *Fars* has been traditionally taken for granted without further arguments. But it is necessary for scholars to argue if we are to understand the philological transition from one culture or language to another. Another vague concept is the historical application of Parsa or Fars, given that it may be used only for the seat or capital of the ancient monarchs and not necessarily as the name for a vast land or the main plateau. During the Sasanian period (third century CE), according to Islamic geographical sources, the term *Iranshahr* was applied to the vast land, not *Fars*. It thus remains a question why the Europeans continuously used *Persia* and not *Iran* or *Iranshahr*. The flow of Europeans after the Middle Ages toward the Orient gradually made them aware of many historical changes of which they had only had a traditional knowledge. For example, in the travel chronicles of Jean Baptiste Tavernier and Sir John Chardin (both seventeenth-century European travelers), reference is made to the name *Iran*, although in an insignificant manner, since they knew the land only by the

---

[4] Malcolm, *The History of Persia*, I, p. 1; Browne, I, pp. 4–5; George Rawlinson, *The Seventh Great Oriental Monarchy*, pp. 16–17, 572.

[5] Barthold, *A Historical Geography of Iran*, p. 148; see also Andrew Boyle, "The Evolution of Iran as a National State," p. 327; Browne, I, p. 4.

[6] Mostaufi, *Nodhat ul-Qulub*, p. 135.

name *Perse* or *Persia*.[7] In the late eighteenth century, the term *Iran* is dealt with in a scholarly fashion by Silvestre de Sacy as a result of his reading of the Sasanian inscriptions.[8] Gradually, after the nineteenth century, the term *Iran* came to be used interchangeably with *Persia*, although at times inaccurately, thus causing confusion by giving the impression that Iran was inside Persia or that Persia was inside Iran or that Persia was named after the Aryans, and so on.[9] It was then safe to think that *Iran,* after its introduction to European intellectual circles, had been the name of the land since ancient times, as the statement by J. Malcolm in the nineteenth century confirms: "Iran has been from the most ancient times to the present day, the term by which the Persians call their country."[10] However, applying *Iran* in such a way that Persia was accommodated within it from the linguistic, ethnic, and cultural perspective was left to subsequent scholars.

The other misconception is rooted in the appellation *Persian,* derived from *Persia.* Often the term *Persian* has been used to characterize people and language as well as culture and tradition. The West, unaware of the complexity of the sociocultural components of what they called Persia, simply called everything in the region Persian; whereas this crude perception failed to distinguish the areas of culture, language, and ethnicity. Although *Iran* has been substituted for *Persia* and *Iranian* for *Persian* in recent times, the word *Persian* is still used for language and for certain cultural traditions to emphasize the continuity of Persian dominance. There are some problems posed by using *Persian* so loosely, however. To begin with, the inhabitants of so-called Persia were called Persians by the Europeans prior to the twentieth century (some still call them Persians), although these people did not have any linguistic correspondence with the inhabitants of

---

[7] Tavernier, *Voyages en Perse*, p. 22; see also Chardin, *Travels in Persia*, II, p. 4.

[8] de Sacy, *Mémoires sur Diverses Antiquités de la Perse*, pp. 1–270.

[9] Malcolm, I, p. 1; Flandin, *Voyages en Perse*, II, p. 407; see also Tavernier, p. 22; A. H. Sayce, *The Ancient Empires of the East*, p. 234; Chardin, II, pp. 4–5.

[10] Malcolm, I, p. 1.

Persia themselves. If we consider Fars synonymous with Persia, all the people of Persia could not have been called Fars or Farsis because Fars was only a region of the land (Iran/Persia). Furthermore, there were other regions and linguistic communities such as the Baluchis, Kurds, and Turks that did not fit the Fars or Persian category. (Therefore, in subsequent scholarship they were given the designation *Iranian* rather than *Persian.*) Pietro della Valle, a traveler from Rome in the early seventeenth century interestingly describes inhabitants of Persia who are of several kinds and are the foreigners of different nations.[11] He adds that the real Persians *(veritables Persans)* who continue to live on the land are only living in three or four cities, including Isfahan (the capital of the Safavid dynasty).[12] Father Krusinski, a Jesuit priest, observed in the early eighteenth century: "There is hardly a country inhabited by so many different nations as Persia."[13] In the mid-nineteenth century, Eugene Flandin refers to Persians in general but then at times uses (for example) the Kurds in place of the Persians, as if the author is aware of its difference of identity and yet ambiguously puts both as part of one large entity (without using the general designation *Iranian*).[14]

Thus, *Persian* was an obscure term that hardly explained the multiethnic population and did not correspond to anything in a general scale of identity that the local inhabitants would refer to. It should also be noted that, if *Persian* was borrowed from ancient sources just as *Persia* was, the change of the name to *Iran* simply ignored the changes of culture and languages and the constant new migrations, occupations, and transitions of intervening centuries. It would be far-fetched and anachronistic to believe that peoples of pre-Iran or Iran (pre-Islamic or Islamic) continuously viewed themselves as possessing one unique identity in various regions, whether it be a native Khurāsān, Kurdistan, or Fars. So one widely disseminated aspect of 'Persian' identity does not properly reflect the complex multilayered issue of identity that underlies it except

---

[11] *Voyages de Pietro della Valle*, II, pp. 386–409, 323–325.

[12] Ibid., p. 387.

[13] Krusinski, *History of the Late Revolutions of Persia*, pp. 120–121.

[14] Flandin, I pp. 117–119; II, p. 409.

for purposes of convenience. However, as time went by *Persian* gradually came to be used for the language designation and less for the ethnic.

In the early Islamic period, from the seventh to ninth centuries, the languages of the region underwent a sharp transition and synthesized new languages under Arabic alphabetical and stylistic auspices. Farsi, the language that developed in the post-Islamic period, is generally referred to as Persian. But the designation *Persian* for *Farsi* (the language) and for the people of Persia (who potentially speak Farsi) creates a confusion in designating a broad identity for the speakers of Farsi outside Persia proper such as people in regions of Transoxiana (Tajikistan, Afghanistan). Could these people be called Persians because they were (are) speakers of Farsi? No technically satisfactory answer was provided until the modern concept of nationality and geographical identity took precedence over other vague cultural affiliations. The Persian designation for both the people and the language also raises questions as to how and why, if the Farsi language was formed between seventh and ninth centuries,[15] the ancient term *Persian* (derived from Persis) was conveniently used for a much younger language? Furthermore, the ancient appellation *Persian*, at least in the European sources, indicated an ethnic designation, not necessarily a language. The uninformed use of *Persian* for the *Farsi* language by the Orientalists was based on nothing but an imagined continuity of the people and the language from ancient times, particularly from the Sasanian period. It was through this reasoning that the Farsi language (Persian) was seen in its third phase after having gone from 'Old Persian' of the Achaemenid to 'Middle Persian' of the Sasanian (as Browne states, this development is "quite analogous to the expressions 'Old English,' 'Middle English,' and 'Modern English'").[16]

Again, the designation of 'Old' and 'Middle' for these languages has had at least two consequences. First, the philologists

---

[15] Lazard, "The Rise of the New Persian Language," 4, p. 595. First composed Farsi poetry was in Marv in 809; see also Darmesteter, *Les Origines de la Poesie Persane*, pp. 3–4.

[16] Browne, I, p. 82.

(e.g., Darmesteter) conclusively stated that due to borrowed words from various languages, modern Farsi differs structurally and grammatically from those ancient languages. Nonetheless, it was seen as an extension of them and not other regional languages, probably for mustering the conception of continuity from antiquity on, in a national context. Second, by having said this, the Orientalists established the necessary link between the pre-Islamic and Islamic periods — particularly in culture and language — although in fact these differed sharply from one another. Still, the evident distance between the so-called Persians of the Achaemenid period of half a millennium BCE and the speakers of Farsi of, say, the fourteenth century CE as a widespread and continental (not national) grouping had to be bridged both in technical scholarship and in nationalistic historical thinking. It should be acknowledged that the Farsi language is a symbol of continuity for over a millennium (even from what has been borrowed from the common languages of the Sasanian period), but such continuity does not guarantee continuity for the culture or the ethnicity inside Iran proper. Thus the designation *Persian* for all the elements, including language, culture, and ethnicity, without considering the selective and discontinued aspects culture and ethnicity leads to seriously contradictory conclusions. The challenge in working out the classifications and construct of national religion, history, and languages was undertaken in the painstaking studies of A. V. W. Jackson, James Darmesteter, F. H. Weibach, E. W. West, F. Spiegel, F. Justi, T. Nöldeke, K. F. Geldner, K. Salemann, E. Herzfeld, E. G. Browne, and later eminent scholars.

Subsequently, the broad 'national' term *Persian*, which has been used for the language and its speakers, technically excluded other ethnic populations of Iran whose mother tongue is other than Farsi (Persian). When the term *Iran* came to be substituted for the term *Persia* in Western literature, the concept *Iranian* was equally poised to replace *Persian*, but *Iran* became a broad historical category to nourish the nationalistic necessities of many groups of which Persians were only one.

THE APPEARANCE AND SIGNIFICANCE OF THE TERM *IRAN*

The designation of names for geographical locations is a universal phenomenon from ancient times. Besides more complex motivations, people seem moved by the convenience of finding or positioning themselves with some precision on this vast planet. In a broad sense, all geographical names are only words; as Edward Said points out, the geographical sectors Orient and Occident are manmade and only relative to each other.[17] These concepts and names only find particular significance as a result of the meanings and interpretations we give them. In tracing the name *Iran*, we must not imagine that we are acting in a historical vacuum with a case of simple invention and application of a name; we must also argue and reargue the meanings and interpretations that were given to it — especially during the period of open racism and nationalism. The anachronistic and unwarranted use of the term *Iran* to construct tradition, history, and ideas in a national context has been substantially taken for granted by scholars. However, future critical studies may shed light on many historical circumstances in a more faithful manner. Here we provide a sketch of the appearance of the term *Iran* and attempt to expose the extravagant inventions of a certain kind of scholarship purporting to demonstrate the existence of racial, national, and cultural consciousness on the part of the inhabitants of Iran in a crude Iranian context.

As noted before, various European travelers prior to the eighteenth century became acquainted with the name *Iran* and reported it in their diaries next to *Persia*. The serious study of the term *Iran* came in two consecutive phases. During the first, the European scholars were simultaneously developing the preliminary stage of Aryan studies, in the late 1700s through early 1800s. The second phase was when extreme Aryanism dominated the scholarship from the mid-nineteenth century on.

The first European to uncover the term *Iran* in the future academic and Orientalist work (after the painstaking data-gathering efforts of others) was Antoine-Isaac Silvestre de Sacy[18] in 1790. It was de Sacy, apart from his massive works on Arabic literature and Islam, who for the first time produced a consequential work on the

---

[17] Said, p. 5.

[18] To learn more about the period, school, and ideas of de Sacy see Said, pp. 123–130; Bernal, p. 234.

inscriptions of the Sasanian dynasty of Persia (225–650 CE).[19] Actually de Sacy produced the first methodic study on the philology of antiquity and therefore deserves close scrutiny. His *Mémoires sur Diverses Antiquités de la Perse,* published in Paris in 1793, was a pioneer of philological excavation emphasizing the national framework of Iran. This book contained two parts, the first focusing on "Iranian national consciousness" during the Sasanian period and the second focusing on "nationalist historiographical consciousness" (for which de Sacy translated the out-of-context Sasanian history recorded in Mirkhond's collection of historical writings).[20] In the first part, de Sacy's deciphering of the inscriptions of Naqsh-e Rustam, Persepolis, Kirmānshāh, and the medallions of the Sasanian kings extracted the term *Iran* as standing for both the land and the people in the Sasanian period.[21] The emblematic royal statement *Malcan Malca Iran ve Aniran* (first known to have appeared with Ardeshir I, then by Shapur I) was converted through ideogram to correspond with "King of the Kings of Iran and Turan." At least this is the interpretation de Sacy provided, saying that *Iran* in the inscription stood for Iran proper while *Aniran* (the negative) stood for beyond and the enemy of Iran — in this case Turān.[22]

Although argument is quite extensive about the interpretation of *Iran* and *Aniran* among subsequent scholars during the life of and after de Sacy, his interpretation was established because it had ethnic, geographical, and political resonance. Quatremère, another eminent Orientalist of the early nineteenth century, contested the

---

[19] Gignoux, "Middle Persian Inscription," p. 1206; Browne, I, p. 59; MacDonald Kinneir, *A Geographical Memoir of the Persian Empire,* pp. 136–137, and Massé, "Les Sassanides," p. 121, indicate de Sacy was the first to decipher the Sasanian inscriptions.

[20] Pedro Texeira in the mid-1600s had already undertaken this initiative in translating part of Mirkhond's work on the kings of Persia (Fars); see his *Voyages de Texeira ou l'Histoire des Rois de Perse* (Paris, 1681).

[21] de Sacy, *Mémoires sur Diverses Antiquités de la Perse,* pp. 38, 47, 52, 88, 89, 101, 102, 110, 111, 247.

[22] Ibid. See also pp. 183, 185–186; see also Sadik Isfahani, *A Critical Essay on Various Manuscript Works, Arabic and Persian,* pp. 6–7.

interpretation of de Sacy but only within its larger racial and national context, changing the inscription's translation to "King of Kings of Medes and Persians."[23] Quatremère believed that the two rival races of Medes and Persians *Ari* and *Anari* in a broad sense conformed to the interpretation.[24] This interpretation was taken as a partial explanation for the Sasanian politics in which the Parthians, vanquished at the hands of Sasanians (who were Persians), were invited to share in the name of the empire to prevent the revolt by constituents of the recently lost Arsacid empire (who were supposedly Medes). The appearance of the Persians in the second place in the emblem was the strategy.[25] The question was how the faded Medes of centuries ago were to fit into the Parthian argument. Such arguments by Eugene Bore, Quatremère, and others eventually led to contradictory conclusions.

Sir John Malcolm took de Sacy's translation and interpretation of the inscription to Moulla Firooz in Bombay (apparently in the early 1800s) to scrutinize its accuracy. Firooz interpreted the word *Aniran* to mean unbeliever, as Malcolm adds: "*Eer* he informed me was a Pahlevee word, which signified believer; *Eeran* was its plural." Firooz then translated the royal emblem apart from its Zoroastrian (the state religion) reference point to include its geopolitical context: "King of believers and unbelievers, or of Persia and other Nations."[26] Such elaboration bypassed racial interpretation but retained the essence of its national interpretation. The religious interpretation of *Iran* and *Aniran* in the poems of *Shāhnāmeh* (the version DuPerron brought from India) had portrayed that *Iran* was the practitioner of Zoroastrian laws and *Aniran* simply was not.

---

[23] Dubeux, "Lettre à M. le rédacteur du journal asiatique, sur un article de M. Eugène Boré relatif aux inscription Pehlvies de Kermânchâh traduites par M. Silvestre de Sacy," pp. 53, 57–58.

[24] Ibid., p. 58.

[25] Ibid., pp. 61–63.

[26] Malcolm, *The History of Persia,* I, p. 548; see also Dubeux, pp. 40–41 (notes); de Sacy, pp. 184–185.

If you do not have any knowledge of Aniran and Iran,
I will inform you about them.

Aniran do not carry the Kosti belt respectably,
But, Iran carry it nobly.

Like the men of faith and saints of religion,
They carry the Kosti belt as prescribed by religion.[27]

If this perspective is accurate, then *Iran* and *Aniran* may not be understood correctly by either racial or national reasoning. Within the Sasanian Empire there were simply Zoroastrian citizens and non-Zoroastrians, regardless of their ethnic or geographical origin. Having said that, it is not necessary to assume that all the Persians were Zoroastrian and that all the non-Iranians were non-Zoroastrian. Although one can argue that Zoroastrianism was tied to ethnic and linguistic affiliation, this again does not necessarily support an argument in a national context. There must have been a mixture such that the title King of Kings of Iran and Aniran could possibly have meant, as interpreted in *Shāhnāmeh*, "King of Kings of Zoroastrian believers and non-Zoroastrian believers" — that is, the sovereign of all subjects. Again, this is supported by the multiplicity of religious practices of Buddhism, Judaism, Gnosticism, and other religious traditions in the Sasanian Empire.[28]

The word *Aniran* has received still other interpretations: Birunī (d. c. 1048) interprets it as the thirtieth day of the month in the Zoroastrian rites.[29] According to Anquetil Du Perron, Hyde, and de Sacy respectively, *Aniran* also means first (or limitless) light, an *ized* presiding over marriage; and the day that Zoroaster announced his doctrine.[30] De Sacy claimed too that *Aniran* is

---

[27] de Sacy, pp. 184 (notes), 422. (The Kosti belt worn by men of Iran may have a Hindu parallel of the sacred thread worn by people of Brahmin caste of India.)

[28] Puech, "La situation Religieuse dans l'Iran Occidental à l'Avènement des Sassanides," *La Civilisation Iranienne*, pp. 123–128.

[29] Biruni, *Chronology of Ancient Nations*, p. 215; see also de Sacy, p. 185.

[30] de Sacy, p. 185.

synonymous with *outsiders,* and he drew an analogy between it and *barbarian* in Greeks and *'Ajam* in Arabic.[31]

In appraising the symbolic meaning or consciousness of the Sasanian use of *Iran* and *Aniran* in Zoroastrian terms, we must recall the antagonistic position of the Sasanians vis-à-vis the converted Christian Roman Empire. In subsequent periods the threat of Christianity on one hand and the Manichaean and Mazdakite religions as a threat to the hierarchy of religious aristocracy on the other may have encouraged the Sasanian propaganda on behalf of Zoroastrian tradition.[32] (See Epilogue for an update).

We now return to de Sacy's interpretation of *Aniran* — that it stood for Turān, the non-Iranian region and population. According to Firdowsī's epical tradition, Turān was the enemy of Iran;[33] furthermore, when the Iranian philological classifications were being formed in the nineteenth and twentieth centuries Turān, due to perhaps phonetic similarity, was interpreted as the Turkish population[34] of Central Asia, who according to the Orientalist did not belong to the so-called Indo-Iranian or Aryan world. Based on this tradition, if we assume that Turān did not belong to the Iranian world, we face a geopolitical as well as philological paradox: There is convincing geographical evidence that, during Firdowsī's time (tenth to eleventh centuries) and possibly even prior to that, Turān was a well-known country that included the Baluchistan region.[35]

Moreover, Turān was included under the governorship of Sistān during the Sasanian period.[36] Since (as linguists believe) the Baluchi language and its related dialects are part of the Iranian

---

[31] de Sacy, p. 183.

[32] Gnoli, *The Idea of Iran,* pp. 139, 162, 166.

[33] See Bosworth, *The Ghaznavids: Their Empire* in *Afghanistan and Eastern Iran,* pp. 205–206.

[34] Ibid.

[35] *Yaqut al-Hamawi,* p. 128; W. Barthold, p.75.

[36] Frye, *The Golden Age of Persia,* p. 14; Frye, "The Political History of Iran under Sasanians," p. 121.

language family,[37] Turān, as the central part of Baluchistan, could not have been outside the Iranian world. Furthermore, during the period of Firdowsī and of the Ghaznavid dynasty of the eleventh century, Turān and its principal city, Qūsdār, recognized only the authority of the caliph of Baghdad; and for this reason Sultan Mahmud had launched attacks against Turān.[38] It is certainly *possible* that Firdowsī had used Turān as the enemy in a metaphorical sense in his construct of epic through poetry, and had used as the enemy of the rightful sovereign the opponent of Sultan Mahmud of Ghazna (his patron).

Thus, de Sacy's interpretation of *Aniran* meaning Turān may be contradicted if Turān is considered part of Iran itself, as the subsequent Orientalists who further constructed the national languages for Iran seem to have done. Along the same lines, if *Aniran* is interpreted as the enemy of *Iran* in its nationalistic aspect, we run into the same collision of theories. Tabaristān (modern day Māzandarān), as part of Iran geographically and according to the Orientalists, philologically, had always been a challenge and may have been an enemy to the empires inside Iran proper from the Achaemenids to the Sasanians, to be incorporated under their rule.[39] However, Ibn Isfandīyār, author of *Tārīkh-e Tabaristān* in the thirteenth century, and Ibn Rusta, author of *al-'Alaq al-Nafīsa* in the tenth century, indicate that Tabaristān remained a distinct kingdom until the Islamic period.[40] In fact, Tabaristān never showed any sense of unity with the rest of the empire and remained distinct until the Il-Khanids emerged in the thirteenth century, when the region was incorporated into the empire.[41] The 'national' Iranian consciousness as portrayed by the Orientalists and nationalist

---

[37] Farhang-e Farsi, xxvii–xxviii; see also Safa, *Tārīkh-e Ulum va Adabiyāt-e Irani*, p. 121.

[38] Barthold, p. 75.

[39] Ibid., pp. 230–231.

[40] Ibn Isfandiyar, *Tārīkh-e Tabaristān*, p. 41; Ibn Rusta, *al-'A'laq al-Nafīsa*, p. 178; see also Abol-Ghassemi, *Gilan az Aqaz ta Enghlab-i-Mashroteh*, pp. 32, 34, 39.

[41] Abol-Ghassemi, p. 112. (Some indicate Tabaristān adjoined the mainland in the Safavid period.)

authors does not support the theory of Iran versus Aniran as a
clear cut scenario. The same racial or philological classification
could again be used in arguing about why the Sasanians (as
Iranians) chose Iraq — the verge of the so-called Semitic world, as
Istakhrī (d. 346/957) put it — as the heart of their empire?[42]

It is interesting in this regard to recall the ancient biblical
division of the world's races and regions among the three sons of
Noah. H. Mostaufi informs us that Iran belonged to Shem,[43] and
was traditionally known as the Semitic region. Perhaps it is fair to
say that nationalist doctrine and national identity, in a modern
sense, is the by-product of what we have constructed and produced
in the field of social sciences in the past two centuries, rather than
the characteristics of people of the past, like Mostaufi.

Thus, in attaching the terms *Iran* and *Aniran* to nationalistic
motives of the Sasanians may be utterly improper and fallacious. As
a name for the geographical and to some extent jurisdictional
location of the Sasanians, however, a similar term is used by the
empire: *Iranshahr*. Although we will deal with this name in a
historical-geographical context later, it suffices now to mention that
the assigning of such a name by the Sasanians may have been
related to propagating the Zoroastrian tradition. *Iranshahr* was the
intended and given name of the land that through time may have
changed to *Iranzamin* and then been cut short to *Iran* — not
originally having been *Iran* alone. It must be borne in mind that
merely assigning a name to a land does not create a homogeneous
population on that land, despite the fact that many Orientalists
have concerned themselves with seeing a national culture and
tradition — notably an Iranian one.[44] In other words, the name of
the land, *Iranshahr*, had nothing to do with the broad question of

---

[42] See Mostaufi, *Nodhat ul-Qulub*, p. 29, Istakhrī, *Masālik wa Mamālik*,
pp. 86, 122; see also Birunī, p. 122.

[43] Mostaufi, *Nodhat ul-Qulub*, p. 20.

[44] See Rawlinson, pp. 24–27; Frye, *The Golden Age*, pp. 7–26; see also
Christensen, *L'Iran Sous les Sassanides*.

the national identity of the vast heterogeneous population and ethnic composition of the Sasanian Empire.[45]

IRAN AND THE ARYAN HYPOTHESIS

It is time now to investigate the post-de Sacy period, when the term *arya* found significance in both Indo-European studies and as the base for the emergence of Iranian national aspirations. This is a period when Aryanism in scholarship became a force for distinguishing races as well as nations from one another.

A debate on the question of the Aryans of Asia — namely, the Indo-Iranians — is philologically, rather technical. However, regarding the speculations that have accompanied the Aryan hypothesis within the racial and national context of Iran there are general deficiencies that we will scrutinize here.

We will also focus on the question of whether the term *Iran* is derived from *arya* and whether the so-called early Western Asian Aryan tribes (specifically the Persians and the Medes) tried among the complex mixed population in the first millennium BCE to rise up and establish their own distinct national state and empire. As already mentioned, several Orientalists (primarily philologists, and archaeologists including Adolphe Pictet,[46] A. H. Sayce,[47] and E. Herzfeld)[48] proposed that the name *Iran* is derived from the establishment of Aryans in the region. The question of the name of the land before it was called Iran — *Elam*,[49] some have proposed — is a separate issue. Of course, many Orientalists do not concern themselves much with the name of the land, taking it for granted that it was called Iran, but rather pay attention to the ethnicity of the early Aryan settlers, who distinctly became known as Iranians. George Rawlinson, a nineteenth-century historian; W. Barthold, a

---

[45] Rahimi-Laridjani, *Die Entwicklung der Bewässerungslandwirtschaft in Iran bis in sasanidisch-frühislamische Zeit*, p. 23.

[46] Pictet, p. 39.

[47] Sayce, p. 234.

[48] Gnoli, pp. 1–10.

[49] Contenau, "L'archéologie de la Perse des origines à l'époque d'Alexandre," *Société des Études Iraniennes*, p. 3; Kinneir, p. 2; Birunī, p. 110, indicates *Elan* instead of *Elam*.

historian/geographer, Roman Ghirshman, an archaeologist; and Albert Olmstead, a historian, all in the twentieth century, developed an avalanche of ideas regarding the distinct Iranian ethnic, linguistic, and cultural consciousness as the "superior" Aryans of ancient times; they convinced a wide audience of students, scholars, nationalist government officials, and the public at large that the Aryans or Iranians had made Iran their homeland.[50]

There are, however, several general weaknesses in this hypothesis. First of all, it is difficult to believe that a segment of a population, in this case the Aryans, could remain ethnically and culturally autonomous from the rest of the indigenous population for nearly a millennium. Then, this precise segment of people with their photographic historical memories and self-consciousness of their Aryan ancestry supposedly built their own empire and called it Iran or a similar name. Such a linear vision in history can only be thought valid by those who unreasoningly wish to believe it. Second, the theory of the Aryan race is based entirely on linguistic conceptions that cannot support it as a whole. The nineteenth-century designation of Aryan for the entire Indo-European language family was arbitrary, and the assumption that Sanskrit was the oldest Indo-European language (primarily propagated by A. Pictet) has been proved wrong.[51] In the early stages of Indo-European studies, the Medes were thought to be of the Aramaic or Semitic race.[52] Only later were the Medes deemed to be of Aryan descent, based on the speculative etymologies of a handful of names and words they left behind.

The connection of the Medo-Persian population of the western part of present Iran to the eastern part — the Indian

---

[50] Rawlinson, pp. 1–29; Barthold, p. 4; Ghirshman, *L'Iran et la migration des Indo-Aryen et des Iranien*, pp. 45–77; Olmstead, *History of the Persian Empire*, pp. 16–24.

[51] Schmitt, "Aryans," *Encyclopedia Iranica*, p. 684.

[52] See Malcolm, I, pp. 479–480. Gobineau in the mid-nineteenth century regards the Medes as the superior Aryans who came and mixed themselves with the Mesopotamian population, where they failed in their primitive superiority; see Boisset, pp. 202–203.

population — and finally to the European communities was formulated on the assumption that at one point in history they had all spoken a proto-Indo-European language and only later did they disperse. So far, this hypothesis has not been able to gather enough evidence to answer various fundamental questions. "The directions and the time of their migration cannot be adequately treated unless relevant data at the disposal of other sciences is made use of."[53] Furthermore, the linguistic conception (discussed in Chapter 1) has been challenged and modified by certain philologists who have demonstrated similarities among many languages that largely change the status of the Indo-European structure, which has racist coloring. Thus, the concept of *arya* as a racial phenomenon could not have been the foundation for envisaging a nation (in modern sense) in ancient times.

Third, the crude juxtaposition of the historical anecdotes of thousands of years ago to serve nationalistic and race-oriented consciousness and perceptions of the modern type is depressingly anachronistic. In other words, the early Medo-Persian population who conceived the so-called nation of Arya or Iran are now being falsely given all kinds of racist and nationalist characteristics (e.g., Rawlinson). In fact, *arya* found racial definition only from the nineteenth century on. To substantiate all three general discrepancies in the formation of the nation of Iran from the Aryanist point of view, let us discuss a few examples to further our evaluation of the commonly represented history of Iran.

In this discussion, to solve the problem of whether the idea of Iran was conceived by the early so-called Aryan settlers who eventually gave rise to the Achaemenid Empire, we must reexamine the "facts" presented by certain Orientalists so that we can curb the anachronistic construct of Iran as the name for the land and people. The common belief among the Orientalists is that the Persians and the Medes were early settlers of Aryan stock in the western plateau of Iran who separated from their Indian counterparts at an unknown date and location. The necessary connection between the Western Aryans or Iranians (Medes and

---

[53] Gafurov, "The Study of Aryan Problems in USSR," pp. 15–17; see also Schmitt, pp. 684–685.

Persians) and the Eastern Aryans was made by tracing certain religious, mythical, and epic words in the Veda, Avesta, or a handful of other sources. For example, *asura* in Indic and *ahura* in Old Persian as the name of the God are believed not only to be etymologically of the same roots but also to indicate (as Max Müller proposed)[54] common religious rites and practice. Such an assumption, although serviceable to the Aryan hypothesis, requires a wider scope of interpretation than is offered by a narrow and somewhat absolutist vision of Aryanism. Not only that, but also, as T. Burrow warns us, "The Indo-Aryan nature of the Aryan vestige in the Near East is established both on the basis of the language and religion, but the material is still remarkably small."[55] Another theory concerns the date of the appearance of Zoroaster in the East and the movement of the Persians and Medes from the East toward the West. Generally, 600 BCE has been accepted by certain scholars as the birth of Zoroastrianism (although others, like Boyce, date it earlier). Meanwhile, the earliest mention of the Medes and the Persians in the West occurs in Assyrian annals of the mid-ninth century BCE. Two abstractions without detailed arguments could be made from the above revelations. One is that, if the Medo-Persians were the worshipers of Ahuramazda, the Zoroastrian God, as some scholars have suggested, then either the date of the propagation of Zoroastrian doctrine must be changed to prior to the ninth century BCE (the Medes are mentioned in an inscription as early as 1100 BCE),[56] which rules out 600 BCE, or the conversion of the Medo-Persians to Zoroastrianism in the East before coming to the West must be doubted. On the other hand, it is possible that Medo-Persian stock may have migrated westward before the *Farvardin Yast* (a legendary material of early Zoroastrian faith) was compiled.[57] It is also clear that the Medes and the Persians are not mentioned in the Avesta; thus the designation Avestan peoples or *arya* becomes obscure, in Avestan geographical

---

[54] See Browne, I, p. 34.

[55] Burrow, "The Proto-IndoAryans," pp. 123–124.

[56] Spiegel, *Erânische Alterthumskunde*, II, 246 quoted by Browne, I, p. 20.

[57] Burrow, pp. 136–140; see also G. Gnoli, pp. 62–64; Schmitt, p. 685.

(ethnic) terms, with regard to the Medo-Persian population of the West. This issue leads us to the second abstraction.

The equivalent term appears as *arya* in Old Persian; *ari, arya* in Indian materials; and *airya* in Younger Avestan Yasts, in different passages and contexts in different periods, for which an absolute chronology is lacking; in addition, their common source and original meaning cannot be established with continuity as well as etymologically. Moreover, the variations in meaning and interpretation in Indian materials, as well as the different connotations of the term *arya* in Avestan and Old Persian, has hindered solving the problem of the Aryans of the West (Medes and Persians) in the ethnic sense.[58] Furthermore, Gnoli indicates that the Elamite and Greek usage and meaning of *arya* adds more fuel to the problem of conceiving a common root and meaning for this term.[59] The Avestan version *Aîryana väejah* is referred to by some scholars as the homeland of the Iranians or Indo-Iranians (Frye, Boyce, Morgenstierne), and yet it is emphasized as the homeland of Zoroastrians (who resided in the eastern territory — Afghanistan) rather than of Iranians (Nyberg, Henning, Gnoli).[60] As noted before, the Medo-Persians (the so-called early or Western Iranians (in Iran proper) in the Avestan geography of the Aryans) may not be included in the Aryan bond.[61]

In Elamite, however, according to Gnoli, there are references to the Aribi in the Assyrian annals that may very well document the existence of Arabs in the eighth century BCE in the central plateau (present-day Iran).[62] F. C. Andreas' observation of the term *Aribi* made him propose that it was an Elamite plural of the name of the Aryans; this view was accepted and maintained by E. Meyer, A. Christensen, and a few others. Others did not want to say that

---

[58] Bailey, "Arya," *Encyclopedia Iranica*, II, p. 682; Gnoli, pp. 8, 30, 32–35.

[59] Gnoli, pp. 8, 13, 18, 29–31.

[60] Ibid., p. 50; Duchsne-Guillemin, *Zoroastrianism: Symbols and Values*, p. 5; see also Lars-Ivar Ringbom, "The Seven Keshvars of the Earth," p. 15.

[61] Burrow, pp. 136–140; Gnoli, pp. 62–64.

[62] Gnoli, p. 8.

there were Arabs in Iran in the first half of the first millennium
BCE but claimed there were "nomads" and "shepherds."[63] The
early mixture of the Arabs (as Semitic) and Iranians (as Aryans) was
controversial in light of what had been distinctively constructed for
the "Aryans of Iran" and the Aryan hypothesis altogether. In fact,
it has been proposed that the word *ari* or *arya* may very well be a
Near Eastern loan word, a common Hamito-Semitic vocable, or an
Egyptian loan word in Ugaritic.[64] All of these prototype words, in
sum, have caused a collision of opinions, but in all circumstances,
the ethnic Aryanness of the Medo-Persian population has been the
dominant view. It is, however, from such point of view the
Achaemenid dynasty is seen as the beginning of the Aryan empire
and the early establishment of Iran and the Iranian nation.

E. Herzfeld, an archaeologist, propagated that the term *Iranian*
is derived from the political and geographical name of *Aryanam
Khshathram* — The Empire of the Aryans — used in Achaemenid
inscriptions. (It does not occur.) The Czech scholar Otakar Klima
concludes that, first, the Achaemenids had no official name or title
as far as we know; second, the expression *Khshayathiay Parsaiy*
should not be interpreted as the name of the empire but of the
state, since the term *empire* does not occur at all in the inscription.[65]
Furthermore, *Parsa* (from which *Persia* or *Persian* is conceived in
Herodotian terms) was most likely used in a political sense and
Achaemenid in a tribal sense rather than *arya*. Although *arya* does
appear, for example in the inscription of Darius at Naqsh-e Rustam
and Xerxes at Persepolis (where the king proclaims himself *Arya
ciça*, its meaning may be sought in broad, but obscure cultural and
religious contexts.[66] Zoroastrianism found its way to the state of
the Achaemenids, but as the scholar Muhammad Dandamaev
informs us about the religious politics of the empire, they
worshiped and respected Egyptian, Babylonian, and Elamite gods,
too, and many people worshiped other elementary divinities of

---

[63] Gnoli, pp. 8–11.

[64] Ibid., p. 30.

[65] Klima, "The Official Name of the Pre-Islamic Iranian State,"
pp. 144–146.

[66] Gnoli, pp. 16–17, 22–23.

nature.[67] Thus it is difficult to believe that *arya* in the Avestan sense in a multicultural empire was only used in a religious sense, to emphasize purity and piety by Darius rather than using it possibly as a political tool to establish genealogical legitimacy from his Zoroastrian subjects. Darius himself speaks in the inscriptions of being the king of numerous communities,[68] and thus it would be unlikely that Darius conceptualized his empire as Aryans, an alleged unique race.

In a broader cultural sense, the Achaemenids may not be looked at as pure promoters of Aryan civilization or of Iranian civilization as it has been conceived by racially-oriented and nationalist individuals, but rather as the cosmopolitan bearers of the previous civilizations. In supporting the thesis for the lack of cultural purity of Achaemenids in giving rise to a civilization that has been labeled Aryan or Iranian by the Orientalists, the following indications are only the tip of an iceberg. As for the assumption that the Achaemenids spoke Old Persian: First, this language did not have an alphabet of its own, but rather used the Aramean alphabet (so-called Semitic) for writing; second and more important, as Roman Ghirshman reports, out of 30,000 tablets found in Persepolis, not one was in Old Persian; a few were in Aramean but most were in Elamite.[69] Some scholars even held that the names Cyrus and Cambyses seemed to be Elamite derivations.[70] The Akkadian, Assyrian, Chaldean, and Egyptian influences in art and architecture, apart from in language, were so evident that they made some elements of nineteenth-century opinion favor the thesis that the Medes, as counterparts of the Persians, were Aramaic, Elamite, Turanian, or Semitic.[71] It thus comes as no surprise that the architectural style of the so-called tomb of Cyrus (not all

---

[67] Dandamaev, "La Politique Religieuse des Achaemenides," pp. 193–200; Duchesne-Guillemin, "Le dieu de Cyrus," pp. 11–21.

[68] Benveniste, "Les Langues de l'Iran Ancien," p. 37.

[69] Ghirshman, *L'Iran des Origines à l'Islam*, pp. 158–159.

[70] Sayce, p. 240; see also Browne, I, p. 55.

[71] Ibid., pp. 235, 240, 270–273; see also Malcolm, I, pp. 479–480; Oppert, "le Peuple et la Langue des Medes," II, pp. 10–15; Browne, I, pp. 23–24, 36, 60.

scholars have accepted this tomb as that of Cyrus; the native people considered it to be the tomb of Solomon's mother)[72] is said to be an Egyptian imitation. This is explained by the royal marriage of Cyrus to an Egyptian princess.[73] In the linguistic realm, it has been argued that the stylistic elements of Aramaic and Biblical Hebrew had their impact on certain words and verbs in Old Persian.[74]

These instances underline the intercultural and intellectual interaction of various cultures (whether Mesopotamian, Achaemenid, or other) in a wide multiethnic area and show their significance. This approach to complex historical processes rules out any narrow national, ethnic, or anachronistic attribution to one community or another, particularly in the more heterogeneous regions. Thus, to apply the term *arya* to a race and to some embryonic notion of an early nation of Iran is an act of historical blindness influenced by extreme Aryanism in scholarship. As Gnoli demonstrated in his painstaking study, *arya* neither stood for Iran nor was synonymous with Parsa; and it would be a sheer anachronism to consider Achaemenids the historical source of Iranian national aspirations.[75]

The Parthians, who succeeded the Seleucids (Greeks) after the latter had conquered the Achaemenids, are believed to have come from *l'Iran extérieur*. According to G. Contenau and R. Grousset, this marks the return to an "Oriental national ideal."[76] There is a twofold argument against the Parthians' use of *Iran* or similar names or being the guarantors of Iranian or Aryan heritage and continuity. First, the idea that the Parthians used the phrase *Empire of the Aryans* just as the Achaemenids supposedly did is, as Gnoli

---

[72] This is an indication of the lack of historical consciousness of people of the past who only recently were awakened to their pre-Islamic and historical glory in a national context.

[73] Barthold, pp. 149–150.

[74] Greenfield, "Iranian or Semitic," pp. 311–316.

[75] Gnoli, p. 26–27, 175–177.

[76] Contenau, "Status Élemites d'époque Parthe," p. 231; Grousset, "L'âme de l'Iran et l'humanism," pp. 35–36.

argues, without foundation.[77] Second, their loose return to Zoroastrianism[78] did not completely put them in the Avestan *arya* category, nor is there any trace of evidence that the Parthians had an *arya* ethnic awareness. As D'iakonov indicates, the existence of many ethnic groups in Parthian territory leaves us to believe that a single ethnic and national designation and consciousness were lacking among the Parthians.[79] Furthermore, their heterogeneous decentralized form of petty princes or *Muluk al-Tawāif*[80] government could not have provided a basis for national unity anyway. On the other hand, Ehsan Yarshater indicates that the Parthians experienced a complete loss of memory of the Achaemenids, since the authors of *Khwaday Namag (Book of Monarchs – Shāhnāmeh)* had no information before Alexander[81] (this may very well be attributed to the Sasanians since they were the compiler of the legend). This rules out the earlier hypothesis of the return to an Oriental national idea by the Parthians.

It has also been argued that the Parthians used the title *Shahanshah Eran* (or *Shahanshah Aryan*), King of Kings of Iran. Those who believed that such a title existed in the Parthian period were misled by an erroneous reading of the drachma inscription of the reign of Gotarzes II. In fact, this was an anachronistic forgery of the idea of the Sasanian title King of Kings of Iran, which has no Parthian precedent.[82] Thus, based on this interpretation, the Parthians could not have used the term *arya* as the source of Iran and did not have any memory of the Achaemenids to use as a basis for pursuing the continuity of Iranian consciousness. However, the attribution of Iranism to both the Achaemenids and the Parthians by the Orientalists is uniquely due to philological findings, since the Medo-Persians of the Achaemenid Empire were considered

---

[77] Gnoli, p. 103.

[78] Ibid., pp. 113, 116.

[79] D'iakonov, *Ashkanian*, pp. 122–123.

[80] Biruni, p. 17; H. Mostaufi, *Tārīkh-i Gozīdeh*, p. 97; see also Hamza Isfahānī, *Tārīkh-i Sini Muluk al-Arz wal-Anbiā*, p. 44; Christensen, p. 34.

[81] Yarshater, "Iranian National History," pp. 359–366; see also Frye, "The Political History of Iran Under Sasanian," p. 116; Christensen, p. 79.

[82] Gnoli, pp. 120, 129–130.

Western Iranians and the Parthians were considered Eastern Iranians.[83]

From this assumption the hypothetical affinity of Aryans or Iranians for each other was conceived as a basis for maintaining a distinct national entity. Considering the lack of evidence and what has just been argued, we should be skeptical of the imaginative and rhetorical projections of certain Orientalists that the Parthians restored Achaemenid Iranism, a questionable issue itself.

Let us now turn to the Sasanian period, during which time the term *Iran, Eran,* or *Iranshahr* was adopted in one way or another. Although we have already discussed the origin of the term in the inscriptions translated by de Sacy in the late eighteenth century, we still need to clarify the inconsistencies in the adaptation of *Iran* for geographical, political, and ethnic purposes that has been attributed to the Sasanians.

The term *Iran* was not an evolved form of *arya* in an ethnic sense; the emphasis was more on its Zoroastrian political propaganda aspect, appearing as *Iran* and *Aniran* in the Sasanian literature. From such an origin, it is difficult to connect *Iran* to a geographical designation or to an ethnic one, as de Sacy and subsequent scholars proposed. For the geographical designation we have a term that appears in many post-Sasanian sources — *Iranshahr* or *Eranshahr* — which corresponds more or less to present-day Iran.[84] The term is obviously combined from *Iran* and *Shahr* meaning province or land, which again may be connected to Zoroastrian religious-political motives. By investigating variations in geographical designations and the frequent appearance of *Iranshahr* interchangeably with *Fars* in the post-Sasanian sources, we can establish an account whereby the term was not strictly used in correspondence to an ethnic community perceived to be Iranian by certain Orientalists.

---

[83] Ghirshman, *L'Iran et la migration des Indo-Aryens*, pp. 45–46.

[84] *Tārīkh-i Sistān,* pp. 23–24 (considers the western Iranian plateau as *Iranshahr*); Gnoli, pp. 137, 157 quoting *Letter of Tansar,* mentions that *Iranshahr* was a designation for both the west of Iran proper and Fars.

CHAPTER 4
IRANSHAHR
AND SYNONYMOUS DESIGNATIONS:
A POLITICAL-HISTORICAL INQUIRY

The first meaning of *Iranshahr* (used by the Sasanians) or of *Iranzamin, Iran, Fars,* or *'Ajam* (used by others in the Islamic period), was the name of the land, and not a political or ethnic concept. Although the question of the nationalist historiography of Iran is discussed in the following chapters, here attention is given to the geographical names of Iran rather than to the terms' sociopolitical aspects. From the viewpoint of twentieth-century nationalist-oriented scholars, of course, the name of the land and the socio-political dimension were inseparable.

In tracing the name *Iranshahr* used by Sasanians, the Danish scholar Arthur Christensen relates an account about Shahpur I, the Sasanian sovereign who ordered the destruction of Susa and the killing of its inhabitants in response to an uprising and then had the city reconstructed under the name *Iranshahr*.[1] This account does not, however, sufficiently explain the broader usage of *Iranshahr.* Furthermore, Sasanians made use of the word *Iran* in naming other cities (e.g., *Iran-Khuarreh-Kard,* north of *Iranshahr)* as well as in naming individuals (e.g., *Iran-Dukht)* and in administrative and

---

[1] Christensen, *L'Iran Sous les Sassanides*, pp. 247–248; see also Mostaufī, *Tārīkh-i Gozīdeh,* p. 76; Gnoli, *The Idea of Iran,* p. 131; Rahimi-Laridjani, *Die Enturickling der Bewässerungslandwirschaft im Iran bis in sasanidisch-frühislamische Zeit,* p. 39.

military official titles (e.g., *Iran-Sepahbadh*).[2] It thus appears that the widespread use of the word *Iran* by the Sasanians, either in honorific titles (King of Kings of *Iran* and *Aniran*) or in geographical designations, eventually found its way in the Islamic period into historical documents as the name of the land — especially in the name of *Iranshahr* (and Iran) — and not of its inhabitants.

It is interesting also to note another geographical designation whose roots lie most probably in Sasanian administrative codes — namely, Iraq — since the Sasanians' core of government was based in the present-day Iraq (Ctesiphon, the capital of the Sasanian empire, was on the Tigris River near present-day Baghdad). The reason for the similarity of the names *Iran* and *Iraq* has been the subject of debate. It has been said that *Ir* must be the root for both *Iran* and *Iraq*.[3] Ali Akbar Dehkhoda in his massive Farsi lexicon *(Lughat Nāmeh)* indicates that *Irāh* was originally a Sasanian term meaning "place near the sea"; it had been Arabicized by having its *aleph* changed to *'a'in* and its *ha* changed to *ghaf*, and therefore *Irah* became *'Arāgh* or *Iraq*.[4] Sir John Chardin, however, indicates that the term *Erec* or *Arāc* (probably meaning *Iraq* or the ancient city of Erech) could be found in the tenth book of Genesis.[5] If Chardin correctly read and understood the etymology of this name, then the history of the name of *Iraq* antedated the Sasanian period. It seems from certain sources that *Babylonia* was the old name for Iraq; some Islamic sources mention that Babylonia became Iraq under Iraj, and others say that it was renamed Fars or *Iranshahr*.[6] In any case, Iraq was seen as a region within *Iranshahr* by later sources.[7] Some modern commentators have argued that certain medieval Islamic

---

[2] Christensen, pp. 94, 102, passim; Gnoli, p.130; Chardin, *Travels in Persia*, II, p. 4.

[3] Gnoli, p. 147; Shushtari, *Davāzdah Maghāleh-i Tārīkhī*, p. 176.

[4] Dehkhoda, *Lughat Nāmeh*, s.v. "Irah".

[5] Chardin, II, p. 7.

[6] Mas'udī, *Muruj ul-Dhahab*, I, pp. 264–265; Ya'qubī, *Tārīkh*, I, pp. 175–176; Tabarī, *Tārīkh*, I, p. 154; Isfahānī, p. 33; Istakhrī, *Masālik wa-Mamālik*, p. 5; Birunī, *The Chronology of Ancient Nations*, p. 122.

[7] Mostaufī, *Nodhat ul-Qulub*, pp. 29, 46; *Tārīkh-i Sistān*, p. 25.

geographers of a so-called Iraqi school have purposefully recognized Iraq and *Iranshahr* as synonymous.[8]

Returning to the topic of the roots of *Iran* or *Iranshahr*, particularly in the Arab-Farsi Islamic sources, we come to learn of a tradition that is reflected in many of the sources. This tradition, which may be based on mythological anecdotes, indicates the division of the world among the three sons of Feraidūn — Salm, Tur, and Iraj. Salm was given the West, Tur the East (Turān), and Iraj the middle section, which was named Iran or *Iranshahr* after him.[9] Masʿudī (d. 345/956) in his *Muruj ul Dhahab*, indicates that the letter *j* was replaced with *n* and the name *Iraj* changed to *Iran* or *Iranshahr*, with *shahr* meaning land.[10] The dictionary of *Borhān-e Qāte* (1062/1651) attributes the emergence of the name of *Iran* to Siyāmak, son of Kayūmarth; others credit Hushang, the king of Pishdadians.[11] It is equally interesting to note that certain sources refer to *Khunirath* or *Hunira* as the old name of Iran proper. Among these sources, Avesta, Abu Mansuri's *Shāhnāmeh*, Jāhiz's *Kitāb al-Tarbī' wal-Tadwir*, Masʿudī's *al-Tanbīh wal Ashrāf*, and Tabarī refer to *Khunirath*, while Hamza Isfahānī and the author of *Majmal al-Tawārīkh* refer to *Hunirah*.[12] Perhaps further research into these names will one day explain historical circumstances that render ordinary nationalistic concepts obsolete.

The name *Iranshahr* next to *Fars* nonetheless appears in other accounts prior to Firdowsī, the eleventh-century poet. Ibn Rusta, who finished his *al-ʿAlāq al-Nafisa* around 290/902, makes

---

[8] Tashnar, *Tarikhche-i Jughraphia dar Tamadon Islami*, pp. 19–33.

[9] Tabarī, I, p. 54; Masʿudī, *Muruj ul-Dhahab*, I, pp. 265–266; lsfahānī, p. 33; Birunī, p. 110; Masʿudī, *al-Tanbih wal-Ashrāf*, p. 34; Mostaufi, *Nodhat ul-Qulub*, pp. 19–20; Ibn Balkhi, *Fars Nāma*, p. 17; see also Gnoli, pp. 56–57, 135; Kinneir, p. 2. The tradition also exists in Avesta and Firdowsī's account; see Wolff, *Glossar zu Firdosis Schahname*, pp. 91, 614.

[10] Masʿudī, *Muruj ul-Dhahab*, I, p. 266.

[11] Mostaufi, *Nodhat ul-Qulub, p.* 20.

[12] Masʿudī, *al-Tanbih wal-Ashrāf*, p. 32; Tabarī, I, p. 154; Isfahānī, pp. 20, 32; see also p. 21 annotations; Ringbom, "The Seven Keshvars of the Earth," pp. 11–16.

reference to *Iranshahr* and its provinces.[13] Tabarī (d. 310/923), Istakhrī (d. 346/975) in *Masālik wa Mamālik*, Jayhānī (d. 365/975) in *Ashkāl al-'Alam*, and Mas'udī (d. 345/956) all mention *Iranshahr* and its extent.[14] Firdowsī refers to both *Iranshahr* and *Iranzamin*.[15] Later, Birunī (d. c. 1048) in *Athār al-Bāqīya* makes various references to *Iranshahr*.[16] However, in Birunī's map of the seas in his *Kitāb al-Tafhīm* (c. 420/1028), *Fars* appears to have stood for the land.[17] The unknown author of *Tārīkh-i Sistān*, compiled sometime between the eleventh and fourteenth centuries, geographically locates *Iranshahr* and Arab Iraq (as opposed to 'Ajam Iraq), its heartland, in the western part of Iran proper; he also identifies Khurāsān as a distinct region and country in the eastern part.[18] Hamdullāh Mostaufī Qazvīnī (d. 740/1340) in *Nodhat ul-Qulub*, a geographical account based extensively on earlier works, perhaps in imitation of Firdowsī, prefers *Iranzamin* over *Iranshahr*.[19]

None of these sources (with the exception of Firdowsī) refers to the name of the land and to the identity of its inhabitants synonymously. The geographical designations thus do not seem to have stood for people's identity, especially in a national context. In other words, nobody was called *Iranshahri* or *Iranian*. The genealogical attributes of a tribe, town, or region given to individuals for a certain kind of parochial identity (e.g., Isfahāni, Baghdadi, Salman Farsi) is an interesting but separate question.

The problem of using the name Fars during the Islamic period instead of *Iranshahr* is a historical curiosity. Since *Fars* even today refers to a region in the south-western part of Iran proper, it was more common in the Islamic period to call all of the land Fars,

---

[13] Ibn Rusta, *al-'Alāq al-Nafīsa*, pp. 119–120.

[14] Tabarī, I. p. 154; Istakhrī, pp. 5, 11; Jayhānī, *Ashkāl al-'Alam*, pp. 34, 35, 121; Mas'udī, *Muruj ul-Dhahab*, I, p. 266; see also Mahmoud Al Sayyad, *Min Wajhat ul-Jughrāphia*, pp. 28, 89, referring to Istakhrī and Qilqashandi's indication of *Iranshahr* and *Iran* as one of the lands of Islam.

[15] Wolff, pp. 81–91.

[16] Birunī, pp. 111, 205, 209, 212, 215.

[17] See Tashnar, p. 82.

[18] *Tārīkh-I Sistān*, p p. 23–25.

[19] Mostaufī, pp. 19–21.

particularly when many of the sources of this period referred to the Sasanian kingdom. This simultaneous use of *Fars* and *Iranshahr* raises a question regarding what role the region of Fars played in the politics of the Sasanians, given that it had been more in the front line of usage than the Sasanian's own term *Iranshahr.*

It may be that the Sasanian court (for religious propaganda) had an agreement with high-ranking priests from Fars, or this usage of *Fars* may have resulted from the early years of the new dynasty's origin in Fars.[20] The preference for using *al-Fars* or *al-'Ajam* over *Iranshahr* or *Iran* in the Islamic period, as Gnoli indicates, may be because *Iran* had an unpleasant echo of Sasanians and Zoroastrianism.[21]

The persisting puzzle is why the Sasanians' seat of government (which was in present-day Iraq or the Kurdish region) was identified with Fars. We have no clear record of the underlying complex geographical reasoning and transition. Istakhrī may be making a cautious hint when he says that Babylonia was called *Pars* (Fars) and was the seat of *Iranshahr.*[22] Firdowsī, however, often uses *Pars* (Fars) for the province in the west; he only uses *Pars* for Sasanians of Istakhr.[23] If we consider *Furs* the plural of *Fars* as a general ethnic designation, then it is assumed the terms' roots must be laid in the region of Fars. In summarizing the legends of the Kings of Fars, or Persians (*Muluk al-Furs*), Mas'udī relates a far-fetched but interesting story about the name *Fars* drawing on both biblical and Arab traditions. In brief, he says that one of the sons of either Abraham or Shem (son of Noah) who was called Furs fathered ten sons who all became awesome horse-riders, and since horse-rider is translated *Faris* in Arabic, their country was called Fars.[24]

There is an account as early as Ibn Ishāq (d. 150/767), the first biographer of Muhammad, the prophet of Islam, relating the Sasanians to the Furs, and referring to the land of Fars rather than

---

[20] Gnoli, p. 151.

[21] Ibid., p. 139.

[22] Istakhrī, p. 5; see also Jayhānī, p. 34.

[23] Wolff, p. 177.

[24] Mas'udī, *Muruj ul-Dhahb*, I, p. 278.

to *Iranshahr*. Ibn Ishāq, according to the tradition of Ibn Hishām (d.
218/833), reported that during his prophecy in Mecca, Muhammad
was mocked by the people of the market; one time al-Nadr b. al-
Hārith is said to have spoken about Rustam the hero, and Isfandyār
and the Kings of Fars, *Muluk al-Furs*, emphasizing to Muhammad
and his audience that he could tell a better story than
Muhammad.[25] Although in an anecdotal and stereotypical way, this
story signifies the familiarity of Nadr and of certain Arabs in Mecca
with Sasanian legend perhaps due to geographical proximity or
travel in the region. It also acknowledges the mythical and
legendary tales that Firdowsī put into epic poetry in the eleventh
century — a favorable phenomenon in both the Sasanian court and
its periphery, as reflected in early sources of the Islamic period. It
also seems that in the Arab tradition (whether in Mecca or in other
towns), Fars had always maintained powerful empires in their
eastern region. Thus, *Fars* (in relation to Furs) historically was a
more tangible name to use in identifying the empire to the east of
Arabia than the one to the northwest that they called *Rum* (Rome).

We have evidence that many Arabo-Islamic sources used *Fars*
(or sometimes *Pars* — e.g., Tabarī) instead of *Iranshahr* or *Iran* to
describe the dynasty of the Sasanians and even the dynasties before
them (e.g., Pishdādiān, Kayāniān, Ashkāniān). The title *Kitāb Sirat
al-Muluk al-Furs* was used for many books that were either
translated or authored about the Kings of Fars [Persians] in the
Islamic period — among them Ibn al-Muqaffaʿ, Muhammad ibn
Jahm Barmakī, Zadwiya ibn Shahwiya Isfahānī, and Muhammad
ibn Bahrām ibn Mutayyār Isfahānī.[26] A book titled *Tārīkh-e Muluk
Banu Sāsān* (History of Sasanian Kings) by Hisham ibn Qāsim
Isfahānī[27] refers to the dynasty without indicating its geographic
origin.

From these examples and others, a historico-geographical line
of reasoning may be established: the origin of these kings,
dynasties, and rulers, whether through accurate investigation or
not, was thought to be in *Fars*, a name that may have been familiar

---

[25] Ibn Hishām, *Sirat al-Nabī*, Vol. I, p. 373.
[26] Hamza Isfahānī, p. 7.
[27] Ibid.

for a long period of time, rather than in *Iranshahr,* which was used
to describe a broader geographical territory and may have been a
younger name than *Fars.* In the same fashion, *Rome,* the name of a
city or district at one stage in a gradual historical process, came to
be used for large portions of both the western and eastern Roman
empires. Many Islamic sources (Hamza Isfahānī, Mas'udī, Tabarī,
etc.) use the name *Rum* (Rome) or *Qustantanīya* (Constantinople) to
represent the historical empire or dynasty rather than the actual
name of the territories involved. We also learn that the name of the
region may have been used symbolically to identify the empire, not
necessarily to fix its limits, which constantly fluctuated with new
conquests and losses. Nor should *Furs* or *Rumi* as an ethnic
designation for people belonging to regions other than *Pars* or
Rome obscure the identity question in a historical sense.

Although the geographical extent of *Iranshahr* has been
explained to some extent in various early and late sources,[28] there is
still no consensus on this point in measuring and arguing which
name mattered from their standpoint. Thus the identification of
the empire with *Pars* left a dismaying gap, although the nationalist
historians of the nineteenth and twentieth centuries connected and
interchangeably used *Pars* with Iran as part of constructing a
national history. Consequently, by translating *Fars* as *Iran,* they
paved the way for themselves and others who wished to promote
nationalist historiography.

Leaving the name *Fars,* we come across *Diyār al-'Ajam* (land of
'Ajam) used in certain sources synonymously with the name *Iran.*
The term *al-'Ajam,* apparently an early Arab designation for all non-
Arabs, gradually came to be applied to the land of and people of
Iranshahr. Nāsir Khusrau in the eleventh century, Sa'dī in the
thirteenth century, and Hafiz in the fourteenth century use *'Ajam*
instead of *Iran.*[29] In the sixteenth century, Ali Akbar Khatāi from
Istanbul divided Iran into three parts: Arabistan, Rum and 'Ajam.
From his treatment we learn that present-day Iran was called

---

[28] Istakhrī, pp. 5–6; Mostaufī, pp. 20–28; see also Frye, *Golden Age of
Persia,* pp. 12–14; Rahimi-Laridjani, p. 23.

[29] Koichi, "Meanings of Iran: Preliminary Essay on the Emergence of
'Iranian' Consciousness," p. 188.

'Ajam.[30] Contemporaneous reports and travel chronicles of certain Europeans passing through the region (although perhaps unreliable) indicate that the people called their land and themselves, respectively, 'Ajam and 'Ajami, according to such sources as Pietro della Valle and Pedro Texeira in the early 1600s.[31] On the other hand, Chardin informs us that the people called their land Iran or Iroun, and he refers to two main regions of Iran proper: Iraq Arab and Iraq 'Ajam.[32] The term *'Ajam* could have been used to distinguish the non-Arabic speaking regions of Iran and Iraq from the Arabic-speaking regions. We will later consider the letter of the Ottoman Sultans to the Safavid monarchs in which the term *'Ajam* is frequently used.[33]

Judging from certain geographical and historical works of the Mongolian and post-Mongolian periods, the term *Iran* apparently became the primary designation for the land. Mirkhond, the other historian of the fifteenth century besides Mostaufī, in the segment of his history covering the Turkish Saljuq, refers to Iran three times solely as the name of the land (with no political significance) next to Iraq and Khurāsān.[34] In his history of the Sāmānid dynasty, however, there is no mention of Iran.[35] Another account of Saljuq history by Ibn Bībī refers to such provincial regions as Kirmān, Fars, Khurāsān, and Iraq, rather than using *Iran* in a larger context.[36] The seventeenth-century geographical work of Sādik Isfahānī explicitly refers to Iran and its limits.[37]

---

[30] Koichi, p. 188, quoting Ali Akbar Khatai, *Khatai Nama,* Bibliothèque Nationale Ms. Supplement Persan 1354, f. 3b.

[31] Texeira, *Voyages de Texeira ou l'Histoir e des Rois des Perse,* p. 52; *Voyages de pietro della valle,* II, pp. 386–409.

[32] Chardin, II, pp. 4–7; see also Mostaufī, p. 51.

[33] See Navai, *Shah Abbas,* Vol. I, and *Shah Isma'il Safa vi,* Qa'im, Maqami, *Yek Sad-u Panjāh Sanad-i Tārikhī.*

[34] Mirchondi, *Historia Seldschukidarum,* pp. 15, 107, 162; Mostaufī, p. 27, also agrees that Khurāsān was a region separate from Iran.

[35] See Mirchondi, *Historia Samanidarum* (Goettingen, 1808).

[36] Ibn Bibi, *Histoire des Seldjoucides d'Asie Minore,* IV, p. 237.

[37] Sādik Isfahānī, *The Geographical Works,* pp. 6–7.

IRAN AND ITS POLITICAL USE

The reality of the name *Iran* for the land became clearer in historical writings and names such as *Fars* and *'Ajam* gradually faded away. But it is extremely important to bear in mind that the land of Iran, from the time of the Arab conquest in the mid-seventh century to the rise of the Safavids at the turn of the sixteenth century, was under either the Umayyad (661–750) or the Abbasid (750–1258) caliphate (at least until the first quarter of the Abbasid) or was fragmented under different dynasties. Such fragmentation in a complex historical process is significant for a twofold reason. First, the name *Iran* was not the determining factor in the legitimacy of any dynasty or ruler, as it came to be in modern times — in other words, the aim of any political group in the Islamic period was not to conquer Iran and to establish a national state but rather to conquer more land in any given direction to expand the dynasties' jurisdiction. Second, there was neither a homogeneous population inhabiting Iran nor a modern nationalist ideology promulgated by the dynasties to prevent its fragmentation.

Thus, although using the name of the land to legitimize the political process in a patriotic framework has been the focus of the modern period, it must be remembered this was not the case in the medieval period. One may argue that poets such as Firdowsī and Nizāmī supply ample examples of the medieval type of "cultural nationalism" by praising the land of Iran. This is the subject of the next chapter, but it is sufficient to mention here that there is equal evidence that other Farsi-speaking (Persian) poets, such as Amīr Khusrau Dehlavī and Abdulfeiz Feizī (both from India), praise India and Delhi as the real paradise rather than Iran.[38] We should be aware that much poetry of this kind has only rhetorical rather than political value. Furthermore, it indicates that Farsi (a transnational language) and the land of Iran do not have a particularly special relationship or are not exclusively synonymous as modern nationalist scholars have portrayed it.

---

[38] Ansari, "Amir Khusrau, the Poet and the Patriot," pp. 88–99; see also Chibli, "Nazari bi Nil Deman Feizi," pp. 118–123.

It is important not to confuse the geographic designation of Iran with its political meaning, which it was given in the era of nationalism. The various post-Islamic dynasties who ruled in different corners of Iran in different periods — the Tāhirids, Safavids, Sāmānids, Ghaznavids, and Buyids — all the way to the Safavid period did not use the name *Iran* for political ends or to try to gain legitimacy. In the coinage of all post-Islamic dynasties, even until the Qājār period, not one coin carries the name *Iran*. The policy was that the common logo or inscription on almost all the coinage would be the names of God (Allah) and the Prophet (Muhammad), together with a few Koranic words or the names of the first four caliphs and at times the name of the sovereign or city.[39] Eminent Orientalists have tried to knit together historical documents to identify the Farsi language with the land of Iran and to create a textual argument that the various dynasties in the post-Islamic period were connected and each sought to revive the old "Iranian" culture. It is true that re-archaization and the borrowing of ideas from the past have been a strategy for various dynasties to gain legitimacy in the eyes of their subjects, and this should not be seen as a nationalistic attempt. E. G. Browne, V. Minorsky, C. E. Bosworth, R. Frye, and several others whose works will be evaluated in the next two chapters emphasized such dynastic connections in the context of Iranian heritage. The gaps in their textual analysis were due to the fact that the name *Iran* had nothing to do with the goals and policies of various dynasties during the times when these dynasties confronted each other simultaneously. The allegiance of each dynasty's subjects in each period is a question that textual arguments simply cannot answer concretely. In simple terms, it is anachronistic and historically naïve to think that the people of each region and dynasty gave their allegiance to a geographic name whose limits and meaning were obscure — even more far-fetched to an imagined Iranian nation.

---

[39] Lane-Poole, *The Coins of the Mohammadan Dynasties*; S. Lane-Poole, *The Coins of the Mongols*; Marsden, *The Plates of the Oriental Coins*; for Safavid coinage only see also Chardin, II, pp. 332–333; Tavernier, pp. 346–347.

MAMALIK MAHRUSE-E IRAN

From the seventh century until the intertribal wars began in the fifteenth century, the Iranian plateau was not under one ruler or dynasty (except under the Il-Khanids). This is why, when the Venetian traveler, Marco Polo, crossed what he thought was called Persia (never using the term Iran) in the late thirteenth century, he reported that there were eight kingdoms in Persia, each under a different name.[40] The period between the Il-Khanid and Timurid dynasties is marked by a hundred years of war, when the political vacuum set the stage for the Safavids to come to power at the turn of the sixteenth century. The religious and political propaganda of the Sufis had brought the known although contested seven prestigious Turkish tribes of Shāmlu, Rūmlu, Ustāglu, Tekelu, Afshār, Qājār, and Zolqadr into a political coalition; and in later years the Tāleshān tribe joined them and made the governments of Qara Qoyūnlu (1378–1468) and Āq Qoyūnlu (1378–1502) into a new Safavid government in 1501.[41] It was then, for the second time (the first time was under the Il-Khanids, but no one has made anything of that), that the main plateau of Iran and its regional peripheries were brought under a unified dynasty.

The new dynasty, occurring as it did in the era of new diplomatic relations with neighboring and European empires, still used the name *Iran* in a basically nonpolitical way. In a collection of more than a hundred original letters, decrees, and protocols of the Safavid kings and officials, the name *Iran* appears only a dozen times. It could be asserted from the context of certain documents that the name *Iran* was being used for the land and not necessarily for the government. Meanwhile, some letters by the Ottoman sultans to the Āq Qoyūnlu or to the Safavid kings, refer to the sovereign as King of 'Ajam or King of the land of 'Ajam, although

---

[40] Yule, *The Book of Ser Marco Polo*, Book I, Chapter XV, pp. 78–84. To know more about Marco Polo's family, travels, and contacts with the East see Navai, *Iran va Jahan*, pp. 35–37.

[41] Savory, "L'Empire du Lion et du Soleil," *L'Islam d'Hier à Aujourd'hui*, pp. 282–284; see also Petrushevsky, *Islam in Iran*, p. 388.

less as King of the land of Iran and King of the land of Islam.[42] By
the late Safavid period, according to the letters (particularly those
written during the reign of Sultan Husayn, the last Safavid
monarch) carried by both foreign and domestic couriers, the
administrative title *mamālik* or *velāyāt mahruse-e Iran* (protected
provinces/kingdoms of Iran) was used a title that was carried over
to the Zand and Qājār dynasties.[43]

It is interesting to periodize or categorize the evolution of the
usage of the name *Iran* in the Safavid period, as the Japanese
scholar Haneda Koichi has suggested. There are three phases in
which the name *Iran* appears in the documents: first, *Iran* is used as
the name of the land in relation to others; second, *Iran*
rudimentarily connotes the idea of nation or country; third, in the
late Safavid period *Iran* is used for the nation. Koichi asserts that
the second and third phases indicate that the elites and governing
class of the Safavids were aware of the existence of the land and
nation of Iran.[44] For Koichi to use the word *nation* in this regard is
rather strong and anachronistic, considering that the Safavids called
it *mamālik* (kingdoms) *mahruse-e Iran*. The Safavids may have
measured the unity of their subjects through the medium of their
massive forced conversion to Shi'ism rather than supposing the
existence of a homogeneous national Iranian consciousness among
a culturally heterogeneous population. On the other hand,
examining the emerging consciousness among the folk of remote
areas and their affiliation with the word *Iran* is an integral but
separate responsibility, if we are to understand the mixing of the
name of the land with patriotic political propaganda during the
Safavid period. From coins and other sources, we can assess the
political conduct of the Safavids — namely, that Islam was their
political doctrine and *Iran* a land to practice it on.

---

[42] Navai, *Shah Abbas,* pp. 46, 49, 59; Navai, *Shah Isma'il,* pp. 22, 26, 63,
143, 152, 157.

[43] Qa'im Maqami, *Yek Sad-u Panjah Sanad-e Tarikhi,* see footnote 33,
pp. 67, 70, 81, 83, 105; Varheram, *Tārikh-i Siyāsī va Ijtemā'i Iran dar Asr-i
Zand,* p. 126.

[44] Koichi, "Meaning of Iran ...," pp. 188–193.

During the Zand period (1749–1785), the decree of Ali Murād Khan (1782–1785) uses the Safavid title *mamālik mahruse-e Iran*.[45] Adoption of the name *Iran* in royal letters or administrative texts became a trend to which the Qājār dynasty (which ruled after the Zand dynasty) subscribed. Many early Qājār sources — for example, those in the compilation of historical documents by Qa'im Maqami and in *Afzal al-Tawārīkh* by Afzal ul-Mulk — lead us to believe that the term *Iran* was still being used for administrative and geographical designations.[46] In many contacts with Europe during the mid-Qājār period, when a modern bureaucracy, modern army, telegraph, and so on were established, the logo "Government of Iran," *Dowlat-e Iran*, appears,[47] although the title *mamālik mahruse-e Iran* remains. The 1881 Qājār postal stamps, which had bilingual writings on them, appeared with *mamālik mahruse-e Iran* in Farsi and *Poste Persane* in French. Later the Qājārs decided to change the French singular form of "post of Iran" to a plural, which obviously referred to the plurality of its kingdoms and populations. Thus, in the 1894 series, it appeared as *Postes Persannes* and the series was more or less carried forward to the Pahlavi era, when in 1929–1935 it appeared as *Poste Iraniennes;* it was changed to *Poste Iran* only in 1936–1937.[48]

The end of the Qājār period was marked by two important events: the Constitutional Revolution (1906) and the emergence of European nationalism. Together, these events tried to unify the land and its diverse inhabitants in order to control the affairs of the region. This was the beginning of the time during which *Iran,* a geographic designation, gradually found new sociopolitical meanings — a process that accelerated during the Pahlavi era. Not only did internal factors and the international situation require the buildup of a nation-state to safeguard political and strategic interests, but the works of the Europeans in the fields of Iranian Studies in its nationalist context also became grounds for

---

[45] Qa'im Maqami, p. 105.

[46] Qa'im Maqami, pp. 111–380; Afzal ul-Mulk, *Afzal ul-Tawārīkh*, pp. 298–302.

[47] See, for example, Qa'im Maqami, p. 153.

[48] Gnoli, p. 180, notes.

solidifying and filling the minds of many people with belief in the
pre-existence of Iran as a distinct nation and civilization. This and
other factors for the emergence of modern Iranian consciousness
are the topics of the remaining chapters, which will develop the
argument that the terms *Iran* and *Iranian*, although obscure, found
their political, cultural, and social meaning only in the twentieth
century, not in the past.

Chapter 5
Problems and Context of National Historiography and the Invention of an Iranian Identity

Having discussed the significance and status of the term *Iran*, we should now scrutinize its historical application. The preceding inquiry has determined that historically this geographical designation was not used to represent a race, a language, or a unique culture. It is now appropriate to address the theoretical and textual aspects of certain prominent Orientalists who staunchly believed in the homogeneity and Iranianness of communities who lived in the land of Iran in different historical periods.

The most important single problem in assessing the notion that there has always been an Iranian entity lies in understanding the nationalistic methodology of historiography introduced by nineteenth-century Orientalists followed by the nationalist thinkers of Iran. The root of this problem can be found both in the Aryan school and in the nationalistic orientations of the scholars themselves (at times these two are indistinguishable).

The nationalistic methodology of Western Orientalist scholars may have been inevitable and even, to a certain degree, natural after Europe had gone through the historical experiences that led to the formation of national identities in a narrow context. The development of these identities determined the point of view and ideology of European literary circles in expounding their theories of history. The easy first-hand access Europeans had to Oriental documents encouraged Orientalists to use an authoritative academic approach to construct the past and model the Orient on the European experience. What little contemporaneous Western criticism there was is expressed by Marx and Engels, by Tocqueville's letters to Gobineau,[1] and by certain other Europeans of the nineteenth and twentieth centuries to the European nations that were influencing and transforming the globe.

The application of racial theories to the historical description of certain peoples or events (in this case the Aryan race for Iran) has implied a racial consciousness by ancient people such as the Medes and the Persians vis-à-vis the Semitic world. In fact, however, the Aryan theory is merely a construct of the eighteenth and nineteenth centuries, not necessarily a phenomenon known to ancient peoples. Hertz states in his *Race and Civilization:* "The primal Aryan race is a purely hypothetical conception as Indo-European is a mere linguistic conception."[2] It is true that the appearance of vernacular languages was one of the major factors in the emergence of nations in Europe, but racial sentiment became one of the elements that made up a national sentiment and united people in a cohesive way.[3] Orientalists, under the influence of mainstream Western academia and the Aryan model, began to look into the past of peoples with complex backgrounds and tried to work out (at times imaginatively) such modern issues as race and national identity for communities of the remote past whose consciousness was conditioned by non-modern ideas. With regard to the construct of Aryan communities in Iran, unsupported assumptions and hypotheses gained more and more currency, even though there is still no hard evidence to provide a solid basis for such arbitrary speculation. One cannot fail to be reminded of Berlin's remark, which suits this and other historical constructs: "Without sufficient knowledge of facts a historical construction may be no more than a coherent fiction, a work of the romantic imagination."[4]

Race and national identity are the two interrelated issues apart from religious studies that preoccupied the works of the Orientalists on Iran. Philology covering the pre-Islamic period, and

---

[1] Kohn, *Age of Nationalism*, pp. 75–76.

[2] Hertz, *Race and Civilization*, p. 77, quoted by Joseph, *Nationality: Its Nature and Problems*, pp. 43–44.

[3] Joseph, p. 34.

[4] Berlin, *Concepts and Categories*, p. 133.

the philosophy behind a national identity concurrent with the appearance of vernacular languages for the Islamic era, accommodated both a vision and a theory of historiography of Iran. Delatinization and the escape from the Church's domination in the West were taken as an analogous form of historical expression to dearabization and the emergence of local dynasties to bypass the combination of the caliphate. But although the two approaches appear similar, they involve two historical circumstances several centuries and two continents apart, therefore representing two nonparallel cultures and circumstances. The appearance of the Farsi language around the ninth century during the first several decades of Abbasid rule onward and the growth of power of local dynasties within or on the periphery of the Iranian plateau have been characterized as expressions of national revivalism in its Iranian framework by the Orientalists. Western Orientalism used European historical logic and equations to examine and construct a national history for the peoples of an old empire and a vast land who historically had displayed no Iranian sentiment or identity.

National identity and nationalism are quite new tendencies. It is a grave mistake to relate them to the remote past. Hobsbawm in *The Invention of Tradition* makes a comment that fits this argument and is directly applicable to the anachronistic approach of Orientalists to national identity and nationalism in relation to the complex historical process of the Iranian plateau: "Traditions which appear to claim to be old are often quite recent in origin and sometimes invented."[5] In this regard and in the context of the rise of the new philosophy of history, Kant also suggested that the transmission of history from the oldest times of which the records are lost is only conducted from the point of view of what interests us.[6]

The method of historiography and the conceptualization of the past of the peoples of the Iranian plateau in a national context

---

[5] Hobsbawm, "Introduction: Inventing Tradition," *The Invention of Tradition*, Hobsbawm and T. Ranger (eds.), pp. 1, 6.

[6] Kant, "Idea of a Universal History from a Cosmopolitan Point of View," *Theories of History*, Patrick Gardiner (ed.), pp. 21, 33.

call for scrutiny in quest of understanding their effect on the historiography of the twentieth-century historians of Iran and on its subsequent stereotyping and propagation by existing Iranian governments. It will be useful here to descriptively analyze some of the more significant issues that certain Orientalists established as the basis for Iranian national identity and nationalism. The magnitude and painstaking efforts of Orientalists will not and cannot be belittled or condemned; only their pattern and methods are criticized. Again, the purpose is to open avenues for new approaches to the issues under scrutiny.

THE SCOPE OF THE PROBLEM

The Western national historiography of Iran suffers both from crude periodization and from its attempt to connect the cultural components of a given community in a given period with the surrounding geographical region that inherently invented a national identity. The periodization into pre-Islamic and Islamic eras as a basis for conceptualizing a history for Iran encourages the belief that there has always been a continuity of the people and culture on the Iranian plateau. It is true that the elements of continuity from the pre-Islamic to the Islamic period perhaps have not been overlooked, but its nationalistic categorization is rather questionable. Implicit in this depiction lies the notion that the Islamic period changed very little if any of the character and nature of the Iranian community, which sought to preserve its identity in the face of Arab and Turkish domination. This view, however, demonstrates a profound contempt for dynamic phenomenological principles of history; people do not remain statically concerned with a unique and unchanging political and racial consciousness throughout a long and tumultuous historical journey. How would the ordinary people of a particular generation, with their own immediate sociopolitical or religious concerns — for instance under the Buyid or Sāmānid dynasties of the tenth century — remain faithful to and conscious of their so-called ancestors the Persians and the Medes, the alleged "inspirers of the Iranian Nation"? Only the historicism of the nineteenth and twentieth centuries could conceive of such a thing. It is highly likely that neither the historical memories nor the interest existed among the common people to detach themselves from their own reality and show an affinity to the doctrine of what in modern times we call nationalism.

The sciences of genealogy and philology existed among Arabs and later among others[7] in the early centuries of Islam, but this tribal form of tradition should not be confused with our concern with geopolitical nationalism. People did not tend to identify themselves on a large or national scale with a land, and they did not retain such a consciousness for complex sociopolitical, religious, and linguistic reasons. The persistence of Zoroastrianism as a religion or as a community of believers in the same fashion as Islam, Christianity, and Judaism should not be overlooked in trying to identify these people with one particular nation. As a matter of fact, it has not been; it is in fact modern scholars who tend to call Zoroastrianism the "national religion."

The method by which Orientalists conceived the continuity of the Iranian world has involved relying on philology for the pre-Islamic era; and for the Islamic period, apart from comparative philology, on the connection of literature in vernacular languages with political events — all in connection with the land of Iran. For the Islamic period, the appearance of the Farsi language and the emergence of local dynasties became primordial signs of national and cultural independence. Part of the problem, discussed in Chapter 3, is attributable to the similarity of the name of the new language in the Islamic period (Farsi) to the region of Fars, the seat of ancient kings and empires. The Farsi language has been noted, although undocumented, to be the language or the dialect of Fars before the Muslim conquest.[8] Allegedly due to Arab control and settlement in the West, it only flourished in the eastern part of Iran during the Muslim rule. (Actually, this assertion has not been confirmed and could be challenged — a point to which we will return.) The identification of *Fars* (as a region) and *'Ajam* (as non-Arab) as having stood equivalent to *Iran* in abstract terms has been extremely misleading. The translation of *Muluk al-Fars* from Muslim sources (often in Arabic) to mean Persian kingdoms or

---

[7] Goldziher, *Muslim Studies*, I, pp. 164–165, 176.

[8] Frye, *Golden Age of Persia*, p. 173; Bailey, "The Persian Language," *Legacy of Persia*, pp. 174–175.

Iranian kingdoms has also been misleading in associating a dynastic history with an imagined national community. The designation in Muslim literature (e.g., Tabarī) of *Muluk al-Roum* for the Roman kingdoms does not refer to people and kings of what is now modern Italy (where Rome is located). Similarly, the Holy Roman Empire of Europe equally accommodated a dynastic designation without referring to anything approximating the modern interpretation of political nationalism. What belonged to the Greco-Roman empires in terms of land and subjects had their own distinct names, cultures, languages, and customs. *Fars*, therefore, was a provincial designation whose name may have originated just as the name *Rome* did.

Materials from the Zoroastrians and other sources were used by various individuals including Firdowsī, a renowned poet (d. c. 1020), to construct *Muluk al-Fars* in epic form, using the medium of the Farsi language. This created a ground for modern historians to link the pre-Islamic tradition with the post-Islamic one. The political conflict among communities and dynasties within the caliphate, such as the dynastic rise of Tāhirids, Saffārids, Sāmānids, and Buyids in the ninth and tenth centuries; the religious and literary debates (e.g., *Shu'ubiya*); and other contrasts provided enough ground to forge a national category for all these historical developments. Obviously, many of these historical arguments in a national category make sense in modern times, especially in light of the "Farsification" of Iran during the Pahlavi era and the ready availability of history books by the authorities of the field. Obviously, to contest all of that would make one an outcast.

Let us by scrutinizing some of the works of the famous Orientalists try to understand the framework of their methodology, their proliferation and propagation of each other's works, and their shortcomings in treating some of the points mentioned above. The inquiry will be in the form of a survey analyzing and questioning the nationalistic conceptualization of Iran in the micro or macro studies of the Iranian topic that have largely contributed to nationalistic historiographical methodology. In doing so, we will contest the approach of these Orientalists, who anachronistically describe the issues of the remote past in modern nationalistic terms.

SCRUTINY OF IRANOLOGY

The first effort to find continuity in the sequence of events from the pre-Islamic period through modern times occurred in the nineteenth century when Sir John Malcolm, an untrained historian, wrote his *History of Persia* (1815). In fact, the interest of Western historians had increased at the time due to Silvestre de Sacy's reading of Sasanian inscriptions and Henry Rawlinson's reading of Persepolis. The Aryan hypothesis was taking new turns, while philologists were working out what became known later as Iranian and Indo-Iranian next to Indo-European languages. The philological gates were opened by William Jones and Anquetil DuPerron, who revealed the Sanskrit and Avestan languages to the Europeans[9] in the eighteenth century. Subsequently, the Semitic, Indian, and Iranian language families were identified. In the Iranian language family, F. Spiegel worked on Old Iranian languages (Bactrian); A. V. W. Jackson and F. Justi on Zend and Old Persian; J. Oppert on Median; K. Geldner on Avestan; and W. Gieger, E. West, and T. Nöldeke on Pahlavi. Other scholars' efforts also contributed to the growth of the Aryan hypothesis and to language classification.

James Darmesteter produced a synthesis of the works of these eminent philologists in his two-volume *Études Iraniennes* (1883). The first volume deals with the history of the grammar of "Persian" languages from the Achaemenid to the present time. The second volume contains five parts, of which at least three deal with the history of Iran and its relations with literature, legend, and mythology (e.g., Avesta, *Shāhnāmeh*).[10] Darmesteter's accomplishment not only consolidated the recent works of his philologist colleagues, it also opened more avenues for subsequent Iranian studies. The works of the eminent scholar Italo Pizzi on the history of Persian poetry and literature should not be ignored. His two-volume *Storia della Poesia Persiana* (1894) followed his *Manuale di letteratura Persiana* (1887), *Firdusi il libra dei Re* (1886–1889), and

---

[9] See Said, *Orientalism*, pp. 22, 51; Poliakov, *The Aryan Myth*, pp. 189–190.

[10] Darmesteter, *Études Iraniennes*, I, pp. vii–ix.

Antalogia Epica (1891). All of these language materials in connection with the land of Iran maintained the importance of creating a national chemistry during the ancient and pre-modern periods. In the early twentieth century Edward G. Browne produced his monumental and popular four volumes of *A Literary History of Persia* (1902–1924). He had intended to title it *The History of Persian Literature*, but Browne's own introduction suggests that he had two models of history before him — that of Green's *Short History of the English People* and that of Jusserand's *Literary History of the English People* — and thus Browne decided not to write the history of the poets but instead, after his models, to write about the "national genius" of Persia and Persians in the fields of religion, philosophy, science, and literature.[11]

The work of Browne remains among the most original and influential of Iranian studies. His innovations included connecting literary achievements with political upheaval from the ancient period on. Browne's mentality, conditioned with the European notion of language as the basis of national identity, led him to interpret the appearance of the Farsi language as a sign of the "national revival" of Iranism. Browne both supports Darmesteter's philological conclusions and opens the gates for his own historiographical hypothesis about Iran: "The Persian language of today, *Farsi*, the language of Fars, is the lineal offspring of the language which Cyrus and Darius spoke, and in which the proclamations engraved by their commands on the rocks of Behistun and Naqsh-i Rustam and the walls and columns of Persepolis, are drawn up."[12]

Browne's work could be said to be based on philological finds and divisions into ancient and Islamic periods, on literary production in the Farsi language, and on a political history that augmented what Italo Pizzi had initiated. Browne's creative adaptability in linking literature to political history extended the European vision of history as a linear national progression.

Let us return to the work of Sir John Malcolm, who in the two massive volumes of his *History of Persia* (1815) made a

---

[11] See Browne, *A Literary History of Persia*, I, pp. vii–ix.
[12] Ibid., pp. 4–5.

remarkable impact on both the European knowledge of Persia (Iran) and of course subsequently on the native historians of Iran. It must be noted that at the time Malcolm began to write (around 1808) his national history, his contemporaries were working out the Aryan hypothesis on one hand and were trying to connect the western languages of Iran to the eastern ones in making the Iranian language family. Such initiatives obviously would have made the writing of a national history more coherent, as Malcolm thought that without it the history of Persia would be incomplete. Malcolm mentions the thirty years of visits to Persia by the European inquirers and says of their observations: "Hence while some scholars, according to their tastes and habitual predilection, have made the eastern account of ancient Persia give way to the western, or the western to the eastern ... [they] have sought out and fancied they have discovered certain points of contact between them."[13]

Due to the lack of sufficient information and unsophistication of the available philological and historical information about the pre-Islamic era, Malcolm relied on legendary accounts and anecdotes about the Pishdādiān, Kīyāniān, Ashkāniān, and Sāsāniān dynasties to reconstruct that period. For example, he uses the authority of Firdowsī and Khondamir and works like *Zīnat ul-Tawārīk* and *Ruzat ul-Safā* extensively for the construction of pre-Islamic history. Orientalism was in its premature stage and political nationalism had not picked up the necessary enthusiasm in Europe at the time of Malcolm. The question then is why Malcolm devoted his time to writing a relatively voluminous national history of Iran. Malcolm was actually assigned by the British colonial government of India as an agent to collect information (along with two other officers) about regions on the western extent of India because of the danger of Napoleonic invasions. Iran was assigned to Malcolm; and consequently, as it has been said, "the writing of history was a sort of paid holiday for Malcolm."[14] Thus, Malcolm's mission to Persia on several occasions had to do with the urgency of collecting information about the people, customs, languages, and history to

---

[13] Malcolm, *The History of Persia*, I, p. 476.

[14] Yapp, "Two British Historians of Persia," *Historians of the Middle East*, p. 343; see also pp. 344–356.

serve a specific and immediate political purpose. Furthermore, the British seemed more attracted to the pattern of national history writing than the Germans and the French.

It is not irrelevant that John MacDonald Kinneir was a political assistant to Malcolm in their mission to the court of Persia. Kinneir's *A Geographical Memoir of the Persian Empire* (1813) may not be a detached example of what colonialism asked for and what scholarship could produce.

About a century after Malcolm, Sir Percy Sykes, also a British official, wrote his two-volume *A History of Persia* (1915).[15] In the years between Malcolm (1815) and Sykes (1915) many gaps in scholarship, particularly with respect to Iranian studies, had been filled. Thus, Sykes' modern selections and interpretations, although now outdated themselves, certainly made the work of Malcolm obsolete. At any rate, after Malcolm, other figures who (unlike him) were trained Orientalists made consequential contributions to the field of Orientalism and Iranology. F. Spiegel produced a volume on the religion, history, and antiquity of Iran from earliest times until the end of Sasanian dynasty titled *Erânische Alterthumskunde* (1871–1878). Theodor Nöldeke, a pioneer in many subfields of Orientalism, produced works on Iran such as *Geschichte der Perser und Araber zu Zeit der Sasaniden* (1879), *Persische Studien* (1888 and 1892), *Das Iranische Nationalepos* (1896), and *Sketches from Eastern History* (1892). Then there was George Rawlinson, an Oxford history professor, whose monumental historical works on pre-Islamic Iran were instrumental in consolidating national and racial thinking in both historiography and ideology in general. Rawlinson, an Aryanist, a scholar who never bothered to hide his racist remarks, produced three sets of histories of the Orient; he diminished his scholarship, however, by putting down non-Aryans and by promoting the idea of a national and racial continuity in Iranian civilization. Rawlinson's *Five Great Monarchies of the Ancient Eastern World* (1871) deals with the antiquities of Assyria, Babylon, Chaldea, Media, and Persia. His *Sixth Great Oriental Monarchy* (1873) deals with Parthia. Finally, his *Seventh Great Oriental Monarchy* (1876)

---

[15] Ibid.

deals with the Sasanian Empire; it was translated in part into Farsi and published in Iran.[16]

Rawlinson is notable for the crude and dry language he used to describe the ethnic communities of the East as well as his sometimes disjointed approach to making national connections with historical events. For example, in describing the Aryan physiognomy, Rawlinson has the nerve to state this about the Persian look: "expression is not full of life and genius, it is intellectual and indicative of reflection."[17] Examples of the typical approach of uninhibited derogatory remarks, nationalist Orientalism are numerous in Rawlinson's work. The following quotation is representative of the Aryan supremacist school to which he belonged, except that Rawlinson expressed his opinions more explicitly than others:

> The Aryan family is the one which of all the races of mankind, is the most self-asserting, and has the greatest strength, physical, moral, and intellectual. The Iranian branch of it, where to the Persians belonged, is not perhaps so gifted as some others; but it has qualities which place it above most of those by which western Asia was anciently peopled.[18]

The offensive and judgmental remarks of Rawlinson deserve nothing but dismissal. About a decade later another British philologist, A. H. Sayce, in his *The Ancient Empires of the East* (1885) perpetuated a similarly racist attitude in scholarship by making this somewhat offensive remark in his description of the Persian people and empire: "In short, the empire contained within it from the first all the elements of decay, and the Persian character was one which could with difficulty be respected and never loved."[19]

A critique of these prejudiced scholars and their disparaging statements would not lead to any vibrant intellectual discourse nor should it be tempered by any overriding acknowledgment of their

---

[16] Adamiyat, "Problems in Iranian Historiography," p. 137.

[17] Rawlinson, *The Seventh Great Oriental Monarchy*, p. 24 (notes). Rawlinson is possibly referring to European Aryans.

[18] Ibid.

[19] Sayce, *The Ancient Empires of the East*, p. 275.

eminence. The fundamental flaw that concerns us here is indeed the nationalist methodology of which Rawlinson is the champion. With regard to the emergence of the Sasanian dynasty, Rawlinson boldly asserts that a sense of racial and national consciousness already existed among the Sasanian elites and rulers who brought the empire back to the original glory it had achieved during the period of the Achaemenids: "The great Asiatic revolution of the year 226 AD marks a revival of the Iranic nationality from the depressed state into which it had sunk for more than five hundred years."[20]

What "Iranic nationality" does Rawlinson have in mind? Were not the Parthians, in European terms, philologically part of the Iranian world? Thus, misunderstandings arise in measuring what fits into the Iranian category and then in applying Rawlinson's own anachronistic approach of nationalistic assessment to a dynastic triumph. Furthermore, neither the Parthians nor the Sasanians had any concrete memory (at least not racial or national) of the faded Achaemenids.[21]

Other historians who developed more Europe-centric interpretations of history in its Iranian or Persian national context include R. G. Watson, author of *A History of Persia from the Beginning of the Nineteenth Century to the Year 1858* (1866), and Clement Markham, author of *General Sketch of the History of Persia* (1874).

We would be remiss not to mention the contributions of E. M. Quatremère and J. A. de Gobineau in this context. Quatremère was primarily an eminent Orientalist, like Ernest Renan, in Semitic studies, but his focus on Iranian studies was noticeable. His unique translation of *Histoire des Mongols de la Perse* (1836) from Rashīd al-Dīn (1247–1318) *Jāmi' al-Tawārīkh (Universal History)* in a bilingual Farsi and French edition in a large, elegantly decorated folio had a purpose of giving it national character. But Quatremère's out-of-context emphasis on the necessity of understanding Mongol rule (which had no particular national boundary) in a national realm violated Rashīd al-Dīn's intention,

---

[20] Rawlinson, p. 29.

[21] See Chapter 3; see also Yarshater, "The Absence of Median and Achaemenid Kings in Iran's Traditional History," p. 209.

which was not to write a national history. It may be true that Mongol rule did acquire certain characteristics in various regions, whether in China, Southern Russia, or Iran, but these acquired characteristics should not be defined in boundary-oriented modern nationalistic terms. Quatremère and Jules Mohl had the *Journal Asiatique* at their disposal to develop and to promote a national historiographical method for better understanding history.[22] The *Journal Asiatique* became an important scholarly vehicle in Europe that produced lasting notions of the people, literature, philosophy, and history of the Orient. In its entirety, the journal became the bible of facts about the Orient. Jules Mohl, apart from his contribution to the *Journal Asiatique,* published a seven-volume edition of the *Shāhnāmeh* by Firdowsī, with French translation and commentary, between 1837 and 1878. The introduction of the *Shāhnāmeh* into the European academic circle helped link the legendary mythology to national history — as became evident in the works by Orientalists from Malcolm to Roman Girshman[23] all the way to contemporary scholars.

Joseph Arthur, Comte de Gobineau, is remembered not only in Europe but also in the Orient. His devotion to biological racism and Aryan-ness energized him to write enthusiastically what came to be known as the bible of racism, *Introduction à l'Essai sur l'inégalité des races humaines* (1854). Gobineau's diplomatic career had blossomed from 1848 through 1877, under Louis Napoleon's second empire and the reactionary monarchist rule of Marie Edme Patrice Maurice de MacMahon, and it has been said that he wrote his book in response to the revolution of 1848.[24] Whatever the vision of this rebellious, racially prejudiced diplomat may have been, he left behind impressions of Asia and Iran that are still used

---

[22] See Quatremère, "De l'ouvrage Persan qui a pour titre Moudjmel-attawarikh, Somnnaire des histoires," 246–288; see also Mohl, "Extraits du Modjmel el-Tewarikh, relatifs a l'histoire de la Perse," pp. 385–432.

[23] Malcolm, I, p. 502; Ghirshman, *L'Iran et La Migration des Indo-Aryens et des Iraniens*, p. 74.

[24] Anderson, *Imagined Communities,* p. 136 (notes); see also Poliakov, Chapter 10.

as a source by social scientists. Gobineau's primary concerns were race, civilizations, and the reasons for their downfalls. His infatuation with Iran had much to do with supposed Aryan myths of the past. To Gobineau, the rise of the Persian Empire was a movement of a "small number of men (Aryan) among a bulk of (racially distinct) masses (Semitic) who created a nation."[25] Gobineau was not the last person in the era of racism and nationalism to conceptualize the Aryans of Iran in such fashion. The twentieth-century racially-oriented nationalist mood was no different. This is what J. H. Iliffe in his essay "Persia and the Ancient World" had similarly to say about the Aryans of Iran: "They were now to impress on the world the simple and manly qualities which they had brought with them from their ancient home."[26]

Gobineau in his prejudiced mind was curious about the fall of the Aryan empires and was influenced in his understanding by Gibbon's *The Decline and Fall of the Roman Empire*.[27] Gobineau's explanation of the defeat of the Persians at the hands of the Macedonians was that the mixture of the Persians with the inferior and indigenous "Semitic" people led to their downfall, as it subsequently occasioned the downfall of both the Greeks and the Romans in their turn.[28] His ambivalence toward Asia and his affinity for the historical Aryans of Asia made him suspicious of "poisonous" racial mixture with Asia's non-Aryans. In his *Trois Ans en Asie* he issues a warning about Asia's power of seduction.[29] The web of unscrupulous remarks exhibited in Gobineau's attitude, his academic knowledge, and what he transmitted to the field of social science must either be treated with serious criticism or simply imputed to his obsolete reactionary attitude. It is true that Gobineau's impressions and notes enhance our understanding

---

[25] Boisset, *Gobineau l'Orient et l'Iran*, p. 205; see also Gobineau, *l'Essai sur l'inégalité*, p. 380.

[26] Iliffe, "Persia and the Ancient World," *Legacy of Persia*, p. 5.

[27] Boisset, p. 403.

[28] Gobineau, *Trois ans en Asie*, p. 332; Boisset, pp. 206–207.

[29] "Je me borne donné à constater ce fait que l'Asie est un mets très séduisant, mais qui empoisonne ce qui le mangent," Gobineau, p. 336.

about events in mid-nineteenth century Iran and other regions of central Asia; nonetheless, we must carefully distinguish between what actually happened and how Gobineau interpreted it.

The transmission of racial and national methodology based on Europe-centered political ideology from the nineteenth to the twentieth century is inescapable. There was no major breakthrough in the works of the typical twentieth-century Orientalists whose scholarly works have been looked upon as bibles in the field of Orientalism and Iranology, among them E. G. Browne, W. Barthold, V. Minorsky, A. Christensen, E. Herzfeld, R. Ghirshman, A. J. Arberry, B. Spuler, C. E. Bosworth, R. Frye, R. Grousset, H. Masse, and L. Massignon. This generation of scholars was entrusted with the task of refining what had already been established by its predecessors. The Aryan notion, however, remained firm (but more implicit) in twentieth-century scholarship. The pieces of the Aryan model in a national context were arranged to accommodate the secular history for Iran next to an already existing broad Islamic historiography.[30] In fact, during this period methodology and the exaltation of pre-Islamic glory generated a growth of nationalistic sentiment in Iran.[31]

In any discussion of turn-of-the-century scholarship, a return to E. G. Browne's ideas is inevitable. From the period of Browne on, a formative process is evident in using the Aryan hypothesis, connecting the Farsi language with Iran (as its homeland and its national language) and at times bundling disjointed historical developments into a national category, all in the new direction of embryonic Iranian nationalism. Browne's efforts were devoted to assimilating what had already been established. His faithfulness to the Aryan school makes him repeat the previous unproved opinion that the name *Iran* was derived from *Aryan* or from *Airya* of Avesta.[32] The trend did not end with Browne. The Russian scholar W. Barthold cannot resist mustering the Aryan element in his assessment of Iranians: "In the ethnic sense, the term 'Iranian' as is well known, denotes that branch of Aryans who are closely related

---

[30] See Adamiyat, "Problems," pp. 133–134.

[31] Enayat, "Politics of Iranology," p. 11.

[32] Browne, I, p. 4.

to those of India."[33] Barthold reminds us that the "Iran/Aryan" notion is "well known" — but, it should be noted, only among the propagators of Aryanism and Iranian nationalism.

Browne confesses that he has no expertise in the ancient languages of Iran and thus claims to limit the scope of his study to the Islamic period. However, he finds it difficult to construct his account of history and his hypothesis of continuity on a national scale without reverting to the pre-Islamic time. Thus he devotes some four chapters to the ancient period, from the Achaemenids to the advent of Islam, during the course of which he establishes the notion of continuity for a racial group that survived the Muslim conquest with their language — Farsi — intact. Alessandro Bausani made a similar undertaking in his *Storia della Letteratura Persiana* (1960) to connect the Farsi language with political events and the Iranian geographic zone. The significance of this book, which Browne could not do alone in presenting pre-Islamic literature in connection with the Islamic, was that Bausani's co-author, Antonino Pagliaro, elaborated on the pre-Islamic languages in the Iranian context.[34] In other words, the speakers of Farsi, particularly inside Iran proper (a relatively smaller percentage than neighboring Tajikistan and Afghanistan), according to Browne, Bausani, Pagliaro, and other Aryanist Orientalists, were the heirs of the ethnic and linguistic nationality of the Aryans of Iran. Such an assumption has two flaws: firstly the language has nothing to do with ethnicity, and secondly, Farsi had become a transnational language — the *lingua franca* from India all the way to the Ottoman lands. But although the alleged ancient Aryans were settled in the western plateau of Iran, the Farsi language (a much younger language) in the Islamic period flourished in the eastern part of Iran, in the Transoxiana and Khurāsān regions as opposed to the *Pars* and Mesopotamian regions. The ongoing hypothesis has been that, with the advent of Islam from the west, there was less Arab cultural pressure on the eastern regions; thus it became fertile ground for a revival of old cultures and languages.

---

[33] Barthold, *An Historical Geography of Iran*, p. 4.

[34] Browne, I, pp. 39–185; Bausani and Pagliaro, *Storia della Letteratura Persiana*, see particularly pp. 151–204.

The formation of the Farsi language and the puzzle of east-west migration will be argued later, but clearly Browne's intention to connect the "revival" of the Farsi language to the emergence of dynasties in the eastern part of the Iranian plateau (although in an imprecise and fluctuating political geography) had much to do with his loyalty to the national methodological framework. Identification of the Farsi language with Iranian geographical limits was a natural step, given the cultural and political nationalism of Europe, even though it was clear to Browne that speakers of Farsi were not exclusive to eastern Iran but also resided in central Asia, India, and (in later centuries) the Ottoman lands. However, Browne showed no fear of contradiction or distortion in connecting the Farsi language with a circumscribed physical and far more important national geography. With regard to the speakers of Farsi in other lands, Browne says, "India, for example, has produced an extensive literature of which the language is Persian, but which is not a reflex of the Persian mind, and the same holds good in lesser degree of several branches of the Turkish race."[35]

Browne's arbitrary and 'pro-Iranian' remarks should be dismissed as biased and disrespectful. It also represents a claim about the existence of a "national spirit" expressed through the Farsi language. From another approach, it can be understood that the existence of other linguistic communities in the Iranian plateau did not matter to Browne as 'national' languages. For Browne, the Farsi language held the same place with regard to Iran that the German language did in the minds of Herder and Fichte as the basis for national unity and distinction; other languages and "harsh dialects" and categories, therefore, should submit to its supremacy. This viewpoint explains why Browne convinced himself to write *A Literary History of Persia* and not *A History of Persian Literature;* one is the history of a nation while the other is the history of a language (although Browne in fact combined the two, since he did not want to limit himself only to language).

---

[35] Ibid., p. 3.

"MEN OF PERSIAN BLOOD"

In surveying the concept of language and nationality in the works of the Orientalists one often encounters disputes over what have been the Arab and what the Persian achievements and contributions in the melting pot of the Islamic empire. Pizzi, Goldziher, Browne, and Arberry are among many who make assertions about such national or ethnic achievements. For example, they mention that it was the Persians who produced Arabic literature.[36] The parameters used to designate an identity for a multilingual community can perhaps be ascertained by reviewing the controversy of *Shu'ubiya* — particularly the view expressed by Goldziher, who dedicates two chapters of his first volume of *Muslim Studies (Muhammedanische Studien)* to this topic. Keeping track of genealogical accounts and linguistic differences within the large Muslim community had certainly fostered a competition among them, as in the case of north and south Arabs,[37] but this should not be confused with the hostility against so-called Arab political domination and the demand for equal status that, apart from literary debates, was by and large the argument of the *Shu'ubiya*. At any rate, the identification of individuals in national or ethnic terms based on their speech is both misleading and unsubstantiated. The following statement by Arberry recognizes that the search for cultural and ethnic purity in the Muslim community is unrealistic (although he subsequently attempts it himself): "To diagnose and isolate the specifically Persian (or Iranian) elements in that culture and its literature is an impossible task, for Arab civilization drew upon many sources, and these sources were considerably contaminated already at the birth of Islam."[38]

If a person such as Browne is convinced that those who speak Farsi are Iranians or Persians, although others in other lands may

---

[36] Pizzi, *Storia della Poesia Persiana*, I, pp. 124–127; Goldziher, *Muslim Studies*, I, pp. 149, 227; Browne, I, p. 89; Arberry, "Persian Literature," *Legacy of Persia*, pp. 204–205; see also Safa, *Tārīkh-i Adabiyāt dar Iran*, I, pp. 637–645; II, pp. 1037–1040; this became a pattern among other scholars.

[37] Goldziher, I, pp. 164–165.

[38] Arberry, pp. 204–205.

speak it as well, the status of those who speak Arabic in Iran or elsewhere is not of concern — because it is clear that the national category for the language is not exclusively the Arabian Peninsula (the same is true about Turkish) and must be worked out. Then again the question is who is an Arab and who is an Iranian? A partial explanation may be found in the science of tribal genealogy, which has no national significance, but the question is answered largely in contemporary terms. In the same fashion, the presence of Muslims in Spain from the eighth to the fifteenth centuries has been a puzzle for modern scholars trying to determine whether a particular element or achievement was Castilian, Catalan, Berber, Arab, or other. This detective work is a labor often undertaken in modern times to promote national distinction, ethnic achievements, and personal satisfaction.

In criticizing the assertions of Browne (and probably of Goldziher in his discussion of *Shu'ubiya*) as a source of national aspiration, we must inquire into the issue of the Iranian people and identity, from the advent of Islam to later centuries. Roy Mottahedeh begins his article about the *Shu'ubiya* controversy by quoting Edmond Burke: "There is no such thing as a people ... it is wholly artificial; and made, like all other legal fictions, by common agreement." In regard to Iranians, Mottahedeh himself then states: "Whether the Iranians in the early Islamic period — that is, the period from the seventh to the twelfth century — were in Burke's sense a 'people' is a question that the cautious scholar would be eager to disregard and loath to handle."[39] Whether cautious scholars have disregarded the question or not, the identity question is all over the scholarship and has not *yet* been curbed. The basis for Orientalists to conceive an Iranian identity for the pre-modern period is the linguistic classification of Farsi and other languages that recently became known and categorized in the Iranian language family. It may be anachronous to attribute such linguistic conceptions to the consciousness of pre-modern masses who neither recognized an Iranian language family nor were familiar with the nationalist doctrine of modern times. The construct of

---

[39] Mottahedeh, "The Shu'ubiyah Controversy and the Social History of Early Islamic Iran," p. 161.

national identity is merely a hypothetical and artificial concept that many Orientalists of different caliber have yet to escape. This is what David Morgan, contemporary academic, had to improvise about the notion of Iranian identity: "There does in fact appear to be a Persian consciousness of identity — *iraniyyat* — that runs right through the country's history, or so western historians seem to suppose."[40] It is more appropriate to believe that the construct of "Iranian" identity is the supposition of Western historians and the norm of modern nationalism.

Let us continue to put into perspective what is meant by the Persian contribution to Islamic civilization. Arberry, espousing a theory of biological and cultural purity in describing the contributions of fellow Muslims to Arabic literature refers to "the contributions made by men of Persian blood to Arabic literature."[41] The attribution "men of Persian blood" of course carries an attached set of values that has been developed explicitly and continually in the textual analysis of identity by Orientalists like Arberry. Investigations of the Persian mind and Persian spirit as opposed to the Arab mind or Bedouin mind, according to Arberry (and let us not forget Browne), have given the advantage to the Persians as "talented converts whose works decisively influenced the shape and structure of Arabic culture"[42] as well as his own. Arberry then provides a catalogue of names of men, seemingly of Persian blood, who wrote in Arabic and were medieval grammarians, historians, theologians, scientists, and philosophers; among them are Bukhārī (d. 870), Abu Hanīfa (d. 767), Baladhurī (d. 892), Birunī (d. c. 1048), and Avicenna (d. 1037). What we are primarily concerned with here is not the fabrication of historical reality but the invention of national divisions whereby historians deposit certain achievements and people into the treasury of a "national heritage" of particular modern nations — in this case, Iran.

Louis Massignon, apart from his expertise in Sufism, was — like Arberry — more Arabist than Iranologist. Nonetheless, in an

---

[40] Morgan, *Medieval Persia 1040–1797*, p. 7.

[41] Arberry, p. 199.

[42] Ibid., pp. 204–206.

essay titled *"Les penseurs iraniens et l'éssor de la civilisation arabe"* he strikingly reveals his Aryan sympathy for Iran and for the "intellectual superiority of Iranians," attributed once again to their Aryanness vis-à-vis the Semitic Arab world.[43]

The debate was wide open for other Orientalists to rejoice in their nationalist prejudices under an academic cover. The racist and nationalist fervor equally involved the modern Iranian belletrists and can at times be quite revealing. Abdul Husayn Zarinkub in his well-known book *Doo Gharn Soukut (Two Centuries of Silence,* 1957) contains extensive unacceptable remarks against the "Arab intruders;" indeed, the title refers to two centuries of suppression by the invaders until the "Iranian renaissance."[44] Isa Sadiq is another who falls into the chauvinist category for crediting the "talented Iranians" at the expense of the "evil" neighbors and intruders.[45] Such scholarship demonstrates the damage that Orientalism and the harsh nationalism of the Pahlavi dynasty inflicted on sociopolitical thought in Iran. (In Chapter 7 we focus on Iranian historiography.)

Giving credit to the Iranian contribution to whatever the topic might be in the complex Muslim civilization was the semantic work of a few Orientalists. The "Persian contribution to historiography" in general or to "Arab historiography" or to "Muslim historiography" is an indication of how prejudicially certain scholars have tried over time to distinguish the "Iranian" world from the "Arab" world or the world of other Muslims. The universal history or *Tārīkh* of Tabarī (d. 923) is often categorized as Iranian, even though the history is written in Arabic. Tabarī's native land, Tabaristān, is connected to the Iranian world only by the geographical fact that Tabaristān is a region near the Caspian Sea in Iran proper today. Because Bal'amī, under Mansur b. Nuh (961–976) of the Sāmānids, translated Tabarī's history into Farsi,

---

[43] Massignon, "Les penseurs iraniens et l'essor de la civilisation arabe," *L'Âme de l'Iran,* pp. 69–90; see particularly pages 70, 71, 75, 76, 79, 83, 84, 89; see also Said, p. 268.

[44] Zarinkub, *Doo Gharn Soukut* (Tehran, 1336/ 1957), pp. 68, 83, 106, passim.

[45] See Sadiq, *Tārīkh-i Farhang-i Iran,* Chapter 7.

Carl Brockelmann indicated that he thus "became the founder of Persian historiography."[46] Unquestionably, when the earlier generations of Orientalists were convinced that the Farsi language had been irrefutably connected to Persian ethnicity and therefore to the Iranian plateau, it was easier to conceive of anything that was produced in Farsi — whether inside or outside Iran proper — as Iranian. The conclusions of Pizzi, Browne, and Brockelmann led to distinct essays and arguments by Spuler, Arberry, and Bosworth elaborating the notion of a distinct "Persian contribution to historiography" in the Islamic period.[47] This comment by Arberry sounds a common theme of confusing language and national influence in developing both technique and works of historiography: "The Persian contribution to the Arab conception of history was undoubtedly massive."[48] The development of historical writing dates back (according to Franz Rosenthal) to ancient times, and even the root of the term *Tārīkh* (chronology or history) probably finds its source in Akkadian, Aramaic, Hebrew, Ethiopic, and south Arabic; (in fact, there is no word in Farsi for *history* of so-called Iranian etymology) and historical writing in Farsi and Turkish came, respectively, around the tenth and fifteenth centuries.[49] Contrary to what Arberry said about Persian eminence in historical writing, this is what Rosenthal, who sought to conceive of a Muslim category of historiographical works rather than a national category, has to say:

> The predominance of Arabic might be considered assured also in the case of historiography although historical works soon were written in the native languages of individual rulers and regions, and there exists an important Persian historical

---

[46] Brockelmann, *History of the Islamic Peoples*, p. 167.

[47] Ibid., pp. 166–167, 170–172, 174–175; Spuler, "The Evolution of Persian Historiography," *Historians of the Middle East, pp.* 126–132; Arberry, "Persian Literature," pp. 204–207; Bosworth, "The Persian Contribution to Historiography," *Levi della Vida Conference*, UCLA, 1991.

[48] Arberry, p. 205; see also Browne, I, p. 358, quoting Brockelmann.

[49] Rosenthal, *A History of Muslim Historiography*, pp. 7–15.

literature since the tenth century, beginning with a free translation of al-Tabari's history.[50]

Thus Arberry's assertions about the ethnic and national contribution of the Persians to the Arab conception of history do not match the historical records. In fact, the Farsi language historiographical consciousness began to grow only after Bal'ami's translation of Tabari.[51] The Arabic language continued to dominate until the thirteenth century, when Farsi was used to write history. Thereafter, Farsi was not a language of historiography exclusively in Iran proper but was also used in the regions of India-Pakistan from the time of the Timurid rule (around the fifteenth century), and in such a manner the Farsi language gained a continental significance, particularly under the Turks.[52] Indeed, Farsi maintained its status in part of India until the nineteenth century, when the British replaced it with English and Urdu.[53]

Determining the national categories of achievements and individuals, in modern terms, remains subject to confusing criteria. For example, there have been literary figures from Turkish or Arabic-speaking tribes who were born outside Iran proper but whose skillful use of the Farsi language led to their being unwarrantedly categorized as part of Iranian literature. Amīr Khusrau Dehlavī, of Turkish descent from Delhi, and Saif-e Farghānī from Aksaraiy (in modern Turkey), both in the thirteenth

---

[50] Rosenthal, p. 7, quoting Storey, *Persian Literature*.

[51] The existence of *Khwaday Namag* (Book of Kings) and other Zoroastrian materials should not be confused with the historiographical method of universal history writings in the Islamic period. Moreover, the new linguistic community of the Islamic period — namely, Farsi-speaking — was still only on the verge of making advances in literary fields, including historiography. Spuler actually comments that no works of historiography existed in pre-Islamic Persia; see Spuler, "The Evolution of Persian Historiography," p. 126.

[52] Asghar, *Persian Historiography* in *Indo-Pakistan*, introduction; for Ghaznavid centers of Farsi learning and usage, see Bosworth, *The Ghaznavids,* pp. 129–144; Morgan, *Medieval Persia*, pp. 3, 21–22.

[53] Amalendu De, "Persian in Our Life," p. 59. 54. See Safa, III (1), p. 623; III (2), pp. 771–797; IV, pp. 133–146.

century; Sultan Salīm, of Ottoman stock, in the early 1500s; and many others outside Iran proper to whom Zabīhullāh Safā refers as *Farsi Gouy* (Farsi-speaker) are categorized as part of the Iranian heritage in Safā's voluminous *Tārīkh-i Adabiyāt dar Iran*.[54] Francesco Gabrieli proposed a correction and caution about "Arabic literature "by suggesting that scholars avoid possible misconceptions by instead using the term *literature in Arabic*."[55] The same stricture should apply to Farsi, and it would be better to say literature in Farsi (Persian) than Persian literature, to avoid ethnic and national biases and discrepancies. In the same manner, the terms *Turkish literature*, and *Arabic literature*, in a modern nationalistic approach, might be taken to imply that the literature belonged to modern Turkey and to Saudi Arabia and possibly other Arab countries.

Consequently the production of works in Farsi bypassed any given political boundaries and de-emphasized any national significance of this language. Indeed, any national tag, whether Iranian or Persian, fails to do justice not only to the intellectual community that has enjoyed and continues to enjoy the fruits of works produced by the great scientific and literary communities of the medieval period, whose works recognized no boundary, but also to the congregation of Arabic-speaking and other groups who are to this day being intimidated by national and racist attributions to such figures (e.g., "men of Persian blood"). The problem is not merely the connection by Orientalists of Farsi to Persia or Iran. It also involves the disagreement among Orientalists about the formation of the Farsi language itself, which evokes the national conception.

THE FARSI LANGUAGE

To curb and explain the wide and often contradictory assertions made about the origin and evolution of Farsi is a necessary but separate task. To establish the place of Farsi in a historical context, a few points must first be brought to light simply in order to

---

[54] See Safa, III (1), p. 623; III (2), pp. 771–797; IV, pp. 133–146.

[55] Gabrieli, "Literary Tendencies," *Unity and Variety in Muslim Civilization*, p. 88.

identify the source of confusion in formation and the character of the language.

Darmesteter, Browne, and a few others asserted that the Farsi language was an extension of Middle Persian, which was itself an extension of Old Persian. This assertion, though arbitrary, was worked out philologically and has been more or less accepted as the frame-work for considering the roots of Farsi. Based on such a conception, scholars like Frye, Bailey, and Lazard indicate that the region of Fars — the land where both the Achaemenid (Old Persian) and the Sasanian (Middle Persian) dynasties originated — must be the source for the Farsi language.[56] In addition to the philological explanation, Muslim sources have to a certain extent been exploited to consolidate this theory. In the account of Ibn Nadīm's *al-Fihrist,* which cites Ibn Muqaffaʿ as a source, five languages and seven forms of script existed at the end of the Sasanian period.[57] These five languages were Pahlavi (or Fahlavi), Dari, Pārsī, Suryānī, and Khuzī; in the opinion of Lazard they were spoken, respectively, in Fahla country (ancient Media), by the people of the capital, by the *mobeds* and scholars, by the people in Sawād, and by the people of Khuzistān (the last two of which Lazard identifies as "non-Iranian" and "Semitic").[58] Frye, however, claims that Dari was spoken both in the west (the Sasanian seat) and in the east, where it had to compete with Soghdian, Khawrazmian, Bactrian, and Parthian.[59]

Based on what has been reported, we must ask about other languages of the Sasanian period that Ibn Muqaffaʿ in the Ibn Nadīm tradition does not report — for example Kurdish, Luri, Gilaki, and other regional languages and dialects spoken in the Iranian plateau. Of Kurdish and Luri, Parviz Khanlari indicates that they were referred to in other records but that, since these languages were not used in writing, however, they lost their

---

[56] Frye, *Golden Ag e,* p. 173; Bailey, "The Persian Language," *Legacy of Persia,* pp. 174–175; Lazard, "The Rise of the New Persian Language," *Cambridge History of Iran,* IV, p. 598.

[57] Ibn Nadim, *al-Fihrist,* pp. 22, 195; see also Lazard, pp. 598–601.

[58] Lazard, p. 600.

[59] Frye, p. 173.

importance.[60] This indication is only hypothetical, however, and it may be challenged and clarified in the future. Moreover, the Sasanian base for over three centuries was around the Kurdish regions of present Iran and Iraq. Many cities in these Kurdish regions (e.g., Kirmānshāh)[61] were first built by Sasanian monarchs. Consequently, it is difficult to believe that the indigenous Kurdish language, customs, epic tradition, and other dominant cultural phenomena could have been utterly ignored by the Sasanian court. As a matter of fact, sociologically and anthropologically, such a result is impossible, given that for several centuries the Sasanian dynasty's central government lay surrounded by Kurdish culture. This suggestion does not mean that Ibn Muqaffa' (whose account refers to the Sasanian languages) is wrong, but rather that the information gathered in the Islamic period was incomplete. Adding Khawrazmian, Soghdian, and other Eastern languages that are absent from Ibn Muqaffa's list is again important to make one cautious about the non-absoluteness of his historical information. The adoption of *Middle Persian* as the name for one of the languages of the Sasanian period, when the proper name of this language escapes us, should be attributed to shortcomings in the transmission of historical information. As a result of these shortcomings, the Orientalists felt free to adopt *Middle Persian* and to filter Sasanian traditions through modern dominant cultural characteristics, namely by forging the Farsi language (New Persian) as a medium.

There is no general consensus among scholars about how the modern Farsi language was synthesized and took its current grammatical and stylistic form. The question still to be resolved is whether and how Farsi as the language of the western Sasanian dynasty of Iran appeared and flourished in the extreme eastern part of the plateau. It seems that despite similarities in vocabulary between Middle Persian and New Persian (Farsi) — even though phraseology, grammar, and style are influenced tremendously by the Soghdian of the east — there is something a bit mechanical in

---

[60] Khanlari, *Zabān Shenāsī va Zabān-i Farsi*, p. 85.

[61] Mostuafī, p. 128; see Morony, *Iraq after the Muslim Conquest*, pp. 265–266 for the Kurdish stock of Iraq during the Sasanian period.

imagining that during the Muslim conquest this language, after about a century and half, should be transplanted into eastern Iran (Khurāsān and Transoxiana). The first definite appearance of Farsi poems in the form of the *Qasīda*, using the Arabic alphabet, was in Marv in 193/809 at the time of the caliphate of Ma'mun, reported in the *Lubāb al-albāb* of Muhammad Aufī (d. 618 /1221),[62] although there are sketchy reports (e.g., by Tabarī) indicating that the oldest Farsi record dates back to the late seventh century CE from Basra and (later) Balkh.[63] Frye quotes the *History of Sistān* as having reported that the first to compose a poem in Farsi was Muhammad b. Wāsif in 867.[64]

Some scholars felt comfortable in connecting the Dari language (as known in Afghanistan and Tajikistan) to the basis of Farsi development. Lazard, for example, assumes that Dari was the language of everyday life in the Sasanian period.[65] The suggested presence of Dari in the Khurāsān and Transoxiana regions justifies the argument that the Dari language underwent a transition in the east during the Islamic period. This transition entailed heavy borrowings from Soghdian, Parthian, and other eastern dialects and languages.[66] But granting all that, how did Dari as an imported language from western Iran defeat the already existing languages of Transoxiana and establish itself as a dominant language that to a great audience became known as Farsi? It must be strongly stated that Farsi and Dari are one and the same language, only spoken with different dialects. Let us not forget, too, that apart from the mélange of thousands of Arabic words (including Aramaic and Turkish words), Farsi seems to have borrowed from Arabic "literary kinds and rules, stylistic themes, and models, metrics and rhetoric, a scientific and artistic terminology"[67] as well.

---

[62] Lazard, p. 595; Pizzi, *Storia della Poesia,* I, p. 66.

[63] Zarinkub, pp. 121–123; see also Tabarī, VII, p. 2884; IX, pp. 4079–4080; Bahar, *Sabk Shenāsī,* I, p. 231.

[64] Frye, *Golden Age,* p. 173.

[65] Lazard, p. 601.

[66] Ibid., pp. 597–601.

[67] Gabrieli, "Literary Tendencies," p. 98; see also Bailey, p. 199; Lazard, p. 612.

To answer the above question, we must take into consideration a three-fold observation about the meaning of having accepted that the roots of Dari and Farsi are the same. First, it has been suggested that Farsi or Dari is closer to Soghdian than to any other language;[68] second, the Farsi language (as well as other components of a major culture or subculture in any given region of Iran proper, particularly in the east) is a by-product of synthesis and encounter among languages and cultures in both ancient and contemporary settings, and thus Farsi and its evolution could be considered signs of the emergence of a new culture; third, as some have suggested, Dari was only formed in the Islamic period in Central Asia (present-day Tajikistan and Afghanistan) along with other languages, and thus Farsi or Dari is a new language synthesized from several disparate languages on the basis of one dialect. Hence B. G. Gafurov argues that "as a result [of the tendency of various people of Transoxiana to unite economically, politically, and culturally] the development of east Iranian dialects and languages, evidently on the basis of one of the dialects located in the territory where Soghdian, Tukhāristān, and Khurāsān adjoin, was to form the common language of the Tajiks, which at that time was called Dari."[69]

If Farsi-Dari (in a national context) is credited to be a Tajik innovation, then its connection to Sasanian — or for that matter to the region of Fars, which is inside Iran proper — creates a confusing nationalist rivalry between the historians of Tajikistan and of Iran (see, e.g., Gafurov), not even mentioning Afghanistan. The difficulty is that one cannot confirm that Farsi's place of origin is necessarily Fars. The other aspect, as was discussed in the previous chapter, is that historically the Orientalists have identified Farsi (Persian) with Persian people in an accordingly distinct Persia proper, which by and large is a crude assumption. Furthermore, the linguistic designation for a community (in this case, Farsi) is not necessarily coincident with an ethnic or tribal designation, and especially in modern times the concept of nationality has bypassed

---

[68] Humai, *Tārīkh-i Adabiyāt-i Iran*, II, p. 264; see also Bailey, p. 188.

[69] Frye, "Soviet Historiography on the Islamic Orient," *Historians of the Middle East*, p. 372.

all these designations, creating even more confusion. Over the past several years, there have been a few publications in Farsi about Iranian identity and the Farsi language,[70] and all of these fail to distinguish historically and to substantiate the differences and antecedents involved in the formation of a language as opposed to the formation of a modern nation-state.

The issue that gave additional grounds to certain Orientalists and nationalist thinkers for equating Farsi with Iran was the *Shāhnāmeh* of Firdowsī. The *Shāhnāmeh* was a source of ancient epic stories of the Zoroastrians and other ancient myths of the kings of Fars. It assumed special importance in the light of a new language of the Islamic era (Farsi), and through time — particularly during the nationalist era — the epic stories, Farsi, and Iran came to be identified as synonymous. A brief discussion may clarify certain convictions and principles of the storyteller Firdowsī and may offer some insight into the substance and significance of his story *Shāhnāmeh*.

FIRDOWSĪ: A NATIONAL CHAUVINIST?

A practical incentive to formulate the national heritage of Iran has always been attributed to Firdowsī as a result of his references to the land of Iran and its heroes, even though all this is done in a mythological sense. At the centers of Arabic and Farsi learning between the ninth and eleventh centuries, many works were translated into these languages. The translation of a certain work — particularly *Khwaday Namag*, a mythical royal account of history compiled at the end of Sasanian times and translated from Middle Persian into Arabic by Ibn Muqaffa' (d. 757) — is believed to have provided major sources that Firdowsī (d. c. 1020) used for his 50,000- or 60,000-verse epic poetry. Rudakī, the poet of the Sāmānid period of the tenth century, likewise translated the Arabic text of *Kalila wa Dimna* into Farsi poetic verses. *Kalila wa Dimna* was originally a work adopted from Indian literature and was translated

---

[70] Meskub, *Zabān va Melliat*, 2nd edition; Nima publication, *Zabān va Huviyat Mellī*; see also Wickens, "Persian Literature: an Affirmation of Identity," *Introduction to Islamic Civilization*, Savory (ed.), pp. 71–77.

into Middle Persian during the late Sasanian period. Balʻamī translated Tabarī's history from Arabic into Farsi during the time of the Sāmānids. The Ghaznavid period, during which Ghazna was the center of Farsi learning, produced more work in Farsi and more poets in the language than ever before. However, the form of the romantic epic was to some extent conceived in the Sāmānids milieu[71] and then further refined during the Ghaznavids.

Daqīqī (c. 976–997), apparently a Zoroastrian poet, was assigned by the Sāmānids to undertake writing in verse form the epic story. Before he could finish, though, he was assassinated. Prior to Firdowsī's attempt, there were actually five sources and attempts at versions of a *Shāhnāmeh;* these planted the necessary seeds for Firdowsī's monumental work. Consider the following sources: (1) *Khwaday Namag;* (2) Abul Muʻyyad of Balkh (365–87/976–97) or Masʻudī Marvazī; (3) Abu Ali of Balkh (no trace is left); (4) a college of four Zoroastrians compiled under the governor of Tus, Abu Mansur Muhammad b. Abd al-Razzāq (346/957), for which account many sources including *Khwaday Namag* were used; (5) Daqīqī. The last two sources had used relatively few Arabic words.[72] Thus an epic style relying on few or no Arabic words (although such assertion is controversial) was already established. Firdowsī only attempted and could finish the *Shāhnāmeh* (some even doubt that Firdowsī called it *Shāhnāmeh)* after receiving the support of the aristocracy of Tus and the powerful Sultan Mahmud of Ghazna.[73]

The purpose of the present discussion is not to analyze the literary qualities of the legendary *Shāhnāmeh* but to inquire into the intentions of its author. The craving to produce a legendary work in an epic style had emerged, reflecting the poetical taste of the aristocracy in a few short generations. It was not the personal idea of Firdowsī to write the *Shāhnāmeh;* he was only the supporter of the notion and the story-teller, since the idea and material were already there. Firdowsī combined the two in a celebrated and most

---

[71] Bosworth, *Ghaznavid,* p. 134, quoting Rypka.

[72] Minorsky, "The Older Preface to Shahnama," pp. 260–261; Lazard, pp. 625–627; Massé, *Firdousi L'Epopée Nationale,* p. 45; Safa, p. 153.

[73] Lazard, pp. 625–627.

awe-inspiring fashion. There was just as much urge during this era, however, to put the Indian-origin *Kalila wa Dimna* into Farsi verses as to put the Zoroastrian *Khwaday Namag* (or mythical stories of kings of the pre-Islamic era) into Farsi. The intention was not to make a special connection between Farsi and the particular past of an alleged nation (in modern terms, India or Iran); nevertheless, in a general context, the land of Iran became a more fertile soil to receive such legendary works in the service of nationalist doctrine.

As a result of praising the land of Iran (which again may have a Zoroastrian connotation, since the term *Iran* has its roots in the Zoroastrian Sasanians), Firdowsī has unfortunately come to be identified with the promotion of modern nationalist terms. It must be borne in mind that the vast Iranian plateau had not been under any unified political leadership since the Muslim conquest of the seventh century and would not be for almost another three centuries after the time of Firdowsī, notably under the Il-Khanids of the thirteenth century. Therefore, realistically, Firdowsī could not have implied any kind of political nationalism. We will turn to this point later.

In terms of what Firdowsī himself believed and what he portrayed and praised in his poems, Theodor Nöldeke in his *Das Iranische Nationalepos* (1896) and Henry Massé in his *Firdousi l'Epopée Nationale* (1934) provide us with numerous insights. Firstly, Firdowsī's strong and incontrovertible religious and monotheistic Islamic belief has been fully established not only by these two scholars[74] but also by a wide range of readers. But opinions differ as to whether Firdowsī's specific faith was Shi'i Islam. Nöldeke indicates that Firdowsī's Shi'i ideas and devotion to the household of Ali had at some point angered Sultan Mahmud as a Sunni Muslim.[75] One of the most popular conclusions drawn from his poetry is that Firdowsī implies his dislike of the Arabs and the Turks (Turānians) and only praises the "Iranians." But it remains as yet a puzzle, if Firdowsī meant to portray the Arabs and the Turks derogatorily, that his own affinity was toward the Arab prophet, household, and religion and that his patron, Sultan Mahmud, was

---

[74] Nöldeke, *Das Iranische Nationalepos*, p. 36; Massé, *Firdousi*, p. 234.

[75] Nöldeke, pp. 39–40.

of Turkish origin. How could Mahmud have learned about the kings of Fars (allegedly Iran) and their glorious and punishing wars against the Turānians, had he not known about the *Shāhnāmeh*'s epic and mythical nature?[76] As was discussed in Chapter 3, it is quite possible that certain parts of the *Shāhnāmeh* may have sustained rather than challenged the political order of the period. For example, Mahmud's confrontation with the Turānians of Qusdar could have been interpreted in favor of Firdowsī's patron, Mahmud, who was a king facing the enemy.

In other sections, Firdowsī attacks Christianity, a biblical religion, in his poems, which in principle could be considered un-Islamic. But it may be that the sources and myths had originally portrayed the Christian Romans who were at war with the Zoroastrian Sasanians[77] giving the impression that Firdowsī equally shared the belief in the propriety of attacking Christianity. It is clear, however, that such rhetoric does not necessarily put him in defense of the Zoroastrians (who were said to worship fire) nor in enmity with Christianity, which in Islamic tradition is considered an accepted biblical religion.[78] Nor does Firdowsī's defense of Alexander the Great, the Macedonian conqueror of the Achaemenids (allegedly an Iranian Empire, as opposed to a foreign one), as a legitimate religious ruler imply that he supports Greek hegemony over the native Achaemenids of Fars or Persia proper. This is only a compiled story with consciousness of the people of Late Antiquity, and Firdowsī is *only* its orator. On the question of Alexander and national identity, the legitimacy of Alexander's rule is also affirmed by other poets such as Nizāmī, Jāmī, and Amīr Khusrau.[79] Nizāmī, in fact, in his twelfth-century *Eskandar Nama (Book of Alexander)* refers to Alexander as a "God worshiper" who decimated the false creed of the pagan *(kāfir)* Persians.[80]

---

[76] Ibid., p. 28.

[77] Duchesne-Guillemin, *Zoroastrianism Symbols and Values*, p. 9.

[78] Ibid., pp. 36–38.

[79] Hanaway, "Alexander and the Question of National Identity," p. 99; Nöldeke, pp. 36–37.

[80] Browne, I, pp. 118–119. (The name *Eskandar* [Alexander] became common in Iran due to an apparent legitimization of Alexander's seizure

As for the lack of treatment of Achaemenid kings in the *Shāhnāmeh*, a fact noted by Yarshater, Firdowsī should not take any blame. Indeed, in the compilation of *Khwaday Namag* and other related Avestan myths, the Sasanian recollection did not include the Achaemenid period.[81] Firdowsī obviously reported and mythologized what was available to him at the time.

Let us now come back to the issue of Firdowsī's praise for the land of Iran, which has given modern society and governments quotations to adopt and apply to their nationalist ideology. It is dubious, as discussed in Chapter 3, to suggest that any of the dynasties of the East — whether Tāhirid, Saffārid, Sāmānid, or Ghaznavid (at the time of Firdowsī) — ever used or exploited the term *Iran* for political and cultural purposes. The appearance and (often) praise of the land seem to have been a pattern used by a number of poets who may have desired to express sentiments that in modern interpretation could be labeled cultural nationalism. Let us consider a few poems by the Farsi-language poets:

Be Iran Paradise or the Rose Garden
The fragrance of musk comes from the Rose Garden.
  [Firdowsī]

Do not scorn the land of Iran in contempt
Because one town of it is better than the whole of China and
  Trans-China. [Asadī]

In modern terms, these poems seem to possess a strong nationalist tendency, but we must consider that in the era of each of these poets Iran was never under a unified government or empire. And if one does not stubbornly cling to the modern Iranian nationalist interpretation, one may encounter Farsi-language poets who equally praised other lands or geographical regions. Thus, Sa'dī in the thirteenth century praises Iraq (although one may object that Iraq lay inside Iran proper [Iraq-'Ajam]):

---

of the previous empire, the Achaemenid, on the same basis that the name *Changiz* (Gengis [Khan]) became common among the people.)

[81] Yarshater, "The Absence of Median and Achaemenid Kings in Iran's Traditional History," p. 209; see also Massé, pp. 17–19.

Beyond Iraq no climate suits
O musician, play the song of Iraqi melody. [Sa'dī]

Similarly, Amīr Khusrau of the thirteenth century left behind a series of passionate and enthusiastic poems about India, leading one contemporary commentator to express this opinion: "Even the comparative dark Indian beauty was more captivating for his eyes and more enchanting for his heart than the white soulless and ice-cold beauty of Iran and Turkistan."[82]

At any rate, the following poem by Amīr Khusrau about India is a direct response and challenge to those who might have thought that for Amīr Khusrau Iran represents beauty:

Such is the comparison pertaining to Indian goddesses,
A hair of them is equal to a hundred kingdoms of China.

Amīr Khusrau (a venerated Sufi saint in India) goes on to praise the Indian language (Sanskrit) and other aspects of life in India, and he suggests that those who cross India will never enjoy Iran or Khurāsān again:

Anybody who passed time in this land [India],
Has his heart turned away from Khurāsān.[83]

Sixteenth-century poet Abdul Feiz Feizī, like Amir Khusrau, remembers India with warmth and love:

This thread has been spun with Indian magic.
This Orchard has been planted in the Indian soil.
All its soil is love, atom by atom;
Each atom of it being light of nine heavens.
This flame is fervently rising in India.
It is here, where the sun gives its warmth.[84]

---

[82] Ansari, "Amir Khusrau, the Poet and the Patriot," p. 89.
[83] For all Amir Khusrau's poems see Ibid., pp. 89–99.
[84] Chibli, "Nazari bi Diman Feizi, pp. 118–123 (in Farsi). All poetry translation has been by this author with the generous help of Dr. Ravan Farhadi.

Firdowsī, Amīr Khusrau, and other poets naturally expressed their tastes, preferences, and sense of romance in their own poetic style. It would be a sheer anachronism, however, to judge these poets, who cherished a region for its beauty and colorful nature, as being nationalistic. Their poetry was rhetorical rather than political. Furthermore, there is relevant correlation between local patriotism and a *hadīth* (saying) attributed to Muhammad, the Prophet of Islam: "Love of the fatherland is prescribed by faith."

The term *Iran* used by Firdowsī must be largely understood in its Zoroastrian and mythical context of Sasanian mindset than Firdowsī's own initiative to pour out verses on and about Iran. In the case of Firdowsī's attributed 'nationalist' tendencies, (from a modern point of view), Mottahedeh, by using Fritz Wolff's *Shāhnāmeh* glossary, has demonstrated that the use of various so-called nationalist terms by Firdowsī has been selectively noted and misconstrued. Firdowsī's conception of Iran should be put into perspective so that we may realize and compare what he meant then to what we understand today. For the term *nation* (which constitutes the nation of modern Iran) Firdowsī never used terms such as *millat*, *qaum*, *vatan*, or *umma*, all of which are Arabic. Instead, the terms *kishvar* and *mīhan* occur in the *Shāhnāmeh*. *Mīhan*, which in its modern sense means native land, occurs three times — twice in the sense of house and once in the sense of extended family. *Kishvar* (country) occurs more frequently but is often used as a synonym for region or zone, as in the phrase *haft kishvar* (seven regions).[85]

Taking into consideration what has been said about Firdowsī's religious commitment, his mastery of the Farsi language, and his imposition of a unique epic style, it appears that his masterpiece had significance only in literary circles and rulers; but for the political and nationalist implication of the *Shāhnāmeh* the explanation should be sought in twentieth-century consciousness. The concept of Iranism or the restoration of a supposed ancient sovereignty of Iran or the rearchaization of the political system by what is understood from the *Shāhnāmeh*, whether by Sāmānids and Ghaznavids in the east or by Buyids in the west, was not a concern.

---

[85] Mottahedeh, "The Shu'ubiyah Controversy," p. 172.

In each of these dynasties, territorialization of political orders did not involve ruling precisely over a given geographical designation (in this case Iran) or necessarily over a cohesive population, but rather emphasized sketching jurisdiction for the dynasty to gain strength. It is far-fetched to believe that both Firdowsī and the dynasties ruling over parts of Iran wanted to denounce Islam in order to bring back the old Zoroastrian beliefs and thus promote Iranism. The historical myth that Firdowsī preached should not be confused either with his own beliefs or with the political strategy of the day.

Apart from its mythical character, it is quite possible that the *Shāhnāmeh* was a means of preserving traditional knowledge about the past. It was also a history book for the rulers and aristocracy, rather than for the masses, since history books were never written for the masses in pre-modern times. It was more of a lesson for the rulers — particularly the theme of *Shāhnāmeh*. The importance of the *Shāhnāmeh* was carried to the subsequent rulers who read Farsi. Subsequently, the Mongol rulers added illustrations to the *Shāhnāmeh*'s story and cherished it. Zand and other eighteenth-century rulers recited parts of the *Shāhnāmeh* before battles to boost the morale of their army.[86] But what impact did the *Shāhnāmeh*, with all its details of traditional history, have on the formation of national identity and nationalism? Ann Lambton, in her studies of nineteenth-century Iran, expresses the view that it largely remained in the literary tradition and simply did not have an adequate basis for emphasizing nationality or nationalism in a modern sense.[87] It is fair to say that, when nationalism and national identity became concerns in the twentieth century, the *Shāhnāmeh* certainly served as the traditional folk source of such modern notions. It was thus not without political purpose for the Pahlavi regime to organize a millenary celebration for Firdowsī in 1937 in Tehran and Tus (Firdowsī's native town).

The singling out of particularly exciting heroic episodes from the great body of the *Shāhnāmeh* by the traditional local orators

---

[86] Boyle, "The Evolution of Iran as a National State," p. 338.

[87] Lambton, "Social Change in Persia in the Nineteenth Century," p. 128.

(naqāl) to tell to their audiences in the early twentieth century (or previously) has probably been mainly to take advantage of the inherent excitement of these themes (as in the story of Rustam and Sohrāb) rather than to emphasize the work's modern historical and political dimensions: the survival of Iran as a sociopolitical entity. Any assertion that the *Shāhnāmeh* was read by the general masses (other than rulers and literary elites) in pre-modern times, in association with the popular and mystical poems of Hafiz, Rumi, and the educational verses of Sa'dī, should be questioned. In other words, were Hafiz and Sa'dī more read among the ordinary masses or was Firdowsī? Again we have to be careful not to assess the value and weight of the *Shāhnāmeh* during those periods from a modern nationalistic standpoint. Certainly, the Firdowsī phenomenon has nicely corresponded to the needs of current secular nationalism and national pride. Still, in order to expand the argument it is now time to discuss the basis on which historians and Orientalists consolidated their theory of continuity and dynastic connection in the Iranian category in order to understand precisely the constructed historicity of Iranian national identity.

CHAPTER 6
DYNASTIC CONNECTION AND IDENTITY CONSTRUCT

All of the arguments outlined on the preceding pages should be viewed against the background of a whole series of Orientalists' methodology and vision in their conceptualization of Iran as a persistent sociocultural and political entity by excluding other regions and communities. The dynastic connection — whether in the pre-Islamic period (briefly discussed earlier) or in the post-Islamic period — had been the most familiar methodology for constructing a political history of a modern nation-state (in this case, the old imperial Iran). The complex past had to be given meaning from the stores of historical information compiled together over several centuries. It was the job of the Orientalists to select and interpret the assembled material in a way that would provide the necessary "national" meanings. In this part of our discussion we will simultaneously view the construct of dynasties in a national context and take up the names of the most prominent Orientalists involved in this enterprise.

In pursuing the thread connecting the main personalities of academia in the nineteenth and twentieth centuries, one must take into account the significant contribution of the Russian Orientalist Vladimir Minorsky. Minorsky, a graduate of the Lazarev Institute of Moscow (1903), studied Oriental languages after having studied law at the University of Moscow. E. G. Browne's studies of Bābīs had turned the mind of young Minorsky to the study of the Ahl-i Haqq as another esoteric sect. Minorsky's first publication on Iran appeared in Russian in 1911 on an esoteric sect of Ahl-i Haqq or Ali Allāhī, about which a series of articles continued to appear until the late 1920s. His academic career was relocated from Russia after the revolution of 1917 to Western Europe, chiefly Paris and

135

London. During the next forty years, by using the established methodologies of Europeans, he developed his interests in the historical geography, ethnology, political history, literature, and antiquities of Iran, contributing articles about these to more than 200 publications.[1]

Relevant to our discussion is Minorsky's work on the minor dynasties of the Caspian region, which appeared in Paris under the title *La Domination des Dailamites* (1932). Minorsky's original treatment of this subject did more than a little to institutionalize the minor dynasties in the Iranian plateau as part of "national Iranian history." The Dailamites had not previously received a refined national treatment. Browne devoted few pages to the Buyids and Ziyarids in his *A Literary History of Persia* (1902).[2] Sykes dedicates only three pages to the Buyids.[3] George S. A. Ranking's *A History of the Minor Dynasties of Persia* (1910) was basically an extract from the *History of Habīb us-Siyyār* of Khondamir Ghīyas al-Dīn. None of these works made the necessary links with the category of national Iranian historiography. Although H. L. Rabino's studies in the 1920s of the Dailamites and the Caspian region were authentic enough, they did not emphasize the national thesis.

In Minorsky's approach to the Dailamites' political enterprise, the minor tribal dynasties of Kākoyids, Muzaffarids, and others are treated, but the Zīyārid and Buyid dynasties are given the significant national title Iranian. In fact, Minorsky considers the Zīyārid (928–1042) the "first Iranian dynasty" in the West, corresponding to the Sāmānids of the East.[4] Minorsky describes the Zīyārids, along with the Buyids (932–1055) and other minor dynastic affiliates as having created a consolidated Dailamite culture that opened the gates of national Iranian consciousness in all Iran. The Buyids' introduction of Shi'ism (Buyids were reportedly a Zaydiyya Shi'i sect) as the national religion, according to Minorsky (although it had nothing to do with Persian

---

[1] For a list of his publications see V. Minorsky, *Iranica, Twenty Articles*, Publication of the University of Tehran, vol. 775 (1964), pp. xi–xxvi.

[2] Browne, *A Literary History of Persia*, I, pp. 364–365, 367.

[3] Sykes, *A History of Persia*, I, pp. 23–26.

[4] Minorsky, *La Domination des Dailamites*, p. 9.

nationality) provided a basis for the region not to be absorbed into an "abstract Islam" and into the "Turkish ocean," as well as furnishing grounds for the Safavids to reestablish this again.[5] The Buyids' expansion of jurisdiction all the way to Baghdad, the seat of the caliphate, without any intention of abolishing the caliphate, is viewed by Minorsky as the liquidation of Arab rule; meanwhile, he considers their 110 years of rule as having been dedicated to glorifying the pre-Islamic Iranian tradition.[6] The assumption of the title *Shāhanshāh* by Bahā ud-dawla, the Buyid sovereign, was the first time it had been used since the time of the Sasanians.[7] (According to Mostaufi, the Caliph al-Qādir gave him this title.)[8] The topic of the assumption of the title of *Shāhanshāh* was exploited in a series of discussions and articles (which we will refer to later on) to establish the notion of the Buyids' solid "Iranian" base. In elaborating on other pre-Islamic traditions practiced or promoted by the Buyids, Bertold Spuler in his essay "Iran: The Persistent Heritage" adduces several points in this regard — for example, the court festival of coronation with *tāj* (crown) and the celebrations of Mihrigān and Nawruz, with its traditional distribution of gifts.[9] Furthermore, many (including Minorsky) relate that the visit of A'zad ud-dawla to Persepolis and the inscription in his commemoration appear to be an imitation of Sasanian forms.[10]

In an evident contradiction in terms, Minorsky asserts that the Dailamites during the Islamic era had become Iranized, despite the fact that their regions were never solidly conquered by the pre-Islamic Achaemenid and Sasanian dynasties.[11] What may be

---

[5] Ibid., pp. 1, 19, 21; see also Minorsky, "Iran: Opposition, Martyrdom and Revolt," *Unity and Variety in Muslim Civilization*, pp. 194–195.

[6] Minorsky, "Iran: Opposition, Martyrdom, and Revolt," p. 186.

[7] Minorsky, *La Domination*, p. 18; see also Minorsky, "Geographical Factors in Persian Art," *Iranica*, p. 44.

[8] Mostaufi, *Tārikh-i Gozīdeh*, p. 423.

[9] Spuler, "Iran: The Persistent Heritage," *Unity and Variety in Muslim Civilization*, p. 177; see also Morgan, *Medieval Persia*, pp. 23–24.

[10] Minorsky, "Geographical Factors in Persian Art," p. 44.

[11] Minorsky, *La Domination*, pp. 3–5.

Iranization according to Minorsky is one thing; but that he lacks historical reasoning and a concrete notion of what the Iranian components may have been during the Islamic period when things by and large had an Islamic color is another. According to Minorsky, the simultaneous appearance of Buyids in the West and Sāmānids in the East created an "Iranian intermezzo" between the period of Arab control and the subsequent Turkish rule until the rise of the Safavids.[12]

A few of the points outlined above should be reassessed in order to help us understand the nationally unstructured behavior of the Dailamites. With regard to their adoption of pre-Islamic festivals and ceremonies, it is clear that the wide jurisdiction of the Buyids in the West all the way to Baghdad had brought various ethnic, cultural, and religious communities under their control. Their respect for the rites and festivals of Zoroastrians (at that time a large community) had tactical links with their commemoration of the Muharram mourning for various sects of Shi'ites, including the Zaydites, due to satisfying the two large communities. In fact, the Zīyārids and the 'Alavī Sayyids were more concerned with promoting Shi'ism[13] than with developing an alleged form of national Iranian revivalism. Moreover, the reception of the Zoroastrian New Year was not unique to the Buyids. During the first decades of the Muslim conquest, the Arab officials and even the Abbasids themselves sponsored the new year ceremony for the recently conquered people, perhaps out of respect for their traditions and because they received gifts and set the date for *Kharāj* (poll-tax).[14] This should not be mistaken as evidence that Umayyad or Abbasid officials were interested in reviving pre-Islamic traditions. This Umayyad and Buyid gesture was motivated much more by a spirit of diplomacy and tolerance than by anything else.

As to Minorsky's reference to the Buyids as being Iranized in the Islamic period, it is unanimously agreed that the Buyids'

---

[12] Ibid., p. 21; see also "Iran: Opposition, Martyrdom, and Revolt," pp. 186–187, 13; Browne, I, pp. 348–349.

[13] Browne, I, pp. 348–349.

[14] Morony, *Iraq after the Muslim Conquest*, p. 73; see also, Levy, "Persia and the Arabs," *Legacy of Persia*, pp. 65–66.

patronage of literature and science at their court in Shiraz was all given to Arabic, and indeed Shiraz actually produced the greatest of poets in Arabic.[15]

In contrast, the Ghaznavids in the east, who were Turkish émigrés (rhetorically speaking, non-Iranians) patronized poets and a learning center for Farsi rather than Arabic. It is worth mentioning that the A'zad ud-dawla commemorative inscription at Persepolis was in Arabic[16] (not necessarily an appropriate choice if it was a nationalistic Sasanian imitation, as Browne says). The only rational explanation is that the Buyids did not have the alleged Iranian national consciousness attributed to them by Minorsky.

The event that most nurtured the Orientalists' thought about the Buyids' being Iranian was the Buyids' assumption of the title of *Shāhanshāh* (King of Kings). The question is why this particular occurrence was so carefully scrutinized and treated as significant. And just because the title King of Kings is identical with the Sasanian title, why is this "Iranian"? Again, based on the assumption that the Sasanians were the guarantors of Iranism against the Semitic and other non-Iranian elements, the reference to the title *Shāhanshāh* has certainly led many Orientalists not to treat this issue with nonchalant generalities. Individual scholars such as Amedroz, Minorsky, Frye, Bosworth, and (in particular) Madelung[17] have catalogued this parallel to emphasize the secular Iranian side of the Buyids in contrast to their religious Shi'i side.

However, the Buyid sovereigns and their rivals used all kinds of supreme and royal titles besides *Shāhanshāh*, including *Falak al-Umma*, *Amīr ul-Umarā*, and *Malik al-Muluk*.[18] In coinage the titles varied, depending on the reigning sovereign. On Bahā ud-dawla's

---

[15] Bosworth, "The Heritage of Rulership in Early Islamic Iran and Search for Dynastic Connection," p. 57; see also Frye, *Golden Age*, p. 211.

[16] Barthold, *An Historical Geography of Iran*, p. 151.

[17] Amedroz, "The Assumption of the Title Shahanshah by the Buwayid Rulers," *Numismatic Chronicle*, pp. 1393–1399; Frye, *Golden Age*, p. 210; Bosworth, "Heritage of Rulership," p. 57; Madelung, "The Assumption of the Title Shahanshah by the Buyids" and the "Reign of the Daylam (Dawlat al-Daylam)," pp. 168–183.

[18] Madelung, pp. 170–172, 181–183.

silver and gold coins, for example, next to the silver coins of Sultan ud-dawla the title *Shāhanshāh* appears.[19] For a number of other Buyids, the title *Amīr ul-Umarā* (among others) appears on coins.[20] For Bahā ud-dawla, the title *Amīr ul-Mu'minīn* (Lord of Believers) was used.[21] Many of these titles are Arab usage for religious or theocratic leaders — particularly the last title, which was used for the grand caliphs. The use of such Arabo-Islamic titles and the conversion of the Buyids to Shi'ism, an Arab religion, at the very least provide evidence of strong countervailing trends in sharp contrast to the alleged pre-Islamic and Sasanian or Iranic tendencies. In this regard, let us reiterate Minorsky's proposition that the Dailamites had become Iranized during the Islamic period; and the use of the title of *Shāhanshāh*, according to Madelung, is one of the elements of this development: "The title of *Shāhanshāh* first revived under Islam as a symbol of Persian revolt against Arab Islam and the Caliphate."[22]

Such speculation perhaps should be viewed against the background and mainstream of nationalist Orientalism rather than in light of any new historical findings that would help us understand the collective behavior of the Buyids, which was certainly complex. The lack of intention to overthrow the Sunni caliphate in Baghdad, the promotion of Shi'i as well as Zoroastrian rites, the assumption of various titles, and the patronage of science and literature in the Arabic language all in all do not point to a simple explanation about the nature of the Buyid rule, particularly in a national context. Furthermore, as noted, there were no homogeneous Iranian people or nation either at the time of the Buyids or before. Thus there is said to be ample evidence that the people of southwest Iran, when they were ruled by the Dailamites

---

[19] Lane-Poole, *The Coins of Mohammadan Dynasties*, pp. 213–217.

[20] Ibid., pp. 191–193, 197.

[21] Madelung, pp. 176, 178, 179 notes.

[22] Madelung, p. 183. Many such titles were also given to Mahmud of Ghazna; *Shahanshah-i Ālam, Khudāvand-i Khurāsān va Shahanshah-i Iraq*, etc.; see Bosworth, "Heritage of Rulership," p. 61.

of the Caspian region, thought of the latter as outsiders.[23] Here again, to say the least, the Orientalists are confusing the geographic heritage or land and the old imperial rule of Iran with the sociocultural and political affairs of a dynasty in a way that more nearly resembles the retroactive European injection of nationalism into the past than historical reality.

EASTERN DYNASTIES

In passing we will consider examples of other minor dynasties in relation to their adoption and patronage of the Farsi language as well as to their political line, since these features in the opinion of the Orientalists qualified these dynasties as being of Iranian origin. The Ṭāhirid dynasty (821–873) is supposedly the earliest autonomous governorship in Khurāsān in the vast Abbasid Empire. Its hegemony went far beyond Khurāsān and covered a great portion of the Iranian plateau but, while some scholars have put this dynasty into the line of anti-caliphate and national-Persianized dynasties,[24] such a view can be contested from several perspectives.

In the civil war of 811 between the rival brother caliphs, al-Amīn and al-Ma'mun, Ṭāhir sided with the latter. When al-Ma'mun triumphed, Ṭāhir was rewarded with a prominent position in Iraq and Syria. The family of the Ṭāhirids by and large retained their positions within the caliphate while the Saffārids in the Khurāsān and Sistān regions were pushing them on the marginal political line. The Ṭāhirid policies of suppressing the Khawārij and the Shi'ites[25] matched those of the caliphs. Their coins even bore the name of the caliph,[26] just as did other Abbasid coins during this period.[27] The Ṭāhirids were highly Arabized in culture and intellectual

---

[23] Mottahedeh, "The Shu'ubiyah Controversy and the Social History of Early Islamic Iran," p. 173, quoting Mahmud b. Uthman, *Die Vita des Scheich Abu Isahq al-Kazaruni* (Leipzig, 1948).

[24] Browne, I, p. 346; Morgan, p. 19.

[25] Bosworth, "The Tahirids and Arabic Culture," *Medieval Arabic Culture and Administration*, p. 53.

[26] Lane-Poole, p. 73.

[27] Frye, *Golden Age*, p. 191.

activities.[28] With regard to their alleged veneration of pre-Islamic traditions, certain historical allegations suggest a very different case. Frye and Browne indicated that various sources described how Tāhirids had ordered Pahlavi books to be burned or thrown into the water, on grounds that the Koran and *hadīths* (sayings and deeds of the Prophet) would suffice.[29] (This and other actions are believed to have caused the eradication of Pahlavi inscriptions and the spread of Pahlavi script in the face of Arabic.) Bosworth disputes this claim about a policy of destroying Zoroastrian and Pahlavi books and claims that, although they played no role in new Persian (Farsi) literature, the Tāhirids were not positively anti-Iranian.[30] Meanwhile, the Orientalists have magnified the Tāhirids' Iranian genealogy in the historical context of national determination far more than the Tāhirids themselves chose to do; the Tāhirids preferred linkage and clientage with an Arab tribe of Khuza'a that had been more prestigious than the Quraysh tribe of the Prophet. Various assertions have been made by poets and others that the lineage of Tāhirids reached back to the Kisrā of 'Ajam (Persian King) and even Rustam.[31]

Due to the many uncertainties, Frye cautiously prefers to consider the Tāhirids an intermediate step between governors appointed by Baghdad and independent rulers of the area in its Iranian form.[32]

More important, the penetrating study of the Tāhirids by Mongi Kaabi tells us that the arguments of Orientalist historians on the continuity of the Persian struggle to govern local affairs independently from the Arabs (e.g., Abu Muslim, Barmakids, and Banu Sahl) have led to contradictory conclusions. Furthermore,

---

[28] Morgan, p. 19; Bosworth, "The Heritage of Rulership," p. 56; Frye, *Golden Age*, pp. 191–192; Bosworth, "The Tahirids and Arabic Culture," pp. 59–63, 67.

[29] Frye, *Golden Age*, p. 192; see also Browne, I, p. 347.

[30] Bosworth, "The Tahirids and Persian Literature," *The Medieval History of Iran, Afghanistan, and Central Asia*, pp. 103–106.

[31] Bosworth, "The Heritage of Rulership," p. 56; Bosworth, "The Tahirids and Arabic Culture," pp. 51–53.

[32] Frye, *Golden Age*, p. 191.

Kaabi argues that the Tāhirids were not products of a struggle against Baghdad but in fact evidenced the continuity of the Khurāsān *Wilāya* (governorship) installed since the conquest, and that its dichotomy was a consequence of crisis with the caliphate.[33] He further elaborates that, contrary to the views of some,[34] the Tāhirids had no affiliation with the *Shu'ubiya*[35] — a literary movement that had attempted to subdue certain Arab claims.

The Saffārid dynasty in the ninth century, according to Frye, Stern, and others, constituted "more of an Iranian national dynasty than the Tāhirids, for not only did they rise from the people, but the inability of Ya'qub to understand Arabic is cited as the reason for the development of Persian poetry in Seistan."[36] Obviously here the rise of a new language — namely, Farsi — to prominence is, according to the Orientalist's criteria, a sign of national feeling. Some even suggest that the Persian language saved the Persian nation.[37] We might wish that the question of language and national identity were that simple. In light of what has been discussed so far, it is clear that we must carefully distinguish the history of a language from the physical geography of the place where it occurs, as well as from the political history of a coinciding dynasty (Farsi, Iran, and Saffārid). An effort to prevent any anachronistic attributions to the events of the medieval period would require separate studies of Farsi language, dynastic history, a geographical region and culture. This pattern again and again warns us not to believe that the development and flourishing of Farsi literature — whether in Sistān or later in India — need be exclusively bound up

---

[33] Kaabi, *Les Tahirides au H̱urasan et en Iraq*, pp. 403–405.

[34] Stern, "Ya'qub the Coppersmith and Persian National Sentiment," *Iran and Islam*, p. 538; see also Bosworth, "The Tahirids and Arabic Culture," p. 49.

[35] Kaabi, pp. 404–405.

[36] Frye, *Golden Age*, p. 199; Stern, "Ya'qub the Coppersmith," pp. 545–552; Bosworth, "Heritage of Rulership," pp. 59–60; Morgan, p. 20; see also *Tārīkh-i Sistān*, p. 209. It refers to Ya'qub's remark about not understanding Arabic.

[37] Boyle, "The Evolution of Iran as a National State," p. 327; Wickens, "Persian Literature: An Affirmation of Identity," pp. 71–72.

with a modern geographical designation or with the political ideology, military goals, and Islamic orientation of a remote dynasty (in this case, the Saffārids). Patronage of Farsi-language literature and poets by the Saffārid sovereigns was a linguistic choice and not necessarily an expression of political ideology — at least not as anachronously connected by Orientalists to a preconceived pre-Islamic Iranian consciousness.

Attributing an Iranian national identity to the Saffārid dynasty is belied by the fact that this dynasty ruled under no national title except the banner of whatever suited its purpose and political ends. Theodor Nöldeke's work, although a bit dated, provides a well-rounded account of the Saffārids regarding their bargain for rulership with the caliphs of Baghdad. He properly called the Saffārid realm a Sistanese kingdom. According to the author, Ya'qub ibn Laith's campaigns against the non-Muslims (Hindu-Buddhist) who lived in the vicinity of present-day Kabul and his suppression of the Khawārij movement had already made him the champion of conventional Islam. It is even said that Ya'qub aimed for Tabaristān, which was in the hands of Shi'i Zaidīya.[38] Had Ya'qub succeeded in toppling the early Dailamites of Tabaristān (an accomplishment that would have pleased the Sunni caliphate), then Minorsky's suggestion of Shi'ism as a factor in the formation of Iranian national consciousness as well as the revival of Iranian sentiment by the two warring dynasties would have proved to be uneven and contradictory. The two alleged champion Iranian dynasties, the Dailamites and the Saffārids, had two separate ideologies and strategies. Thus, bundling these two dynasties together as being so-called Iranian is historically inconsistent and clashing. Furthermore, to emphasize the role of Islam in these dynastic histories which often times has been ignored by nationalist authors and a number of Orientalists, Ya'qub and other Saffārid rulers, according to Tabarī, used to send lofty and symbolic gifts of

---

[38] Nöldeke, *Sketches from Eastern History*, pp. 176–183; *Tārīkh-i Sistān*, pp. 206–212, 223–224.

loyalty to the caliphs of Baghdad.[39] In addition, the Saffārids acknowledged the caliphs by putting their names on their coins.[40]

These points about the Saffārids' attitude toward the caliphate are only an interpretation intended to avoid the trappings of national development promoted by the above-mentioned Orientalists, since the Saffārids were primarily Muslims rather than representatives of any national entity. Besides, many dynasties (including the Saffārids) during the period of power struggle were more properly military entities than hierarchical state organizations engaged in promoting culture. The following statement expresses the opinion of one scholar: "Ya'qub and Amr were continually in the field, there was not much time or leisure to promote culture."[41] In being patrons of poets, Farsi or other, the Saffārids like other sovereigns were indulging themselves by encouraging the flattery and compliments of poets. As to their alleged genealogy, the information we have is rather ambiguous. It has been mentioned that the lineage of the Saffārids can be traced back to the ancient or Sasanian kings.[42] Even we accept this, it is not a "national" evidence because the ancient kings did not have any national designation. Moreover, in general terms, most supreme rulers wished to connect themselves with noble and royal roots. Thus it is a misconception to view the Saffārids or any other royal genealogical fabrication as a sign of a national tendency.

In the methodological sense, the rise and inner development of the Sāmānids of the tenth century in Transoxiana were seen as Iranian, as subsequent to the already underway Persian Renaissance, and as an eclipse for western Iranians.[43] It is again Minorsky who places the Sāmānids next to the Buyids as an Iranian shield vis-à-vis the Arab caliphate. The Sāmānids of Bukhara

---

[39] Tabari, *Tārīkh*, XIV, pp. 6278, 6272–6280; XV, pp. 6439–6468; see also Nöldeke, pp. 181, 182.

[40] Lane-Poole, pp. 75–78; see also Morgan, p. 20.

[41] Frye, *Golden Age*, p. 199; see also Stern, p. 538.

[42] Bosworth, "The Heritage of Rulership," pp. 59–60; Stern, pp. 541–545; *Tarikh-i Sistan*, pp. 200–202.

[43] Minorsky, *La Domination*, p. 1; Brockelmann, *History of Islamic Peoples*, p. 166; Grousset, "L'âme de l'Iran et l'humanisme," *L'Âme de l'Iran*, p. 36.

established their feudatories alongside the Turkish-speaking aristocracy, Ilak Khan or Qarakhānids. Thus there were dichotomies on both sides' religious, economic, and cultural orientations, but Minorsky collates all this in a crude national context. Minorsky obliquely refers to such dichotomies and to the vigorous Qarakhānid pushing back of the Sāmānids by claiming that the Sunni clergy of the Sāmānids "showed a complete lack of national ideas and sacrificed the Sāmānids to the Turkish outsiders."[44] With regard to Minorsky's quest for cultural and political purity, as evidenced by his reference to the "Turkish outsiders," these Turkish elements were natives of Soghdiana and Central Asia — the same home for the Sāmānids. Only the Qarakhānids defeated the Sāmānids. The ill-founded contempt of historiographers for the existence since pre-Islamic times of Turkish elements in that region[45] has notably led Iranologists like Minorsky to contrast in a historically specious manner the presence of Turkish outsiders with the Iranian purity of the Sāmānids.

Since Arabic culture apparently influenced the Sāmānids less than it did the Tāhirids,[46] the Sāmānids made an effort to support the development of Farsi literature. Their use of the Arabic language even at the governmental level encouraged Spuler to express an inherently self-contradictory statement about the national identity of the Sāmānids: "Reinstatement of Arabic as the language of government by Sāmānids did not influence their Iranian conception of the state."[47] This is also followed by another speculative assertion by Morgan in comparing the Saffārid and Sāmānid dynasties in their so-called nation-building: "Sāmānids did not labor their Persian identity in quite Saffārid style."[48]

From the standpoint of Soviet or Marxist methodology, the emergence of the above-mentioned dynasties of the ninth and tenth centuries in the face of a powerful centralized caliphate was

---

[44] Minorsky, "Iran: Opposition, Martyrdom, and Revolt," p. 185.

[45] Frye, "Soviet Historiography," p. 373.

[46] Bosworth, "The Heritage of Rulership," p. 58.

[47] See the discussion by Spuler followed by the essay by Minorsky, "Iran: Opposition, Martyrdom, and Revolt," p. 202.

[48] Morgan, p. 21.

the result of the rapid resurrection of feudalism in Central Asia that could be characterized as a victory of the local aristocracy over the caliphate.[49] Such an approach, which disputably lays significant emphasis on economic factors, certainly bypasses the national motivations of these dynasties. It was accordingly the class of the *dihqān* (landed aristocracy) that gave rise to the Sāmānids; and it was through the dominance of this group that Islamic cultural phenomena were synthesized with local interests that largely differed from the interests of the Arab caliphate. This has led Western Orientalists to perceive this episode as an instance of national defiance against the caliphate. The closest national affiliation Orientalists found was Iran, due perhaps to well-hidden political agendas of the past two centuries. Had Khurāsān and Transoxiana historically emerged as a distinct political unit in modern times, it would have been easier to catalogue many of these events under the Khurāsānian national banner. Mostaufī informs us, however, that Khurāsān maintained a separate kingdom from Iran under the Il-Khanids.[50] The emergence of Afghanistan as a political entity along with Tajikistan as parts of Great Khurāsān (northern Afghanistan) and Transoxiana (as the result of external interventions) was, at least during the zenith of Orientalism, too insignificant politically to require an accounting next to the established stronghold of Iranology in the authoritarian field of Orientalism.

To say the least, careful attention to the art, culture, and fabric of Khurāsān and Transoxiana would indicate to us that what has been deliberately constructed as a national Iranian heritage belonged to other lands. In many of the archaeological finds in these regions and in parts of Central Asia the date and origin of the artifacts cannot be determined;[51] other finds suggest that Indian, Chinese, Turkish, and Buddhist influences have been present in those regions.[52] Therefore, transgressing against the diverse and

---

[49] Frye, "Soviet Historiography," pp. 367, 371.

[50] Mostaufī, *Nodhat ul-Qulub*, p. 27.

[51] Frye, *Golden Age*, p. 207.

[52] Bosworth, *The Ghaznavids*, pp. 146–147; Minorsky, "Geographical Factors," p. 58.

creative civilization of the Sāmānids of Khurāsān and Transoxiana is an unavoidable byproduct of the nationalistic attempt to acknowledge and place them in an Iranian category. This historical inconsistency has been overshadowed, of course, by the Sāmānid patronage of Farsi literature, which was taken as an Iranian proof by the believers in the theory of the national soul based on patronage of a vernacular language. It is also fair to ask, if what took place in the eastern plateau of Iran has been known dynastically and literarily as Iranian, what parallels are found in the western plateau of Iran on the same artistic, intellectual, or political scale. Although the question is complex and diverts the focus of our argument, it is nonetheless an issue worth mentioning to determine the scholarly basis of the Iranian categorization of complex historical events.

The eastern Iranian plateau, including Khurāsān and Transoxiana, without any boundary prejudice is attached to the Central Asian, Turkish, Chinese, and Hindu-Buddhist worlds from which this region has elegantly extracted and exchanged historical antecedents. In contrast, the western regions of Iran gained their character through ancient influences of Sumerians, Babylonians, Assyrians, Achaemenids, Sasanians, and later the Arabs, whose strongholds and centers lay mostly in the west. Thus the historical experiences of Kurdistan and Khuzistān in the West and of Transoxiana and Khurāsān in the East cannot easily be forced into clear-cut Iranian national terms, at least without doing substantial violence to anthropological and sociological principles.

These arguments are not new; scholars such as M. Hartmann, J. Strzygowski, Herzfeld, Diez, and Barthold have tried in one way or another to challenge the conventional Orientalist interpretation of the east and west issues. However, with regard to the arguments of these scholars, Minorsky reveals his own inability to consolidate his theory in the face of discrepancies and contradictions. How to conceive a unified field for the existence of an Iranian culture and for the interdependence of eastern and western Iran, according to Minorsky, has remained obscure, and there simply is not sufficient knowledge for assessing the role of east-west ties in creating that unified field.[53] The archaeologist Roman Ghirshman has been less prudent and more assertive than most in assuming that eastern Iran has played the role of catalyst in the "national awakening" and in claiming that the Tāhirids, Saffārids, and Sāmānid have been the expression of a "True Iranian Renaissance."[54] Of course, by doing so, Ghirshman has already counted on the western dynasties of the pre-Islamic period to balance the national equation in different periods. Such an approach is obviously both anachronous and uneven in linking the diverse civilizations of different regions and times together for the sake of stressing an interregional unity of late antiquity in modern terms of nationalism.

Let us now return to the dynastic connection in its Iranian aspect and the employment of nationalistic methodology by the Orientalists. After the fall of both the Buyids in the West and the Sāmānids in the East, the Ghaznavid (Turkish) dynasty was emerging and subsequently supplanted by the Seljuqs; both events occurred in the eleventh century and ended with a monopoly of power by the latter in the Iranian plateau. Then came the Mongolian takeover, beginning in the mid-1200s. This period of Turko-Mongolian domination was effective until, as Minorsky suggests, the rise of the Safavids at the turn of the sixteenth century, which he interprets as a turning point for the "Persian nation to assert its originality."[55] Although the early administrators under the Safavids, the Qizilbāsh, were all Turkish-speaking, and although the Eastern Arabian and Syrian-imported theologians were Arabic-speaking, many Orientalists would like to refer to the Safavids as a "national" and "Iranian" governing body whose political meanings have to be found in the subsequent uninterrupted geopolitical unity of Iran, along with the designation of the Shiʻi sect of Islam that eventually helped distinguish it from the neighboring lands. On the other hand, Morgan believes that the Turkish domination in some sense remained in Iran until 1925, when the last Qājārs were overthrown by the Pahlavi dynasty.[56]

---

[53] Minorsky, "Geographical Factors," pp. 57–63.

[54] Ghirshman, *I'Iran et la migration*, p. 77.

[55] Minorsky, "Iran: Opposition," p. 194.

[56] Morgan, p. 25.

The linguistic and ethnic diversity in the plateau at the levels of the masses and the ruling elites — particularly in the presence of massive Turkish-speaking segments — has convinced such Orientalists as Bosworth and Grousset to propose the terms *Iranization* and *Persianization* for these Turkish and other elements in order to construct a national historical continuity.[57] In this framework, it would be appropriate to ask what exactly is meant by an Iranization process, and what its standard characteristics are. Apart from adoption of the Farsi language, Bosworth tells us that the taking of Iranian names is another element. But if that is so, then taking Arab names must, according to the same equation, signal an Arabization process, and consequently all Muslims who have taken Arab names have become Arabized. Goldziher, however, strongly argues the *Shu'ubiya* and Arab/non-Arab issues, rightly saying "names are but symbols and marks" and "thus names cannot be used as proof or disproof of any national descent."[58] True, the transitions, inter-borrowings, and syntheses of customs and traditions in the broad context in which they are exercised culturally have constantly been taking place, but this process should not all be ascribed to a single cultural entity whose very basis is subject to question — that is to say, Iranian.

The Turkish tribal dynasties that ruled various parts or all of Iran from the Ghaznavid period of the eleventh century on should each be scrutinized separately in order to detach such dynastic groups from the national conception. However, a few of the derogatory remarks of the Orientalists about the Turkish settlement of the Iranian plateau should be viewed as 'pro-Iranian' bias, and to distinguish the Iranian world from the Turkish one into which it dissolved. The notorious remarks and examples demonstrating the prejudiced tradition in early Orientalism and in modern scholarship are many and unjustified; the following are only a few of them. Minorsky, referring to the settlement of the Turks and to Turkish hegemony on the Iranian plateau, anachronistically conceives the existence of a sociopolitical body he

---

[57] Bosworth, "Heritage of Rulership," pp. 60–61; Grousset, "L'âme de l'Iran et l'humanisme," p. 37.

[58] Goldziher, *Muslim Studies,* I, p. 185.

calls Iranian that he says rendered "some service to the people in civilizing the invaders and smoothing the harshness of the barbarous and foreign administration."[59] The same discriminatory remark Minorsky made about the Turks in Iran is repeated in a chapter title by Morgan: "The Barbarians Civilized?"[60] Bosworth's assessment of the Turks is no less demeaning than that of other Orientalists when he says that the Turks "for some hundreds of years to come, were, it is true, gradually permeated by the superior culture of Persia."[61] Not only has the approach been cynical and somewhat insulting toward the Turks and the Mongolians, but the coming of Arabs to Iran and the Muslim conquest have been subject to the same denunciations — of course, with a cautious view toward the doctrine of Islam, which the conquerors brought and to which they converted the conquered people. Here is a representative example of Arberry's one-sided treatment of the Muslim conquest of Iran and the defeat of the Sasanians: "After the catastrophes of Qādisīya (635) and Nahāvand (642) ..."[62] Catastrophes for whom? Whose side Arberry is taking is not the question; the unfair and judgmental points of view of Arberry and the like are the serious problems that the works of many Orientalists are not totally free from. It remains to be asked why these historians show such obvious affinity for Iran in such imprecise fashion without including the views from other lands and peoples in their construction of history. The general answer could be found and described by the philosophy hidden behind the curtains of Aryanism that have so widely entangled the scholars and scholarship.

Western Orientalism obviously has been at one and the same time a progeny of colonialism, an exercise in cultural and intellectual competition, and a haughty expression of superiority to others. It is in such a frame of mind that cultural competition for superiority in an ethnic and national context are fostered between the so-called Iranians and the Arabs, Turks, Mongolians, and

---

[59] Minorsky, "Iran: Opposition," p. 199.

[60] Morgan, Chapter 8.

[61] Bosworth, "The Heritage of Rulership," p. 62.

[62] Arberry, "Persian Literature," p. 204.

others. The alleged Iranians, due to their purported Aryan
background and their historical culture (in Gobineau's sense) are
treated as respectable members of the Aryan family who have
legitimate ancestors, as opposed to other peoples and cultures of
the Orient. It comes as no surprise when John Andrew Boyle uses
Firdowsī's *Shāhnāmeh* as documentation of a legitimate ancestral
tree for the Iranians in the face of "rootless Arabs":

> It is because of the *Shāhnāmeh* that the ordinary Persian, unlike
> the ordinary Egyptian, Syrian, or Iraqi, knows and has always
> known, that the history of his country does not begin with the
> flight from Mecca to Medina; he can trace it back through the
> historical Sasanians and an Iranized Alexander (the son of
> Philip by an Iranian princess), not indeed to Cyrus the Great,
> but to the legendary Jamshid and Feridun, who are in fact
> Aryan deities.[63]

This and many other impudent slanders have gone unchallenged —
particularly by the modern scholars of Iran, whose resulting sense
of historical grandeur has overshadowed their sense of unbiased
objectivity. The self-generated perceptions of certain Orientalists
have been no accident; they constitute a pattern for creating a
national genealogical structure. Such a pattern is discernible in the
works of Grousset, Spuler, and Corbin, in which arbitrary
nationalist fancies have managed to be accommodating to and
consistent with the ongoing tenets of modern nationalism and
racism. For these Orientalists the question of continuity looms
larger than the question of change. Grousset, for example, comes
out with an astronomical figure of fifty centuries of Iranian
continuity.[64] Like Spuler, Grousset firmly believes that the distant
dominant characteristics of the primordial Iranian nation were all
translated into Islamic practices in the Islamic period.[65] The
prominent Islamicist Henry Corbin's four-volume study *En Islam
Iranien* (1971–1972) makes innumerable assertions about the

---

[63] Boyle, "The Evolution of Iran as a National State," p. 328.

[64] Grousset, "L'âme de l'Iran," p. 35.

[65] Spuler, "The Persistent Heritage," *Unity and Variety in Muslim
Civilization*, pp. 167–179; Grousset, pp. 35–38.

conjunction and continuity of pre-Islamic (Zoroastrian-Mazdean) mysticism and esotericism into Shi'ism. According to Corbin, these took a peculiar national Iranian coloring. This conception not only implies that Iranian religious history has not undergone drastic change in developing this national character, but seriously brings into question what he conceives of as the characteristics of Arab Islam.[66]

The production of such national categories, along with the knitting together of historical events in connection with a geographical designation, has encouraged Orientalists in their cultural and racial biases to conceive what they have conceived. Connections identified or fabricated between pre-Islamic and post-Islamic dynasties and other cultural and political happenings in the Iranian plateau have authenticated an argument about Iranian history and identity. This putative account of national history has been geared toward historicity and the self-perpetuation of other historical events that the Orientalists have had to create national motivation for. Apart from the *Shu'ubiya* debate, one may point to the religiopolitical movements during the first century of the Abbasid empire after Abu Muslim (such as those of Bih-āfarīd, al-Muqanna, Ishaq Turk, Sinbād, Ustādhsis, Māzīyār and Bābāk) which Browne and Goldziher interpret as "undisguised manifestations of the old Persian racial and religious spirit — actual attempts to destroy the supremacy of the Arab and of Islam and to restore the power of the ancient rulers and teachers of Persia."[67] The idea behind such oppositions may have been anti-Islamic, or anti-caliphate inspired by certain religious and regional fervor but it could not have been precisely "national" or "Iranian."

The same national attribution has been given to the Abu Muslim uprising against the Umayyad Caliphate, which resulted in

---

[66] See Henry Corbin, *En Islam Iranien,* Vol. I–IV (Paris: Gallimard, 1971–1972); see also Hamid Algar, "The Study of Islam: The Work of Henry Corbin," pp. 85–91.

[67] Browne, I, p. 336, quoting Goldziher's reference to Shu'ubiya in *Muhammedanische Studien;* see also Massé, *Firdousi et l'Epoée Nationale,* pp. 17–19, 29; about these individuals a book in Farsi was written by Parviz, *Qiyām Iranian dar Rāh-i Tajdīd Mahd va Azemat-i Iran,* pp. 58–104.

its downfall and in the establishment of the Abbasid rule. Any investigation of the network of opposition against the Umayyad Caliphate, however, should be sensitive to the complexity of its religious-political-economic basis rather than being devoted to elaborating on a superficial and anachronous national basis.[68] The movements following Abu Muslim mentioned above have been discussed by Nizām al-Mulk in his *Sīyāsat Nāma,* by Shahrastānī in his *al-Milal wal-Nihal,* and by Rashīd al-Dīn Fazlullāh in his *Jāmi' al-Tawārīkh.* Although in a certain sense heretical, these movements had a Manichaean, Mazdaki, and Shi'i (Ismā'īlī) formation and orientation against the status quo.[69] Certain Orientalists have labeled these culturally and politically complex movements as national because they have extracted the pre-Islamic elements to demonstrate their defiance to Muslim or Abbasid hegemony. But the mere presence of pre-Islamic elements (or any given religious forms) should not convince us to treat these elements as national or particularly as Iranian. The opposition against both the Umayyad and the Abbasid empires in fact recognized no national criteria. It is the consciousness of modern times that has defined these medieval movements in national terms.

Because of the developed network of inter-referential Orientalist works, it has become extremely difficult if not impossible to impede and challenge the flow of historical assertions and publications on the nationalist theme of Iranian studies. The dynastic connection and a superficial overview of Iranian national identity in terms of certain cultural or political behaviors observable in some corner of the Iranian plateau have presented a massive amount of work that needs to be critically traced, checked for factual accuracy, and undercut in order to better grasp the true unfolding of history as against indigenous or national claims.

---

[68] Moscati, "Per una storia dell'antica Si'a," p. 265; see also Vaziri, *The Emergence of Islam: Prophecy, Imamate, and Messianism in Perspective,* pp. 120–126, 153–154.

[69] Nizām ul-Mulk, *Sīyāsat Nāma* pp. 23–238; Shahrastānī, *al-Milal wal Nihal,* I, pp. 200–201; Rashīd al-Dīn Fazlullāh, *Jami' al-Tawārīkh* (section on Hasan Sabah), pp. 72–74; see also Vaziri, pp. 157–159.

MORE ORIENTALISTS

In light of what has been addressed thus far in the themes and names of western academicians, a few more names and topics of study should also be considered. The Danish philologist Arthur Christensen is one of the most influential Orientalists of the twentieth century. His work on the Sasanian dynasty, *L'Iran sous les Sassanides* (1936) — even apart from his other publications — was an edifice unequaled in its time. Through this work Christensen interposed the philological readings at the Naqsh-i Rustam and other pre-Islamic sites with Aryan concepts to create an imaginary nation of Arya (Iran) in the Achaemenid period[70] as a precedent to the establishment of the Sasanians in a national context. Although the textual research done by Christensen was an academic triumph, one must say with dismay that it fell ultimately into the same dismal category as other academic works along racial and national lines. That the Sasanian work kept its high and unique status in the bibliographies of post-Christensen scholars is an indication that *L'Iran sous les Sassanides* was the only comprehensive and viable source on the topic.

Christensen's work received virtually no criticism and was treated as a bible in the field. But the chief shortcomings (without detailed arguments) of Christensen's approach obviously were his solid conviction about the legitimacy of the Aryan hypothesis and his disregard for dynastic historiography as an alternative to the national conceptualization of the Sasanians, whose geographical and organic expansion went far beyond Iran proper (see the epilogue of the present book). The problem partly arises from the fact that, like others, Christensen took the name *Iran* for granted. As has been indicated previously, the Arab sources used *Fars* as a dynastic designation; Christensen simply translated Fars as Iran.

In the field of art and architecture, the scholar who comes to mind first is the eminent Arthur Pope. His authorship and editorship produced voluminous works on Persian art and architecture linking the distant past with the modern era that guaranteed continuity of "Persian art" in a national context. The

---

[70] Christensen, *L'Iran sous Les Sassanides*, pp. 13–14, 85–88.

title of this famous six-volume work is *A Survey of Persian Art from Prehistoric Times to the Present* (1938–1939). Without detailed discussion, it is clear that there could not have been anything uniquely Persian either in prehistoric times or in later periods. As suggested in Chapter 3, Achaemenid's art and architecture, for example, reflected a multiplicity of influences from previous civilizations and from within the existing communities of the Achaemenid empire; these elements could not have produced a narrow and single ethnic art in the Iranian plateau, then or later. The national conceptualization of multiformat art in the vast Iranian plateau convinced Pope to produce other works on the topic, including *Masterpieces of Persian Art* (1945) and *Persian Architecture: The Triumph of Form and Color* (1965). Pope gained considerable attention in Iran and was quoted by numerous scholars there; thus he supplied the missing link in creating a comprehensive national heritage. Pope's major shortcoming is his relentless usage of "Persian" for the complex art of the Near East.

Among the well-known Orientalists, A. E. Olmstead should be cited for his production of works on ancient Iran. In some sense it could be said that he was the heir of G. Rawlinson of the nineteenth century on the topic and 'school' of Aryan historiography. Olmstead died in 1945; his most famous work, *History of the Persian Empire*, was published in 1948. In this work he reemphasized the Aryanness of the Persians, taking the terms *Iran* and *Iranian* for granted and using them interchangeably throughout the text with *Persia, Persians*, and *Aryans*.[71] This work, however, filled the scholarly time gap in the West since Rawlinson in refining and repeating the account of Achaemenid history in a racial and national context.

Many other Orientalists wrote about the history of Persia or Iran, emphasizing its dynastic ancestral background, but Donald N. Wilber is typical for both his generalist/popular approach to history and his connection of environmental, geological, and developmental factors to customs, people, dynasties, and political systems in the Iranian plateau. His *Iran Past and Present* (1948), of which nine editions have come out — the most recent (1981) including a

---

[71] For example see Olmstead, *History of the Persian Empire*, pp. 16–24.

chapter on the Islamic Republic since 1979 — offers a market display of all items from 4000 BCE to the present. The combination of the name Donald Wilber, the publisher Princeton University Press, and the overflow of generalities have given this book a wide audience. The book is without footnotes, self-serving, and far too general, with all kinds of uncorroborated nationalistic assertions — particularly in the third chapter, where the author emphasizes patterns of continuity in culture, history, religion, and language:

> Since the rise of the Achaemenid Empire some thirty-three dynasties ruled Iran ... . [All the outsiders who came to Iran] were all absorbed by and became a part of Iranian civilization. ... This capacity for absorbing foreign blood and adapting foreign influences was due both to the topology of the land and to the vitality of its inhabitants ... Iran's civilization has its own distinctive character ... . The history of Iranian culture exhibits a remarkable persistence and continuity.[72]

Wilber did not invent these ideas, but he has provided the dubious service of cataloguing numerous (and often obsolete) nationalistic ideas into a book. Of course, between 1955 and 1969, Wilber also contributed a few books on the subjects of the architecture and archeology of Iran. His other books, particularly *Four Hundred Forty-Six Kings of Iran* (1972), are still in the mainstream of the nationalistic approach.

The proliferation of scholars and publications in the twentieth century has offered ample authority for others to admit the power of academia and lend themselves to submission. Unfortunately, many more publications and Orientalists who are worthy of scrutiny — particularly on the subject of Iran — due to limited space must be left out of this discussion. In the next chapter, we investigate the direct impact of Western methodology and nationalistic conceptions of Iran on modern belletrists and historians inside Iran, who imported and imitated this methodology in twentieth-century Iran. Of course the focus remains how such a method of historiography constructed and reinforced the historicity of Iranian national identity.

---

[72] Wilber, *Iran Past and Present*, pp. 74–78.

CHAPTER 7
NATIONALISTIC HISTORIOGRAPHY AND IDENTITY CONSTRUCT IN IRAN

Once the Western methodology for the nationalistic conceptualization of Iran was established in the nineteenth century, the twentieth century saw the consolidation of such methodology and acceleration of publications on various topics about Iran. The emergence of Asian (and in particular Iranian) nationalism in the twentieth century coincided with the nationalistic approach to Iranian culture, society, history, and languages developed by the Western Orientalists. This approach provided the ground and the necessary ingredients to emphasize these subjects even more. (The emergence of nationalist doctrine inside Iran and the imposition of national identity are investigated in Chapter 8 for understanding their connection with the works of academia.) In the present discussion we are interested solely in scrutinizing the methodology and the output of certain individuals who promoted the Western method of national identity in both historiography and sociopolitical theory in Iran.

For nationalistic or patriotic reasons or when they saw an impasse in trying to initiate anything else, these native writers elected to portray Iran's place in history and to reassert its legacy in Orientalist terms — with the difference that the language of description they used was Farsi. This does not exclude the nationalist movement in Iran which bolstered the promotion of Iranian identity in their approach to historical writings. Western sources, however, served as catalogues of historical reference, whether the writers/historians were independent or state-sponsored. The importation of Western methodology was one thing, its imitation and promotion another.

PROBLEMS POINTED OUT

In the early 1960s and 1970s, three articles appeared in English in Western publications by, respectively, Firouz Kazemzadeh, Fereydoun Adamiyat, and Hamid Enayat. The common theme of all three emphasis on the problems and poor state of historiography and Iranology in Iran. Although none of the articles deal with the anachronism of using a nationalistic conceptualization of past events in the Iranian plateau, each does touch on the lack of originality and fresh contributions to the designated fields.

In a general sense, both Kazemzadeh and Adamiyat actually direct little criticism toward those who venerated the pre-Islamic heritage, which was a particular interest of those wishing to vitalize Iranian nationalism.[1] The problem referred to by Enayat is the use of Western sources without any criticism by the Iranian authors: "The greatest shortcoming was, therefore, the absence of any background of criticism and evaluation of Western Orientalism."[2] Adamiyat's observation is somewhat similar when he notes that few Iranian historians are familiar with sociology and philosophy of history. Furthermore, he adds, "Their judgments are often more like the flatteries and slanders of poets than historical evaluation."[3]

The framework of Iranian scholars' historiography and Iranology in the twentieth century is basically modeled on European-centered methodology; that is to say, issues are textually researched, and (as Kazemzadeh points out) the fable is detached from reality.[4] This school heavily depended on textual construction, along with racial and national biases, in vitiating universalistic approaches to history in general. Even the Hegelian, Marxian, and Weberian schools, with their slogans of universalism and value

---

[1] Kazemzadeh, "Iranian Historiography," pp. 431–433; Adamiyat, "Problems in Iranian Historiography," p. 138.

[2] Enayat, "Politics of Iranology," p. 7.

[3] Adamiyat, pp. 144–145.

[4] Kazemzadeh, p. 431.

detachment, could not bypass the influence of the European situation.[5]

Historians and historiography in Iran have been deeply affected by Western historical, archaeological, and philological finds and have put very little effort into developing their own systematic study of history, whether about Iran or about the outside world. It is true, as Adamiyat claims, that Iranian historians have not taken the initiative to deal with the history of most Asian countries, and what has been written about the Western countries hardly exceeds the level of secondary school textbooks.[6] In research about Iran itself, the criticism is equally valid: "The historical writings of many of our historians are insignificant. Perhaps ten or fifteen books, monographs, and articles (in Persian and Western languages) can in fact be considered of real historical value."[7] Of course, since the time Adamiyat made his assertion the number of valuable books and articles has increased — although perhaps not at the same ratio as ill-conceived and unwarranted ones because not only are they unable to address and contribute to the field but by their method of un-evaluating compilation of historical writings they add to historical misconceptions. In response to several decades of history-writing based on Western conceptions, only a handful of individuals have strongly criticized Western works.

Among them, Khunjī is notable for having strongly criticized Dyakonov's *History of Media*.[8] In Adamiyat's opinion, "the true pioneer in criticizing the tradition of historical writing was Mīrzā Fath Ali Akhundzādeh," who wrote his *Irādāt (Objections)* in 1862, directing criticism to all historians of the literature of Iran.[9] Mīrzā Āqā Khan Kirmānī's contribution to historical thinking should not be ignored either.[10]

---

[5] Enayat, pp. 9–10.
[6] Adamiyat, p. 145.
[7] Ibid., p. 142.
[8] Enayat, p. 17.
[9] Adamiyat, p. 141.
[10] Ibid.

One serious problem has been the absence of any background evaluation of the historical works of the Western Orientalists, which has led either to flattery or polemical conclusions by a certain number of Iranian writers. Enayat's criticism is directed toward only three authors, whereas it ought to have been extended to many more: "Ahmad Kasravī's *Āyīn* (Tehran 1932), Sayyid Fakhrud-dīn Shamdān's *Taskhīr Tamaddun-i Farangī* (Tehran 1946), and Jālāl āl-Ahmad's *Gharbzadegī* were far too polemical or ethico-political in their approach to impress the scholarly community which would dismiss any argument not accompanied by detailed documentation and textual citation."[11]

Due to these shortcomings and to the lack of creativity in developing new approaches to historical thinking, many young scholars from Iran became heirs of the Western method of scholarship, if they possessed the credentials. In addition, aside from the historical naiveté of the Iranian scholars in trying to write a secular history of Iran, the method of historiography in its religious (Islamic) context has been neither a significant field in modern times nor free from political biases and sectarian dogmas.[12] Although Adamiyat believes that Sayyid Jāmāl al-Dīn Assadābādī (al-Afghānī) was perhaps the first person in the modern era to promote the notion of a history of Islamic culture and civilization,[13] this assertion has yet to be argued and proved.

Given the problems posed by the domination of Western Orientalism and the lack of critical works by Iranians in the fields of history and historiography, the nationalistic methodology has not had difficulty perpetuating itself.

Let us highlight some of the works produced by number of Iranians who may be classified as historians, belletrists, and academicians, in order to detect their imitation of Western nationalistic, racial methodology in conceptualizing the national

---

[11] Enayat, p. 7; see also F. Adamiyat, "Āsheftegī dar Fikr-i Tārīkhī," pp. 14–24.

[12] See Vaziri, "Dogma Islamico e Problemi di Storiografia," pp. 29–33.

[13] Adamiyat, p. 141. (Adamiyat adds that Sayyid Jamal must have borrowed his point of view from Guizot, who researched for Western civilization in Christendom.)

history of Iran in which historicity of Iranian identity was celebrated. We must first acknowledge the fact that both the influence of Western academia and the nationalist disposition of the nineteenth–twentieth century inside Iran contributed to the current state of affairs in indigenous Iranology, then we can establish the pattern that actually developed among historians in Iran as newcomers to the field and in the mind of their audience. In this regard, Franz Rosenthal makes a striking point in the first paragraph of his book, which elucidates this concept:

> Writing about the writing of history by any particular group or in any particular period means only one thing: To show the development which the concept of history underwent in the thinking and in the scholarly approach of the historians of that particular group or period...[14]

THE DAWN OF NATIONALISTIC HISTORICAL WRITINGS IN IRAN

The twentieth century began with an outburst of nationalistic sentiments, along with the first reproduction of European nationalist historical works in Iran and other regions of Asia. It would be impertinent to ignore other lands in an attempt to single out Iran as the focus of such a historical transformation. Other lands of Asia generally followed the same pattern in feeding the flame of nationalism, with Western academic works as its fuel. For example, Sir William Jones and other founding European scholars of the Asiatic Society of Bengal in 1784 eventually yielded a sizable accumulation of knowledge about the history of India. In this manner "educated Indians increasingly were to learn about their own culture through the mediation of European ideas and scholarship." Then, in these circumstances, "Indians began to write history in the European mode."[15] The grouping together of the vast and diverse multiple civilizations of the Indian subcontinent not only demonstrates the distorting effects of nationalist doctrinal

---

[14] Rosenthal, *A History of Muslim Historiography*, p. 3; see also p. 8.

[15] Cohn, "Representing Authority in Victorian India," *Invention of Tradition*, pp. 182–183.

restrictions but also reveals an overarching contempt for sound and principled methods of historiography. Bernard Joseph has described the magnitude of the problem involved in conceptualizing India in a nationalistic framework:

> One cannot help wondering whether the Indians have not been misled by the mistake of Europeans — based on ignorance of the facts — of describing all the inhabitants of the country as Indians, without taking into account their severance into different groups. India is, in truth, more than a country. The assertion that all the inhabitants of India are from a single nationality is inadmissible.[16]

Thus India became the subject of rigidly maintained misconceptions among its native scholars as well as among Western historians who conceptualized India in a nationalistic context. In the same fashion, Iran, at the turn of the century — despite all the political friction against the West as well as Anglophobia and Russophobia — tended to welcome Western methods of research and national historiography warmly. The conceptualization of Iranian identity in the Orientalist works was especially hailed during the peak age of nationalism. This academically imposed viewpoint on elite and government levels in Iran gradually and profoundly corrupted and changed the mood of religious and patriotic masses, who in a peculiar way saw a link between Shi'ism and secular Iranian nationalism. It is then fair to say that Western academia in some sense colonized Iran and that no thorough effort has yet been attempted to decolonize its history and nationalistic methodology.

In general terms, the writing of history during the Qājār period, particularly in the nineteenth century, was a fairly simple matter. The philosophy was to describe events (around the Shah) from day to day or from year to year; and the authors were usually not historians but, as Kazemzadeh indicates, essentially

---

[16] Joseph, *Nationality: Its Nature and Problems*, pp. 234–235, 223; see also Kohn, *History of Nationalism in the East*, p. 349, although Kohn has a different approach to this issue.

chroniclers.[17] Besides, there exists a considerable literature in the field of history from the historians, of the Abbasid, Turko-Mongol, and even Safavid periods. Most of this consists of either universal or dynastic history; none of it actually deals exclusively with Iran as a distinct nation. Only at the turn of the century was the need for a new style of nationalistic historical writings stimulated and acted upon. In a nutshell, Iranian nationalism was tightly interwoven with the Orientalist material and later with modern Iranian writings regarding an 'ancient Iranian nation' and Aryan identity, a web from which it could not easily be extricated.

At the turn of the century, men of letters such as Mīrzā Malkum Khan, Ali Akbar Dehkhodā, Mīrzā Muhammad Husayn Kahn, Zakā ul-Mulk (known as Foroughī), and Hasan Pīrnīyā (known as Mushīr ul-Dawla) — not all of them fully committed to history — introduced and used Western methodology and models to approach history and historiography. Dehkhodā's co-editorship with Mīrzā Jahāngīr Khan in publishing the post-Constitutional Revolution journal *Sur-Isrāfil* (1907–1909) produced a document of patriotic and nationalistic rhetoric in its Iranian context. Dehkhodā's articles and writings are symbols of dependence on and adoration of modern Western democracies and scholarship. His successful accomplishment of producing the comprehensive Farsi lexicon *Lughat Nāmeh* demonstrates his extensive knowledge and use of Western scholarly sources to substantiate his explanations of various terms and topics (e.g., Arya). His attempt to produce a lexicon in the Farsi language came after observing French, Russian, Ukrainian, and German lexicons served as national symbols in a linguistic and cultural sense. Dehkhodā felt that a series (in some editions, fifty-two volumes) was necessary to establish the cohesion of language and land in a realm of cultural nationalism. (The undertaking of writing and/or compiling encyclopedias in philosophy, theology, administration, natural sciences, and other general topics dates to the ninth through fourteenth centuries; the first Farsi language encyclopedia appeared

---

[17] Kazemzadeh, p. 430.

in the eleventh century.)[18] Thus, while Dehkhodā was not a historian, he had much to do with importing and encouraging the Western nationalistic approach to society and culture in Iran at large, an undertaking that heightened Iranian consciousness as Farsi being the nucleus of it all.

Malkum Khan's cultural influence and sociopolitical doctrine deserve more attention. His contribution to the consolidation of nationalist beliefs in Iran was central to his activities. As early as 1890 he published a journal in London called *Qānun (The Law);* its nationalistic, state-oriented, and civic rhetoric is discussed in the next chapter. But the development of civic and legal standards provided another framework for nationalism and citizenship backed by the rule of law — one that already existed in Europe — and Malkum introduced it to the intelligentsia in Iran. Malkum was apparently the first to propagate Masonic teachings in Iran, which had a correlation with his translating into Farsi of the address by Mirabeau to the French National Assembly on liberty and with his being motivated to import Western knowledge and civilization into Iran.[19] Malkum sought to bridge the changing society under Qājār rule with European sociopolitical notions, among which nationalism was prominent. Actually, the role of Malkum and his contemporaries in influencing the outcome of the Constitutional Revolution of 1905–1906 and in promoting secular thinking was instrumental in the rise of national thinking in Iran.

Zakā ul-Mulk (Foroughī) had a more direct hand in writing history, producing one of the earliest nationalistic historiographical works. As early as 1901, Foroughī wrote a history textbook, *Tārīkh-i Iran (History of Iran)* for the newly established *Madrassa Ulūm Siyāsī*

---

[18] The earliest Farsi dictionary, the *Lughat-i Furs* of Asadī, was compiled toward the middle of eleventh century for poetical purposes. See Lazard, "The Rise of the New Persian Language," *Cambridge History of Iran* vol. 4, p. 606; see also Živa Vesel, *Les Encyclopédies Persanes* (Paris: Edition Recherche-Sur les Civilisations, 1986).

[19] Algar, *Religion and State in Iran 1785–1906*, pp. 185–193; see also Algar, *Mirza Malkum Khan* (Los Angeles, California: University of California Press, 1973).

(School of Political Science),[20] which trained diplomats for the foreign service. This volume, although a relatively simple account of history, is significant in two respects: First, it is one of the earliest works of national history in its Iranian framework; second, it incorporates the Western accounts of pre-Islamic dynasties (Achaemenid, Seleucid, Parthian, and Sasanian) alongside traditional Eastern descriptions of pre-Islamic dynasties (Pīshdādiān, Kīyāniān, and Sāsāniān) and goes on to link these to the Islamic dynasties of the Iranian plateau. Foroughī, however, confesses that in outlining the pre-Islamic dynasties recently uncovered by Western scholarship, he consulted English and French books.[21] The volume itself is rather simple and depends on both Western writing and Eastern mythical information. The methodology it uses in connecting a geographical zone to political history is Western and successfully established; however, it lacks footnotes, textual documentation, a bibliography, and acknowledgments. It appeared in Iran a year before the first volume of Browne's history appeared in London, and thus was an early manifestation of state-sponsored nationalism promoted through the academic network. Obviously, such networks among the intelligentsia were going to be effective in proliferating the notions and sense of national identity that subjects of the dynasty previously lacked.

Foroughī's revised text was reprinted in 1917. This volume was slightly refined and contained portraits of kings of various pre-Islamic and Islamic dynasties. The book actually covered the historical events all the way to the author's own time and period — the period of turmoil following the coup attempt by Muhammad Ali Shah around 1907–1908.[22]

The next person of prominence is Hasan Pīrnīyā, who undertook his monumental three-volume work on ancient Iran at the end of his political career, around 1925. The timing of the project and the gap in actual historical records required a work dedicated to generating more pride and a sense of historical

---

[20] See Foroughī, *Tārīkh-i Iran*, I, p. 390.

[21] Ibid., p. 43.

[22] Foroughī, *Tārīkh-i Iran*, II, part 3, p. 147.

identity. By 1930, Pīrnīyā had completed two books on ancient Iran. The development of the subject matter in Pīrnīyā's mind and the beginning of Reza Shah's nationalist policies encouraged Pīrnīyā to intermingle his personal convictions with a design of institutionalized nationalism and national identity in attempting to write a comprehensive history from the beginning to the end of the Sasanian period or the advent of Islam. He completed the three volumes of *Iran Bāstān (Ancient Iran)* in about 2700 pages, only covering the years until the end of the Parthian period. He never reached the Sasanian era, although his notes remained after his death; and Saīd Nafīsī, his close associate, published two hundred pages of these before publication was aborted due to the high cost of paper during World War II.[23] Pīrnīyā was educated in Russia and pursued a career in politics with parliamentary and premiership positions; he then applied himself to scholarship. He received his academic inspiration mostly from European sources in the fields of philology, archaeology, and history. The three massive volumes by G. Rawlinson in the nineteenth century had covered all antiquity up to the end of Sasanian period next to the work of F. Spiegel. The authenticity of Pīrnīyā's work lay in its combination of major European philological finds about the ancient periods of the Iranian plateau with a nationalistic method of historiography that was for the first time written and published in Farsi. This new enterprise gained considerable attention.[24]

Pīrnīyā's historical vision and his faithfulness to the Aryan theory were bound to the Western method of historiography to such an extent that he became critical of traditional Oriental-history writing. It even became questionable whether Pīrnīyā could distinguish between mythology and empirical history. For example, Pīrnīyā criticized and rejected sources such as Firdowsī's *Shāhnāmeh*, claiming that they contained erroneous accounts of history and were confusing.[25] On the other hand, his nationalistic consciousness sometimes overrode his caution. For example,

---

[23] Pīrnīyā, *Iran Bāstān*, Vol. I; see the preface by Bastani Parizi, pp. cxxvi–cxliv.

[24] Ibid., pp. cxxxviii–cxxxix.

[25] Kazemzadeh, pp. 430–431.

contrary to some traditional sources and poetical works that treat Alexander of Macedonia as a legitimate ruler of the Orient, Pīrnīyā considers him a womanizer, cruel, and a staunch enemy of Iran.[26] This is most probably because Pīrnīyā considers the Achaemenids and their last monarch, Darius III, to be Iranian and Alexander the Macedonian to be a foreigner. Such descriptions of remote historical individuals and peoples strip away many elements of complexity and ambiguity in order to redefine them in modern nationalistic terms.

Pīrnīyā also made some contribution to the educational system by providing school textbooks. By 1927, the requirement of the government ministry was to have a series of texts to cover the entire history of Iran up to the Constitutional Revolution. Pīrnīyā was assigned to write on the period from earliest antiquity until the Muslim conquest (of which the Sasanian part, as noted, was never done). Hasan Taqīzādeh was assigned the period from the Muslim conquest to the Mongolian invasion, and Abbas Iqbāl was assigned the Mongolian period and to carry the work through to the Constitutional period (of which he finished only one volume).[27]

Other important nationalist historiographical works appeared after Pīrnīyā's. But translation and adaptation of European historical writings was used as a mechanism to legitimate the nationalist approach, introducing purportedly sophisticated European-researched books in order to familiarize the audience with the various tenets of nationalist historiography. Parts of the history books of Malcolm and Rawlinson had already been translated into Farsi. Then the two volumes of Sir Percy Sykes' *A History of Persia* were translated in 1944 and 1951, respectively, into Farsi.

One prominent contemporary of Pīrnīyā should be mentioned: Ibrāhīm Pourdāvood. His field of study was the ancient languages and religions of Iran. Farsi-language scholarship was now in high gear to fill the remaining gaps of the nationalistic approach to history. One of the earliest attempts to write a history of Farsi literature was made in 1929–1930 by Jālāl al-dīn Humāi Isfahānī. It

---

[26] Pīrnīyā, II, pp. 1635–1656; see also Vol. I, p. cxxxix.

[27] Pīrnīyā, I, pp. cxxx, cxxxiv.

is tempting to say that E. G. Browne may have been the primary model or the source of inspiration for Humāi Isfahānī; but, although Browne is referred to as one such source, the work's conventional language and its mixture of diverse philological material with history and poetry flavored with personal opinions mark it as a very individual melding of scholarship and sentimental Farsi-based nationalism. The author's extensive personal and nationalist (and racially-biased) remarks[28] are nonetheless clearly rooted in the racism and chauvinism of his period.

In the introduction of the first volume to his *Tārīkh-i Adabīyāt-i Iran (History of Iranian Literature)*, Humāi proposes a breakdown of history into five periods, from antiquity to his own time. Humāi devotes the second half of his first volume to discussing the science of philology and pre-Islamic languages in the same fashion as Darmesteter and Browne had done, to connect these ancient languages and to conceive Farsi as an extension of them. This not only convinces us that the Aryan model was now preeminent in Iranian scholarship but also underscores how the language, Farsi, was linked to the land, Iran, to reinforce cultural nationalism. Humāi, a high school teacher in Tabriz, is unsophisticated in his scholarship and his work lacks proper references, but his writing style is informative for general readers and does not obscure his nationalistic intent and point throughout the text.

The most intriguing personality in the field of history and other sociopolitical issues during the 1930s and 1940s was Ahmad Kasravī. His works on various socio-intellectual topics such as Islam and Baha'ism sought to provide a portrayal of good and evil, right and wrong like a fashionable intellectual. As an untrained historian, he made a significant impact on historical thinking and on popular knowledge about the recent and (to some extent) medieval history of Iran. After publication of his two-volume *Tārīkh-i Hijdah Sāle Azarbāijān (Eighteen Years of History of Azarbaijan)* in 1937, Kasravī began to understand an adequate correlation

---

[28] Humāī Isfahānī, *Tārīkh-i Adabīyāt-i Iran* (Tabriz, 1930), I, pp. 56–57, 59–64, passim. This must have been meant to be treated in five volumes. I have had access only to the first two volumes and cannot confirm whether the other volumes ever followed.

between Azarbaijan's affairs with the constitutional movement. He then committed himself to write a complete account of constitutionalism, *Tārīkh-i Mashroteh-i Iran (History of Constitutionalism in Iran)* (Tehran, 1940). Kasravī's foremost achievement was to bring for the first time the heroic story of the constitutional movement into the homes of people in Iran. In introducing his work, Kasravī confesses is that he does not consider himself a historian and indicates that the information presented in it is derived from his own personal knowledge and from inquiries he has made.[29] He does not provide acknowledgments, references, or a bibliography. The resulting self-contained form of history makes the task of weighing what Kasravī himself was worried about and addressed difficult for inquisitive historians.[30] The reported accounts, allegations, and accusations are at times used misleadingly in order to make a point.

Kasravī wanted people to be alert and skeptical toward what had been written about his subjects, and he himself feared that if he did not write his account of history as appeared accurate to him, others might write it differently.[31] It is fair to say that Kasravī actually wanted to tell his own story in a historical context, since he was a young man observing the tumultuous period. It should be noted that prior to Kasravī's undertaking, two books in Europe had already been published on the subject of the constitutional movement: *The Persian Revolution of 1905–1909* (Cambridge, 1910) by E. G. Browne, and *Revolution de la Perse* (Paris, 1910) by Victor Berard.

In the work by Kasravī, Browne is referred to about half a dozen times, without any proper reference notes.[32] The same is true of other individuals and sources, and there is no way of knowing the faithfulness of the text to the accuracy of the reported events. Kasravī's historiographical method is positively non-scholarly. The periodization breakdown sometimes involves day-to-day or stage-to-stage reports, and in general it represents a well-

---

[29] Kasravi, *Tārīkh-i Mashruti-i Iran*, I, p. 6.

[30] Ibid., p. 4.

[31] Ibid., pp. 3–5.

[32] Ibid., II, pp. 596, 624, 644, 798, 809, 846.

organized attempt to compile personal and academic sources in a conventional fashion. Finally, the nature of the constitutional event and the nature of the subject matter, along with the rhetoric and the language of Kasravī, make it fully clear that Iranian identity and a sense of patriotism in the upheaval are being traced and highlighted.

In the post-Kasravī period, two other influential people enjoyed considerable fame in their nationalist approach to historical topics, Isā Sadīq and Said Nafīsī. Although these two scholars pursued different topics, they reserved a similar place for themselves as purveyors of a bombastic nationalist promotion of history and national heritage. Nafīsī's two volumes of *Tārīkh-i Ijtemāʿī va Siyāsī-i Iran (Social and Political History of Iran)* (1956, 1965) provide an interesting account of Qājār dynastic policies in a national context from the beginning to the mid-nineteenth century, by and large covering the Irano-Russian wars and treaties. Nafīsī's construct of history was based on a series of articles he had prepared for the army on request, but it was also a symbol of an urge for historicism to curb historical wrongdoings as well as to put sociopolitical issues in a national context as a patriotic historian. Nafīsī's contempt for social history (due to his lack of training in sociology) contrary to the title of his book, confuses a history of dynastic warfare with another imperial power, (Russia) with an account of the social-cultural changes that were occurring in certain regions and in the Iranian plateau at large for complex reasons. His obvious unsuccessful effort was, in the modern sense, to connect the social background with the military and dynastic campaign in order to foster a sense that the two were attributable to a single cause — the Iranian one. This approach is obviously overlooked in the anachronistic method used by Nafīsī, which in his time was not exclusive to him.

Isā Sadīq played, one may say, a more consequential role in consolidating the national and racial sentiments expressed in academic work. In his writings Sadīq often shows his nationalist ideas superseding his academic objectivity. His background as a politician and an accomplished academician led him to undertake writing a series of articles and books as early as 1920, a project he continued through the 1970s. They are mostly documents praising the "national Iranian Civilization" and Iran's contribution to world culture and even to the Renaissance.[33] His most prominent work is *Tārīkh-i Farhang-i Iran (History of Education in Iran)* (Tehran, 1957), which was reprinted seven times until 1975 and was used as a university textbook. In this book, Sadīq's out-of-context citations from foreign sources to boast about and sharply distinguish the Iranian world and culture from others is quite notable. By exploiting Western academic sources to promote his anti-Arab rhetoric and his love for Iran, Sadīq developed a strong nationalist language for describing the historical process by which an indestructible Iranian entity gracefully survived and dissolved all foreign elements within it. His idols as foreign sources of reference were E. G. Browne, A. J. Arberry, A. U. Pope, R. Ghirshman, and a few others who represented the Aryan and national school of Western Orientalism. In a general sense, the works of Sadīq, although personally satisfying, left a distinguishable impression in the minds and the hearts of many of his readers, who began to preach and murmur about the "grandeur and superiority of Iranian culture and civilization" vis-à-vis if not the world at least the neighboring Asian and North African lands.

In 1957, Abdul Husayn Zarīnkub wrote the famous and still-popular *Doo Gharn Sukout (Two Centuries of Silence)*. The connotation of the title is to disparage the time between the Muslim conquest and the emergence of local dynasties in the eastern parts of the Iranian plateau and the attendant rise of the new Farsi language. During this time, according to the author, the Iranian world was sunk in the Arab-Islamic world. Zarīnkub's level of scholarship surpasses Sadīq's, but in opinionated rhetoric they match each other. Zarīnkub's exaggerated and offensive remarks against the Arab culture and language[34] were a means of expressing adoration for and glorification of the Farsi language and, more generally, Iranian culture. The book had five goals: (1) to identify the Farsi language with the Iranian plateau, which was not

---

[33] Sadīq, "Le Role de l'Iran dans la Renaissance," pp. 381–397; see also Sadīq, *Tārīkh-i Farhangi-i Iran*, pp. 426–471.

[34] Zarīnkub, Doo *Gharn Soukut*, pp. 71, 83, 106–107, 110–111, passim.

uncommon; (2) to portray the restoration of local autonomy as an inevitable consequence of the magnificent and forceful culture and national spirit of Iran; (3) to establish that, as some Europeans had suggested, Iranians soon gained control of and manipulated the entire Islamic empire; (4) to emphasize the persistence and continuity of the Iranian entity to the present time (which led Zarīnkub to miss the reverse equation that the modern construct of such an entity in the past is based on present circumstances and consciousness); (5) to attack imported Arab values as having been responsible for the violent overthrow of the ancient Sasanian Empire and for the subsequent Arab domination of the region. All these points manifest intentions to promote nationalistic ideas and reveal the influence of existing propaganda disseminated either through scholarship or through the state enterprise. Nevertheless, Zarīnkub's essay was considered strong enough in nationalistic and scholarly terms to be included in its English version as a chapter in the *Cambridge History of Iran* (Vol. 4, 1975) under the title of "The Arab Conquest of Iran and Its Aftermath."

The Pahlavi regime promoted these and other publications through university presses and imperial academies, encouraging work that filled gaps in the national framework history of Iran, whether in archaeology, philosophy, art, or literature. This effort became particularly strong when the Pahlavi regime sought to represent itself as an extension of the tradition of monarchical continuity in Iran. Perhaps the most comprehensive national catalogue on Iran, appearing in two volumes (about 2040 pages), was *Iranshahr* (Tehran, 1963, 1964). This massive project was carried out under the direction of the national commission of UNESCO in Iran, and it received particular attention from the Shah and various government ministries. Literally nothing could be named that these two volumes did not cover. The range of topics covered political history, ethnic composition, language, script, music, architecture, and theater to topics such as climate, fish, geology, infrastructure, army, and other aspects of life in Iran. These two inexhaustible volumes included a substantial historical background on each subject matter under scrutiny.

The authors assigned to research and write *Iranshahr* were a mixture of Iranians and Westerners. The clever methodology adopted by the authors (with the support of the officials) was to bridge the diverse elements of life in a given physical geographical or ecological zone — in this case the Iranian plateau, including the Caspian Sea to the north and Persian Gulf to the south — with political, cultural, social, and religious organizations represented in a complex historical process to achieve their nationalist goal. The characterization of geographical conditions and their link to various institutional developments in the region in all its heterogeneity is nothing but simple slanted nationalism.[35] Of course, the fact that *Iranshahr* was produced by a number of credible scholars under the auspices of the highly respected international organization of UNESCO, quite apart from its useful information, served elegantly to fulfill the nationalist goal the Pahlavi government had in mind.

It would be impossible not to mention here the two living legends of cultural nationalism, Zabīhullāh Safā and Ehsan Yarshater. Through painstaking studies and credible scholarship, both have maintained the nationalist methodology — Safā in literature and Yarshater in history and languages. Safā, with his voluminous contribution of *Tārīkh-i Adabīyāt dar Iran (History of Literature in Iran)* (1953–1985) in some 5320 pages, provides an awesome reference source on literature. His other publications in the field certainly qualify him as a foremost authority in the field of Farsi literature. His faithful patriotic conception of history has convinced him to ignore the transnational approach to constructing a history of Farsi literature; instead, he has categorized all the achievements in Farsi, whether in Iran proper or elsewhere, under the heading of Iranian literature.

Yarshater's numerous publications inside and outside Iran and his editorship in many topics of Iranian studies have won him many domestic and international awards, including in his retirement the Levi della Vida award in 1991. His conceptual framework in reformulating the accounts of ancient Iran, whether in philology, folklore, or historiography (although he is quite able in using primary sources), is largely based and dependent on Orientalist/nationalist methodology and scholarship. His construct

---

[35] For a more stimulating account of the argument concerning continuity, see Morony, *Iraq after the Muslim Conquest* (Princeton: Princeton University Press, 1984), see also the introduction ("Question of Continuity").

of traditional national history aims to bypass unscrupulous assertions and to clarify the relationship between mythical and empirical history. Indeed, he honestly admits the mythical dimension of such history by saying that "our exploration [of history] must therefore be based on inferential evidence."[36] Nevertheless Yarshater, having recognized the gray area of this pre-Islamic topic, still concludes that a fair account of history necessitates use of a national context. His editorship of the latest volumes of the *Cambridge History of Iran* and of the new *Encyclopedia Iranica* has made him the most respected Iranologist of our time. The continuation of the old nationalist structure and the massive number of publications it has produced, however, have left very little room for other points of view to flourish. Although Yarshater is articulate, faithful to accuracy, and devoted to sound pedagogical methods of research, his commitment to nationalistic scholarship may inherently impede change toward a less nationalistic approach to history. Such a transformation of course requires a change in self-examining, nationalist political motives and a new era of reexamining Western Orientalism to achieve the ideal results.

Our scrutiny of nationalistic methodology as applied by historians of Iran leaves many names still to be explored. In addition to the list of individuals who paid their dues in academic or literary circles by offering tributes to "Iranian" civilization, a few more should be identified without discussing their works: Iraj Afshār, Muhammad Javad Mashkur, Abdul Rafi' Haqiqat, Abbas Parviz, and a few other academics and independent writers deserve mention for their efforts. There are, however, countless polemical and chauvinist writers, operating with very little knowledge of history and less depth, who have tried to promote certain obsolete ideas through their own personal or ideological convictions. These individuals should remain unacknowledged in their respective fields.

---

[36] Yarshater, "Iranian National History," *Cambridge History of Iran*, Vol. 3(1), p. 359.

A FINAL COMMENT

The widespread use of nationalist methodology, along with existing nationalist governments and the patriotic sentiments of the authors, has not necessarily falsified history altogether; rather, it has drastically changed the direction of historical thinking and cosmopolitanism. The West has influenced and transformed historiography in Iran and elsewhere, as Kazemzadeh says: "It would not be an exaggeration to state that over the last generation the influence of the West has utterly changed the nature of Iranian historiography."[37]

The debacle in early-twentieth century Iran may have involved a choice between continuing the traditional discipline of history (which was a by-product, in some sense, of literature) or giving in to the Western methodology of historiography (which may have appeared more substantial and practical). Having said that, we must look to the development and sociopolitical changes occurring during the first decade of the twentieth century, as well as to the importance of Western ideas along with preparation for the rise of the nationalist regime of Reza Shah in the 1920s. In this regard, Western academia, it seems, was steadily establishing a place among influential circles and individuals of the time in Iran. The seeds of the Aryan hypothesis and of the nationalist conception of Iranian history were planted without opposition, and at times were even dogmatically boasted of and cherished by its propagators in Iran.

The universal medieval history books written by authors like Tabarī, Mas'udī, Bayhaqī, and Mostaufī first began to be viewed as obsolete and were then used as catalogues of historical information from which later writers could construct any historical account they wished; and the most familiar of these were accounts in a nationalist framework. Clear evidence that the medieval authors had no consciousness or intention of writing national histories (although regional histories such as *Tārīkh-i Sistān* and *Tārīkh-i Tabaristān* were undertaken) did not convince the twentieth-century native historians that nations in a modern sense never existed in that period. Thus it became a preoccupation in modern times to

---

[37] Kazemzadeh, p. 430.

show an affinity for writing national histories. As Rosenthal tells us, the medieval type of historiography was bound by its own series of preoccupations and issues of significance.

These issues and topics, apart from either a universal or a parochial approach, often found expression in historical materials that corresponded to the reporting of genealogy, biography, cosmography, astrology, and philology which fitted in various forms of periodization under a dynastic or annalistic format.[38] Thus it only became a subject of modern emphasis to write a distinct national Iranian history, much of it based on political events.

Another aspect of applying the nationalist methodology of history to Iran is that it tends to marginalize religious history. Attaching pre-Islamic accounts to the political events of the Islamic period created a monumental secular history that promoted to the validity of an "unbroken" monarchical tradition. This historical assumption convinced the Shah and his entourage to engage in a theatrical celebration of such a history of twenty-five hundred years. This costly undertaking took place in 1971 before the Shah's international royal guests at Persepolis and was nationally televised.

Finally, it would be an oversimplification to claim that Iranian nationalism was invented by the nationalist historiographical approach. It is true that the question of identity was forged and linked to historiography, but it is safe to say that nationalism was already becoming a tool of activists in Iran and in exile to change the status quo, and the historical materials of first the Western Orientalists and then those produced in Iran were used as fuel. Thus, the importance of nationalism to Iran and with construction of Iranian national identity became intertwined and gave rise to an era in search of the meaning of the newly gained identity. However, the particular circumstances under which Iranian national consciousness emerged are the subject of the next chapter.

---

[38] Rosenthal, Chapters 3 and 4.

CHAPTER 8
THE EMERGENCE
OF IRANIAN IDENTITY

Despite the publication of many monographs and articles on the subject of Iran, regrettably, up until 1992 and the original release of this book, no serious attempt had been made to treat and dispute the traditional reasoning regarding the historicism of an Iranian identity. In considering the emergence of an Iranian identity in connection with the emergence of Iranian nationalism during the modern period in this short chapter, we can only briefly investigate the main factors involved. As we proceed, connections between these matters and other chapters of this book will strengthen the hypothesis that Iranian identity is a modern concept in its secular context and is not necessarily applicable to the remote past. The primary purpose of this chapter, however, is to discuss the issue of an Iranian identity in two consecutive phases of its development: first, with regard to the origin and roots of the secular perception of this identity, based on territorial boundaries; second, with regard to its intense popularization under subsequent political conditions. The first phase may thus be considered to extend from the early nineteenth century to the ·eve of the Pahlavis' rise to power and the second to cover the Pahlavis' national-chauvinist policies of the 1920s through the 1970s.

BACKGROUND
Prior to the Safavid rise to power, the disintegration that occurred between 1335 CE (Il-Khanid) and 1381–1404 (Timur-i Lang), resulting from devastating military campaigns and tribal warfare,

left both a political confusion[1] and grounds for a lack of common identity among the inhabitants of Iran. In an investigation of the nature of national consciousness in the pre-Qājār era — the important period of the Safavids (1501–1722), when territorial consolidation gave Shiʻism the main unifying authority — the question becomes acute in two senses. First, did the consolidation of rule over the territory of Iran under a single monarch provide a mechanism for territorial identity among the inhabitants? Second, did Shiʻism provide a unique cultural identity and collective consciousness among all the inhabitants of the empire? With regard to religious identity, Eugene Aubin indicates that Shiʻism brought one of the most ethnically diverse regions of Asia under a single religious cover and guided its direction toward a single destiny,[2] although various ethnic minorities were almost entirely left out. Mir Ahmadi similarly emphasizes the impact of Shiʻism in the sociopolitical upheavals of the Safavid era, whose effects lasted until the Qājār period. She also claims that in the Safavid era there was more *Islamiyat* (Islamism) than *Iraniyat*[3] (Iranism), which suggests that identity was more cultural or religious than clearly territorial until the late Qājār period. The royalty and their genealogical constructs, as referred to by European travelers such as della Valle and Krusinski, were traced to Arabs from the household of Ali and the Imams rather than to local (so-called Iranian) dynasties of the past.[4] This must have been used as a tactic to provide legitimacy for the kings in an Islamic rather than the so-called ancient Iranian context. Furthermore, the territorial extent and conquest of the Safavids was determined by accident (as they aimed to conquer Anatolia and Central Asia, rather than by design, notably to conquer only Iran.

The propagation of cultural identity in a Shiʻi context must have had political advantages for the Safavids. However, the goals, ideals, and consciousness of the state seem to have changed after

---

[1] Savory, "L'Empire du Lion et du Soleil," pp. 283–84.

[2] Aubin, *La Perse d'Aujourd'hui*, p. 150.

[3] Mirahmadi, *Din va Madhab dar Asr-i Safavi*, p. 124.

[4] *Voyages de Pietro della Valle*, III, pp. 34, 130–32; Krusinski, *History of the Late Revolutions of Persia*, p. 3.

the Safavids, when Nadir Shah (d. 1747) concluded a peace treaty
with the Ottomans and proposed the unification of the two Islamic
sects (a unification that never actually occurred).[5] The inconsistent
so-called national cultural identity between the Ottoman and Nadir
must equally raise doubts about whether this identity was shared in
its national context among the vast and tribally diverse population
of Iran, considering that other religious minorities including
Zoroastrian, Armenian, Jewish and Sunnis inhabited the Iranian
plateau. The concept of Iranian territorial identity thus seems
unlikely to have existed except in the form of a monarchical or
dynastic identification tied to the royal house that systematically
subjugated the Iranian plateau under its reign.

It has been asserted in general terms that, during the Qājār
period, territorial identity did not exist and that patriotism (cultural
identity) assumed the form of religious sentiment.[6] This assertion
may be true only for the early Qājār period. The religiosity of the
Shiʿites and their preoccupation with the affairs of the twelve
Imams clearly took precedence over their so-called national
concerns.

Such observations of the Shiʿites can be found in the travel
chronicles of Francklin, Flandin, and Gobineau.[7] However,
Gobineau, relying on various preconceptions of his own, refers to
the "Iranian nation" as a combination of two ethnic populations:
(1) Farsi, Lur, and Kurd; (2) Turk. The model he uses here is clearly
the two groups contained in the French nation, the neo-Latin and
Gallo-German populations.[8] In contrast, Flandin speaks of civil
wars attributable to the heterogeneity of national factions,
languages, socioeconomic class hierarchy, and other regional

---

[5] Goldziher, *Le Dogme et la Loi de l'Islam*, p. 248.

[6] Lambton, *Qajar Persia, Eleven Studies*, pp. 301, 320; see also Gnoli, *The Idea of Iran*, p. 180 quoting Lambton. Professor Lambton only refers to nationalism, patriotism, and their forms — not necessarily to national identity.

[7] Francklin, *Observations Made on a Tour from Bengal to Persia*, pp. 176–183; Flandin *Voyages en Perse*, I, p. 250; Gobineau, *Trois Ans en Asie*, pp. 207, 217, 268.

[8] Gobineau, *Trois Ans en Asie*, p. 212.

elements within Iran.[9] The question is whether any national identity in a meaningful fashion based on the supposed territorial and cultural cohesion of the Iranian region existed in the late Qājār period and, if so, how it surfaced. Before we discuss the origin of the emergence of Iranian identity, it would be useful to shed some light on the mechanism and elements involved in the perception of national identity in its modern form by its promoters.

THE MECHANISM OF PERCEIVING AN IRANIAN IDENTITY

From a tribal, ethnic, regional, religious, or even political standpoint, it is an impossible task (at least in this study) to sort out the multilayered complex of loyalties and identities possessed by the population of Iran in the nineteenth century. In any case, however, the focus must be on the categories of individuals and institutions that promoted the concept of territorial (Iranian) identity as the ultimate category of group identity, regardless of all existing differences among peoples in the region. The marginalization of the old systems by the gradual imposition of modern forms of statism should also be put in perspective as having laid the foundation for a new sense of secular realm and identity.

The clerical dogmatic style of conceptualization characteristic of the Shi'i community, as opposed to the approaches of Sunni, Armenian, Jewish, Zoroastrian, and other religious sects, imposed one strain on efforts to create and maintain a common national consciousness; the diversity of ethnic-lingual groupings as well as the heterogeneity of tribal cultural ties imposed another. The killing of the Sufis, the destruction of Armenian properties, the cursing of the Sunnis, and the terrorizing of the Zoroastrians by thugs allied with various local clerics — in addition to the frictions with Bābīs and the sometimes serious conflicts between the state and the clergy[10] and the lack of tribal allegiance and consciousness of belonging to one single nation — are all indications of weak

---

[9] Flandin, II, pp. 409–412.

[10] Nateq, *Iran dar Rāh Yābī Farhangī 1834–1848*, pp. 35–49; see also Algar, *Religion and State in Iran*, pp. 45–122.

statehood and the presence of a multitude of dissonant identities, both religious and ethnic. The assertion that Iran and Shi'ism (Islam) are inextricably intertwined is evidently a by-product of the Constitutional Revolution,[11] and its application to the past is sheer anachronism.

The connection between Shi'ism and Iran in a national context was first observed by the European travelers and only later by scholars. Ann Lambton and others who share her views argue that the Shi'i world separated from the Sunni territorially and that Shi'ism was thus the mechanism for nationalism.[12] Such views are suspect, however, because they rely on the attribution of modern concepts such as national identity and/or even patriotism (in its religious or territorial context) to the people of the nineteenth and earlier centuries. Moreover, they ignore the pan-Islamic tendencies of the late-nineteenth century, when the *ulamā* (clergy) and the Shi'i people in Iran regularly rendered homage to the Shi'i shrines and centers of Iraq and kept up their contacts with the Shi'ites who lived there, in this way showing more affinity and kinship with their Arabic-speaking counterparts in Iraq than with their non-Shi'i neighbors at home. A language barrier between, say, a Farsi-speaking Shi'i of Iran and an Arabic-speaking Shi'i of Iraq may have justified a separate linguistic identity or consciousness; but as regards a proto-national or territorial identity, the same language barriers existed throughout Iran itself anyway. Perhaps the dichotomy involved in having a Shi'i monarch in Iran and a Sunni sultan in the Ottoman Empire had led to some divergence if any, in the sense of monarchical loyalty, between the Shi'i communities of the two territories. But extreme caution is warranted in equating religious identity (known to be broad and boundaryless in pre-modern times) with territorial identity in Iran prior to the twentieth century.

The transitional period from a traditional monarchical kingdom to a more modern state was basically a time of searching

---

[11] Hairi, *Shi'ism and Constitutionalism in Iran*, pp. 89, 126–136, 282, 304.

[12] Lambton, *Qajar Persia,* p. 280; see also Young, "Interaction of Islamic and Western Thought in Iran," *Near Eastern Culture and Society*. This opinion is actually held by many scholars.

for a new conception of identity in Iran. This does not mean that the Muslim identity was surrendering its place in people's minds, but the newer mechanism of identity had to be able to entertain and accommodate all kinds of identities in Iran. One product of modern nationalism and the state apparatus is the imbuing of citizens with a common identity characteristically associated with a particular geographical zone. The passage to a new era of nationalism in Iran was caused by internal forces and global upheaval as well as by the ruthless abuses of the British and Russian empire-builders. By and large, the mechanism under which the modern Iranian identity emerged can be categorized under four headings: secularism, the already unified territorial zone of Iran, the Farsi language, and constitutional/democratic movements.

Secularism

The realm of intellectual and social development in Iran until, at least the nineteenth century was mainly in the fields of metaphysics, literature, theology, and Islamic philosophy. The state mechanism lacked the expertise needed to improve the organizational bureaucracy and establish new institutions. The infiltration and domination of the Europeans had left few viable alternatives for improvement. In this regard, it is interesting to note Gobineau's proposal of alternatives for the Asian countries: either to vegetate, as in previous centuries, or to accept domination by the Europeans.[13] In the case of Iran, events were strongly affected by the appearance of Western-educated natives who tried to storm the sociopolitical machinery in order to place Iran in the line of European nations.

Because the Shi'i religion was a shadowy and unorganized institution, unlike the church in Europe in pre-modern times, it served as a peculiar core for the intermingling of religion and politics in Iran. The king was considered the shadow of God and thus responsible for keeping the affairs of society in order, according to the tenets of the Koran and the *Shari'a* (Islamic

---

[13] Gobineau, *Trois Ans en Asie*, pp. 330–331.

laws).[14] The mass of people looked to the *ulamā* for guidance in education, marriage, all kinds of transactions, and even personal protection.[15] The father figure in its despotic aspect was personified by the Shah, who was often called *Pādishāh-i Islam* (King of Islam) or some similar title.[16] At any rate, the nineteenth-century sociopolitical principles and practices remained tremendously influenced by the Shi'i sect the Safavids had left behind. The clerical class lacked any reform package for modernizing the government or updating it to respond to the new needs of the society; yet the clergy were poised to combat any change that might lead to a deterioration of the fabric of the government's foundation or threaten their own position.

The need for technological modernization was felt during the foreign wars of the eighteenth and early nineteenth centuries, at least as regards the army infrastructure. The traveling of natives of Iran to Europe and even their exposure to European modes of life inside Iran had fostered a desire among the elites to reform the government's affairs-not purely for the love of progress, but perhaps out of a wish to imitate the West. Thus the emerging consciousness of impending change among individuals such as Abbas Mīrzā, Mīrzā Sāleh Shīrāzī, and Amir Kabīr set a precedent for gradual modernization (or, rather, Europeanization). The first attempt came in 1811, when the first organized group of students was sent to Europe to study European sciences and techniques and to return with the skills needed to shape various affairs of the country. The student expeditions to Europe continued as an avalanche of European notions (as well as the sociopolitical

---

[14] Watson, *A History of Persia from the Beginning of the Nineteenth Century to the Year 1858*, pp. 12–17; see also Lambton, *Qajar Persia*, p. 280.

[15] Lambton, pp. 281–283; Flandin, I, p. 141; see also Nateq, pp. 54–55, who indicates that organized criminal activities in certain circumstances were carried out under the protection of the clergy for justified reasons.

[16] Kirmānī, *Tārikh-i Bīdāri Iranian*, I, pp. 24, 28, 40, 42–44, passim; Muhammad Rahim, *Makhzan al-Inshā*, pp. 5, 94, 183, 187; Lambton, "Social Change in Persia," p. 128.

development of the neighboring Ottoman Empire) inundated the system of government and awakened a new consciousness in Iran.

To achieve reforms without resorting to absurd extremes of effort, the secular movement and the streams of self-reform were taking their own particular colorings. The Bābī movement attempted to introduce reforms. This movement with its messianic fervor stressed politico-economic reforms and national unity against the dominant traditional and corrupted culture of the clergy.[17]

Identifying the European roots of certain notions in the Bābī movement is a controversial and somewhat questionable undertaking. But the series of ministerial, legal, and educational programs introduced by other modernizing agents can without serious dispute be attributed to European and Ottoman sources. This is definitely true of notions that had a direct correlation with European democracies, parliamentary systems, and the belief in the equality of men before the law. Such ideals also carried a message either of anticlericalism (since clerics were ready neither to accept manmade laws nor to accept the notion of equality between a Muslim and a non-Muslim) or of overtures toward compromise with the clergy; this struggle continued until the Constitutional period, 1905–1906.

The European secular movements had been successful in establishing sociopolitical institutions that not only guaranteed the loyalty of the citizens to the state and fatherland but also transmuted religious loyalty and authority into national form of religion (e.g., the Anglican Church). The Ottoman versions of European-inspired reforms, whether administrative or legal, required a concomitant marginalizing of the authority of the clerical class in order to ensure the loyalty of all the empire's non-Muslim subjects. In Iran, the transformation of the traditional system, with its multi-religious and multiethnic communities, into a modern state had to proceed in the same manner that had already been tested in the Ottoman Empire (although non-Muslims in Iran were less numerous) and in Europe — a secular direction. Among the

---

[17] Keddie, "Religion and Irreligion in Early Iranian Nationalism," pp. 269–270.

intelligentsia and political leadership, secular values had engendered aspirations to create a unique supreme identity for all inhabitants of Iran rather than to reinforce a parochial or religious identity.

Territorial Zone of Iran

The discussion in this book has focused on the rise of the name *Iran* from designating a geographical zone to identifying a sociopolitical entity fraught with various psychological and historical echoes. Naturally, whatever their specifics, reforms were aimed to change the shape of the state and society and had to involve the territorial and demographic boundaries within Iran proper. The creation of a modern nation-state in Iran did not require territorial consolidation unlike in some European states (such as Italy and Germany); the land was there, and it was simply a matter of time and effort to convert this imaginary boundary into a common territorial Iranian identity for the heterogeneous masses.

Much the same changes had to take place in the Ottoman territorial sovereignty. Although the Ottoman designation referred to a person (Usmān), all its territories from the Balkans to the Iranian border, regardless of their regional names, were identified as Ottoman. Similarly, all the people, in spite of sharp and longstanding differences among them, were somewhat identified in common as Ottomans. The Turkish patrons equally called themselves Ottomans, since the designation *Turk* was used for country villagers.[18] Thus, Ottomanism although it was a late development as an identity, surpassed all identities as Muslims (Sunni or Shiʻi), Christians, or Jews as well as all identities as Turks, Arabs, Kurds, or other ethnic/tribal affiliations. All were required to give their primary allegiance to the homeland (*vatan*). It is true that the secession of various Balkan regions and Greece in the nineteenth century was a challenge to the political authority of the Ottomans that consequently meant a crisis of identity.

---

[18] Keddie, "Pan-Islam as Proto-Nationalism," p. 17; see also Birnbaum, "Turkey: From Cosmopolitan Empire to Nation-State," *Introduction to Islamic Civilization*, p. 182.

In nineteenth-century Iran, whether individual's primary identification was with religion or with the state or with a specific region depended on the political thinking of the masses at a given time. The state and the masses had little intercommunication, and as a result people were not addressed as Iranian in a collective fashion. Perhaps people did not perceive themselves as Iranians, either. It was the job of the intelligentsia and of the channels of communication (e.g., newspapers and schools) that they opened to address the inhabitants of Iranian territory — whether Turk, Baluchi, Arab, or something else — as Iranians and to inculcate them with this identity. The political thinking of the masses in the pre-secular era seems to have been restricted to the familiar subjects of metaphysics, mysticism, and the vital question of the Prophet's succession (a popular theme between the Sunnis and Shi'ites).[19] It would be far-fetched to believe that the secular history of Iran or the political controversies of the pre-Islamic period were of any significance or concern to the masses or to anyone else there except for a handful of Western-educated individuals toward the end of the nineteenth century. Thus it appears that religious and local matters formed the basis of people's historical consciousness rather than the wide range of events over many centuries that happened to occur within an imaginary historical boundary called Iran.

Nevertheless, changes, reforms, and the modernization process in general began to have an impact on the formation of territorial consciousness among certain categories of reformers — the more so when frictions with imperialist powers increased. The concept of Iran or Iranism thus became the preoccupation of activists, the intelligentsia, and especially the secularists. All of the various religious, ethnic, and regional communities that fell within the state's borders were to be accommodated under the canopy of Iranian identity, just as had been done by the Ottomans in setting the precedent.

---

[19] Young, "Interaction of Islamic and Western Thought," p. 136, quoting Browne.

Farsi Language and Enforcement of National Identity

The Iranian plateau hosts various linguistic entities apart from altogether distinct dialects. From the secularist standpoint, sufficient links among these communities — which were often tribal, geographically remote, and without easy access — had been considered obstacles to the construction of a modern nation-state. The European successes in overcoming the discrepancies of national identity have been due in almost every case to the enforcement of a national language. Thus, "It was the aim of the French revolution to impose a central national language on all the people of France,"[20] in order not only to homogenize non-French-speaking people inside France but also to delatinize it in making a Frenchman out of a Catholic.

The Farsi language has been a powerful language of literature and administration in Iran, as well as among its eastern neighbors, at least since the time of the Turko-Mongol domination in those regions. Farsi's status in modern times in Iran led to its being used as the medium for carrying out secular programs; by promoting it throughout the territory of Iran, the secularists hoped to link diverse groups in Iran together. For their purposes, it was necessary that people understand each other, in order to share and cherish the same myths, history, and heritage. But the common bond within the Iranian territory had to be created. All inhabitants — Turks, Baluchis, Gilakis, and Kurds — must be required to learn the national language in order to give birth to a new consciousness. This new consciousness was not merely territorial but also cultural and above all secular, and its proponents recognized that it was only possible through a printed language. It should be noted that there had been hardly any literary use of the other languages in Iran; it was perhaps natural that Farsi should be the medium *par excellence*.

With the proliferation of newspapers, books, and educational establishments organized by the state or by other reforming individuals or institutions, the Farsi language served as a strong language linking people by the printed word. But, just as important,

---

[20] Emerson, *From Empire to Nation*, p. 134.

it also carried cultural, rhetorical, and historical themes that connected it with the developing concept of Iran in a profound way. In subsequent years of the nineteenth and early twentieth centuries, books and newspapers proudly reported evidence of past accomplishments, whether from the Achaemenids and the Sasanians of Iran or the later literary figures whose achievements occurred in Iran or were expressed in Farsi. To heighten national consciousness, new avenues were opened to learn about the past, about present culture, and about other national phenomena by means of the Farsi language alone. Although some Iranian newspapers were printed in other languages (such as Turkish), they gradually lost their strength as a result of cultural pressures and the imposition of Farsi.[21]

The Farsi language historically possessed no national homeland, and its speakers had never searched for a national homeland in modern times (unlike, for example, the German language and Germany). Farsi had been an indigenous language in regions of Iran, Afghanistan, Tajikistan, India, and other outlying areas, but the Orientalists and the nationalist government of Iran expended great efforts to make the Farsi language and Iran synonymous. Through these efforts, Farsi became not only the historical property of Iran but also a national language that all its inhabitants were obliged to learn. The educational establishment, the political press, and the literature of the turn of the century were all saturated with a sense of their being uniquely Iranian[22] — particularly among the educated, the leaders, and the white-collar elite. The subsequent imposition of Farsi under a centralized state apparatus to enforce uniformity of language within the territorial state depended on the success of the educational programs and network of the Pahlavi dynasty. (The subject of language and Persian identity is further treated in the epilogue.)

---

[21] For a list of all the newspapers in late nineteenth and early twentieth centuries, see Browne, *The Press and Poetry of Modern Persia*, pp. 27–153.

[22] Arasteh, *Education and Social Awakening in Iran*, p. 99.

Constitution and Democracy:
Legal Bond of National Identity

To make the transition from an empire with its archaic characteristics to a modern nation-state, from a geographical expression to meaningful homeland, Iran had to undergo drastic measures to achieve modernity. One norm of modernity was a constitutional and legal arrangement that would guarantee the rights and equality of all inhabitants of Iran. In other words, both the state and the population had to be given responsibilities vis-à-vis each other in order to keep the two poles in check and in balance. The formation of a constitution, of administrative units, of political parties, and of other national institutions provided the fundamental basis of a common destiny. Patriotic definitions had to find their place gradually in the institution of the state territory rather than in other unassembled cultural or political entities.

The secular imitation of parliamentary and democratic forms present in the Ottoman Empire and the West at first intimidated the clergy but eventually provided the basis for a breakthrough in engaging in mass politics. The Constitutional Revolution of 1905 became a mechanism for expressing aspirations that possessed many dimensions and were subject to a multitude of interpretations. The significant ones included controlling state affairs through mass representation, guaranteeing personal freedoms, halting imperialist plunder, exercising manmade (secular) laws while devoting special attention to Shi'i jurisprudence, and involving all the people in their national destiny, all of which carried an inseparable message of territorial consciousness. Thus, the various inhabitants of Iran, regardless of their particular denominations, were now territorially and constitutionally termed *Iranians*. By means of educational and state propaganda, a notion of belonging — ourness and us — was to be created, and an adequate foundation for the nucleus of Iranian identity was laid. Having highlighted the basis of identity construction it is now time to investigate the origin of that Iranian identity and the circumstances by which it came into existence before we go on to discuss its popularization by the Pahlavi regime.

ORIGINS OF THE FORMATION OF IRANIAN IDENTITY

In this section we review highlights of the movement for modernization that arose in the last hundred years of the Qājār period, under which Iran's territorial identity merged with its state-imposed cultural identity. This progression involved various issues, personalities, and stages instrumental in the transformation from traditional to modern systems of government, education, and sociopolitical consciousness. The pattern and mechanism for realizing Iranian identity, whether intentionally or not, fell into the same categories of secularism, Iranism (geographical zone), Farsi language, and constitutional norms that have already been discussed.

The tangible aspirations for change were first felt when the elite natives became aware of the sharp differences between their institutions and those of the Europeans and the Ottomans. A vast land with a loose government, Iran was open to the traffic of European entrepreneurs, military officials, and diplomats to pursue their affairs.[23] The corruption and disorder in the system had previously encountered no criticism or any other comparable system. For full-fledged change to become possible in Iran, the exposure of Western-educated children of the aristocracy to the European and Ottoman systems was necessary, as was a desire on their part to achieve efficient change by formulating a new system of rules. These new rules set the sociopolitical stage to bring Iran out of dynastic traditionalism, parochial Islamism, and regional tribalism.

The early nineteenth century may be identified as the beginning of a new era of modernity, with its early figures such as Mīrzā Bozorg and Abbas Mīrzā.[24] The first group of students went to Europe in 1811, followed in 1815 and 1819 by more students who were sent both to Europe and (later) to the Ottoman Empire

---

[23] Lambton, "Social Change in Persia," p. 135, indicates that the number of Europeans in Iran in the mid-nineteenth century was 150; it increased to 800 by the 1890s and to 1000 by 1900.

[24] Adamiyat, *Fikr-i Āzādī va Muqadami-yi Nihzat-i Mashrutīyat*, pp. 22–23.

and Egypt to study.[25] The fascination with European science and the European mode of administration had put two returned students from the class of 1819 in the forefront of the movement toward reform: Mīrzā Ja'far Muhandis and Mīrzā Sāleh Shirāzī. It was actually Mīrzā Sāleh who took allegedly the first anticlerical position, when he expressed his admiration for the European democracies, particularly the British. As he attempted to familiarize Iran with European principles and institutions, he took two important initiatives to promote new ideas and awareness. First, he established a print shop in the 1830s; second, he printed the first Farsi newspaper in Iran in 1837.[26] (The first Farsi newspaper ever printed anywhere was in India in 1822, and the second was also in India.)[27] It is interesting to note that the first Turkish-language newspaper in the Ottoman Empire and the first Arabic-language newspaper in Egypt were printed in 1831 and 1828, respectively.[28] Mīrzā Sāleh's use of Western printing techniques to promote Western-inspired conceptions flourished in subsequent years as his readership increased. Although one reference states that Iran possessed a Farsi font and press as far back as 1629 (when these were introduced by the Carmelites) they were evidently not used.[29] The need for and effect of newspapers were felt by the renowned reformist premier Amir Kabīr in the early 1850s.[30] Newspapers continued to transmit Western thoughts into Iran.[31] The gradual movement of literate people was toward a common consciousness, and a preliminary stage of nationalism was being set. What Gabriel

---

[25] Ibid., pp. 24–25, 41–42; see also Hairi, pp. 11–12.

[26] Adamiyat, *Amir Kabīr va Iran*, pp. 362–364; Arasteh, p. 99; Hairi, p. 12.

[27] Amalendu De, "Persian in our life," p. 60; Adamiyat, *Amir Kabīr*, p. 362.

[28] Adamiyat, *Amir Kabīr*, p. 364.

[29] Young, "Interaction of Islamic and Western...," p. 134.

[30] Adamiyat, *Amir Kabīr*, p. 365; see also Kohn, *A History of Nationalism in the East*, p. 319.

[31] Young, p. 135.

Tarde said of the newspaper should not be taken lightly: "The idea of nationalism has been the product of the newspapers."[32]

Secular political thinking was being effectively spread to the small number of literate groups in Iran. The quest for national resurgence multiplied the publication of newspapers both there and abroad. Between 1875 and 1900, the important newspapers *Hablul-Matīn* in India; *Hikmat, Surayā*, and *Parvarish* in Egypt; *Akhtar* in the Ottoman Empire; *Qānun* in London; and *La Patrie-vatan* (a bilingual Franco-Farsi paper) in Tehran had a strong rhetorical and intellectual impact on political lines of thinking.[33] In essence, the art of journalism was articulating reforms and making early contributions to language's role as the basis of national identity. In addition to newspapers, the telegraph (which began to function in 1865) opened another line of communication both for government status checks of the provinces and for information on the outside world[34] in the form of news and messages. The old crippled dynastic empire of Iran was on the verge of modernizing and connecting all corners of its territory together — it was now ready to become a nation-state.

The latter, in the crucial years of the Constitutional period, proved to be vital. The channels of communication inevitably provided a new awareness, quite unlike the traditional channels of clerical links between the state and the people that existed during the Safavid period.[35]

The opening of Western-style schools in the mid-nineteenth century, particularly through the efforts of missionaries, which reached a total number of fifty by 1929, served as another channel

---

[32] Gökalp, *Turkish Nationalism and Western Civilization*, p. 71, quoting G. Tarde.

[33] See Hairi, pp. 16–17; Adamiyat, *Fikr-i Āzādī*, pp. 202–203; Algar, *Mirza Malkum Khan*, pp. 186–187; Banani, *The Modernization of Iran 1921–1941*, p. 22; see also Browne, *The Press and Poetry*, pp. 27–154; Arasteh, p. 100.

[34] Lambton, "Social Change in Persia," p. 136; Algar, *Malkum Khan*, pp. 25–26.

[35] Arasteh, p. 98.

of new awareness.[36] The opening of the famous college of Dār ul-Funun (Center of Arts) in 1851 in Tehran and other colleges in various cities represented a real breakthrough from the traditional religion-oriented type of education and the meticulously Western academic courses now offered. Acceptance of the new secular type of education brought the class of intelligentsia closer to the West and to Western concepts. On the other hand, the power of the clergy in education remained to be dealt with. The educational reforms of the turn of the century continued to give full weight to the study and exclusivity of Shi'i religious sciences.[37] The other step toward secular modernization was the struggle to constitute a promising and practical legal and administrative order that had proved successful in Europe and later in the Ottoman Empire, India, and Egypt. Attempts to introduce a body of laws and councils in imitation of Franco-British and Ottoman models, starting in 1855 and continuing through the 1890s, were either abortive or insubstantial.[38] In fact, when Mīrzā Husayn Khan Sepahsālār (1863–1870), as minister of justice, had proposed to centralize the administration of justice and to have stamp duties for documents and deeds take effect and to address disputes over land in the department of justice itself, these plans brought him into conflict with the *ulamā*.[39] Although strongly supported by the modernizers, such proposals still met with an irreconcilable hostility from the clergy, which was loath to surrender its comfortable network of authority to a Western-inspired yoke.

During the avalanche of new ideas and the battle of minds that ensued over which of the proposed changes were desirable, possible, and permitted, one person deserves attention for his tremendous impact on the process of secular modernization: the notable Malkum Khan. After completing his studies and returning to Iran from France in 1851, already infatuated with European systems, Malkum engaged in various literary and sociopolitical activities. Employed in the newly established Dār ul-Funun college

---

[36] Banani, p. 89.

[37] Ibid., p. 90.

[38] Lambton, *Qajar Persia*, pp. 291–292.

[39] Ibid.

as an interpreter to foreign teachers, he brought himself to the attention of Nāsir ul-Dīn Shah. Malkum also took an interest in Masonic activities, probably due to French influence, as a means of achieving sociopolitical actions and reforms.[40] His active mind searched for alternatives to reform Iran.

After spending some time in Istanbul upon his return in 1858, he wrote a treatise (one of many that he subsequently wrote) called *Kitābche-yi Ghaybī* (*A Booklet Inspired from the Unseen World*). Using confident language, Malkum proposed political-administrative reforms to the Shah.[41] The key terms used in his treatise, including *tanzīmāt* (reforms) and *qānun* (law), were taken from the Ottoman (Turkish) vocabulary; for the remainder of the nineteenth century, the whole political vocabulary used among the intelligentsia in Iran was derived from Ottoman words and phrases.[42] In this connection, it should be said that, during his expatriate years in Istanbul, Malkum had assimilated various Ottoman ideological influences as well as reflecting on the phases of the constitutional movements of the 1860s there. In his treatise *Politik hā-yi Dawlatī (International Politics)*, Malkum claimed that Ottoman politics were linked to Iran in a thousand different ways.[43] Such an assessment in weighing the similarities between the Ottoman Empire and Iran must largely be attributed to the fact that both lands had a multiethnic and multi-religious population and both systems had to make the transition from old Muslim imperial models to modern nation-states. Ottoman terms such as *vatan* (fatherland) and *millet* (nation), which were used to help impose the concept of unity among heterogeneous people within its empire, served the same purpose when they were used in political vocabularies in Iran.[44]

Malkum's vision in bringing unity, mobilizing the masses and modernizing the state infrastructure was focused largely on

---

[40] Algar, *Malkum Khan*, p. 25.

[41] Ibid., pp. 26–27.

[42] Ibid., pp. 27, 29, 67, 190.

[43] Ibid., pp. 27, 67–68; see also Hairi, pp. 40–41; for partial reference see Adamiyat, *Fikr-i Āzādī*, p. 200.

[44] The terms *vatan* and *millet* both came to Iran via the Ottoman Empire; see Adamiyat, *Andishehā-yi Tālibov Tabrīzī*, p. 90.

introducing the body of laws (*qānun*). Law and order would provide the basis on which the masses would give their allegiance and obedience to the system-by creating coherence between the government and the governed. It was with reference to this concept that Malkum, in his exile years in London, published a newspaper called *Qānun* beginning in 1890.

In the forty-one numbers of this paper one can observe the proliferation of national slogans and messages that formed the components of an emerging national consciousness. Although the tone and the message of each issue of this paper varied depending on contemporaneous events, it nonetheless consistently called on the leaders and people of Iran to restore equality and justice by introducing laws. On the concept of *vatan* and patriotism as discussed in the various numbers of *Qānun*, Malkum invites all the inhabitants of Iran to collaborate (with special reference to women in number 7) by using such phrases as *Khalq-i Iran* (People of Iran), *Khāk-i Iran* (Soil of Iran), and *Iran Khān-i māst* (Iran is our home).[45] To Malkum, the establishment of legal processes and reforms served as the means and proof of territorial patriotism. Thus Malkum praises the Ottoman sultan for his understanding and respect of the law, for the sake of his country.[46]

Actually, Malkum was addressing his proposals to members of the literate community who had access to and could read his newspaper, as well as to the officials of government so that it might indirectly know about these demands. For the rest, Malkum was talking to an imaginary population in Iran, since the majority were illiterate and it is possible that about more than half did not even know Farsi. Malkum and reformers like him understood themselves and each other quite well when it came to modern political doctrines such as nationalism, modernism, and constitutionalism, but it is not at all certain that ordinary people who heard about them understood them completely.

The other group to whom Malkum had to make himself clear was the *ulamā*. One thing that Malkum failed to clarify, perhaps

---

[45] *Qānun*, No. 1, p. 1; No. 2, pp. 1–2; No. 3, p. 3; No. 7, p. 3; No. 16, p. 3; No. 34, pp. 1, 4.

[46] *Qānun*, No. 3, p. 2.

intentionally, was the secular nature of law he was prescribing and its points of tension or collision with *Shari'a*, the Islamic law.[47] In several issues of *Qānun* Malkum specifically praised the *ulamā* and their potential role in reforming the government and implementing Islamic laws.[48] This is characteristic of Malkum's politics, both to provoke the *ulamā* in an attack against the government and to side in general terms with the reality of the traditional Islamic society he was addressing. Malkum seems to have been clear about what he wanted for Iran; he simply put it in different and discrete terms. For example, the issue of pan-Islamism and the union of all Muslim lands, together with the designation of its capital, was the subject of number 18 of *Qānun*. In joining the ongoing argument, Malkum "neutrally" claimed that all valuable lands of Islam that had been conquered with the shedding of Muslim blood obviously belonged to Muslims, but he asserted that the issue of unity in such questions should be referred to and judged by the *ulamā*. He then put the matter in his own patriotic terms by saying "but Iran is the poorest of all Muslim lands."[49]

In the face of widespread resistance to westernization and his promotion of patriotic and national sentiments, Malkum was not only discouraged but had even newer ideas for changing Iran as well. Besides being one of the earliest advocates of fundamental change in the educational program,[50] he jointly (with Fath-Ali Akhundzādeh) proposed to reform the Arabic alphabet in Farsi.[51] Jalāl al-Dīn Mīrzā, a correspondent of Akhundzādeh, who shared his hatred of Islam and of the Arabs, wanted to rid Farsi of loan words from Arabic and develop a "pure Persian." The 1868 proposal of a prototype disjointed alphabet by Malkum and Akhundzādeh and their advice that it be taught in schools[52]

---

[47] Algar, *Malkum Khan*, p. 29.

[48] *Qānun*, No. 18; No. 2, pp. 1–2; No. 21, p. 1; No. 24, p. 2; No. 25, p. 2.

[49] *Qānun*, No. 18, p. 1.

[50] Algar, *Malkum Khan*, p. 32.

[51] Algar, "Malkum Khan, Akhundzada and the Proposed Reform of the Arabic Alphabet, "pp. 116–130; Adamiyat, *Fikr-i Azadi*, pp. 178–179.

[52] Algar, *Malkum Khan*, pp. 37–38, 90–91, 159–162.

promised more de-Arabization and further distinction from the Arab-Islamic world. Such initiatives, adopted through the efforts of Munif Pasha, though on a restricted scale, had been enacted in the Ottoman Empire primarily to create room for more modernization without further arousing the suspicion of non-Muslims who might hesitate to give their oath of allegiance to the state.

Neither Malkum's disjointed alphabet proposal nor Akhundzādeh's final project of a mixed Roman and Cyrillic alphabet worked in Iran, although subsequently a Roman and Cyrillic alphabet successfully replaced the Arabic alphabet in modern Turkey and in Akhundzādeh's native Caucasus.[53] But in those days the difficult question was how this proposal of script reform would alter the people's connection to their Islamic faith. The bond of Arabic script, whether in Farsi or in Turkish, must have carried a feeling of direct affiliation with Koranic or Islamic script, since its implications led to abandonment of the script reform in Iran and even the successful effort in Turkey has created a backlash in modern times.

Another historical witness stands out as a medium of exchange in the interaction of Iran with the Ottoman Empire: Mīrzā Husayn Khan Sepahsālār (Mushīr ul-Dawla). After his posts in Bombay and Tiflis, Mīrzā Husayn Khan spent twelve years of his diplomatic mission in the Ottoman Empire. His friendship with statesmen and participants in the *tanzīmāt* movement and subsequently in the constitutional movement — in particular, Fuad Pasha and Aali Pasha — as well as his time spent observing the sociopolitical upheavals in that land compelled Mīrzā Husayn Khan as an influential and patriotic man to write to Nāsir ul-Dīn Shah about the various Ottoman parliamentary initiatives. These, he reported, would embody and unify the state's many nationalities and religious minorities, all of whom were represented in government and were treated as equal before the law.[54] These reforms exalted a secular feeling of patriotism and would have

---

[53] Algar, "Malkum Khan, Akhundzadeh and the Proposed Reform," p. 128.

[54] Adamiyat, *Fikr-i Āzādī*, pp. 57–64; Hairi, pp. 31–32; Algar, *Malkum Khan*, pp. 65–67.

forced a transition from the traditional dynastic kingdom or from sectarian religious beliefs to a modern territorial fidelity, but it was difficult to ask the Shah to give up his absolutism in order to mobilize the masses to control the state and to cherish a common principle. Nāsir ul-Dīn Shah was reputedly a pious and devoted monarch who even went so far as to make the birthdays of Ali and Husayn (the first and third Shi'i Imams) official festival days.[55] His opposition on the one hand and the power and reaction of the *ulamā*, who feared the corruption of Islamic culture by foreign elements, on the other hand combined to keep these reform proposals in check until the next stage.

Modernization initiatives and secularization were expressed by different individuals in various ways. Another striking personality of the latter part of the nineteenth century was Mīrzā Yusuf Khan Mostashār ul-Dawla (d. 1895). As a government official, he had spent many years abroad and had become enamored with the constitution of France and other Western features. His attraction to representative government made him propose adoption of one, as well as a legal system in Iran. He also proposed a nationwide program to construct railroads, but this idea met with opposition because critics thought that such a network would allow foreigners to penetrate and circulate too easily.[56] The contradiction of patriotic sentiment on the one hand and a lack of coherence in ideology and in the proposed methods of modernization on the other synthesized a strange coalition. Indeed, due to the new awareness, the need for reform was recognized by all the camps (notably by the secular and religious), and an ill-defined nationalistic sentiment was aroused.

The reformer, Mīrzā Abdul Rahīm Tālibov's assessment of the emergence of this nationalistic sentiment identified it as being the consequence of two phenomena: first, the emergence of anti-Western sentiments; second, the formation of new sociopolitical ideas and values.[57] Thus, as a reaction to imperialism in the nineteenth century, national loyalties began to grow — largely at

---

[55] Algar, *Malkum Khan*, p. 101.

[56] Adamiyat, *Fikr-i Āzādi*, pp. 183–32–33, 199, 200; Hairi, pp. 32–40.

[57] Adamiyat, *Andisheha-yi Tālibov*, pp. 88–89.

the expense of loyalty to the Islamic community as a whole.[58] Obviously such individuals as Tālibov (1834–1911), Āqā Khan Kirmānī (1853- 1896), and Akhundzādeh (1812–1878) pursued nationalistic and secular values at the expense of Islamic ones for patriotic reasons.

On the religious side, the most influential personality of the nineteenth century, Sayyid Jamāl al-Dīn al-Afghani (1838–1897), appeared as the champion of the pan-Islamic movement. His main objective was to revive traditional religious values and reunite the Muslim world, in order to create a united front against Western political-cultural invasion and to reform the sociopolitical apparatus of Muslim societies. If we consider the pan-Islamic phenomenon as another form of Muslim nationalism, with the exclusion of non-Muslims (in a literal sense) as one of its primary aims, the problematic nature of the diversity of communities had made al-Afghani and those like him want at least to de-secularize territorial nationalism.[59]

The fifteen years after 1890 proved a crucial period in the formation of a vague nationalistic sentiment along with religious fervor among members of the leading clerical class. The 1890 tobacco boycott throughout Iran, which was declared by the clergy in response to the government's granting a tobacco concession to a British company, demonstrated the strength and desire of this class to protect the common interest of the Muslim people of Iran and to maintain the territorial integrity of Iran. The anti-foreign camp of the clergy had created a mechanism in which patriotic rhetoric was used to secure religious values. In other words, at this early stage the clerics still preferred Islamism at the expense of Iranism and saw the two concepts as potentially conflicting.

The gradual involvement of members of the clergy in political affairs simultaneously created friction between them and the Western-inspired principles of the secularist thinkers. One of these principles was the need for a constitution. The notion of introducing a body of laws and institutions had already been planted by secularists in the nineteenth century; it simply gained

---

[58] Keddie, "Pan-Islam as Proto-Nationalism," p. 18.

[59] See Cottam, *Nationalism in Iran,* p. 138; see also Arasteh, p. 99.

momentum during the first four years of the twentieth century. Significant controversies and debates took place over whether a constitution that was derived from Western sources could be compatible with Shiʻi principles. The original purpose underlying the foundation of the constitution was not to serve the interests of Shiʻism but to bring the entire population of Iran into the orbit of its provisions. However, a major shift by the clerics in interpreting the value of the constitution occurred: They determined that it was a good idea, but only under certain conditions. Although the explanation is controversial, the correlation of secular ideas to the religious interpretation behind this shift suggests the influence of secret Bābī infiltration in the clerical circle.[60] Whatever the reason, powerful theologians supported the establishment of the constitution in 1906, which in itself was a victory for the coalition of political forces dedicated to territorial patriotism and the equality of all inhabitants of Iran. Even so, the debate over the question of equality continued to be pressed by certain clerics like Fazlullāh Nurī. In particular, the equality of non-Muslims and Muslims before the law was objectionable to Nurī, but the establishment of the constitution as a triumph of manmade laws was also in contrast with Islamic tenets.[61] The philosophical debate over the legitimacy of the constitution from a religious standpoint was worked out by Mīrzā Muhammad Husayn Nāʼīnī. According to Haʼiri's study, the compatibility of the constitutional system with Shiʻi theology was demonstrated by Nāʼīnī,[62] who further elaborated the particularity and importance of the constitution within the Iranian boundary.[63] In fact, Nāʼīnī claimed to recognize no distinction between the interests of religion *(dīn dārī)* and of [territorial] patriotism *(vatan khāhī)* — in whose name he postulated the principles of national government and democracy.[64] At this point, it could be asserted, the way in which the temporal and spiritual senses of government

---

[60] See Keddie, "Religion and Irreligion in Early Iranian Nationalism," pp. 271–272.

[61] See Hairi, pp. 299–300, 304–305.

[62] Ibid., Chapter 5.

[63] Ibid., Chapter 6.

[64] Ibid., pp. 282–283.

were combined already defined a national identity in modern times for Iran.[65] This was a breakthrough in creating a modern nation-state. The nation and the faith, at least from the Shi'i standpoint, were becoming indivisible although the limits of the concept of nation were still ill-defined. But in general terms, the constitutional movement was essentially a nationalist phenomenon with some strong religious elements present in it.[66] Consequently, in a complex sociopolitical atmosphere, Iranism and Islamism mixed to a sufficient extent that the Iranian identity carried a twofold notion of Shi'i thought and of the secular monarchical tradition of the region, which was subsequently elaborated. Obviously, constitutional rights and Iranism did not carry the same message to the country's religious minorities as it did to the Shi'ites. The former, small colonies in a Muslim ocean and in fundamental disagreement with Shi'i political thought, became more attached to the concept of Iran. (The 1979 Islamic revolution may be examined from this perspective.)

The Constitutional Revolution transformed Shi'i beliefs into national political doctrine. The elucidation of this transformation is recorded by Nāzim ul-Islam Kirmānī, who shortly after the Constitutional Revolution began to write his *Tārīkh-i Bīdārī Iranian (History of the Awakening of the Iranians)*. Use of the term 'Iranian' by Kirmānī in this case may be interpreted as signaling the beginning of a movement toward unity and progress rather than as describing a unique, fully developed historical identity for all the inhabitants of Iran. By "awakening" Kirmānī also alludes to progress and modernization rather than necessarily to a historical effort by Iranians to regain their patrimonial identity. Nonetheless, the constitutional setup did create elements of mutuality of territorial consciousness between the clerical and secular classes.

On the other side, the outpouring of European scholarship about ancient history and Iranian civilization, though it proved distasteful to the clergy, provided the secular intelligentsia with even better reasons to nurture and adopt nationalistic and (gradually) racist notions. Subsequently, many European books

---

[65] See Millward, "Iran," *Introduction to Islamic Civilization*, p. 174.

[66] Lambton, *Qajar Persia*, p. 277; Cottam, p. 145.

about the secular and racial theories about Iran were translated into Farsi.[67] During the post-Constitutional period, nationalistic rhetoric in its Iranian and self-praising slogans were expressed in the form of poetry, journal articles, and textbooks (discussed in the preceding chapter).

National and patriotic praise making special reference to ancient Iranian language, religion, and civilization and to a search for a Pure Persian language are all voiced in the poetry of Pourdāvood in the post-Constitutional period.[68] During this period, the introduction of European discoveries about the ancient civilizations of Iran, the politicization of various classes, and the rise of anti-Arab feeling combined to create an unparalleled consciousness of Iranian territorial identity. The various other pro-constitutional and nationalistic works of poetry printed in Browne's collection testify to this fact.[69]

The outstanding example of a pro-constitutional and nationalistic newspaper after Malkum's *Qānun* was the journal *Sur Isrāfil* (1907–1909), under the co-editorship of an influential personality in secular historical thinking, Ali Akbar Dehkhodā. The common identity of Iranians and their patriotic responsibilities were characteristic themes of this journal.[70] This is reflected not only in the tone but even in the emblem of the journal: an angel carrying a triple political slogan that was a direct translation of the French triumvirate of fraternity *(ukhuvat)*, liberty *(hurriyat)*, and equality *(musāvāt)*. Numbers 18 and 20 of this journal provide particularly clear testimony in describing the historicity of the Iranian identity by stretching the patriotic memories to pre-Islamic times. The language used in vitalizing this political sentiment and in creating a psycho-historical attachment to the imaginary communities of the past is quite strong:

> Oh Iran … A glorious death or an honorable life … Is there not still in the air the smell of blood shed by Achaemenids?

---

[67] Adamiyat, "Problems of Historiography in Iran," p. 137.

[68] Browne, *The Press and Poetry of Modern Persia*, pp. 289–295.

[69] Ibid., pp. 175–306.

[70] See *Sur Isrāfil*, particularly No. 4, pp. 2–3, and No. 5, p. 1.

Has not your soil taken the red color of Arsacid and Sasanian blood? ... The children of Iran for five thousand years with certitude and honor confronted the Greeks, Romans, Turks, Mongolians ... Oh Iran ... our religion, our fatherland, our nation.[71]

The pre-Islamic glory of Cyrus and his conquests, the Sasanian shielding of Iran against the Romans in their aggressions, and the expansion of Malik Shah Saljuq and Nādir Shah all came to be praised in their Iranian context.[72] The ferment of historical information and nationalist thinking was encouraged and increased by early twentieth-century press and literature.[73]

One of the most substantial periodicals of the 1910s was *Kaveh*, a newspaper published in Berlin starting in 1916 that tried to equate the development of national identity with the quest for modernity. In eloquent literary language, the paper covered World War I, literature, history, science, and European scholarship on Iran. Special emphasis was placed on the perspectives of Iranian society, languages, and literary figures with substantial footnotes and documentation, all organized around the unifying idea of reasserting a national culture and common identity.[74] This journal provided translations of the latest Western publications on Iran, with special descriptions of G. Rawlinson and A. Christensen.[75] In *Kaveh*, the achievements of Farsi literary figures such as Firdowsī (obviously for his alleged cultural nationalism) were celebrated for their role in forming and nurturing the rich Iranian culture.[76]

During the first few years of *Kaveh*'s publication, the growing patriotic feeling within Iran coincided with the downfall of the Ottoman system and identity. The fear that Iran, as a multiethnic

---

[71] *Sur Isrāfil*, No. 18, p. 3.

[72] *Sur Isrāfil*, No. 20, pp. 1–2.

[73] *Iranshahr* (1914), No. 1, as well as other widely circulated newspapers.

[74] *Kaveh* (1916–1920), numbers 2, 5–6, 25, 27, 28, 35.

[75] *Kaveh*, numbers 27, 28, 35.

[76] *Kaveh* (1920), numbers 36, 37, 39, 40, 45, 46–47; (1921), numbers 1, 3, 10, 11, 12.

territory and identity, might also fall at the hands of a British conspiracy or of internal upheaval led *Kaveh* to pay tribute to and sympathize with the Ottoman nation and authorities for the difficult time they were experiencing due to British conspiracy. This was real. By 1916, the British were conspiring. (It is relevant that the paper was in Berlin and that Germany was a wartime ally of the Ottomans.) The paper argued that Iran and the Ottoman Empire had common interests and should defend their Islamic lands as allies.[77]

The tumultuous period of the Great War passed at the cost of the dissolution of the Ottoman territory. In Iran, the focus of literature, press, education, state policies, and the intelligentsia continued to be on the questions of how to deal with the external forces of imperialism and how to resolve internal regional and socio-religious issues in order to preserve the unity of Iran. Thus secular propaganda on the one hand and the adaptation of European technological methods by the state in the fields of the army, administration, transportation, and communication on the other had succeeded in bringing the masses of all regions under the banner of Iranism as never before. Still, people who did not read or even speak Farsi and consequently did not receive news and propaganda could hardly have developed the same patriotic sentiment that the intelligentsia and other literate people had. (It is very possible that newspapers were read aloud in teashops to inform and entertain people.)

By examining the three central thoughts of the Ottoman Empire in the nineteenth and early twentieth centuries, we can identify parallel features in Iran. Without obscuring the role of Islam and of the Turkish paternal power in relation to religious and ethnic minorities within the empire, we can say that Ottomanism tried to accommodate all other currents. But the three dominant currents were Ottomanism, Islamism[78] (*ummat*), and Turkism (*millet*). After World War I, Turkism took the leading role (carrying Islam with it) in the movement to establish a more or less

---

[77] *Kaveh* (1916), number 12.

[78] Gökalp, *Turkish Nationalism,* p. 76–77, 82–83; see also Birnbaum, "Turkey," p. 182.

homogeneous home for the Turks — Turkey for the Turks.[79] Pan-Islamism did not succeed for various reasons, and was not welcome for a religious identity among non-Muslims of the Ottoman Empire;[80] that is, the major distinction between people was religious, not ethnic.[81] Thus, the pyramid of identity in the region lost its Ottoman character — though the Turkish pyramid of identity remains unvanquished by impulses toward self-determination among its minorities and by the larger Islamic movement.

Iran's three main currents of identity at the turn of the century consisted of Islamism, Iranism, and regionalism (ethnic heterogeneity). The secular upheaval managed to improve the chances of all the inhabitants to enjoy the same territorial and legal identity, evenly and assuredly, regardless of religious or ethnic identity. Iranism overshadowed Islamism in the peculiar coalition of the two, while regional unrest continually threatened the fragile Iranic stability. Of course, regional and ethnic awareness and identity on a large scale were themselves by-products of the imperialist and strong nationalist claims and assertions of the period. Incidents of regional unrest showed that Iranism was bent at intervals but never broken. The relationship between Islamism and Iranism — their boundaries of consciousness, their authority and sentiment — however, remained a gray area until the 1979 revolution (and indeed continues to be one today, under different circumstances).

A NOTE ABOUT THEORY AND REALITY

The academic reconstruction of Iranian history and civilization has given modern scholars and nationalist thinkers enough grounds to take the historicity of national identity for granted. Scholars such as Richard Cottam and T. Culyer Young (among many others) have

---

[79] Thomas, "The National and International Relations of Turkey," *Near Eastern Culture and Society*, pp. 167–187; Kohn, *History of Nationalism*, pp. 234–234.

[80] Birnbaum, p. 182.

[81] Keddie, "Pan-Islam as Proto-Nationalism," p. 17.

alluded to the received wisdom that Iran's own geographical heritage has contributed to the uniqueness of its culture, history, and national particularism.[82] The presupposition in such definitions of national culture or national particularism is that there is no problem with anachronism in applying modern perceptions of identity to peoples of the past or even to a large and sharply diverse region like Iran. If we take both scholars at their word that nationalism was a product of the twentieth (not the nineteenth) century, then their decision to base their argument on the existence of a historical racial, linguistic, religious, and cultural consciousness that supposedly provided the basis of Iranian identity[83] is inherently contradictory. Cottam, like some other scholars, asserts that the greatness of pre-Islamic history gave nationalism (and national consciousness) vitality, but he also admits that "the uneducated have no idea of Iranian history."[84]

Before assuming that all necessary cultural and communication links were provided within the Iranian geographical zone to enable its inhabitants to conceive a national culture and national particularism, we must recall that the great distances involved over arid and mountainous land had made travel between many regions, even by camel, unthinkable. In fact, these barriers to interaction kept people of remote regions isolated from each other until the era of modern transportation.[85] The movement toward nationalism received its energy from both nonhuman resources (for example, electronic and technological development) and human resources (the educated urban white-collar classes). Cottam's book *Nationalism in Iran* deals primarily with the theoretical issues of modern nationalism without taking cultural and historical phenomena into consideration, nor does it investigate the origin and development of national identity in Iran.

---

[82] Cottam, pp. 23–24; Young, "Interaction of Islamic and Western," p. 131.

[83] Cottam, pp. 25, 26–32; Young, "The National and International Relations of Iran," *Near Eastern Culture and Society*, pp. 189–190, 197.

[84] Cottam, pp. 26, 27, 31, 35.

[85] Ibid., pp. 25–26, notes the lack of roads and climatic harshness in various regions of Iran.

The arguments of the book do not distinguish between the political alignments of regions, parties, and other groups and the national sentiment and its origin.

The problem of how numerous tribally diverse and heterogeneous cultural and linguistic groups came together to feel Iranian strongly suggests that the common denominators must have been provided in recent times. Obviously, the Iranian zone had been the home of its inhabitants for centuries, but the meanings associated with the bounded area involved were redefined, and the inhabitants were encouraged by all available means to feel themselves connected as a single, natural nation. Nonetheless, gaps existed in every direction. Flandin indicates that in the nineteenth century the juxtaposing of urban and rural communities next to purely subsistence-level nomads had created harsh socioeconomic disparities among various populations of Iran.[86] As a phenomenon, nomadism has profoundly disregarded territorial identity. Thus it is highly significant that, in 1800, up to 50 percent of the population inside Iran was nomadic and that, in 1900, between a third and a quarter of the population (perhaps 1.5 million out of 9.9 million) remained unsettled.[87] As of 1956, 70 percent of Iran's population was classified as residing in rural, tribal, or unsettled nomadic areas.[88] Continuing along the same lines, the 1976 census indicated that there were still two million unsettled nomads nationwide.[89] At any rate, the seeming definiteness of territorial identity today, whether on a regional or a national scale, relates to modern political-administrative divisions and should not be allowed to obscure the complex and multilayered identity question. In a linguistic sense, the large communities of Iran — Turkish, Gilaki, Luri, Kurd, Mazandarani, Baluchi, Arabic, Turkoman, and Armenian — maintained their customs, practices, and languages next to smaller groups with

---

[86] Flandin, II, pp. 409–411.

[87] See Halliday, *Iran: Dictatorship and Development*, pp. 11–12. There are, however, disagreements on the exact population on Iran in the 1800s; see *Iranshahr* (UNESCO; Tehran: Tehran University Press, 1963), I, p. 91.

[88] *Iranshahr*, I, p. 101.

[89] Halliday, p. 12.

different languages and dialects, until the central government tried
to use a common language (Farsi) to link Baluchis with Gilakis and
Kurds with Mazandaranis in hopes of creating a common
consciousness in a given Iranian geographical zone. Whether this
effort was successful or not is an interesting but a separate issue.

In expressing a local identity as opposed to a national
territorial one, Kurds of the nineteenth century (according to
Robert Grant Watson) felt their primary loyalty and sense of
identity for the tribe and the chief (with at times a certain allegiance
to the Shah).[90] This mentality evidently has changed very little in
cases where the tribe, family, and religion have been strong bases
of loyalty and identity.[91] Only with the advent of Reza Shah and the
intensely nationalist Pahlavi government did Iran try to debase
tribal (regional) power.[92] Another acute question is to what extent
cultural identity gave rise to political and geographical identity. For
example, was the Mahabad Republic of 1946 (as well as subsequent
Kurdish political movements) representative of a wider Kurdish
geopolitical identity among all the Kurdish-language tribes or was it
merely a political challenge in defiance of Tehran's domination and
imposition of policies? In other words, has the Kurdish
independence movement been more a product of congenial
internal sympathy for unity and common identity among the Kurds
or of antagonistic pressure from outside?

The limits of Baluchi identity as another linguistic group in
Iran should (as Brian Spooner suggests) be searched for and
defined in cultural rather than geographical terms.[93] The Baluchis
are divided territorially among the modern states of Iran, Pakistan,
and Afghanistan. How these political borders have affected their
sense of territorial patriotism on a national scale certainly cannot be
explained in a few lines and without empirical research. Spooner's
assessment of ethnic identity, however, relies on a typical old-

---

[90] Watson, p. 7.

[91] "The Kurds," *The Minority Rights Group Report*, No. 23 (June 1985),
p. 8.

[92] See Cottam, pp. 59–61.

[93] Spooner, "Who are the Baluch? A preliminary investigation into the
dynamics of an ethnic identity from Qajar Iran," *Qajar Iran*, p. 103.

fashioned anthropological analysis that presupposes the common denominator of a shared cultural heritage (at times, it seems in a vacuum), again because of a common language. The sharp diversities that exist among the tribal groups are dismissed in favor of placing a common identity among the Baluchis.

Spooner's crude perception of cultural identity is bound to the description and mental projection that he himself refers to in a different context — namely, that the Baluchi identity developed in the eighteenth century as a result of the rise of its linguistic tribal status supported by the imperialist powers.[94] Thus, it is safe to say that both the common territorial identity and the cultural identity were aspects of a colonial instrumental method that arbitrarily and inadvertently institutionalized the issue of common ethnic identity.

Consequently, in appraising the territorial identity within a given political boundary (such as Iran) scholars should maintain a skeptical position in relation to many undigested theories, bearing in mind that neither political borders nor a particular language per se determines an identity — whether regional or national. Following the Pahlavi rise to power, however, development of sophisticated means of communication, implementation of a strongly secularist educational program, inheritance of patriotic doctrines from the preceding generation, imposition of the Farsi language, and ubiquitous use of state propaganda all aimed to create grounds for tribal, rural, and marginal groups to accept and accommodate the Iranian territorial identity within their belief system. With this clarification in mind, we now need to scrutinize briefly the popularization process of an Iranian identity by the Pahlavi regime.

POPULARIZATION OF AN IRANIAN IDENTITY

The first nationalistic phase was the favoring of modernization and eventually secularization that followed the constitutional movement. This gave sufficient ground to recruit the intelligentsia and also incorporated Western scholarship into a body of beliefs that became known as national or Iranian consciousness. The

---

[94] Spooner, p. 95.

exclusively secular thoughts and perceptions of the intelligentsia of the nineteenth century subsequently found contact with the clerical class, and together they gave expression to the patriotic responsibilities of the leading members of both categories. As Adamiyat indicates, the intelligentsia of the nineteenth and early twentieth centuries maintained no popular bases among the ordinary masses, and yet they founded an enterprise for Western-style modernization in Iran. Moreover, while the introduction of such thoughts is generally attributed to the secularist category, its translation into an organized mass uprising for reform was the work of the clergy.[95]

The entire undertaking to promote both Western modernization and national consciousness was assumed by Reza Khan's strongly established state apparatus, which organized its forces to construct different aspects of national cohesion. In this regard, Rudolph Rocker has said, "The nation is not the cause, but the result, of the state. It is the state which creates the nation, not the nation the state."[96]

When the era of strong statehood over the Iranian territory began in 1925, the task became to denounce archaic norms and values and to bridge existing gaps to create a new and modern nation. Before 1925, despite extensive contact with the West ideologically and technologically, the country was very much the same at the mass level as it had been a century before.[97] Reza Shah's main and immediate policies focused on modernizing the administration, the army, economic development, the judiciary system, education, and communication. The triumph of Reza Shah signified also the triumph of the secular modernists over the conservative clerical class. Although constitutional practices remained in place as the basis of national unity, the reassertion and restoration of the constitution by Reza Shah came only after he had subdued tribal revolts in Fars, Kurdistan, Khurāsān, Luristān, Azarbaijan, and of course Khuzistān under Sheikh Khaz'al.

---

[95] Adamiyat, *Fikr-i Āzādī,* pp. 245, 247.

[96] Emerson, *From Empire to Nation,* p. 114 quoting R. Rocker.

[97] Banani, *The Modernization of Iran 1921–1941,* p. 28.

Reza Shah's key tactical move at this stage was to seek the allegiance of leading members of the Shi'i clergy in Najaf and Karbala in exchange for his promise to protect Islamic principles and values.[98] Not long afterward, however, Reza Shah and his entourage began to attack the mullahs as reactionary elements, while simultaneously trying to glorify the pre-Islamic tradition. This significantly contributed to a revival of anti-Arab (and ambiguously anti-Islamic) feelings traceable to the seventh-century humiliation they had inflicted on the "Iranian" Sasanian Empire.[99] The hatred directed toward Arabs was in a way a by-product of the historiographical method used by Western academia to reconstruct a pre-Islamic Iranian history, as well as of its attribution of Aryan racial status to the inhabitants of Iran. Of course, such anti-Arab feeling among the educated and secular classes implicitly carried with it an underground current of anticlericalism, since the clergy represented Islam as well.[100] The Pahlavi regime was quick to take advantage of the situation, using the hypothetical reconstruction of a remote dynastic connection as the basis of its own legitimacy[101] and of claims about the continuity of monarchical rule in Iran.

Reza Shah's regime began propagating two thoughts in order to maintain the unity of Iran under his rule. First was the idea of transforming Iran through modernization, by building roads, providing public education (only in Farsi), importing Western technology, establishing different kinds of social and economic institutions, and mobilizing the masses to create the national relationship, for example, via mandatory military service for the male population throughout Iran. Second was the doctrinal and ideological idea for which German messianic doctrine and Aryanism became the mechanism. On the ideological front the simple patriotism and unity of the earlier period rapidly passed the

---

[98] Banani, pp. 41–43; Cottam, pp. 147–148; see also Kohn, *History of Nationalism in the East,* p. 340.

[99] Young, "National and International Relations of Iran," p. 197; Cottam, pp. 147–8.

[100] Keddie, "Religion and Irreligion in Early Iranian Nationalism," p. 287.

[101] Gnoli, pp. 178–179.

limits of nationalism and developed into a chauvinism grounded in a supposed superiority to the neighboring states. The media's spirit in the 1920s and 1930s certainly testifies to this development.[102]

Reza Shah positioned himself to be influenced by the prevailing racial thoughts to the extent that his advisers and ideological supporters were mainly Western-educated and subscribed to the racial propaganda. It thus came as no surprise when Ali Dashti, among other protégés of Reza Shah, translated works such as Edmond Demolin's *À quoi tient la Superiorité des Anglo Saxons (The Secret of Anglo-Saxon Superiority)*.[103] The Aryan school in Germany and the Aryan feeling of the Pahlavi regime in Iran had created a closer tie between the two countries. Other Western advisers were constantly being replaced by German ones. The department of press and propaganda installed in Iran was modeled on its counterpart in Germany, which aimed to create a nationalistic spirit in an authoritarian context.[104] "This office issued a multitude of publications dealing with such recurrent themes as the responsibilities of the citizens, the new rights of women and health."[105] In later years, newspaper circulation and the mass availability of transistor radios, the telegraph, telephones, the postal service, and subsequently television in various regions of Iran were used in attempts to bridge existing gaps in the process of popularizing a national consciousness. The rise of nineteenth and twentieth-century national sentiment and the national context of academic Orientalism hand in hand with the strong state of Pahlavi and its nationalist promoters gave a historical meaning to Iran, one of the heterogeneous lands of Western Asia. It did not stop in creating a national consciousness and a historical Iranian identity; it went on to preach racial superiority vis-à-vis neighboring countries.

Modernization and the government's racial doctrinal orientation gave rise to an anticlerical feeling among the Pahlavi elites as well. Given their desire to create an Iranian nation

---

[102] Banani, p. 47; Arasteh, *Education and Social Awakening*, p. 108–109.

[103] Banani, pp. 48–51. Banani erroneously notes that Ali Dashti wrote this book instead of translated it.

[104] Arasteh, p. 106.

[105] Ibid.

defined by a secular history constructed from ancient times and supplemented with aspects of progress in Westernization, the anticlerical position was becoming inevitable. The Western-educated entourage of Reza Shah, such as Taqizadeh, Kazemzadeh-Iranshahr, Ali Akbar Siyasi, Ali Dashti, Mostafa Adl, Amir 'Alam, and Muhammad Sa'ed, became spokesmen for the concept of formulating an Iranian ideology and identity, using (both domestic as well as) Western sources of inspiration.[106] Material progress became increasingly important in shaping the new identity, and gradually the clerics came to be looked upon as anti-progressive. To alienate the clergy further, education — which had previously been marked by the powerful influence of the clerical class — was now used by the state not only to decrease the clergy's cultural role but also to reinforce new secular elements for the nation's indoctrination.

The traditional schools, Madrassa, Maktab, or mosques under the supervision of the clergy served as a first phase of studies, from which promising students moved on for higher education to attend Atabāt (holy centers in Iraq), where they would study Islamic philosophy, literature, science, and mathematics.[107] The establishment in 1851 of Dār ul-Funun made available the first European-style school in Iran. Then, after the settlement of the constitutional government, the provisions for education were assigned. The first provisions of 1907 gave way to the founding in 1910 of the department of elementary education, and by 1911 the law assigned the functions of private and public education. It was, however, during the reign of Reza Pahlavi that the state became the core of a learning system that precipitated the decline of widespread clerical education. Between 1925 and 1928 the elementary and secondary programs for boys and girls were presented; and in 1934 the state directly intervened in the education program.[108] In the 1930s, the curriculum for schools consisted of

---

[106] Banani, pp. 48–51.
[107] Arasteh, p. 13.
[108] Ibid., pp. 53–56, 63.

Farsi, geography, social studies, music, singing (patriotic songs), and Iranian history.[109]

Education in essence became the main channel of communication between the state (which sponsored "socially useful" material) and the masses (who learned it). The integration of the rural and lower classes, which constituted the majority of society, had to assimilate the notion of possessing a common heritage in order to feel that they belonged to a larger community that was termed Iranian. As Arasteh comments, "The extension of public schooling thus opened the way for a common means of communication. Mass media with its stress on a common Iranian heritage now effectively reached numerous literate groups."[110]

The purpose behind the methodology of education was an admixture of technical necessity and state propaganda. Education in the Pahlavi era was taking a direction that literacy aimed to create ideal citizens and civic individuals. The classrooms provided a forum for reciting nationalistic verses, pledging allegiance to the flag,[111] and learning about the Iranian past and its achievements. Reza Shah's governing bodies were thoroughly aware of the importance of creating a link with the past, and the national genealogical construct (though as yet vaguely understood by members of the rural and lower socioeconomic categories) provoked a sense of pride and historical identity. The minister of education in Reza Shah's period put the purpose of education in simple terms: "It follows that an educational program must be built upon the following aims: to create in minds of people a living consciousness of the past by showing the great achievements of the race... to train boys and girls to become good citizens of modern Persia."[112]

Obviously such an attitude gave ample grounds for the educational program to be highly charged with nationalistic and racial assertions in the history, language, and social studies textbooks. It was all meant to heighten the national and racial

---

[109] Banani, p. 92.

[110] Arasteh, p. 56.

[111] Ibid., p. 106.

[112] Banani, pp. 109–110, quoting Isā Sadīq.

consciousness of the youth. Inevitably, the Aryan race and pre-Islamic history (civilization), as the result of the excavations by the Western Orientalists, became the favorite subjects of Pahlavi propaganda to boost the issue of Iranian identity.

Although the Aryan-race concept was hypothesized in the early nineteenth-century Europe, it only found its way into Iran slowly in the early twentieth century — at least textually. One of the earliest references to the division between Aryan and Semitic races and civilizations (with *Aryan* standing for Iran) can be found in Zakā ul-Mulk Foroughī's 1901 history textbook.[113] The Aryan hypothesis was taken seriously in Iran by the secular intelligentsia, who began to base their historical arguments on such conceptions; and in the absence of any strong countervailing theory or opposition, the Aryan racial theory was emphasized in history textbooks of the Reza Shah period[114] and subsequently. This racial theory thus became the back-bone of the new form of history, and the distinction in the Iranian history taught in the history textbooks between the pre-Islamic period and the Islamic period was carefully noted and maintained. It was not, however, irrelevant when Reza Shah demanded that the international community use *Iran* instead of *Persia* for his country, both to emphasize the racial etymology and to underscore the historical significance of the term *Iran* rather than the narrower term *Persia*. It certainly made an impact on the youth to encounter this majestic construct of history under the Iranian banner. The effect was made even more impressive when, in the same textbooks, there appeared a special reference to *vatan* (fatherland): *Iran*, a homeland, a birthplace, and a place to cherish.[115]

The rise of Reza Shah to power itself was an event of high value for publicity. In the 1939 edition of the tenth-grade history textbook the emergence (and anticipated period) of the new regime in power was gloriously characterized as *Gharn-i Pahlavi* (Pahlavi Century). As examples of the high goals and achievements of the

---

[113] Foroughī, *Tārīkh-i Iran*, I, p. 34.

[114] *Tārīkh-i Naw* (Secondary school history textbook) (Tehran, 1309/1930), p. 3.

[115] Ibid., pp. 2, 4.

new regime, the platforms of 1927 were mentioned, including the plan to unify the sharply diverse population of Iran, *motahid ul-shikl shodan-i ahāli-i Iran,* as well as to overthrow the vestiges of feudalism and tribal authority by disarming the forces of such groupings.[116] This indicates a movement toward consolidation of Iranian identity, even by force.

The fast pace of Reza Shah's modernization (in an imitation of Atatürk of Turkey) and mass integration also created an influx of urban middle-class individuals, among whom the meaning and aspects of modern nationalism were gaining strength. Territorial identity came to be incorporated in their conversations, and the cultural achievements of past literary figures were lumped together as part of their territorial Iranian heritage. Due to a high-powered campaign both in education and in other state agencies, the stage had been set for cosmetically decorating the so-called age-old Iranian culture. Between the time of Reza Shah and the early period of his son's reign, the government used the millenary celebration of Firdowsī, Avicenna (Ibn Sīnā), and other figures as an occasion to rebuild their tombs, as well as those of Sa'dī, Hafiz, and Omar Khayyam, to glorify their national cultural achievements. The achievements of people who lived in that geographical zone at different historical periods and spoke languages (Arabic and Farsi) that not all the inhabitants of the lands shared, were now being presented to those linguistically heterogeneous populations as outstanding examples of their national culture.

The Pahlavis' special emphasis on the Farsi language was intended to be the primary linking instrument for creating a national Iranian body on the one hand and for instilling a cultural consciousness that Farsi was the medium that brought cultural glory on the other. In light of the importance of this vernacular against the background of Arab-Islamic culture, the Pahlavi government even decided to set up an academy to purge borrowed Arabic words from Farsi and to replace them with "pure" Farsi

---

[116] *Tārīkh-i Naw* (tenth-grade history textbook) (Tehran, 1318/1939), pp. 127–128.

words,[117] like the nineteenth-century movement in Britain to use Saxon words, rather than Norman-French-derived words. Turkey, in the vanguard of secularization, had already taken such measures to establish a "pure" Turkish language by altering the syllables of Arabic and Farsi borrowings, as well as by determining the proper native terms for non-Turkish words.[118]

In the Pahlavi era, the Farsi language was taken to be historically enlarged as a sign of cultural resistance by the Iranians in the face of the giant Arab culture. In this regard, no explanation was ever provided as to what the birth of a new language (in this case, Farsi) has to do with a political territory or zone-especially when it is put in terms of the modern political boundary of Iran. Forging the concept of language as having properly belonged to a geographical or political zone was a wholesale appropriation of the European notion of national identity, discussed in Chapter 1.

At any rate, as a consequence of many attitudes and factors, the anti-Arab feeling took such a complex direction that the boundary between national/racial and religious sentiment was difficult to recognize.[119] The constitution of a national memory of the glorious past was a central element of Pahlavi policies designed to give a distinct sense of identity to the people of Iran. Pre-Islamic Zoroastrian emblems appeared on government agencies and buildings and special attention was paid to Zoroastrian festivals — all in order to revive the past and to connect with it. Of course, it was again taken for granted that pre-Islamic Zoroastrian religion and traditions were intimately connected and appropriately labeled with the Iranian geographical zone and identity. National biases had blinded the extreme nationalists to the fact that, in the territory before or after it was called Iran, numerous religions and cultural communities besides the Zoroastrians had played a role in the life of that area. Furthermore, the revival of ancient religious traditions should be viewed in a modern sense not as religious but as national. Anyhow, the Zoroastrian religion was viewed as the

---

[117] Young, "Interaction of Islamic and Western Thought in Iran," p. 140.

[118] Kohn, *History of Nationalism*, p. 241.

[119] See Chapter 9 of this book.

ancestral religion of Iranians and the government made certain that
modern Iranians as Muslims felt a special affinity for this tradition.

It is sufficient here to emphasize that the Pahlavi regime
continued to incorporate all the elements it needed to generate a
national doctrine that would provide identity to the people and
legitimacy to itself. The idea of monarchy was excessively exploited
to hammer home the idea that Iran had never been deprived of a
king. In certain ways, the government sought to make patriotism
synonymous with cherishing the monarchy and the monarch. One
eye-catching and ubiquitous slogan in shops and offices was the
triumvirate *Khodā, Shah, Mīhan* (God, King, Fatherland). It was
an advantage to emphasize in the school textbooks the alleged
2500 years of continuous monarchy on Iranian soil. Thus
Muhammad Reza Shah, with the help of his advisers, decided in
1971 to create a milestone in the history of the monarchical
tradition by celebrating 2500 years of Iranian monarchical heritage.
The celebration was not an ordinary one; the setup and the
costumes that attendants wore were reminiscent of previous
dynasties as they paraded before the Shah and his international
guests (mostly monarchs) at Persepolis. Those common folk who
had television sets could watch it and never forget it; others heard
or read about it.

To what extent all this propaganda interested the rural,
nomadic, and remote countryside people and whether they clearly
understood their meaning or not may be separate questions. The
Shah's White Revolution, as a series of reforms that touched the
countryside (particularly via land reform in the 1960s) on the one
hand and as a force for maintaining the unity of Iran (by
suppressing tribal and regional unrest) on the other hand,
established the sole authority of the centralized state and enforced
a single loyalty and identity among these people.

In sum, the commotions and feelings of various people from
different socioeconomic strata about their Iranian identity may be
impossible to analyze; but certainly, with the expansion of
education and the middle class, the national consciousness came to
serve the goals of the state and to consolidate its unity.
Nonetheless, the ill-defined nature of Iranian identity (if not in its
territorial sense, then in its historical, racial, and cultural context)
became evident to the world when the revolution ending the
Pahlavi era preferred to call itself Islamic instead of Iranian.

Popularization of the Iranian identity did not come to an end with the downfall of the Pahlavi regime, but it began to take a different direction with the surfacing of fundamentalist Islamic principles.

THE ISLAMIC REPUBLIC AND IRANIAN IDENTITY

It is not within the scope of this study to analyze the Iranian identity question during the era of the Islamic Republic. What follows is therefore only a note about the attitude of the policymakers, particularly in the field of education, in redefining the Iranian identity by freeing it from secular so called misattributions.

As might be expected, at the beginning of the revolutionary period of 1979, the regional and tribal uprisings for autonomy in Turkoman Sahra, among the Kurds, and in other settlements — whether the result of political intrigue by a few radical activists or an expression of the will of the vast indigenous people — were a clear sign of the potentially crippling effects of separatist national sentiment. In putting down all the unrest that threatened the unity of Iran, the revolutionary government forces naturally turned for justification to the thesis of Islamic brotherhood or national integrity so elaborately developed under the Pahlavis. But the real task before the Islamic regime after its consolidation was to arrest the progress of secular indoctrination about Iranian identity. To accomplish this, the new government tried to propagate the view that patriotism through the regency of Islam was more rewarding in this and the next world than solely cherishing the temporal aspects of modern nationalism.

The redefined component of Iranian identity and culture was formulated in school textbooks outside government channels. The "uncorrupted" children of the Islamic generation struck the Islamic leaders as a more important target than the already-indoctrinated preceding generation, which carried the old propaganda along (many of whom had gone into exile). In general terms, the school textbooks used by the Islamic Republic have tried to marginalize and gradually minimize the significance of the pre-Islamic history of Iran. In the process of doing that, these texts have taken to referring to the inhabitants of Iran as an Islamic community *(Ummati-i Islami)*, not as an Iranian community *(Ummat-i Irani)*.[120]

The reinforcement of historical national identity by the Islamic regime was bound to a common code of culture that was centered on Islam as opposed to the secularism of the Pahlavis.[121] The modification of textbooks' depiction of pre-Islamic Iran (which is presented as tyrannical) is accompanied by a shift in emphasis toward religious science lessons. In the Pahlavi period, the topics on the ancient period accounted for twenty-five lessons or 11 percent of the total. In the Islamic period the figure declined to three lessons or 1 percent. Meanwhile, lessons on religious topics rose from 4 percent of the total during the Pahlavi era to 17 percent under the Islamic Republic.[122]

Thus, by exalting religious culture within the political boundary of Iran, the Islamic Republic has tried to solidify a national identity with a more complicated definition of identity. At least in its first phase of policies, the Islamic regime appears to be attempting to undo the secular and anticlerical knots tied by the previous regime before even thinking about the feasibility of constructing a purely Muslim identity. Such an eventuality would depend on the political situation in the Middle East and on the new urge (after many failed attempts) to achieve Pan-Islamic unity. Having questioned the techniques of the Islamic Republic in creating a new vision of identity, it is also appropriate to ask how the regime has sought to bolster the national identity of non-Shi'ites within Iran now that the Iranian-focused identity is de-emphasized. Iran faces the challenge of taking measures to solve conflicts over regional identities as well as resolve the fragile line between Islamic and Iranian identities within its own borders

---

[120] J. M., "The Textbooks of the Islamic Republic," (in Farsi), pp. 1, 17.

[121] Higgins and Shoar Ghafari, "Changing Perception of Iranian Identity in Elementary Textbooks," *Children of the Middle East Today*, p. 10. (I am most grateful to Professor Higgins for sending me the final draft of this article.)

[122] Ibid., pp. 23–37.

before committing itself to the burden of writing a history that is not religiously or nationally biased.

A FINAL COMMENT

A reversible secular process began slightly more than a century and a half ago to modernize the old and crippled empire of the Qājārs. The aim of this process was initially to reform the archaic administrative network, but it then expanded to embrace reform of the government, the establishment of schools and newspapers, the introduction of new political doctrines, and the creation of a constitution. The reform movement, pursued under the constant threat of Anglo-Russian expansionism, had a profound impact on the political consciousness of the country's sociopolitical leaders. The new political consciousness had been translated into many different concrete forms; but whatever direction it went in, it had to end at the political borders of the empire: Iran. The goals became to reform society for the benefit of the government and the inhabitants of Iran.

Although serious conflicts sometimes arose in defining what the interest of Iran might be, particularly over its points of agreement and disagreement with the interests of Islam, alliances and frictions were resolved (at least temporarily) by focusing on establishing a national assembly, which occurred in 1906. Nevertheless, the rift between the secular and the clerical categories remained tangible. Inescapably, the national assembly became the political institution linking all the opposing forces. At the same time, the development of political notions such as *vatan* (fatherland), nationalist theories derived from Ottoman-Anglo-French sources and Western scholarship in general to develop an elaborate vision of Iranian history all were giving expression to a new and modern attitude about national considerations. To these politically aware individuals and leaders, Iran was the ultimate legitimate political institution and boundary under which all communities — regardless of their religious belief or ethnic background — could be equal in exchange for their loyalty. Theoretically, this secularist notion undertook to transform a geographical expression with its heterogeneous ethnic and linguistic categories into a united, integrated, and unique populace, complete with an ancient and proud cultural identity, a special racial status, and a modern political doctrine. Under such a banner, the territorial (or, rather, Iranian) consciousness was being promoted to take the place of all other identities.

After the seeds of territorial identity were politically established, the cultural aspects were promulgated through modernized schooling and establishment of a single vernacular language — Farsi. The rise of the Pahlavi family to power and its showing affinity to the new nationalist and racial ideas moved the country farther along the path of national indoctrination. The popularization of national identity traveled via several different cultural, social, educational, and political streams, all of which were filtered through the state's propaganda machinery. Iran as a zone was not the cause, but only proved to be the result. Following the European model, Turkish, Iranian, Arab, and Japanese forms provided examples of genuine national chauvinism.

Yet the crude idea of Iranian identity should not have been treated as a payoff and compensation for political gains. The constructed national history, the insertion of racial theory, and the exaltation of national symbols were at the time not thought to be hazardous to the qualitative judgment and vision of people in general. For the modernizing secularists, these developments were meant to express one thing: that men and women living in every corner of the Iranian territory were equally citizens of Iran. But the nationalistic blindness of the secularists in Iran rendered them incapable of creating an atmosphere of inclusiveness in regards to other languages spoken in Iran, yet they were even more contemptuous towards the Shi'i and Sunni discourse in a country with a long and complicated religious history.

Consequently, the internal contradictions and confusion over the issue of national identity — particularly in their expression as Iranism, Islamism, and regionalism — have been the activators of controversy that have caused major side effects and invite the development of a subtler medium of identity.

CHAPTER 9
IRANIAN IDENTITY,
MUSLIM IDENTITY,
AND CULTURAL SCHIZOPHRENIA

The argument of this chapter is based on my own observations having grown up in the last Pahlavi generation. However, these observations could possibly stand true through the present Islamic generation, with some allowance for differences in attitude. It is necessary to examine the attitude of society at large toward the secular Iranian identity and the religious Shi'i Muslim identity, and to assess their correlation and their paradoxical overlaps, which have psychologically and nationally created an unconscious ambivalence among a great many people.

At times excessive love for the fatherland and officially sanctioned cherishing of Iranian civilization and ancestral roots have aroused anti-Arab feelings tied to the humiliation and destruction of the Iranian civilization during the mid-seventh century conquest. This event has been demonized by secular writers so effectively that the inconsistency of embracing and practicing the "Arab" religion of Islam in modern society in Iran has had to be addressed by means of a strategy of separating the account of the doctrine of Islam from any denunciation of the so-called Arab humiliators. Before we discuss the issue historically, two immediate points have to be clarified. First, it would be wrong to think that the seventh-century conquest was exclusively accomplished by an Arab army; it would be considerably more accurate to call it a Muslim conquest, because various non-Arab tribes and groups participated in the campaign on the winning side (potentially all the members of the opposition against the Sasanian court). There seems, however, to have been a racial point to be gained by emphasizing that it was an Arab enterprise to destroy the so-called Aryan or Iranian civilization. Second, the conquest itself brought Islam to Iran, making possible in subsequent generations an emerging pious mood and a mechanism for belonging to the new religion. Furthermore, considering the modern dichotomy in the Iranian attitude toward the Arabs and toward Islam, it is an inescapable fact for the practicing Shi'ites to ponder that Ali, Hasan, and Husayn (the first three Shi'i Imams) were ethnically identical to the Arabs who planned and participated in the suppression of various popular movements of unrest in Dailam, Sistan, and other regions of Iran.[1] The psychological perception of one's religious belief and the awareness of its ideological conflict with the prevailing national sentiment are symptoms of cultural schizophrenia evident in many countries like Iran. The same dichotomy of interest in relation to the preaching of the Catholic Church vis-à-vis the Italian state has persisted to the present time, so that even today the Catholic identity has not fully come to terms with the Italian national identity for many practicing Catholics in that country. Risorgimento was demonized by the Church in 1870 for having caused the destruction and deviation of Catholic tradition no less than the secular propagandists demonized the Muslim conquest in Iran. Perhaps the case of Pakistan, in which the national identity was created squarely on the basis of religion, is somewhat different, but the explanation for the swing within that territory from Muslim to Pakistani identity remains unclear. Similarly, the transition of the Jewish identity as a religious entity *per se* to an Israeli national may present a different issue for the Jews living inside Israel than for Jews living outside. The transformation of Jewish identity in modern times has extended from their earlier national origin — such as Ottoman or Habsburg — to a more modern identity such as Turkish or Austrian Jews and then on, with the establishment of the Jewish state, to the newest identity as Israeli Jews (for those who immigrated there). The longstanding ambiguities of Jewish identity and the issue of ancient Israelite identity propagated by the Zionists have given rise to ambivalence in prioritizing the competing aspects of national and

---

[1] al-Baladhuri, *Futuh ul-Buldan*, section on Iran, pp. 81, 92, 151; see also Vaziri, *The Emergence of Islam*, pp. 76–81.

religious identity, particularly for Jews who are citizens of other countries. Another example is Lebanon. Lebanese swing between the Phoenician racial line (a European invention) and Arab identity has been an evident flaw in modern national identity among the indoctrinated population.

In trying to identify the roots and the symptoms of the cultural dichotomy in attitude toward the Islamic religion (which was of Arab origin) and toward the secular national Iranian identity, we encounter a series of questions that seek answers in future research projects. In every generation, of course, the differences between communities are used to justify their stereotyping of each other. In modern Iran, certain people perhaps continue to stereotype their differences with neighbors or with the rest of the world, but the weight of the stereotyping of Arabs has a particularly ambiguous historical and religious significance (e.g., the Iran-Iraq war). If, as many claim, the animosity between Arab and ʿAjam has been historically consistent, then how can this issue be placed in a modern national Iranian and Arab or religious perspective? How can certain present-day people of Iran in their sober minds simultaneously have faith in Islam and yet express their dislike of the Arabs? And is such dislike addressed to the Arabs who conquered the territory of Iran in the seventh century or to contemporary Arab peoples or to both? How much of this resentment subconsciously connotes anti-Islamic feeling? And how much of this anti-Arab feeling has to do with the products of modern secularism, which have sought to glorify extra-Islamic history (namely, ancient Iranian)?

It is to be hoped that able scholars may shed light on these ambiguous sociological and psychological issues of modern Iran. Whether the swing of identity has any early causes or not it may be worth investigating some of the attributions that have been made in this regard.

Goldziher indicates that historically anti-Arab feeling in the region of Iran dates back even to pre-Islamic times.[2] If this is true, and assuming that the Sasanian stereotyping of the Arabs caused an air of antipathy against them, how can this phenomenon be

---

[2] Goldziher, *Muslim Studies*, I, p. 100.

understood in its ethnic and national framework? No nation and no unique cultural identity existed among the Arabs, nor were there such concepts among the subjects of the Sasanians known as Persians. On the same premise, one could misread Muhammad's anti-Sasanian position in its war with the Romans, as revealed in the Koran (Sura 30-*al-Roum*),[3] as being anti-Persian. To the contrary, as Tabarī reports, the Meccan elites were pro-Persian[4] in the power politics of the region. The attribution of anti-Arab feeling, followed by indiscriminate grouping into rough cultural or national categories, is simply erroneous. It is true that, in many instances, temporary alliances and animosities were influenced or determined by considerations of political philosophy or strategy. Nonetheless, the mere stereotyping of groups in a linguistic, geographical, religious or (to a certain extent) cultural context, although it may have been common, was not necessarily national in character.

In the Islamic period, the interaction of Arabic-speaking Muslims with non-Arabic-speaking ones may have caused friction. The question of *Shu'ubiya* (discussed in Chapter 4), however, cannot again be framed in an imaginary national Iranian context as being against the Arabs in the first four centuries of Islam. Certain instances of pro-Arabism, such as that contained in Ibn Qutayba's writings, did come under attack by Birunī and his contemporaries and were subjects of debate in later generations,[5] but such praise (or opposition to it) should not easily be translated into a plot to promote Arab identity over Iranian (or *vice versa*). The *Shu'ubiya* controversy was as much a literary debate as a political one to demand equal status for non-Arabs with the Arabs. The dislike of Arab hegemony over the vast non-Arab population of the Islamic world often has been interpreted as a dislike of Arab ethnicity, language, or culture, which is not true; the *Shu'ubiya* groups themselves wrote in Arabic.[6] In fact, according to Frye, the Arabic

---

[3] See Tabarī, *Tārīkh*, II, p. 739; see also Vaziri, p. 22.

[4] Tabarī, *Tārīkh*, II, pp. 737–739.

[5] Goldziher, I, pp. 153, 161–162.

[6] Ibid., pp. 191–194; see also Frye, *The Golden Age of Persia*, pp. 121–122.

language was defended and rectified by the Persians (non-Arabs) in Arabic.[7] The praise and the currency of Arabic language and literature (along with the Islamic religion itself, as a so-called Arab religion) are consistent with the positions and attitudes of non-Arabs such as Ibn al-Muqaffaʻ and Birunī.[8]

Other attributions concern the heretical movements of the eighth and ninth centuries, which are considered symbolic of frictions between Arab Muslims and so-called Iranians allegedly seeking to reestablish their ancient "national" way of life. According to general opinion, the movements of Bihāfrid (746–747), Sinbād (755), Ishaq Turk (755–757), Ustādhsis (767–768), al-Muqannaʻ (755–783), and Bābāk (816–838) revolted against the caliphate in order to reestablish the Zoroastrian or Mazdakite faith against the dominant Islamic doctrine. It is true that the name and symbol of Abu Muslim appears in the sources as being one of the focuses of rhetoric in these campaigns against the caliphate (particularly in regard to Abu Muslim's being killed at the hands of Abbasids). But there are still two aspects that need to be considered in treating this issue. First, as indicated earlier, an attempt to revive a religion (in this case, Zoroastrianism) or a political opposition to a dominant religion (in this case, Islam) cannot simply be equated with an Iranian national or territorial movement. Again, this is nothing but an anachronism which violates the order of historical reconstruction. Second, even assuming that these movements were initiated to reestablish the old rule of so-called Iranian life, a two-fold ambiguity remains: (a) Why did other non-Arab (Iranian) contemporaries of these revolutionaries, who must have shared the Iranian national consciousness, refuse to abandon their Islamic faith and practices in favor of Zoroastrian religion and rule (though participation was extremely limited)? (b) How does grouping these heretical movements, which may be said to be anti-Islamic, into the heritage of the Iranian national category help present-day Iranians avoid the conflicting feelings aroused by Islam and by Iranian heroism? This

---

[7] Frye, p. 169.

[8] See *Ibn Muqaffaʻ*, annotated by Abdul Hadi Hairi (Tehran, 1341/1962).

ambiguity has kept a large number of modern Iranians to maintain either an anti-Islamic (as well as pro-Zoroastrian) position, or to be locked in a love and hate position of Islam and Iran.

One of the root causes of cultural and national schizophrenia may be found in the interpretations of historians and social scientists propagated by the government. In the case of Iran, most people could easily have lived as Muslims or national entities in peace without raising the issue of political territory as a home to offend the religion, or *vice versa*. But historical interpretations that distinguished Iranians as an Aryan race and a distinct civilization gradually (particularly as a result of the popularization of such notions during the Pahlavi era) caused the invention and subsequent reinforcement of an old wound on the intellectual and psychological level by presenting to the collective consciousness a "memory" of the attack on and destruction of the old culture of the Iranians by a foreign culture and religion. Books and interpretations like Zarīnkub's *Doo Gharn Soukut,* which asserts that Iranians have been a superior race *(Nejād-i bartar),*[9] or like the hundreds of other writings demonizing the Arabs cannot avoid causing an irreversible cultural swing in identity with regard to Muslims and Iranians. Imaginatively creating a sense of historical nostalgia and resentment (particularly among modern educated people) over something that occurred in the seventh century has also caused gaps among various groups who are trying to achieve a different kind of consciousness, whether religious or national. Yet, although it sounds strange, certain people endorsed both Aryanism and Shi'ism as their source of identity.

Nonetheless, various writers try when interpreting the Muslim conquest of Iran to handle the Islamic doctrine with caution, in view of its functional role in Iran. One interesting example of this technique can be seen in Forough's writing, where he refers to the seventh-century confrontation: "Only out of respect for Islam and for the Muslimness of the Arabs, could one refrain from considering them cruel and brutal."[10] Overall the tension over the

---

[9] Zarīnkub, *Doo Gharn Soukut,* p. 83.

[10] Forough, *Tārīkh-i Iran,* I, p. 130. (In reviewing historical records, the pillaging by Nadir Shah and his army of India in the mid-1700s should

Arab and Iranian issue has caused tension between the secular and the religious classes, as well as between the clergy and the state on a broader scale.

The causes and effects of such contradictions and ambiguities cannot be easily measured, but their existence cannot be denied. They have yielded a fallacious and gossip-laden vision of history; they have stirred up racial and national prejudice; they have encouraged a tormented confusion in people's religious and national sentiment; and they have distanced certain people from each other today purely in order to sympathize with imaginary countrymen from the seventh century. Those who carried contradictory national and religious sentiments over the years perhaps sought to reconcile their Islamic faith with Iran and its glorious past and therefore wanted to avoid being identified with the Arab Muslims.

The revolution of 1979 in certain ways was a reaction of the people's pious perceptions against excessive secular assertions. In other ways, the revolution bruised the historical and secular beliefs of those who felt that their true identity was being consumed by the clergy, if not necessarily by Islam. The revolution created a more tangible cleavage among those who prioritized their strong sense of identity (one way or another) toward Islam and toward Iran. Among these people, a distinction has been asserted between "genuine" Islam and Islam as presented by the clergy. The Islamic Revolution has driven out a large number of people for various reasons, but one significant reason is the conflicting sense of identity people may feel as Muslims and as Iranians.

The gap created between the perception of people living inside and outside Iran, and between the secular and religious people about their identities has obscured the true unity of the society — particularly created by obsolete scholarship and by stereotyping.

---

not be held against the indigenous population of Iran under Nadir Shah or against the modern Iranians for what an alleged Iranian army did to the Indians.)

CONCLUSION

This book is an attempt to analyze the anachronistic construction of Iranian identity along the racial line as well as the various aspects and significance of racism, nationalism, and Western Orientalism. The institutionalization of the ideological aspects of racial theories took place in Europe when the Aryan model differentiated the white man from all others. The form that Orientalism as a scholarly discipline took was a product of the unchallenged exercise of European intellectual authoritarianism over the Orient. We must be aware, however, that the intent of reconstructing and reinterpreting historical episodes in a national and racial context was not to fulfill a premeditated conspiracy but to follow up on scientific research after circumstances had corrupted scholars' methodological consciousness.

There have been two dominant aspects in the methodology of Western Orientalism: nationalism and racial theories. Of course the relationship between these two has been close and has been affected to a tremendous extent by economic, politico-ideological, cultural, and religious factors. Due to the emergence of national and racial dogma, Europe brought about a decisive break in the realm of old Christian historical thinking. Subsequently, scholars gradually debunked the old school, while the new one (nationalistic) gained momentum (despite fragmented challenges) — because of the authoritarian institutions of colonialism and Orientalism.

This study has tried to demonstrate how Western Orientalism misrepresented a historical reconstruction and interpretation along national and racial lines. The dilemma has not involved misrepresentation alone but also its at times appalling progeny: anti-Semitism, racism, and national prejudices. Thus, the method of juxtaposing facts to study the past was not the means used; instead, the past was interpreted in modern terms of nationalism along with racial theories, which thereupon transformed the consciousness of societies in those directions. Having said that, without wishing to hold an insufferably moralistic attitude toward racism or nationalism and without claiming that such an enterprise invariably led to intellectual regression, we should at least criticize the rigid absoluteness of such scholarship and note that it has led to related dogmatic beliefs both in scholarly and in popular communities.

The European projection and imposition of Western historical understanding in the form of a dogmatic paradigm — notably the Aryan model formulated by Schlegel and others — has left a legacy that for two hundred years has continued to proliferate. Of course, the findings related to the Indo-European language family rapidly gave way to an extreme racial conception that introduced another distorting dimension in scholarship. The Aryan race hypothetically replaced the language classification of the Indo-European category, and further elaborations described other distinct language families that were subsequently racially conceived. The scholars' racial consciousness developed terms of racial conceptualization by which to assess various historical events. In fact, philology as a discipline became the basis for retroactively applying racial distinctions to the peoples of antiquity.

In this study, Western scholarship's racial conceptualization of historical developments in the Iranian plateau, from antiquity through the medieval period, has been contested — not only because of its anachronistic attribution of modern concepts to such periods but also because of the shortcomings even today of analyzing (and generalizing about) distinct communities of the past on the basis of philology (or race) without taking into account the complex levels of cultural discourse and exchange within and among these communities. Obviously the alleged racial and national consciousness of these remote communities — specifically of the Iranians — is purely imaginary. Perhaps, however, it was simply misunderstanding on the part of the Orientalists, who took the racial and national consciousness of the modern period as a means to make the highly complex past explicable to themselves.

Many misrepresentations remain to be scrutinized and corrected in the field of Orientalism and specifically in the field of Iranian studies. What was briefly mentioned in this book about the various regions and tribes in Iran and about cultural aspects of various regions and historical periods should be thoroughly and cautiously argued in the future in order to demythologize the crude and arbitrary designation 'Iranian' for these highly complex phenomena. Further elaboration is required on the arbitrary and at times uneven periodization of historical events (e.g., pre-Islamic and Islamic) and on arbitrary terms such as Old Persian (Iranian), Middle Persian (Iranian), and Modern Persian (Iranian) language families that have been used to link remote people, culture, and civilizations together. Cultural anthropology, archaeology, and other fields obviously have been dominated by these rigid nationalistic and racial readings of the long and complex history of various peoples of the Near East and the Iranian plateau.

The singling out of historical anecdotes in order to rebuild a national history and heritage under an exclusively Iranian banner has obscured the monumental cultural interactions of various visiting and indigenous peoples of the plateau. How could it be legitimate to view these interactions in a narrow national context? The experiences, relationships, and commingled elements of multicultural communities in different periods are fully revealed in what is known as Persian literature. The admixtures of Jewish and Zoroastrian elements[1] or of Christian and Mithraist notions present in Farsi literature[2] are only two indications of deeply rooted cultural adaptations which recognize no specific territory or racial genius. The role of imported arts, from Chinese miniatures to Arabic poetical techniques to the role of Buddhism in Islamic mysticism[3] has been immense in the cultural development of the people of the Iranian plateau. The flow of ideas in the region stretching from India to the Mediterranean makes it impossible to draw a narrow conclusion about who was responsible for what developments in a national context over the centuries. It is true, however, that such an undertaking by the Orientalists in the course of reconstructing a

---

[1] Asmussen, "Some Remarks on the Zoroastrian Vocabulary of the Judeo-Persian Poet Šahin-i Sirazi of the 14th Century," pp. 137–143.

[2] Sadjadi, "Mithra et le Christ dans la Poesie de Khaghani: VIᵉ siècle de l'Hegire – XIIᵉ siècle," *Iran Ancien*, pp. 43–51.

[3] Mahdjoub, "The Indian Cultural Heritage and Its Effect on the Enrichment of the Islamic Civilization in Iran," pp. 177–195 (in Farsi); see also Vaziri, *Buddhism in Iran*, chapter 8.

national category of civilization for Iran (in part by disregarding many anthropological and sociological implications) helped the nationalist governments and secular nationalist educators to promote territorial and national identity among diverse people.

Even before the constructed national history had been digested, it became desirable to magnify dominant cultural and historical figures and traits to a national status. As with Dante in Italy and Goethe in Germany, who retroactively became the cultural heroes of their newly emerged nations, it comes as no surprise that Firdowsī became an Iranian one. Despite the argument that Firdowsī's poetry and role may only be understood fully in a cultural sense among Farsi speakers, he was lifted above any subculture or subcategory and given a national Iranian status. It became clear that, in the era of nationalism and of the imposition of Farsi as the national language of Iran, Firdowsī's *Shāhnāmeh* would gain new interpretations. Praise for the legend of Firdowsī now had to be expressed by all the inhabitants of Iran regardless of their ethnic or linguistic origin.

The contradiction in such an attitude was this: People in Iran who did not (and still do not) know Farsi now had to cherish Firdowsī as part of their heritage, while those who spoke and still speak Farsi outside Iran could only read and enjoy him without finding in his work any basis for national pride.

In relation to the *Shāhnāmeh* of Firdowsī, surely a serious scrutiny of the content, motives, and vocabularies involved is required in order to put the literary and political issues in proper perspective. Firdowsī's use of terms like *'Ajam, Farsi, Iran,* and *Fars* in relation to the Zoroastrian material and the current epic style of his time should be understood as originally intended and not necessarily interpreted according to distorted modern nationalist ideas. Nor should many of the rhetorical flourishes in the *Shāhnāmeh* be taken as literal assertions of fact.

In assessing other issues inspired by the Orientalists and subsequently assumed to be settled fact, scholars should carefully investigate regional and tribal matters in relation to national assertions. To elucidate particularly the ambiguities of an alleged Iranian identity among the tribal and ethnic groups of Iran, which have apparently maintained complex layers and levels of identity throughout the centuries, would clarify two important aspects of identity. First, it would uncover the identity question both on a micro level (time-and situation-specific) and on a macro level (tribal and ethnic) within any specific ethnic group. Second, it would clearly evaluate the consciousness of various tribal or ethnic groups vis-à-vis the Iranian identity. Such important studies in the future would also help us understand whether the gathering together of elements of various tribal groups (e.g., Kurds) either for autonomy or opposition has been prompted by outside pressures or by internal ones — and thus whether the unique ethnic identity of those involved is a result of contemporaneous events and lacks a historical basis or whether there are other anthropological explanations behind it. In other words, it is indispensable to understand the identity composition within each ethnicity in its historical and its modern perspective. Of course, with learning the Farsi language, as a means of binding the nation together through modern education and centralized state apparatus with its persuasive nationalist (and religious) promotion, the consciousness of many people within various ethnic groups have gone under a nationalist change.

Another key area to investigate is how, with the rise of a unique ethnic consciousness out of what was before simply a tribal system, each ethnicity's political alignments and oppositions against the central government have contributed to their sense of Iranian identity. The alignments of various ethnic and tribal groups into various factions favoring restoration of the constitutional government after the coup d'état of 1908, together with the countervailing trend evidenced by the sporadic uprisings of these ethnic groups for autonomy or defiance in the 1920s and 1940s, need to be convincingly explored in connection with their sense of identity. It appears that the cohesion that existed might have been achieved as a result of threats or pressure from outside, even though such cohesion would then have been wholly artificial. Certainly, a common historical consciousness is unnecessary to bring the people together under such circumstances. The consciousness might indeed result from the debasement of independent consciousness among the constituent groups. The Jewish national consciousness as Israelis and the subsequent Palestinian identity emerged as a consequence of the perceived threat of degeneration their individual identities faced, and thus they gradually legitimated their claims to special status in a historical context.

It is a question whether, among the Kurds or any other ethnic group in Iran, the sense of identity established under its tribal system (if it involved anything besides a common language) was created as a result of contemporaneous events or whether it had a material historical basis that can be proved. How such ethnic identities were incorporated into a larger (and territorial) Iranian identity is also an acute issue that demands adequate analysis. In attempting to address these questions without becoming entangled in *a priori* assumptions about the sense of historical identity possessed by members of linguistic minorities, as well as in the whole construct of national identity elaborated by Western Orientalists, one should seek out other parameters and criteria in order to construct an unbiased research methodology.

Many more issues could perhaps be brought to light as well in challenging the crude racially-oriented and nationalist paradigm by which the Iranian identity is conceptualized. My hope is that readers might suggest additional valuable topics of study in regard to national identity, not necessarily focused on modern nationality. I have tried to avoid the issue of nationality and to base my argument instead on the constructed historicity of Iranian identity. However, the Orientalist-constructed Iranian identity in its historical sense was in modern times used to forge an Iranian nationality in the world of nation-states. A person's nationality provided a reference point for citizenship or state and political-geographical affiliation, but the unfounded extremes of racial and chauvinist consciousness among indoctrinated Iranians has perverted this conception, so it has become more of a historical identity than a nationality. Similar feelings may be shared by Egyptians, Greeks, and others whose retrospectively constructed histories have encouraged them to view themselves as glorious historical entities rather than simply as members of modern nation-states. Having said that, it should be noted that the terms such as *Greek* (as opposed to *Hellene)* and *Egyptian* (as opposed to *Misr*), in their historical applications and subsequent conceptualization by Orientalists in a national context, should be scrutinized and criticized — just as the term *Iranian* has been investigated in this work.

Finally, this book has attempted to reveal the deleterious effects of racial and national thinking in Orientalist scholarship and to reveal its fallacious and anachronistic attributions of modern ideas to the past. This book has also tried to explore the link between the nineteenth- and twentieth-century nationalist movement and its exploitation of academic writings in promoting the historicity of Iranian identity. It may be within the reasoning power of this and future generations, by rectifying the mistakes and prejudices of ongoing colonial scholarship, to clear the intellectual air for a paradigm shift. This must be done with a goal of achieving an understanding of different peoples unsullied by national biases. This study has not tried to deny the reality of the modern Iranian identity and nation-state. It has only challenged the unwarranted approach to historical reconstruction used in regard to Iranian identity.

EPILOGUE

Twenty years ago, the central thesis of this book challenged the anachronistic construction of Iranian identity, claiming that the nationalist historiography first undertaken by the European Orientalists of the nineteenth and twentieth centuries eventually influenced the modern Iranian nationalist intelligentsia and literati, leading to the adoption of a broad nationalist construction of identity to suit Iranian political and ideological circumstances. This book argued that such a broad-brushed historical and dynastic approach could not have applied to the vast territory inhabited by large multiethnic, multilingual, and multicultural populations in Iran over so many distinct historical periods. The emergence of nationalism and modern Iranian identity in the sociopolitical scene in the late Qājār period was discussed separately, and distinguished from the Orientalist conceptualization of Iranian identity of the remote past created through crude academic use of archaeology, race theory, literature, mythical history, and other broad categories. In the twenty years since this book was first published, obviously much mixed scholarship on the topic of Iranian national identity and nationalism has been produced. But scholarship in Iranian studies apart from a few valuable studies has *generally* remained firm in pursuing its old methodology, which dominates the field and its establishments.

Various publications on the topic of national identity that argue for the historicity of Iranian identity have either flatly dismissed this book without proper evaluation of its arguments, misjudged it, purposefully ignored it, attacked it, referred only minimally to its existence, or placed it decoratively in their bibliography without any reference to it in the text (i.e., A. Marashi and A. Ansari). Others have praised this book and built upon it, used its arguments and sources to pursue their thesis of national identity, and constructively argued against it. Despite the strong forces of nationalism and resistance to ideas that challenge it, this book has both directly and indirectly caused some shifts in attitude among a number of scholars and students towards an Iranian national identity that was previously taken for granted, with its anachronistic historicism and invalid theories, including the Aryan race theory.

It is the nationalist coloring of Iranian identity that has so far prevented new students of history and social sciences from viewing Iran's past in a non-national context. Emerging generations should not be subjected exclusively to one established nationalist interpretation of regional histories. There is strong intellectual and scholarly need for a paradigm shift in order to more accurately interpret the complex Near Eastern, Central Asian, and Southern Persian Gulf cultures, linguistic patterns, and population compositions and bring history more in line with objectivity. But given the present political mood, any criticism against a historically constructed Iranian identity, even though discussions remain academic, faces harsh opposition by those who on political and personal grounds wish to counter the draconian religious politics and policies of the Islamic Republic. Because both the political culture and social opinions are so fragmented, the desire to take refuge in a pre-Islamic heritage simply in order to boost a secular national identity has been heightened inside and outside Iran. Therefore the academic discourse over the historicity of Iranian identity, especially in the Iranian community, is a more grueling task. However, a categorical refusal to engage in this dialogue risks ignoring one of the pending dilemmas of Iranology and Orientalism.

In recent scholarship there is still a disinclination, predominantly on the part of Iranian scholars, to acknowledge the Orientalist flaw which was later imitated by nationalist intellectuals in conceiving an anachronistic Iranian identity covering the last two thousand years. The construction of national identity was bound to the logic of the European concept of nation and was aligned with the late Qājār emergence of nationalism, as opposed to the actual reality of such Iranian identity existing as a historically linear phenomenon linking dynasties and the inhabitants of the plateau for many centuries. All but a few modern academics have continued to utilize the very same old approach, claiming that Iranian distinctiveness today is based on a foundation which has merely shaken off its historical dust. Even though their themes are of an engaging nature with more elaborate information, the outdated methodology still lingers in the background. In contrast, newer reflective studies offer open-minded interpretations of notions of *Iran* as geography and nation, *vatan* (homeland), modernization, nation-state building, and linguistic and cultural unification, or the "Persianization," of Iran of the Qājār and Pahlavi periods.

The newer studies also demonstrate that "Iran" had been used in a political and even literary sense in pre-modern times. Granted, the term "Iran" was used in the political sense by monarchs and historians, sporadically before and systematically after the Safavid period. But the political and historical use of the term *Iran* by the cultural and ruling elites does not represent the deeply rooted Iranian consciousness in pre-modern times among the diverse population that is believed to have lingered after the fall of the Sasanian Empire in the third century. A survey of the term *Iran* and nationalist contentions are not sufficient to support the claims of the existence of pre-modern Iranian identity. Such claims will have to be anthropologically measured against, for example, areas of the Persian Gulf which have been heavily influenced by Indian, Arab, and African cultures among others, and the Khurāsān region, which experienced Sino-Turkish and Indian influences, which cannot all be mechanically brushed away and grouped into a loose, un-examined "Iranian" national category. Many anthropological and sociological studies would need to be undertaken in order to properly substantiate any wide-ranging claims in regard to Iranian identity in pre-modern times.

The issue of identity has to be evaluated from the inside out and not *vice versa*. Until newer sound anthropological studies, instead of ill-defined claims and short footnotes, demonstrate that the notion of *Iran* has had social, cultural, linguistic, and "national" meanings, the central thesis of this book remains the same. In other words, two problems will have to be addressed and proved by social scientists who are eager to believe in the historicism of Iranian identity. First, if there was any meaningful continuity of "Iranian-ness" from pre-Islamic to Islamic all the way to modern times; second, and more important, whether the modern claims of historical national identity on the part of the masses in pre-modern times can ever be examined, or if it is simply that the elites exploited the term *Iran*.

In this Epilogue, the structural challenge to the old nationalist methodology still stands; in addition, arguments in light of newer studies about national identity are addressed. We shall address the following topics: the reaction to and general state of scholarship in the field of Iranian identity; the latest scholarship demonstrating how the nineteenth- and twentieth-century literati constructed Iranian identity; and finally some new perspectives on the study of national identity and reasons for its existence.

NATIONAL IDENTITY STUDIES IN HIGHLIGHT

The leading figure still strongly committed to historicizing, archaizing, and proving Iranian national identity by tying together miscellaneous elements of history, and thus utilizing the old nationalist methodology, is Ahmad Ashraf.[1] It would require a separate article to argue and re-evaluate many of Ashraf's assertions and documentations in the *Encyclopaedia Iranica*. It suffices to say that his articles are more inclusive than most Iranian nationalist authors have ever written, although the approach is familiar: grouping together scattered dynastic, linguistic, geographic, and religious themes without considering or recognizing the necessity for detailed study of each theme in its given context and its historical period. In other words, the appearance of the word "Iran" in scattered documents is no guarantee for the continuity of Iranian identity on a mass level over a period of two thousand years. However, no analysis about the modern discourse of national identity has been more inclusive and balanced than the chapter recently produced by Afshin Matin-Asgari in 2012. In his chapter Matin-Asgari objectively puts major studies of national identity, including the premise of this volume, in perspective and compares

---

[1] See Ashraf, "Iranian Identity i: Perspectives," and "Iranian Identity iii: Medieval Islamic Period," *Encyclopaedia Iranica*.

and weighs the assertions against the rationales and methods of argumentation of their authors.[2]

In attempting to understand the notion of Iranian identity in the past and in modern times, other published analyses of popular and allegorical themes of *vatan* (fatherland, motherland,[3] homeland), Iran and Zoroastrianism, the emergence of Qājār nationalism, and Occidentalism. Much more has been and perhaps will be published because this topic continues to be in demand by the audience for nationalism and the politics of Iranology.[4]

One of the results of tying together scattered events (especially the anti-caliphate or anti-Islamic events) and themes in nationalist methodology in order to demonstrate continuity of Iranian consciousness is inconsistency and oversimplification. A self-contradictory nationalist example is the movement of Bābak

---

[2] Matin-Asgari, "The Academic Debate on Iranian Identity: Nation and Empire Entangled," pp. 171–190.

[3] For an interesting discussion about the premise and psychology of male-based patriotism and gender of homeland, see Najmabadi, "The Erotic Vatan [Homeland] as Beloved and Mother: To Love, to Possess, and to Protect," pp. 442–467; see also Kashani-Sabet, *Frontier Fictions: Shaping the Iranian Nation, 1804–1946*, pp. 137–139, 195–198; see also Tavakoli-Targhi, "From Patriotism to Matriotism: A Tropological Study of Iranian Nationalism, 1870–1909," pp. 217–238.

[4] For another routine nationalist report of Iranian identity, see H. Ahmadi, "Unity Within Diversity: Foundations and Dynamics of National Identity in Iran," pp. 127–147 (one of the premises of this article is to argue against the notion that Westerners or Orientalists had anything to do with the construction of historical national identity in regard to Iran, but it fails to notice that most of its supporting definitions of nation and national identity are based on quotations extracted from Western conceptions. Furthermore, its redundancy of themes is a commonly known narrative which the previous nationalist authors have used in an attempt to historicize and to join together the continuity of disjointed events in Iran); another study is by Farhi, "Crafting National Identity amidst Contentious Politics in Contemporary Iran," pp. 7–22 (this is a mixture of historical and modern claims about the consolidation of identity in Iran).

Khurramdin, who is often heedlessly interpreted in a "national Iranian" vein, as seen in multiple scholarly works. In fact, as Patricia Crone has argued, in this local revolt against the Arab-Muslim warlords, Bābak was confronted and defeated by Afshin, a so-called "Iranian" general leading an army against him.[5] Avoidable negligence, laxity, and sometimes hastiness in interpreting such past events in a dogmatically nationalist light have led to contradictory conclusions.

The other general approach in historical identity construction pertains to the geographical boundary of Iran. Many unyielding promoters of nationalism have neglected to consider its shifting borders and populations in different periods of history. The dominant view in the old school of Iranian nationalist historiography has been to perceive the whole of pre-modern and modern Iran as the basis of a blanket "Iranian" ancestry without any consideration for all the historical shifts and diverse groups in that region. The anthropological impossibility of this view should prod anthropologists[6] to pursue further research into the past cultures within the Iranian plateau in a non-national context. The impossibility of this view must also awaken our natural sense of reason to see how different and alien the communities of the past have been, compared to ours. The study of the past must avoid resorting to a projected nationalist and sentimentalist attitude and judgment.

In order to revisit and debate the problem of historicism of Iranian national identity from different angles, other than what was already presented in the first edition of this book, we will consider the issues involved with reinforcing historical Iranian identity on the basis of the Persian language, the Sasanian-Zoroastrian definition of Iran, and geography in light of newer studies.

---

[5] Crone, "Babak's Revolt," in http://www.parstimes.com/history/ babak.pdf; see also Browne, *A Literary History of Persia*, pp. 331, 334–335.

[6] For fresher and anthropological views on Iran, see Fazeli, *Politics of Culture in Iran: Anthropology, Politics and Society in the Twentieth Century*, particularly chapters 2 and 3: "Anthropology and Iranian Cultures" and "Anthropology and Nationalism."

1. Persian: a Trans-National, not a National, Language

The existence of the Persian language has been exploited to forge a broader historical category of national identity even for those who never spoke it in the Iranian plateau. This nationalist enterprise was largely carried out in the minds of its promoters without having tested the authenticity and realism of their conceptions with the population at large, especially among rural, tribal, linguistically diverse people, asking if they or their ancestors ever spoke Persian. The nineteenth- and early twentieth-century intellectual writing and interpretation of history books and the idea of a national language were elusive but were pushed for acceptance nationwide. In order to make the nationalist case for the Persian language and to give it a potent continuity, a history was constructed for it. The later classification and link between the Achaemenid "Old Persian" (the name of the Achaemenid language is unknown) and New Persian was to a large extent an arbitrary conception[7] that depicted people, language, and land (even the Aryan race) as unremitting historical partners.

The belief that Persian has been the national language of Iran from medieval times onward, and that even the medieval *Shu'ubiya* movement against Arab privileges was based on national and linguistic claims,[8] is erroneous. The *Shu'ubiya* did not stand for a Persian identity contrasted with an Arab identity. This ubiquitous assumption is imprudent scholarship. The strong grievance and opposition against the privileges of the Arabs or Muslims vis-à-vis other groups was similarly an issue in medieval al-Andalus (Spain), where the opposition was not ethnic, but rather political, military, and economic.[9] At a minimum, the boundaries of faith and other loyalties demand newer studies in the anthropology of medieval Iran, rather than simply grouping any opposition — including literary opposition — to the caliphate, Arabs, or Islam together as signs of "Iranian" poise and self-assertion. Besides the *Shu'ubiya*,

---

[7] Daryaee, *Sasanian Persia: The Rise and Fall of Empire*, p. 102.

[8] Richter-Bernburg, "Linguistic Shu'ūbīya and Early Neo-Persian Prose," pp. 55–64.

[9] See Safran, "Identity and Differentiation in Ninth-Century al-Andalus," p. 574.

those who spoke and continue to speak Persian cannot be narrowly associated with Iranian identity or the identity of any particular land, given the widespread history of this language throughout the centuries.

Therefore, let us take a different approach to the problem of the continuing claim of the Persian language as a historical dispositive and basis for a historical Iranian national identity. It is true that New Persian, with its different dialects, has been spoken by pockets of people inside Iran for the last thousand years. Furthermore, much literature inside Iran was produced in Persian. But no less was produced outside Iran in the Persephone regions of Afghanistan, India, Central Asia, and even by the Ottomans.[10] First of all, the development and rise of the Persian language in Khurāsān and Central Asia makes it difficult to trace it to the language of the Sasanians, which came to be constructed among the philologists as "Middle Persian," with "Middle" only an arbitrary designation to emphasize its continuity to "Modern." The two hundred year gap between the fall of the Sasanians in the mid-seventh century and the emergence of New Persian with Arabic alphabets in Afghanistan and Central Asian regions had nothing to do with the suppression of the Persian language by the ruling Arabs. On the contrary, the translation and protection of Middle Persian books were encouraged, and the Zoroastrians continued producing literature at least until the early ninth century. The Orientalist introduction of the idea of a "Persian Renaissance" is also absurd and imaginary if Persian already existed and was fully developed around the ninth century, as it certainly was by the tenth century at the time of Rudakī, Daqīqī, and Firdowsī in Central Asia and Eastern Iran. And if this language did not exist it was not then a "Renaissance."[11] Furthermore, the disharmony in linking the Persian language and Iranian identity is seen with the preference of

---

[10] For the Ottoman use of Persian language and poetry there are many references. See Gábor Ágoston and Bruce Masters (eds.), *Encyclopedia of the Ottoman Empire*, pp. 322–323.

[11] Wilson, "The Formation of Modern Persian, the Beginnings and Progress of the Literature, and the So-Called Renaissance," pp. 215, 222–223.

Arabic over Persian by the tenth-century Buyid dynasty (which in scholarship is seen as the reviver of ancient Iranian tradition and identity) in the western Iranian territory. As Roy Mottahedeh argues, the Buyids' preference for Arabic over Persian was tied to several factors: their own presence in Baghdad and their obvious interest in Arabic; the presence of Zoroastrian priests in western and southern Iran who preferred Pahlavi over New Persian; and possibly also the Buyids' political opposition to the eastern Sāmānid dynasty and their adoption of New Persian.[12] The other issue is that the simultaneous rise of Persian in the ninth century in Central Asia coincided with the decline of the Soghdian language during the same period. The curious similarities of the two languages[13] and the dissociation of New Persian from so-called Middle Persian (Pahlavi) of western Iran call for new research.

Giving the Persian language a national character comes out of the nineteenth-century Orientalist interest in languages and literature in a national context. In the Orientalist writings, Persian literature was fully associated with nowhere else but greater Iranian territory. This was the means of understanding and historicizing nations which later resulted in associating language with the idea of

---

[12] Mottahedeh, "The Idea of Iran in the Buyid Dominions," pp. 157–158. ("All the preceding, and much more, is to say that although the Buyids had a sentimental attachment to the Iranian past and, in particular, to an Iranian tradition of kingship, they were not attracted to the New Persian learning of eastern Iran." p. 155).

The Buyids' affinity towards Iranian heritage has been argued based on very little evidence; there was nothing concretely expressed on what it meant to be 'Iranian' in the tenth century. In addition, the academic claims of the revival of Iranian heritage by the Buyids must be assessed against what the masses understood by the label 'Iranian' in the tenth century. The lack of the Buyids' affinity towards New Persian also seems to have weakened the theory of their "Iranianness," but at the same time it must be borne in mind that in any case the Persian language, due to its continental status, has never been part of Iranian identity until modern times.

[13] For the similarities of vocabulary, see Henning, "Soghdian Loan-words in New Persian," pp. 93–106.

race and eventually territory. The interest in the Iranian and Indian national idea and in Indo-European and Aryan studies was well underway when William Jones,[14] working in Kolkata in 1786 (during the late Zand period), made his landmark claim of similarity between Sanskrit and Latin and Greek.

Another consequential implication found in the work of Orientalism was the confusion between "Persian" as the designation for the language, and "Persia" for the territory. For example, Joseph von Hammer-Purgstall in 1818 when he was finishing his book *Geschichte der Schönen Redekünste Persiens* (The History of Fine Rhetoric of Persia), obviously associated the Persian language with Persia, a precedent that other Orientalists followed despite the fact the name Iran replaced Persia in the next century in the Western vocabulary. The original flaw may even be traced back to the ancient Greeks, who labeled the empire as *Persis*.

As a consequence of this Persian-Persia linguistic-territory conflation, India, Tajikistan, Afghanistan, and other Persephone regions were often ignored and left out in treating the non-national history of the Persian language. In addition, the use of the Central Asian and Afghan term *Dari* for the same language was ignored by the Orientalist and Iranian nationalist authors. The term *Farsi* or *Persian*, not *Dari*, was used and facilitated by the Orientalist and modern Iranian writers, and came to be associated with Persia as its national language. In brief, the etymological similarity between *Persian* and *Persia* in Western use did not exist at all inside Iran, where the language is called *Farsi* and the country *Iran*. In the same manner *Dari* and *Afghanistan* could not be accommodated as a language-land pair.

The formal introduction of Persian in India under the Mughal Empire (1526–1857) (after a brief influx of the Turkish language under the Chagatai Turks) did not mean that Persian had no earlier presence on the Indian subcontinent. On the contrary, many Persian poets came out of India long before the Mughal era (i.e.

---

[14] For an interesting treatment of William Jones' career, see Edgerton, "Sir William Jones: 1746–1794," 230–239.

Amīr Khusrau, 1253–1325).[15] With the development of *maktab* and *madrasa* education in India, Hindus also began to learn Persian on a wide scale. Thus the Mughal rulers meant to bring all elements of India together under one language, as a means of nation-building.[16] Persian remained a strong vernacular language until the nineteenth-century colonization of Persephone Central Asia by the Russians, and India by the British, which reduced and suppressed this once-powerful vernacular language.[17] This transnational decline in other regions reduced the possibility of Persian becoming the national language of India and some Central Asian Republics, but placed Persian in new circumstances with different historical standards in Iran as it gradually became recognized not only as a national language but also as the national property of Iran. According to Bert Fragner, the claim of the Persian language's connection with Persia as the symbol of "Persian Renaissance" is a historical irrelevance.[18] Of course, in treating the Persian language as a continuous Iranian heritage, as discussed in this book, one should not ignore the monumental work in the twentieth century by E. G. Browne, to whom Geoffrey Nash elaborately dedicates a chapter in his 2005 studies of the travellers of the Orient.[19]

Friedrich von Schlegel, one of the proponents of Aryanism in his *Rede über die Mythologie*, in 1800 romanticized the importance of literature and philosophy, particularly in the Orient.[20] This triggered a new interest in literature and language that led to the establishment of literary periodicals engaged in publishing Oriental literature. Joseph von Hammer-Purgstall, the Habsburg diplomat and linguist, founded his journal, *Fundgruben des Orients*, in Munich

---

[15] Alam, "The Pursuit of Persian: Language in Mughal Politics," pp. 317–349.

[16] Ibid., pp. 326–327, 348.

[17] Fragner, "Das Persisch als Hegemonialsprache in der islamischen Geschichte," p. 47.

[18] Fragner, pp. 41, 48.

[19] Nash, *From Empire to Orient: Travellers to the Middle East 1830–1926*, pp. 139–157.

[20] Tzoref-Ashkenazi, "India and the Identity of Europe: The Case of Friedrich Schlegel," pp. 720, 724.

in 1809. This example was followed by the establishment of *Journal Asiatique* in Paris in 1822, *Journal of the Royal Asiatic Society* in London in 1834, and *Zeitschrift der Deutschen Morgenländischen Gesellschaft* in Berlin in 1847.

Hammer-Purgstall actually went on to translate the entire *Divan* of Hafiz from Persian into German; his translation was completed and published in Vienna in 1813. This seminal translation moved Goethe to take a great interest in Hafiz, and to formulate in one of his own poems the marriage between word and mind, a phenomenon found in Hafizian poetry.[21] The European, and even to a degree American, interest in Hafiz continued almost uninterrupted for the next 40 years. Works in a Hafizian style included Goethe's *West-östlicher Divan* in 1819 and another volume in 1827 with more poems, as well as works by Orientalists well-versed in Persian: Friedrich Rückert's *Östlicher Rosen* in 1822; the young August Graf von Platen's *Spiegel des Hafis* and *Ghasalen* in 1821 and 1823.[22] (In fact the passion of Platen for Hafiz can be exemplified in his quest to translate Hafiz's *Divan*: when he could not afford to buy a copy, he sat in the Göttingen library and copied the whole *Divan* by hand.)[23] These European individuals shared a passion for Hafiz with the Persian-speaking inhabitants of Iran, Afghanistan, Central Asia, the Ottoman court and India. In fact, it was a common saying that every literate Indian Muslim household contained two books: the Koran and the *Divan* of Hafiz. Many hand-written copies of the *Divan* are still available in museums in Dhaka, Kolkata, Delhi, and other major cities of India, Bangladesh, and Pakistan. However, for the Europeans, Hafiz and the Persian language were already associated exclusively with Persia or Iran.

---

[21] *Sei das Wort die Braut gennant, Bräutigen der Geist; Diese Hochzeit hat gekannt − Wer Hafisien preist.* (Words being called the bride, the spirit the bridegroom; He who has known this wedding − Is he who knows and praises Hafiz.)

[22] von Hammer-Purgstall, *Der Diwan von Mohammed Schamsed-din Hafis: Aus dem Persischen zum erstemal ganz übersetzt*; Schimmel (ed.), *Friedrich Rückert, 1788–1866: Übersetzungen persischer Poesie*. For more details and a bibliography, see Vaziri, *Quantum Poetry: Verses of Hafiz*, pp. 12–19.

[23] Vaziri, *Quantum Poetry*, p. 19.

The reality of political and cultural life in Iran was a different scenario from the European romantic view of an Iranian society imbued with Persian literacy. The rise of the Turkish Qājār dynasty in 1794 occurred, in the power vacuum created by civil war, through murdering and blinding a great number of local populations and suppressing all political rivals. This period exacerbated previous conditions of civil unrest, poverty, infectious diseases, sectarian conflicts between the Sunnis and Shiʻites, and discord with other religious minorities. The strife was coupled with a lack of infrastructure in the crumbling empire. Furthermore, this weak dynasty seemed to have little interest in or knowledge about the local customs and languages in the geographical boundaries of its new territory. Instead, the culturally apathetic Qājār rulers engaged in defensive and expansionist wars, self-absorption, and pleasure while the rest of the population was left to fend for themselves, following local tribal laws and customs and traditional oral learning.

During this period in Iran it is not clear how many Kurds, Baluchis, Gilakis, Mazandaranis, Azari Turks, and other groups outside of the main Persian-speaking areas spoke Persian or could read Hafiz, or whether they associated the Persian language with a vast land of Iran at all. Was there any awareness among them that Persian, a language that was not their mother tongue, was the national language of Iran? It is not clear whether ordinary people, including even the Persian speakers, gave much thought to a link between the Persian language and Iran in pre-modern times. But it is known that there was massive illiteracy in the nineteenth century. It has to be borne in mind that during the same period when the majority of the inhabitants of Iran did not know Persian, many literate people in India, Afghanistan, and Central Asia spoke Persian and fancied Hafiz's poetry. As an example of how Persian was neglected in nineteenth-century Iran, it is interesting to note that when Nasir al-Din Shah left Tabriz for Tehran he was still not Persephone but *only* Turcophone.[24]

To promote Persian as a natural national language of Iran, nationalist writers frequently link it with Firdowsī's *Shāhnāmeh* and

---

[24] See Amanat, *Pivot of the Universe*, p. 63.

the Sasanians' sponsoring of the original mythical historiography of
Khawday Namag (*Shāhnāmeh*). This approach needs some refinement
here. Because of the Sasanian use of terms such as *Ir* or *Iran*, the
rise of the Sasanian dynasty to power in 224 CE is perceived to be a
hallmark and prototype of Iranian "nationalism" and to be the time
when "Iranian" identity systematically emerged. Among many
Orientalists and custodians of Iranology it is a common belief that
the Sasanian Iranian identity disintegrated after the Arab-Muslim
conquest of Iran, but the writings of Firdowsī revived the dim
memories of Sasanian identity and ancient Iranian identity. Qājār
intellectuals continued to resuscitate this presumably faded and
forgotten identity based on nationalist assertions in the nineteenth
century, putting the Persian language at the center of this lost
identity.

A study by Mohamad Tavakoli-Targhi (2001) claims in the
same vein that the Zoroastrian priests of India, before the impact
of academic Orientalism, played a role in reviving the pre-Islamic
Iranian identity, basing his claim on their preservation of the
Shāhnāmeh and polemicizing against Islam.[25] Despite this claim, the

---

[25] See Tavakoli-Targhi, *Refashioning Iran: Orientalism, Occidentalism, and
Historiography*, pp. 96–101. In his treatment of national identity, Tavakoli-
Targhi eventually has to resort to Qājār intellectuals (i.e. 'Itimad al-Saltana
and Kirmani) to continue the discourse of nationalism stemming from
inside Iran, not India, and to admit the impact of Orientalism on
nationalist historiography in Iran: see pp. 96, 99–100, 143. The
Zoroastrian Parsis, compared to the scientific and academic sources, had
very little, if any, influence on the literati's historical thinking and
approaches to modernity as portrayed in Tavakoli-Targhi's book. In his
detouring to construct national awareness, Tavakoli-Targhi returns to
some ideas familiar from *Iran as Imagined Nation*. As much as Tavakoli-
Targhi tries to take our focus off the real carriers of nationalism, he
occasionally returns to them: "These nationalist historical perspectives
were often informed by and corroborated Orientalist historical writings.
Both nationalist and Orientalist historiography assumed a continuity
between the contemporary and ancient Iran..." (p. 143); "The invention
of a glorious past was contemporaneous with a through restylization of
the Persian language." (p. 104); and some more that can be omitted here.

rise of nationalism or national awareness in Iran was likely based very little, if any, on the work of a small group of Zoroastrians who made some scholarly contribution in the field of Orientalism in India. Instead, the key promoters of nationalism and the *Shāhnāmeh* in Iran exploited Orientalist notions of Iranian and Aryanism. Moreover the use of the term "persianate"[26] by Tavakoli-Targhi for

---

This note is not intended to be a review of Tavakoli-Targhi's book; it suffices to say that, although the chapters are somehow disjointed and independent from the main narrative, his book brings in many interesting elements from Indian Persian heritage and oriental travel diaries of European tours. At the end it must be noted that some of his ideas were already familiar to scholarship. See also Tavakoli-Targhi, "Contested Memories: Narrative Structures and Allegorical Meanings of Iran's Pre-Islamic History," pp. 149–175. The analysis in this article over-emphasizes the role of Zoroastrian literature aimed at polemicizing against Islam and biblical (Adamic) history while trying to legitimize their own history and that of an 'Iranian' nation. But the approach of these Zoroastrians in restructuring pre-Islamic mythical history and maintaining polemics against Islam, especially from their Indian base, could not have been solid enough to either trigger any nationalist Iranian sentiment nor was their material empirical enough to be used as a raw material for the custodians of Iranian nationalism. (The Parsis of India have never shown any interest in returning to Iran. Their primary interests in India, apart from education, have been trade and philanthropy.)

[26] Tavakoli-Targhi, *Refashioning Iran*. The term "persianate" occurs quite frequently throughout the book as a substitute for "Indians" or "Indian Parsis," presumably because the author refused to refer to the Indian contribution to Orientalism from which Anquetil DuPerron and William Jones benefited. For the Orientalists, learning languages and being apprenticed to their Indian teachers, similar to Adam Olearius exchanging German for Persian in the late 1600s with his friend in Iran, does not make their teachers and translators of texts into Persian in India the source of modernism and the "forgotten founders" of Orientalism. Tavakoli also believes the Orient shaped the Occident. But this meager claim cannot be based on a few translations or diaries about the West by the Indians or Iranians. Moreover, Occidentalism does not have the same academic and empirical premise as Orientalism, and it is thus an arbitrary label without widespread acceptance as a serious discipline.

those Indian scholars whose mother tongue or working tongue was Persian would dissociate the Persian language from India and erroneously associate its origin with Persia or Iran. In this context the usage of "persianate" other than referring to Persian speakers is rather ambiguous, and in fact it serves to bypass and ignore the pre-modern identity of other regions, in this case India, just because they happened to be Persian-speaking. The use of "persianate" can misleadingly tie the speakers of Persian with Persia. The Mughal rulers and intellectuals may have dealt with their Persian-speaking counterparts in Iran but never considered themselves to be of "Iranian" origin. This assumption completely ignores the transnational dimension of the Persian language and insists on Persian as the national language exclusively of Iran, and not of India, although the latter was also the proper historical context for the Zoroastrian priests' writings.[27]

The invention of Aryan racial theory occurred in Europe, not in India or Iran. Thus in extracting ideas from European Orientalist sources, modern Iranian cultural frontrunners began to link the *Shāhnāmeh* not only with the ancient roots of the Persian language but also with the idea of an Aryan nation and race. It is the myth and the Indo-Europeanization and Aryanization of history in Iran that "infects some Iranian scholars' view of the *Shāhnāmeh*," as Omidsalar agrees.[28] Attempts by various modern authors and reformers to use Sasanian historiography in connection with Firdowsī were clearly aimed at overthrowing the medieval view of Islamic history and replacing it with an "Iranian" one, albeit mythical. The intricacy of linking the Persian language with Firdowsī's *Shāhnāmeh*, with Sasanian historiography reflected in the *Shāhnāmeh*, and finally the choice of Persian as the Iranian national

---

[27] For Persian works on India and Indian use of the Persian language between the 13th and the 19th centuries, there are some interesting entries on the Perso-Indica website: http://www.perso-indica.net/. In addition, the collection of Mughal texts at the Red Fort (Lāl Qīlā) Museum in Delhi contains copies of the *Divan-e-Hafiz* dating to 1578, Rumi's *Masnavi* dated 1602, and *Shāhnāmeh* dated from the 17ᵗʰ century.

[28] Omidsalar, *Poetics and Politics of Iran's National Epic, The Shāhnāmeh*, p. 3.

language created enough plausible grounds for thinking that the Persian language and Iran have always been concomitant — a nationalist platform through which Afghans, Tajiks, Indians, and others have partially lost their own claims to the Persian language, at least in scholarship.

Thus it can be believed that Persian emerged as the national language of Iran as a consequence of three major modern events: The suppression of the Persian language in India and Central Asia through European colonization; the emergence of intelligentsia as well as a nationalist reform movement in Iran; and the insistence within the field of Orientalism that Persian evolved in different historical stages before taking its final shape of New Persian as the natural property of *Persia*. Not to be ignored, as demonstrated by Denis Hermann, the defiance of Qājār intellectuals against Arabic teaching increased the debate over reducing the power of Arabic and boosting the Persian language in education instead.[29] The modernization of Iran as a nation-state has resulted in a large number of people adhering to the notion that Persian has always been the national language of Iran while ignoring its transnational and historical dimension.

2. Sasanian Iran

Let us now turn our attention to the theme of the Sasanian dynasty in the construction of Iranian identity. The nationalist intellectuals and political leaders, particularly of the Pahlavi period, saw fit to "revive" the Sasanian notion of Iran and give modern Iranian national identity a historical interpretation by indiscriminately including all the inhabitants of Iran ever since the fall of the Sasanians. The Sasanian-Zoroastrian term, *Iranshahr* or *Iranzamin*, took on two levels of interpretation for the Iranian nationalists: *Iran* was used as a Zoroastrian term describing a religious sense of self and sense of foreigners, and also as a territorial specification. The religious-national consciousness of Zoroastrianism during the Sasanian period that was first described by the Orientalists was

---

[29] See Hermann, "La défense de l'enseignement de l'arabe au cours du mouvement constitutionnel iranien," pp. 301–321, esp. pp. 301–304.

then followed by the nationalist scholars in order to forge a territorial Iranian consciousness as far back as the Achaemenids, all the way to the Sasanians. Let us take on this debate from a different angle.

Whatever the origin of "Iran" may have been, it cannot predate the time of Zoroaster and the Achaemenids. Zoroastrianism seems to be the evolution of the older traditions of dualism (Zurvanism) and it is difficult to accept the idea that the Achaemenids were the upholders of Zoroastrianism, since the Avesta never mentioned them.[30] The rigid Zoroastrian-Achaemenid model created by various scholars is problematic: it is circumstantial, not based on concrete evidence.[31] In order to create a national and religious continuity in ancient times, the idea of the Achaemenids being Zoroastrian was promoted by E. Herzfeld.[32] Neither the great deity Ahura Mazda, who antedates Zoroastrianism, nor the Achaemenid rulers themselves created a national order. They did not create a "nation" in which the masses converted to Zoroastrianism, given the lengthy time required for any religion to evolve as well as to communicate its teachings in a territory as vast as the entire Iranian plateau.[33] Furthermore, the ethnic origin, identity, and language of Cyrus, the founder of the "Persian Empire," may have been Elamite (non-Iranian), as a new study by Potts speculates.[34]

Regarding the question of whether Achaemenid or even the Parthian dynasties had any national Aryan consciousness, or used Ērānshahr or similar appellations in the Iranian context, one recent chapter by the late archaeologist Shapur Shahbazi stands out as being rigidly behind this hypothesis. The central purpose of

---

[30] See Daryaee, "National History or Keyanid History? The Nature of Sasanid Zoroastrian Historiography," pp. 138–139.

[31] Skjærvø, "The Achaemenids and the Avesta," in *Birth of the Persian Empire*, pp. 52, 80–81.

[32] Darby Nock, "The Problem of Zoroaster," pp. 273–274, 276, 283.

[33] Ibid., p. 275.

[34] Potts, "Cyrus the Great and the Kingdom of Anshan," in *Birth of the Persian Empire*, pp. 7–28. For an alternative view of Cyrus, see Asgharzadeh, *Iran and the Challenge of Diversity*, pp. 52–53.

Shahbazi's (2005) very short chapter is to challenge G. Gnoli's argument (as well as the arguments of the present book) that there was no "Iranian" consciousness prior to the Sasanians. Shahbazi in his chapter derogatorily refers to *Iran as Imagined Nation* without mentioning its author in the text or bibliography, as if Gnoli is the only party he is arguing with. In any case, Shahbazi tries to revive the already-challenged scholarship, sometimes referring to the Achaemenids as "Persian Rule" and trying to reestablish that Achaemenid, Parthian, and Sasanian dynasties all used "Ariana" and "Iran" in order to maintain Iranian national statehood and society. However, despite his fervent use of archaeological literature, Shahbazi fails in this attempt because of the contradictions between his claims.

The first problem arises when considering Achaemenid use of the Avestan word *Airya* to identify the geographical region and ethnicity in the eastern part of their empire, predominantly Afghanistan and Central Asia. First, Shahbazi notes that the Achaemenids were aware that not all of the inhabitants in their empire were of Aryan heritage. This is followed with an acknowledgement that only Central Asian and Afghanistan regions were called Ariana (Aryan), not the plateau (which was still not called Iran).[35] But Shahbazi cannot explain why, if the Achaemenids were aware of their Aryan ethnicity, Zoroastrianism, and their so-called "Iranian" rule, they would name *eastern* lands Ariana and yet choose to conduct their imperial rule from a so-called non-Aryan territory in the southwestern (Iranian) plateau, the Fars region which is *not* within the Avestan and Aryan ("Iranian") geography. Claims of the Aryanism or Iranism of the Achaemenids are anachronistic, unsubstantiated, and contradictory. Furthermore, using the claim of Herzfeld's idea of the Persian Empire within the Avestan context against Gnoli's denial of it[36] is unsupported.

The second obvious contradiction is about Parthians who "continued to use the name *Ērānšahr* for their original country and

---

[35] Shahbazi, "The History of the Idea of Iran," pp. 103–105.
[36] Shahbazi, p. 105.

its surroundings."[37] Of course this could not be substantiated, yet in the same paragraph it is stated: "Nevertheless, that *Ērānšahr* persisted in oral tradition as the logical historic development of an earlier, Achaemenid *Aryānām xšaçam* — even if it is not attested in the surviving records of the time …"[38] The oral tradition and lack of evidence makes it impossible to support these unwarranted assertions. The arguments of Shahbazi provide no new findings, are rather redundant, and can be considered outdated. Not only does he fail to undo the scholarship of Gnoli, but he tries in vain to recapture Iranian national identity through one thousand years of ancient time with almost no concrete evidence in just nine unconvincingly argued and constructed pages. In brief, the construction of Iranian identity before the Sasanian period is arbitrary and cannot simply be based on archaeological assumptions.

This brings us to the use of *Iran* in the Sasanian period, whether in geographical, religious, or ethnic contexts. Regarding the Sasanian sense of identity, Gnoli in his recent entry in the *Encyclopaedia Iranica* states, "The idea of an 'Iranian' empire or kingdom is a purely Sasanian one," though this statement is supported by the claim that "Aryan" as an "Iranian" ethnicity existed before the Sasanians.[39] Touraj Daryaee, in his research, has tried to demonstrate that the Sasanians used *Ērānshahr* (*Iranshahr*) and *Iran* as designations for the extent of land and its "citizens." These assertions should be examined for their viability.

The confusion in connecting *Iran* with Zoroastrianism arises from the problem that *old* Avesta did not include the territorial notion of *Ērānshahr* and had nothing to do with Iranian geography.[40] We can simply assume that *old* Avestan geography had

---

[37] Ibid., p. 107.

[38] Ibid.

[39] Gnoli, "Iranian Identity ii: Pre-Islamic Period," *Encyclopaedia Iranica*, December 2006, accessed in June 2012.

[40] The Avestan territory of *Airyana vāējah* lies in Central Asia and contains the heartland of Afghanistan. See page 77 of the present edition; see also Grenet, "An Archaeologist's Approach to Avestan Geography," pp. 29–51.

nothing specifically to do with what became known as Iran, other than exploiting the term *arya*. Moreover, Sasanian's *Ērānshahr* and its expansion included the western Asian, Arabian, and even African territories of Egypt, Libya, and Ethiopia.[41] Meanwhile the ancient "citizens" of *Ērān* enjoyed privileges, while others, labeled *an-Ērān* (Aniran/non-Iranians), were denied privileges, either because they lived outside of the territory or on political and religious grounds.[42] This "non-Iranian" status included "Iranian"-born Manichaeans because of their apostasy. Gnoli describes the crises of Manichaeism and Zoroastrianism as the conflict between universalism and nationalism.[43] This is of course a modern formulation of religions, contrasting Zoroastrianism, commonly known as "national or state" religion of the Sasanians, with the Gnostic and universal messages of Manichaeism.

It has been further asserted that Zoroastrianism made no distinction between religion and ethnicity, since the designation of *ēr* was used for Zoroastrians and non-Zoroastrians, whether Christians or Jews.[44] But the meaning of *ir* or *ēr* from most references was religious, not ethnic, and perhaps even referred to monotheists like the Jews and Christians (and unlike the Gnostic Manichaean community) alongside the Zoroastrians. In Islam, *mu'min* and *kāfir* have been used as non-ethnic characterization referring to the faithful and pagan. In the Zoroastrian 'theocratic' context *ir* is used in the same way. *Ir* or *ēr* seems to designate people living under Zoroastrian rule and complying with the Zoroastrian code of non-sinful behavior, which did not include Manichaeans and Mazdakis, the apostates who were figuratively the indigenous citizens of *Iranshahr*. *Ērān* and *an-Ērān*, it is safe to say, were used in a Zoroastrian religious context for friends and enemies of the religious and political establishment. For an antique

---

[41] Daryaee, "Ethnic and Territorial Boundaries in Late Antique and Early Medieval Persia (Third to Tenth Century)," pp. 132, 134.

[42] Daryaee, *Sasanian Persia*, 5, 55–56; Daryaee, "Ethnic and Territorial Boundaries," p. 137.

[43] Gnoli, "Iranian Identity ii: Pre-Islamic Period," *Encyclopaedia Iranica*.

[44] Daryaee, "Ethnic and Territorial Boundaries," 124; Daryaee, *Sasanian Persia*, p. 56.

dynasty such as the Sasanian, applying the term "nation" is an arbitrary and imaginary construction since "nation" is a modern concept, along with national identity and all its modernizing characteristics.[45] This derails and contradicts the claims about Sasanian ethnic or national consciousness, ethnic Aryan identity, and in general about the Iranian identity in a territorial sense, at least during the Sasanian period.

Assuming the correctness of information about the usage of *ēr*, *Ērān*, and *Ērānshahr* by the Sasanian Zoroastrian officials for their land and subjects, one study challenges the notion of Sasanians ever being a centralized state as previously believed. In her 2008 controversial and painstaking studies of the Sasanian era, Parvaneh Pourshariati argues that the defeated Parthians, who never vanished from the political scene, created a confederacy with the Sasanians in control of Eastern Iran and its Central Asian regions. These Parthians were Mithraists, in contrast to the Sasanians, the majority of whom were Zoroastrians. Pourshariati further challenges and renders obsolete the classic Orientalist work of Arthur Christensen, which perceived Sasanians as a highly centralized "Iranian" empire.[46] Even as Daryaee pursues national construction of Iranian identity through continuity of pre-Islamic dynasties, he admits that the elimination of Achaemenid (other than Darius or Dara) and a number of the Parthian kings from *Khuwday Namag* (i.e. *Shāhnāmeh*) had to do with the Zoroastrian religious bias, in their selective historiography, against those kings who were not in favor of Zoroastrianism (similar to the way the Koran included the history of the accepted biblical prophets and excluded all but four non-biblical prophets: Hud, Sālih, Luqman, Dhul-qarnain). So the omission of previous monarchs did not necessarily have anything to do with the lack of monarchical

---

[45] See Wiesehöfer, "Statt einer Einleitung: 'Randkultur' oder 'Nabel der Welt'? Das Sasanidenreich und der Westen. Anmerkungen eines Althistorikers,"pp. 17–18, 20.

[46] See Pourshariati, *Decline and Fall of the Sasanian Empire*. She elaborates on various themes and topics throughout the first few hundred years after the Muslim conquest of Iran and the role of movements in Khurāsān as reminiscent of the Parthian and Mithraist insurgency.

memories of the Sasanians.[47] Pourshariati also believes that the removal of a number of Parthians from Sasanian historiography, reflected in the *Shāhnāmeh,* was intentional and associated with political animosity.[48] In brief, the entire historiographical enterprise of *Shāhnāmeh* was not a "national Iranian" process but a Sasanian-sponsored new Avestan religious undertaking, perhaps explaining the omission of some of the non-Zoroastrian kings and names. In brief, ancient Zoroastrianism developed outside of the Iranian plateau, but then the Sasanians adopted it to the extent that Zoroastrianism became known among the Orientalists as an Iranian religion.

Even regarding the claim that the Parthians were the revivers of Iranian-ness with their approach to the past Achaemenid "Iranian" traditions,[49] the evidence is circumstantial and is based on an assumption that there had always been an Iranian culture and identity before the age of the Parthians, a debate that still continues in the nationalist scholarship. Further studies are also needed to elaborate on the precise influences on iconography, architecture, and other traditions in the western and eastern Sasanian culture.[50]

There is still no concrete evidence that the term *Iran* and its derivatives stood as antecedents for a continuous Iranian identity which was then revived by the Qājār and Pahlavi intellectuals. The assumption of a continuous identity neglects the transition from the Zoroastrian-based Sasanian to the Islamic period and the mass conversion to Islam, and furthermore ignores the complex identity issue of other religious minorities in the Iranian plateau, which again renders the national identity hypothesis weak and untenable.

---

[47] Daryaee, "National History or Keyanid History?" pp. 137–138, 140.

[48] Pourshariati, *Decline and Fall,* pp. 9–11.

[49] Sarkhosh Curtis, "The Iranian Revival in the Parthian Period," pp. 7–25, especially pp. 15, 18, 21–22. The circumstantial evidence includes the Parthians' use of the title "King of Kings" and their costume and coinage, which were passed down to the Sasanids.

[50] A study of Sasanian seals demonstrates that they seem to have been influenced by Mediterranean, Greco-Egyptian motifs: see Gyselen, "Note de Glyptique Sassanide. 6. Phénomène des motifs iconographiques communs à l'Iran Sassanide et au bassin Méditerranéen," pp. 83–104.

3. Geography and Iranian Identity

To return to considering other perspectives on factors that have been used as the basis of claims of Iranian identity, the conception of a continuous geography under the name of *Iran* has played a key role, since — as this book has shown — the foundation of a modern construction of Iranian identity had very much to do with linking the Persian language with the political-geographical territory of Iran. Certainly the link between geographical space and national language was a convenient and effective strategy for the modernizers and nationalists who perceived national identity to be found within the given political borders irrespective of vast differences among its extremely diverse populations. The propagation of notions such as *vatan* (homeland, fatherland, motherland, land of birth, or a land to die for) and *millat* (collective community within the political territory) were all attempts to emphasize the importance of all its inhabitants sharing a common geography regardless of their language or ethnic origin. However, this argument (which has been addressed throughout the book by referring to the geographical term *Iran*, and the theme of territory being a factor for the emergence of Iranian identity during the Qājār period addressed briefly in Chapter 8) has been fully and soundly unraveled by Firoozeh Kashani-Sabet in her 1999 book *Frontier Fictions: Shaping the Iranian Nation, 1804–1946*.

Kashani-Sabet implies the idea that Iranian identity was created by uniting all the semi-autonomous territories and heterogeneous population of Iran and politicizing the notion of *millat*, replacing their parochial loyalties with loyalty to a perceptible geography and greater territory of Iran, and ignores the fact that the umbrella of unity had remained fictional.[51] In other words, the sketch of physical territory above all other agendas of politics and culture was the primary vehicle for the nationalist discourse in Iran. In order to create an Iranian allegiance and sense of *vatan* and sense of others (foreigners and those who lived outside of political

---

[51] For a more detailed and deeper analysis of creating unity within the space of Iranian geography, see Kashani-Sabet, *Frontier Fictions*, pp. 9–10, 18, 42–43, 51–52, 103, 205.

territories), visual evidence of the land was created through map production and surveys.[52] Visualizing a map of Iran gave a concrete focus for expressing patriotism, though a map was a vague drawing in comparison with the vast unstudied terrains and subcultures contained within the territory. Nevertheless, the key figure in linking geography and modern nationalist discourse was the nineteenth-century Mumtahin al-Dawla, followed by Mīrzā Husayn Khan's work including race and Iran's population, which drew on Orientalist works.[53] Through such approaches Iran and all its inhabitants were connected. At the peak of nationalism, all the pieces of national identity were brought together by connecting the pre-Islamic history writing of 'Itimād al-Saltana in the 1890s (and later by Pīrnīyā), Akhundzādeh's linking of land and language, and Kirmānī's elaboration on the Aryan nation. Furthermore, citizenship and the introduction of passports in the mid-nineteenth century bolstered the cultural myth of ancient *Iranzamin*, and eventually, centralization of power and the introduction of law and order throughout the semi-autonomous territories after the Constitutional Revolution paved the way for nation-building under

---

[52] Kashani-Sabet, *Frontier Fictions*, pp. 9–10, 74.

[53] Kashani-Sabet, "Picturing the Homeland: Geography and National Identity in Late Nineteenth and Early Twentieth-century Iran," pp. 415–417, 418–19. Kashani-Sabet has come a long way with the publication of her more recent book to adjust some of her earlier attitude and statements. In her earlier article Kashani-Sabet was more reluctant to admit the viability of the premise of *Iran as Imagined Nation*, in which it is argued that geography and multiethnic communities are in a constant state of flux, and national identities were forged through the nationalist narrative, especially during late Qājār period. She criticizes the idea that Iran's map was "…the consequence of a haphazard act of 'imagination' or 'invention.'" See Kashani-Sabet, "The Frontier Phenomenon: Perceptions of the Land in Iranian Nationalism," p. 26; see also footnote 17. In response to Kashani-Sabet's criticism, it is clear throughout this book that "Iran" as a geographical term and space has been treated as a basis of grouping together languages, culture, and ethnicity to construct an Iranian identity.

the banner of "Iranian-ness" within the borders of Iran.[54] In Kashani-Sabet's words, "the blending of the imagined and the material — helped to forge nations."[55]

In the mid-1800s the Qājār intellectuals attempted to create an image of Iran and an Iranian identity within its historically-fluctuating territory. The formulation of Iranian identity that was molded by thinkers such as the Qājārs' 'Itimād al-Saltana were based upon the continuous monarchy, the Achaemenids, antiquity, and language linkages,[56] none of which were his own findings but were extracted from Orientalist works. This was a period in which the Qājār intellectuals took *complete* liberty with their nationalist rhetoric; a time when they distorted the connection between language and ethnicity, namely the Persian language and Iranian ethnicity. Juan Cole in a 1996 article indicates that Qājār intellectuals imagined an Iranian nation: "Iranian national identity was not an existent that needed to be symbolized, but an idea yet to be realized."[57]

The early Qājār rulers were engaged in an old military style of nation-building, consolidating imperial rule through domination rather than education. The "country" had been plunged into a politically crippled geographical expression by almost any means to represent a homogeneous community of "Iranians." It was the late Qājār intelligentsia that took on the difficult task of uniting people and creating a government with accountability and a system of laws, a task which would limit the Qājārs' fiscal and political recklessness and which eventually created rifts between the palace and the nationalist direction that the succeeding Pahlavi regime on

---

[54] Kashani-Sabet, *Frontier Fictions*, pp. 42–43, 45, 103; Kashani-Sabet, "Picturing the Homeland," pp. 414, 420–422; see also Kashani-Sabet, "Fragile Frontiers: Diminishing Domains of Qajar Iran," pp. 205–234.

[55] Kashani-Sabet, "The Frontier Phenomenon," p. 21.

[56] Cole, "Making Boundaries, Making Time: The Iranian Past and the Construction of the Self by Qajar Thinkers," pp. 52–53.

[57] Cole, pp. 35, 37.

the contrary chose to exploit and align itself with.[58] Thus there is no doubt that the nationalist sentiment and the need to create a proper Iranian nation-state were conceived among the intellectuals and reformers of nineteenth-century Iran, as scholarship has demonstrated. On the political level, the impetus for this constructed national ideology was the need to create a patriotic nation in legal control of the government in the nineteenth century after the Qājārs permitted the imperialists to exploit the country.[59]

This momentum towards a sense of nationhood was valid, but the sentiment was ambitiously consolidated with a deeper and more dangerous enterprise of racial and ancient identity construction for largely agrarian, conservative, often illiterate Muslims. Anne Lambton appropriately enhanced this point about the level of exaggeration in Qājār and Pahlavi nationalism: "National pride was stimulated by the building of a largely imaginary glorious past under the old Persian kings, who were remote enough to enable the need for historical accuracy to be relaxed."[60] The Pahlavi regime realized the significance of such national identity construction for its own legitimacy, and in line with the goal of the unification of all tribes and remote populations required them to learn the Persian language and be identified as "Iranian." Certainly the need to unite the populations of the country and to stand up against foreign exploitation gave rise to nationalism, but the marriage of Iranian national identity with Zoroastrianism, Aryanism, and pre-Islamic heritage only augmented the dispute between the modern and religious-rural-suburban classes of the society which escalated after 1979.

THE PREDICAMENT OF ARCHAEOLOGY AND RACE

Iranian nationalists used most of the ideas they had collected to construct a nation and strong historical national identity against

---

[58] For a more detailed account of Qājār- and Pahlavi-era nation-state building see Marashi, *Nationalizing Iran: Culture, Power, and the State, 1870–1940*. See also A. Ansari, *The Politics of Nationalism in Modern Iran*.

[59] Lambton, "The Impact of the West on Persia," pp. 18–19.

[60] Ibid., p. 23.

imperialist infiltration and even against dictatorship, but they failed to create a democratic system, in part because they adhered to high-risk theories and sometimes self-gratifying national fantasies. This includes the nationalist elites of the Qājār and Pahlavi era as well as some of the modern scholars. The proliferation of modern academic writings on ancient Iranian history owes its key sources to the new unifying political platform of nationalism, and to archaeology, both imported into Iran from the West.[61]

The nationalist arguments of archaeology were bolstered by the rise of divisive racial theories. It is fair to believe that identities in pre-modern times were generally based on languages rather than race, since intermarriage between human populations renders the idea of race ridiculous.[62] The tragic and erosive ideology of race stems from the time of the slave trade in the seventeenth century, as race was a European social invention with no relationship to abilities but instead was rationalized by inequalities, privileges, power, and wealth.[63]

Race theory and archaeology are the products of academia. It must be clear that not everything produced in academic archaeology is necessarily correct in its interpretation, but one would at least expect all arguments to be accountable. Part of the problem with the construction of national identity undertaken by the nationalists is that it has depended on and believed in academia and its outputs, and this practice is still quite common, sometimes without a critical evaluation of the ideas being expressed or the works being used in scholarship. Two of the academic domains that have harmed the nationalist cause and its construction of Iranian identity have been based on archaeological assertions and theorizations about race and what is and is not "Iranian," and the Indo-European and eventually Aryan racial theory in regards to Iran.

Archaeologists in Iran in the first quarter of the twentieth century are largely responsible for boosting nationalist sentiment.

---

[61] Abdi, "Nationalism, Politics, and the Development of Archaeology in Iran," p. 52.

[62] Smedley, "Race and the Construction of Human Identity," p. 691.

[63] Ibid., pp. 690, 694, 698–699.

The manipulation of archaeology for nation-building by inventing nationality and ethnicity on the basis of archaeological evidence for the people of the remote past had already been done in Europe. In other words, nationalist archaeology created nations and national identities that had not previously existed.[64] In Iran, the timely marriage between archaeology and nationalism manipulated perceptions by connecting ethnicity and language using unfounded assumptions. The idea that the Achaemenids were of Indo-European or Aryan stock was based on poorly developed and speculative connections between archaeological interpretation, ethnic groups, and linguistic affiliation.[65] The connection between ethnicity, which is itself a variable concept and prone to constant modification, and language, especially the Indo-Iranian branch of Indo-European, has often been promoted by biased archaeologists, who without anthropological training make speculative allegations rather than produce verifiable theories.[66] For example, the archaeologists of this era often misidentified nearly all non-labeled artifacts of the Near Eastern antiquity as "Iranian," such as the pieces of art that Arthur Upham Pope (1881–1969) found in Iran, which were all catalogued under the new nationalist label of Iranian, despite the possibility of different Near East cultural origins.[67] This nationalizing archaeological enterprise took place in many countries, but Egypt in particular connected their remote

---

[64] Kohl, "Nationalism and Archaeology: On the Constructions of Nations and the Reconstructions of the Remote Past," pp. 223–246.

[65] For the poor state of archaeology in determining and reconstructing the languages and cultures of Indo-Iranian ancestors, see Lamberg-Karlovsky, "Archaeology and Language: The Indo-Iranians," pp. 73–74.

[66] Lamberg-Karlovsky, "Archaeology and Language," pp. 74–75.

[67] See Abdi's article for Pope's approach and how he influenced the fervent nationalism of the day that was fueled by Reza Shah's policies. Moreover, it was Pope's idea to suggest to the former Shah that he celebrate the 2,500th year of Iranian empire and civilization: Abdi, "Nationalism, Politics, and the Development of Archaeology in Iran," pp. 60–62.

antiquity to their Muslim heritage by "Egyptianizing" every artifact.[68]

The messages being propagated by archaeologists and nationalists also gave a new sense to educated Iranians that foreign forces such as the Greeks and the Arabs brought the demise of the Iranian Achaemenid and Sasanid empires. This view neglected any consideration for the complexity of the Near Eastern cultural past and the internal strife that the two empires faced.[69] The Sasanian imperial use of "Iran" or "*Iranshahr*" (similar to Rome's use of "Roman") was politically aimed more at identifying outsiders than at creating "national" cohesion. Additionally, these two allegedly "Iranian" dynasties did not operate on a national level but through the typical expansionist imperial ambitions of ancient times.

The Aryan-ness of the branch of Indo-Iranian groups whose languages and cultures supposedly converged when they immigrated to Iran, proposed with certainty by archaeologists such as Herzfeld, could not be supported by artifacts or physical evidence, and is flatly refuted by recent biological and genetic studies.[70] Similar serious criticism can be leveled against those archaeologists who pushed for racial and later for ethnic identification in Mesopotamia, taxonomies that did not exist in ancient Mesopotamian languages.[71] In the case of populations in Iran and Mesopotamia, the sense of self and others was expressed linguistically, textually, politically, and by other means, but was not racial or ethnic.

The European notion of the Aryan race and the search for extra-European Aryan prototypes led Josef Strzygowski, the "father of racial architecture," to invent the Indo-Germanic artistic superiority, and Iranian architecture was perceived as exemplifying

---

[68] See Goode, *Negotiating for the Past: Archaeology, Nationalism, and Diplomacy in the Middle East, 1919–1941*, p. 117.

[69] Abdi, "Nationalism, Politics...," pp. 51, 73.

[70] Lamberg-Karlovsky, "Archaeology and Language," pp. 74–75.

[71] Bahrani, "Race and Ethnicity in Mesopotamian Antiquity," pp. 48–59.

the Aryan ancestry that Strzygowski had hypothesized.[72] These biological claims of racial Aryanism, combined with the biased claims made by disciplines such as philology and archaeology in order to strengthen the case of nationalism, promoted the idea that a contiguous Iranian identity was conceived a few thousand years ago by a racially-aware group of proto-Iranians.

The usage of the term *arya* (an honorific title 'noble') by the cultural and religious elites of India and Iran in their religious text books and political inscriptions (e.g. Persepolis) was interpreted racially by the Orientalists, who connected Europeans to the category of Indo-Iranian *arya*, which in fact had nothing to do with Europeans. The idea of race was a European invention and the whole Aryan hypothesis brought Europeans who sought a racial identity into an imaginary circle of people whom Orientalists believed to be connected. The European identification with the term *arya* was a self-invitation to belong to the religious or the revered community of the East whom the Orientalists perceived as their racial ancestors.

Aryan racial theory proved to be hurtful to the European continent as well as the Indo-Iranian world. The damage of the Aryan theory brought Europe to practice racism and commit to war. The Aryan racial hypothesis further complicated caste conflict, particularly in modern India.[73] After the introduction of Aryan race theory to India by British imperialists,[74] it was also introduced in Iran, which then, through the educational system and propaganda machinery, spread the idea across several generations, including the present one. This rise of Iranian awareness in the nineteenth and twentieth centuries exploited the nationalistic material of disciplines such as archaeology, historiography, and philology to promote their claims of ancestry back to pre-Islamic times. The origin and spread of Indo-European languages and the Aryan racial theory as a by-product, especially in connection with Iranian nationalism, was

---

[72] Grigor, "Of Aryan Origin(s), Western Canon(s), and Iranian Modernity," pp. 2–5.

[73] Thapar, *Early India*, p. 14

[74] Leopold, "British Applications of the Aryan Theory of Race to India, 1850–1870," pp. 578–603.

discussed in Chapters 1 and 3 of the present book. The recognition and the offending use and abuse of Aryanism in historiography and among the Iranian intelligentsia have been further questioned and explored in a very interesting book by Alireza Asgharzadeh in 2007.[75]

The trend of creating a link between nationalism and archaeology has lingered, and the work of archaeology remains susceptible to political and nationalist influences, largely neglecting anthropological considerations.[76] Race and racism in archaeology have also made harmful contributions.[77] Western archaeologists supported their conception of Iranian identity in a historical framework with massive academic nationalistic crafting that was reinforced by fervent promotion of cultural nationalism, ultimately heavily affecting the work of Reza Shah and the late Shah.

Maintaining an Aryan racial consciousness and superiority complex seemed to make up for all the past social, cultural, and political shortcomings, making Iran a more proud, uncompromising and racially a superior nation compared to its neighbors. But secular Iranian nationalism contained the fatal flaws of engaging with race theory, depending excessively and illusively on a remote past, and excluding many vital, tangible elements of the society — such as Islamic identity and how to bring about Islamic reformation through engagement, the role of other religious identities, and the role of women — from their discourse, which could have shifted the focus to sound intellectualism, pluralism, and nation-building. The high-risk anti-Islamic sentiment of secular Iranian nationalism as an "agent of Enlightenment" provoked an Islamic backfiring and ultimately denied secularists the

---

[75] Asgharzadeh, *Iran and the Challenge of Diversity*; See also Zia-Ebrahimi, "Self-Orientalization and Dislocation: The Uses and Abuses of the 'Aryan' Discourse in Iran," pp. 445–472.

[76] Kohl, "Nationalism and Archaeology," pp. 226, 236. Certainly nationalist archaeology has helped to shape Israel and Israeli national identity (p. 237).

[77] See Gosden, "Race and Racism in Archaeology: Introduction," pp. 1–7.

very thing they wished to deny to others,[78] until eventually such groups were turned into a self-interested, nostalgic cluster banished from the homeland. The battle over the authenticity of historical Iranian national identity has also confused the leaders of the Islamic Republic to the extent that it has kept the rift between the secular and religious camps largely open — but available to be bridged by the new generation, a generation with young unbiased thinkers and artists in a new global setting who are trying to bypass the narrow boundaries of either identity.[79]

THE PROBLEM OF ANCIENT IDENTITY AND ISLAMIC REACTION

The perceivers of ancient Iranian national identity in the nineteenth through twentieth centuries who were convinced of their own narrative failed to have direct experience with their subjects, those Iranians of whom they talked. They simply neglected to fully understand people's attitude toward their own historical identity, and consequently the early intellectuals of national identity failed to participate in the assessment and reflections of those they extrapolated about. The construction of identity should not have been merely an academic task but rather a phenomenon connected with the realities of culture on the ground. But those nationalists who speak of the national character of members of the past and present society have turned away from knowing the inhabitants and have focused on their own epistemology.[80] The discrepancy between the educated and non-educated, urban and rural people of Iran regarding their attitude toward a lost racial and national identity demonstrates self-centeredness on the part of nationalist intellectuals who seem far from grassroots reality.

---

[78] For nationalism and Orientalism and Islamism, see Burke III, "Orientalism and World History: Representing Middle Eastern Nationalism and Islamism in the Twentieth Century," pp. 489–507.

[79] See Kashmirshekan, "The Question of Identity vis-à-vis Exoticism in Contemporary Iranian Art," pp. 489–512.

[80] For an in-depth anthropological and rural study of Iranian national sociolinguistic interpretation and character, see Beeman, "What Is (Iranian) National Character? A Sociolinguistic Approach," pp. 22, 28.

Iran, in pre-modern times and to traditional people up to the present day, was known to be part of the realm of Islam, and its citizens to be predominantly Muslims (despite the presence of the minorities of Jews, Hindus, or Armenians), particularly in trade with others.[81] Sociological and anthropological evidence is lacking regarding nineteenth-century colloquial perception of national identity throughout Iran. Religious debates, predominantly over whether Abu Bakr or Ali was the rightful leader after Muhammad, dominated the mass culture at that time. Shi'ism after the sixteenth century became more associated with Iran, but the question of how Sunnis, Christians, Jews, Armenians, and other minorities expressed their sense of geographical identity, or where their sense of national identity was rooted, cannot be satisfactorily answered.

The anti-Islamic sentiment of certain Orientalists in constructing Iranian history and identity may have stemmed from their own Christian subconscious, or may have been rooted in their anti-religious position in constructing secular histories. The Iranian secular attitude further fueled the isolation of Islamic discourse as a basis of historiography and identity construction. Nevertheless the political error of the nationalists downplaying Islam as a major component of Iranian national identity, and promoting remote Zoroastrianism[82] as the ancient religious heritage of Iranian

---

[81] See Risso, "Muslim Identity in Maritime Trade: General Observation and Some Evidence from the 18th-Century Persian Gulf/Indian Ocean Region," pp. 381–392.

[82] For a link between Iranian nationalism and Zoroastrianism see Ringer, "Iranian Nationalism and Zoroastrian Identity: Between Cyrus and Zoroaster," 265–275. See also Holliday, *Defining Iran: Politics of Resistance*, esp. chapters 2, 3, and 4. Holliday tenaciously and persuasively surveys a series of political themes regarding Islamic and modern Iranian identities, but does not necessarily emphasize the clash of ideas between the historically constructed Zoroastrian-based identity and the Islamic reaction to being left out of Iranian identity construction, whether by the Orientalists or the Qājār, Pahlavi governments and intellectuals. Holliday hardly even addresses the root clash between rural and urban perceptions of Iranian and Islamic identities. The book, however, is worth consulting

civilization, has taken its toll. This non-Islamic yet religious (Zoroastrian) construction of Iranian identity has mostly engaged and mobilized the educated, urban, and paradoxically secular classes (perhaps out of blind defiance against Islam). It is clear that the earliest promoters of Iranian nationalism and national identity such as Mīrzā Aqā Khan Kirmānī (in addition to his Bābī sources) were extracting their anti-religious ideas from European sciences and academic sources.[83] This is not to suggest that including the role of Islam in analysis of the construction of identity would have made it theoretically correct, but this blind nationalist exclusivity inadvertently provoked an Islamic reaction to reassert the significance of Islam in the history of Iran and its identity. The traditional classes and rural-based population with their Islamic convictions consequently pushed back against the secular nationalist classes making non-Islamic claims. In disagreement with the secular, non-Islamic identity construction, the 1979 revolution and its aftermath brought to the forefront the question of the role of Zoroastrianism and Aryanism in Iranian national identity, with efforts to debunk the theory and its promoters. Despite this, in a later tactical move designed to assimilate the urban and secular classes, a number of clever leaders in the government of the Islamic Republic tried to bridge the ancient Iranian identity and the Islamic narrative,[84] something that can only be described as non-oxymoron modern religious nationalism.[85]

---

as a reference for the post-revolutionary national identity conceived by the Islamic Republic leaders, particularly during Khatami's presidency.

[83] For scientific and anti-Islamic (denying Divine Revelation) writings of Kirmani, see Bayat Philipp, "The Concepts of Religion and Government in the Thought of Mīrzā Aqa Khan Kirmani, a Nineteenth-Century Persian Revolutionary," pp. 382, 385, 386, 388–389.

[84] See Ram, "The Immemorial Iranian Nation? School Textbooks and Historical Memory in Post-revolutionary Iran," pp. 67–90. This article is interesting but it needs better analysis and evaluation of the quotations that provides.

[85] Two very stimulating articles about the theories of religious nationalism discuss the Iranian case as well as other nation-states such as Israel that exploit religious narratives to promote modern nationalism:

The experiment of the theory of historical Iranian identity has proven to be an intellectual romantic nationalist ideology based on the pre-Islamic past, ignoring more than a millennium of Islam in Iran and the realities of ordinary people's lives on the ground. The split perception of ancient Iranian identity, caught between the rural and urban, between pious Muslims and the religiously defiant, is so wide that it has divided Iranian political opinion between two extreme poles. From the nineteenth century until the 1960s, when modern education and mass media reached the villages and remote areas of Iran, the construction of pre-Islamic Iranian identity had been mainly the preoccupation of the urban and educated classes of Iran. The boundaries of faith and other loyalties were misjudged and handled condescendingly with loathing by the secular nationalists when it came to dealing with rural people. Not surprisingly, the political divide in the last three decades has partly been due to the polarization of rural-based and urban-based opinions about the content and significance of their past and present identity. In other words, it is doubtful that the significance and the role of Cyrus the Great, Sasanian heritage, Aryanism, and Zoroastrianism in the historical continuity of Iranian identity has gained much adherence among the rural and religiously dedicated people of Iran. It must be borne in mind that before the revolution of 1979, the majority of the population was living in rural areas and was predominantly illiterate. It was only after the revolution that the rural and suburban (*ḥāshīye-neshīnān*) people flooded the cities and took over key positions within the Islamic Republic, creating a tension between the attitude and lifestyle of urban and rural classes — a permeating tension that eventually led to the dominance of suburban and rural people in Iranian financial and political life today.[86] In the same context, the tension in Iran is not necessarily between the secular and religious classes, but rather between the rural and urban categories with arrays of opinions on how domestic

---

Friedland, "Religious Nationalism and the Problem of Collective Representation," pp. 125–152; Friedland, "Money, Sex, and God: The Erotic Logic of Religious Nationalism," pp. 381–425.

[86] The basis of this discussion is extracted from debates with my friend Dr. Asghar Feizi over the course of many years.

and international politics should be handled, which could hypothetically be possible about all countries.

THE GENERAL APPEAL FOR NATIONAL IDENTITY IN MODERN TIMES

Let us briefly discuss the motivation for constructing incontestable national identities that have become ubiquitous in the volatile and competitive world in which we live. Maintaining national identity seems to be inevitable in the modern world. The trick is to discover how far the cultural literati and political leaders have stretched the imaginations of their compatriots in bestowing on them an extraordinary, unique, and ancient identity. The typically anachronous nationalist assertion of Iranian identity in pre-modern times is part of this phenomenon. Nationalists around the world have done this for years, and even today, emerging nations are busy crafting a historical identity for the inhabitants of their countries regardless of their ethnic or linguistic origins. This makes the issue of national identity more of a political reality than a sound anthropological reality, as can be seen from a number of examples.

Cultural and political leaders saw no difficulty in constructing national identities for the ancient civilizations in Asia such as China, Iraq, India, and Iran, because scholars have portrayed such identities as having existed in pre-modern times. But despite China's status as an ancient civilization, newer studies show that its modern national identity was in fact constructed through the re-interpretation of the tenth-century term "China" (Zhong guo). This undertaking, which happened only after 1911, was intended to apply the term *China* to multiethnic communities and under it to conceive a national culture.[87] The evolution from dynasty to state, from mere geography to ethnicity, culture, and national identity, and eventually to nationalism, was disseminated through educational system as it was prepared by the intellectuals of the

---

[87] Zhao, "Reinventing China: Imperial Qing Ideology and the Rise of Modern Chinese National Identity in the Early Twentieth Century," pp. 4, 6–7.

nineteenth century.[88] In other words, there was no *ancient* Chinese national identity.

Iraq also, despite its glorious ancient and medieval histories, had no ancient national identity. It entered its modern nation-state building stage through the amalgamation of groups with conflicting interests and sentiments under the two colonial powers, the Ottomans and the British.[89] The uneasy loyalty and fragile solidarity among the Shiʻites, Sunnis, Jews, Christians, Kurds, and other minorities under the banner of Arabism were all imagined after 1917, when they were sworn to loyalty and renamed as *Iraqis* under a new flag and a newly planted patriotism.[90]

The Indian experiment of establishing a national identity has not been as successful as was originally hoped. The secession of large, linguistically heterogeneous Muslim populations in the east and west in 1947 to create East and West Pakistan was the manifestation of an identity crisis which led to further transformation, East Pakistan becoming Bangladesh because of political conflict and Bengali linguistic consciousness (with the Bengalis' various sub-layers of identities).[91] On the other hand, the obscure "Hindu" label applied by the Muslims and the British to non-Muslims did not stop Brahmins from forming a Hindu identity within the Indian context of nationalism, stimulated by a contrast to Muslim identity.[92] The rise of religious nationalism in India is rooted, as argued by Romila Thapar, in the flaw of the British historical periodization of a dynastic history, namely dividing the history of India into Hindu, Muslim and British periods — such hegemonic textual influence distorted the perception of the historical changes in the Indian subcontinent.[93] Religion was not

---

[88] Ibid., pp. 7–11, 18–23.

[89] Zubaida, "The Fragments Imagine the Nation: The Case of Iraq," pp. 206, 207, 211.

[90] Ibid., pp. 213–214.

[91] Islam, "Islam and National Identity: The Case of Pakistan and Bangladesh," pp. 56–58, 63, 69.

[92] Talbot, "Inscribing the Other, Inscribing the Self: Hindu-Muslim Identities in Pre-Colonial India," pp. 700–701.

[93] Thapar, *Early India*, pp. 5–6, 21.

the sole basis of identity; it was also different ethno-territorial and sociopolitical groups that began to diverge or coalesce.[94] India or *Bharat*, as a large geographical space, held many communities for many centuries. Colonialism temporarily brought them together, but national identity in India has since remained in flux as a non-monolithic phenomenon.

Afghanistan, also known by its ancient and medieval designations Ariana and Khurāsān, because of weak political and tribal systems in the last century and the internal strife of the last three decades has not made as many strong claims about its historical national identity as has Iran, although attempts have been made by Afghans to reconstruct a rich history and identity distinct from their neighbors, particularly from Iran. The fragile Afghan identity was promoted generally through the medium of radio (since mass education was so weak), and through the establishment of the national archaeological museum in 1970 (re-opened in the last decade), which exhibited the identity of the Afghans from prehistoric times to the modern era.[95] Unlike their Iranian counterparts, the Afghan state and its intelligentsia have fallen into disarray, failing to fully exploit the Persian language (*Dari*) as a means to reconstruct a national linguistic and literary tradition next to their rich Zoroastrian, Buddhist, Sufi, and artistic heritage.

Intellectuals and readers of history are the theoretical creators of nations; it is not necessarily the villagers or ordinary people who usually through education consume historical claims about their identities. Intellectuals, especially modern academics, generally pursue their own ideals and produce and transmit ideas, and at the same time often use their advanced education to link themselves to narrower reductionist ideas and categories to which they originally did not belong.[96] The "community of mind"[97] is the theoretical and

---

[94] Talbot, p. 701.

[95] Hatch Dupree, "Cultural Heritage and National Identity in Afghanistan," pp. 977–978, 981, 983.

[96] See Kurzman and Owens, "The Sociology of the Intellectuals," pp. 67, 69.

[97] Cerulo, "Identity Construction: New Issues, New Directions," pp. 386, 397–398.

historical imagination of nationalist authors who group together all groups, even those that don't share common features or that have little connection to communities of the past. In this regard the bold and controversial book of Shlomo Sand, *The Invention of Jewish People* (Hebrew edition 2008, English translation 2009) postulates the invention of Jewish identity as "one folk" out of people of diverse backgrounds in Europe and elsewhere. This task was undertaken by the Europeans who invented, by extracting from mythical sources, a historical identity for all Jews and connected them to a "holy" land that they previously did not expect to settle as one nation[98] — at least not in the near future. If Sand's argument is correct, then the professional historians and Zionists successfully linked the assimilated European Jews to peoples of the remote past and thereby helped create Israel and forged its identity as a Jewish nation-state.

In the final analysis we need to distinguish and separate the importance and necessity of *modern* national identity from exaggerated *historical* identity. Without naively discarding the importance of national identity construction, we can say that apart from romanticizing the imaginary national narrative, national identities are generally constructed for practical internal and external reasons: on the one hand to dominate others, and on the other hand to avoid domination. Fear, power, and historical myths help form identities but can also lead to conflicts with other nations.[99] In avoiding "state-eat-state," or resisting the tendencies of imperialist countries to invade or dominate weaker countries, communities create intergroup behavior by accentuating their similarities rather than their differences for either cooperation or conflict between self and others, but the ethnocentrism of such identity construction has become almost like a "black hole," sucking every view to its center, as a dominant frame of

---

[98] See S. Sand, *The Invention of the Jewish People*. It may be true that religious Jews for centuries expressed a longing to return to the holy land but did not expect it to happen before the coming of the Messiah, until Zionism arose and made it a political possibility.

[99] Mercer, "Anarchy and Identity," p. 243.

reference.[100] Nationalism is a narrow sentiment that sometimes displaces objective scholarship, often out of conviction that does not accommodate impartiality and rationalism in historical investigation, especially in regard to the complexity and exactness of identity in the past. The roots of nationalism and its national identity construction, designed to resist the invasion of colonialism and bring internal order to countries, has at the same time caused proponents to romanticize the past and to fail to broaden and democratize their political and intellectual horizons.

CONCLUSION

Sasanian Iran contained many linguistic and cultural communities to start with, and the land's population became even more diversified after several major invasions that followed. Thus Iran as an open territory became a non-politicized domain to host the newly arrived populations in different periods. Early post-Islamic dynasties ruling different parts of Iran seemed to care more about their imperial expansion than, in the modern sense, politicizing an 'Iranian' nation. Moreover, among the populations of medieval and pre-modern times, due to their linguistic and religious diversities, there were very few cultural media to promote a sense of nationhood. If we use our historical imagination to assess pre-modern national Iranian sentiments, it must be admitted that people in a territory as vast as Iran could not have bred a 'national' bond with each other especially with no centralized or unifying 'national' language, and no actual attempt to indoctrinate the population at large to feel Iranian. The national construction and fusion of Iranian identity, it is fair to say, took place only in modern times.

It is more productive to pursue research in tracing the emergence of Iranian national identity in nineteenth century than to search for it in the remote past, which produces no concrete evidence, but only assumptions and nationalist theories full of holes. The accurate understanding of historical national identity can be put into disarray if scholars continue to ignore their personal

---

[100] Ibid., pp. 233, 241–243.

biases, especially if they dominate the scholarly arena with major periodicals at their disposal. This approach threatens to derail constructive and democratic debate. Stagnation in the old paradigm can only be sustained if the majority continues to come under its influence and endorse it. Currently a large number of Iranian nationalists are the audience and support, and a number of nationalist academics and old-fashioned Orientalists pretentiously abuse history in an individual's or a group's favor and contemptuously craft the old paradigm of national identity, especially when the majority of people automatically approve it. The shortcomings can easily lie in the consciousness of our generation which by and large knows only the power of national thinking. The national interpretation of history has been the fashion of our time. Thapar says this about the failings of the steadfast historians and their historical interpretation: "The inadequacies of their interpretations were often the inadequacies of their time, for historians are frequently more representative of their age than they are aware."[101]

The nonconformist and non-nationalist views such as those presented in this book have been partially marginalized and even trivialized, as seen in the condescending citations of such works in the nationalist school of Iranian studies. Thus in "democratic" academic circles this book and perhaps similar publications, because their investigations lie outside the mainstream, have been perceived and treated as heretical. Such value judgments by certain Iranian and old-school academics would only damage and delay intellectual democracy and the road to tolerance and coexistence in academia as well as in the Iranian world.

The paradigm shift of extricating the national historiography of Iran from the influence of European Orientalism takes time. A non-national approach to history does not mean replacing the history of Iran but instead aims to remove the tyranny of textual history that has distorted the reality on the ground. The old paradigm certainly cannot be maintained merely by providing extra footnotes in an article, or having Ivy League universities in the background to support one's views and as a means of validation.

---

[101] Thapar, *Early India*, p. 28

The danger lies in holding unbending views, whether one is a reputable scholar or an ordinary citizen.

Although it is a bit harsh, there is certainly truth in Ernest Renan's words: "To be right in the long run at times requires accepting the burden of knowing how to resign oneself to being démodé."[102] The first condition for a paradigm shift and iconoclasm lies not in pedantic studies, but in personal de-domestication[103] from the old mode of thinking. At the same time, the re-domestication of one's mind should take shape beyond the realm of preconceived and culture-given beliefs and practices. It is to be noticed that our biology and primordial mode of being have come under a considerable influence of our self-constructed cultures and social contracts to an extent that our human system has been altered and compromised by them.[104] We always have the privilege to argue our views based on books — which sometimes have authority over us and at other times prove their failings and falsities — but eventually we must turn to our natural reason and common sense in dealing with the hypothesis of pre-modern Iranian identity. In this way we can open avenues to debate matters even as "sacred" and "certain" as national identity.

Even false words are true if they lead to enlightenment;

Even true words are false if they breed attachment.

– Zen saying

---

[102] Ernest Renan, quoted in Kohl, "Nationalism and Archaeology," p. 243.

[103] For re-defining the contracts with self, see Ruiz, *Les quatre accords toltèques: La voie de la liberté personnelle.*

[104] See Lorenz, *Der Abbau des Menschlichen.*

SELECTED BIBLIOGRAPHY

Abdi, Kamyar. (2001) 'Nationalism, Politics, and the Development of Archaeology in Iran,' *American Journal of Archaeology* 105/1 January, pp. 51–76.

Abol Ghassemi, Muhammad Taqi. (n.d.) *Gīlān az Āqāz tā Enghilāb-i Mashroteh,* Tehran: Entesharat Hedayat.

Adamiyat, Fereydoun. (1969/1348) *Amir Kabir va Iran,* Tehran: Khrawrazmi.

———. (1984/1363) *Andisheha-yi Talibov Tabrizi,* Tehran: Damavand.

———. (1961/1340) *Fikr-i Āzādī va Muqadami-yi Nihzat Mashrutiyat,* Tehran: Entesharat-i Sokhan.

———. (1985/1364) 'Āsheftegī dar Fikr-i Tārīkhī,' *Millat Bidar* IV, 2, pp. 14–24.

Adamiyat, Fereydoun and Thomas M. Ricks (trans.) (1971) 'Problems in Iranian Historiography,' *Iranian Studies* IV, 4, pp. 132–156.

Adnan Adivar, Abdulhak. (1951) 'The Interaction of Islamic and Western Thought in Turkey,' in T. C. Young (ed.) *Near Eastern Culture and Society,* Princeton: Princeton University Press.

Afnan, Soheil. (1956) *Avicenna: His Life and Works,* London: George Allen & Unwin Ltd.

Afshar, Iraj. (1979/1358) *Nāmehāy-i Siyāsī Dehkhodā,* Tehran.

Afzal ul-Mulk, Mirza Gholam Husayn. (1984/1363) *Afzal ul-Tawārīkh,* Tehran: Nashr-i Tarikh-i Iran.

Ágoston, Gábor and Masters, Bruce (eds.) (2009) *Encyclopedia of the Ottoman Empire,* New York: Facts on File, Inc., pp. 322–323.

Ahmadi, Hamid. (2005) 'Unity Within Diversity: Foundations and Dynamics of National Identity in Iran,' *Critical Middle East Studies* 14/1 Spring, pp. 127–147.

Alam, Muzaffar. (1998) 'The Pursuit of Persian: Language in Mughal Politics,' *Modern Asian Studies* 32/2 May, pp. 317–49.

Al-Baladhuri. (1985/1364) *Futuh ul-Buldan*, (section on Iran) Tehran: Soroush.

Algar, Hamid. (1969) 'Malkum Khan, Akhundzada and the Proposed Reform of the Arabic Alphabet,' *Middle Eastern Studies*, V, 2, pp. 116–130.

——. (1973) *Mirza Malkum Khan*, Berkeley, Los Angeles: University of California Press.

——. (1969) *Religion and State in Iran*, Berkeley, Los Angeles: University of California Press.

——. (1980) 'The Study of Islam: The Work of Henry Corbin,' *Religious Studies Review*, VI, pp. 85–91.

Amanat, Abbas. (1997) *Pivot of the Universe: Nasir al-Din Shah Qajar and the Iranian Monarchy, 1831–1896*, London & New York: I. B. Tauris.

Amedroz, H. F. (1905) 'The Assumption of the Title of Shahnshah by the Buwayid Rulers,' *Numismatic Chronicle*, 4th series, 5, pp. 393–399.

Amin, Samir. (1989) *Eurocentrism*, New York: Monthly Review Press.

Anderson, Benedict. (1990) *Imagined Communities*, London: Verso.

Ansari, Ali M. (2012) *The Politics of Nationalism in Modern Iran*, New York: Cambridge University Press.

Ansari, Noorul Hasan. (1986) 'Amir Khusrau, the Poet and the Patriot,' *Indo-Iranica*, 39, pp. 88–99.

Arasteh, Reza. (1962) *Education and Social Awakening in Iran*, Leiden: E. J. Brill.

Arberry, A. J. (1968) 'Persian Literature,' in A. J. Arberry (ed.) *The Legacy of Persia*, London: Oxford University Press.

Arendt, Hannah. (1977) *Between Past and Future*, New York: Penguin Books Ltd.

Asghar, Aftab. (1985) *Persian Historiography in Indo-Pakistan*, Lahore: Cultural Center, Islamic Republic of Iran.

Asgharzadeh, Alireza. (2007) *Iran and the Challenge of Diversity: Islamic Fundamentalism, Aryanist Racism, and Democratic Struggles*, New York: Palgrave Macmillan.

Ashraf, Ahmad. (2006 updated 2012) 'Iranian Identity i: Perspectives,' *Encyclopaedia Iranica*, Online Edition. http://www.iranicaonline.org/articles/iranian-identity-i-perspectives

——. (2006 updated 2012) 'Iranian Identity iii: Medieval Islamic Period,' *Encyclopaedia Iranica*, Online Edition. http://www.iranicaonline.org/articles/iranian-identity-iii-medieval-islamic-period

Asmussen, J. P. (1967) 'Some Remarks on the Zoroastrian Vocabulary of the Judeo-Persian Poet Šahin-i Širazi of the Fourteenth Century,' *Sir J. J. Zarthoshti Madressa Centenary Volume*, Bombay, pp. 137–143.

Aubin, Eugene. (1908) *La Perse d'Aujourd'hui*, Paris.

Bahar, Muhammad Taqi. (1990/1369) *Sabk Shenāsī*, vols. I–III. Tehran: Amir Kabir.

Bahrani, Zainab. (2006) 'Race and Ethnicity in Mesopotamian Antiquity,' *World Archaeology* 38/1 March, Race, Racism, and Archaeology, pp. 48–59.

Bailey H. W. (1987) 'Arya,' *Encyclopedia Iranica*, E. Yarshater (ed.) Vol. II (97), London and New York: Routledge & Kegan Paul, pp. 681–683.

——. (1968) 'The Persian Language,' in A. J. Arberry (ed.) *The Legacy of Persia*, London: Oxford University Press.

Baker, Ernest. (1948) *National Character*, London: Methuen & Co.

Banani, Amin. (1961) *The Modernization of Iran, 1921–1941*, Stanford, California: Stanford University Press.

Barthold, W. (1984) *An Historical Geography of Iran*, Princeton: Princeton University Press.

Bausani, Alessandro and Antonio Pagliaro. (1960) *Storia della Letteratura Persiana*, Milano: Nuova Academia Editrice.

Bayat Philipp, Mangol. (1974) 'The Concepts of Religion and Government in the Thought of Mirza Aqa Khan Kirmani, a Nineteenth-Century Persian Revolutionary,' *International Journal of Middle East Studies* 5/4 September, pp. 381–400.

Beeman, William O. (1976) 'What Is (Iranian) National Character? A Sociolinguistic Approach,' *Iranian Studies* 9/1 Winter, pp. 22–48.

Benveniste, E. (1952) 'Les Langues de l'Iran Ancien,' in *La Civilisation Iranienne: Perse, Afghanistan, Iran Extérieure*. Paris: Payot.

Berlin, Isaiah. (1979) *Concepts and Categories: Philosophical Essays*, New York: The Viking Press.

——. (1976) *Vico and Herder: Two Studies in the History of Ideas*, New York: The Viking Press.

Bernal, Martin. (1987) *Black Athena*, vol. I, New Brunswick, New Jersey: Rutgers University Press.

Berard, Victor. (1910) *Révolution de la Perse*, Paris.

Birnbaum, Eleazar. (1976) 'Turkey: From Cosmopolitan Empire to Nation-State,' in R. M. Savory (ed.) *Introduction to Islamic Civilization*, Cambridge: Cambridge University Press.

Birunī, Abu Rayhan. (1973/1352) *Āthār ul-Bāqiya*, translated. by A. Danaseresht. Tehran: Ibn Sina Publisher.

———. (1879) *The Chronology of Ancient Nations*, translated by C. E. Sachau. London; reprinted Lahore: Hijra, 1983.

Boas, Franz. (1949) *Race, Language, and Culture*, New York: The Macmillan Co.

Boissel, Jean. (1973) *Gobineau, l'Orient et l'Iran*, Paris: Editions Klincksieck.

Borhān-i Qāte, (1963/1342) Muhammad Moʻin (ed.) Tehran: Ibn Sina Library.

Bosworth, C. E. (1973) 'The Heritage of Rulership in Early Islamic Iran and Search for Dynastic Connection,' *Iran: Journal of the British Institute of Persian Studies*, XI, pp. 51–62.

———. (1973) *The Ghaznavids: Their Empire in Afghanistan and Eastern Iran – 994–1040*, Beirut: Librairie du Liban.

———. (1991) 'The Persian Contribution to Historiography,' *Levi della Vida Conference*, Los Angeles: University of California at Los Angeles.

———. (1977) 'The Tahirids and Persian Literature,' in *The Medieval History of Iran, Afghanistan, and Central Asia*, London: Variorum Reprints.

Boyle, John Andrew. (1974) 'The Evolution of Iran as a National State,' *Hommage Universel*, III, pp. 327–338.

Brockelmann, Carl. (1960) *History of the Islamic Peoples*, New York: Capricorn Books.

Browne, E. G. (1902 & 1956) *A Literary History of Persia*, vols. I–IV. Cambridge: Cambridge University Press.

———. (1910) *The Persian Revolution of 1905–1909*, Cambridge: Cambridge University Press.

———. (1983) *The Press and Poetry of Modern Persia*, London, 1914; reprinted Los Angeles: Kalimat Press.

Burke, Edmund, III. (1998) 'Orientalism and World History: Representing Middle Eastern Nationalism and Islamism in the

Twentieth Century,' *Theory and Society* 27/4 August, pp. 489–507.

Burrow, T. (1973) 'The Proto-Indo Aryans,' *Journal of the Royal Asiatic Society*, 2, pp. 123–140.

Cambridge History of Iran, (1968) vol. I, W. B. Fisher (ed.). Cambridge: Cambridge University Press.

Cerulo, Karen A. (1997) 'Identity Construction: New Issues, New Directions,' *Annual Review of Sociology* 23, pp. 385–409.

Chardin, Sir John. (1720) *The Travels* in *Persia*, vols. I & II. London.

Chibli, Alghama. (1986) 'Nazari bi Nil Deman Feizi,' *Indo-Iranica*, 39, pp. 118–123 (in Farsi).

Childe, Gordon. (1926)*The Aryans: A Study of Indo-European Origins*, London: Kegan Paul, Trench, Trubner & Co. Ltd.

Christensen, Arthur. (1936) *L'Iran sous Les Sassanides*, Copenhagen: Levin & Munksgaard.

Church, William. (1975) 'France,' in Orest Ranum (ed.) *National Consciousness, History, and Political Culture in Early Modern Europe*, Baltimore: The Johns Hopkins University Press.

Cohn, Bernard S. (1983) 'Representing Authority in Victorian India,' in E. Hobsbawm, T. Ranger (eds.)*Invention of Tradition*, Cambridge: Cambridge University Press.

Cole, Juan R. I. (1996) 'Making Boundaries, Making Time: The Iranian Past and the Construction of the Self by Qajar Thinkers,' *Iranian Studies* 29/1–2 Winter–Spring, pp. 35–56.

Conteneau, George. (1931) 'L'Archeologie de la Perse des origines à l'époque d'Alexandre,' in *Societé des Études Iraniennes et l'Art Persane*, Paris: Librairie Oriental et Americaine.

———. (1990) 'Statutes élamites d'époque Parthe,' in *L'Âme de l'Iran*, Sous la direction de R. Grousset, L. Massignon, H. Massé. Paris: Albin Michel.

Corbin, Henry. (1971–1972) *En Islam Iranien*, vols. I–IV. Paris: Gallimard.

Cottam, Richard. (1979) *Nationalism in Iran*, Pittsburgh: University of Pittsburgh Press.

Crone, Patricia. (February 25, 2008) "Babak's Revolt," lecture delivered at UCLA, available at Pars Times, http://www.parstimes.com/history/babak.pdf.

D'iakonov, M. M. (1965/1344) *Ashkānīān*, Tehran: Anjuman Farhangi-i Iran Bastan.

Dandamaev, Muhammad. (1975) 'La politique religieuse des Achaemenides,' *Acta-Iranica*, I, pp. 193–200.

Darmesteter, James. (1877) *Les Origines de la Poésie Persane*. Paris.

———. (1883) *Études Iraniennes*, vols. I, II. Paris.

Daryaee, Touraj. (2005) 'Ethnic and Territorial Boundaries in Late Antique and Early Medieval Persia (Third to Tenth Century),' in Florin Curta (ed.) *Borders, Barriers, and Ethnogenesis: Frontiers in Late Antiquity and the Middle Ages*, New York: Brepols.

———. (1995) 'National History or Keyanid History? The Nature of Sasanid Zoroastrian Historiography,' *Iranian Studies* 28/3–4 Summer–Fall, pp. 129–141.

———. (2010) *Sasanian Persia: The Rise and Fall of Empire*, New York: I. B. Tauris.

Dawson, Christopher. (1980) *Mission to Asia*. Buffalo, New York: Medieval Academy of America.

De, Amalendu. (1986) 'Persian in our Life,' *Indo-Iranica* 39, pp. 59–65.

Dehkhodā, Ali Akbar. (1963/1342) *Lughat Nāmeh*, Muhammad Moʿīn (ed.) Tehran: Sherkat Chap Ofset Golshan.

Dominguez Oritz, Antonio. (1971) *The Golden Age of Spain 1516–1659*, translated. by J. Casey. New York: Basic Books.

Dubeux, Louis. (1834) 'Lettre à M. le rédacteur du journal asiatique, sur un article de M. Eugène Boré Relatif aux inscription Pehlvies de Kirmanschah traduites par M. Silvestre de Sacy,' *Journal Asiatique*, I, pp. 28–72.

Duchesne-Guillemin, Jacques. (1974) 'Le dieu de Cyrus,' *Hommage Universel*, III, pp. 11–21.

———. (1970) *Zoroastrianism: Symbols and Values*, New York: Harper.

Edgerton, Franklin. (1946) 'Sir William Jones: 1746–1794,' *Journal of the American Royal Society* 66/63 July–September, pp. 230–239.

Emmerick, R. E. (1983) 'Buddhism Among Iranian Peoples,' in E. Yarshater (ed.) *Cambridge History of Iran*, vol. 3(2), Cambridge: Cambridge University Press.

Emerson, Rupert. (1960) *From Empire to Nation*, Cambridge: Harvard University Press.

Enayat, Hamid. (1973) 'Politics of Iranology,' *Iranian Studies* VI, pp. 2–20.

Farhi, Farideh. (2005) 'Crafting National Identity amidst Contentious Politics in Contemporary Iran,' *Iranian Studies* 38/1 March, pp. 7–22.

Fazeli, Nematollah. (2006) *Politics of Culture in Iran: Anthropology, Politics and Society in the Twentieth Century*, London and New York: Routledge.

Flandin, Eugene. (1851) *Voyages en Perse*, vols. I & II. Paris.

Foroughī, Zaka ul-Mulk. (1901&1917) *Tārīkh-i Iran*, Tehran.

Francklin, William. (1790) *Observations Made on a Tour from Bengal to Persia*, London.

Fragner, Bert G. (2006) 'Das Persisch als Hegemonialsprache in der islamischen Geschichte,' in Lars Johanson and Christiane Bulut (eds.)*Turkic-Iranian Contact Areas: Historical and Linguistic Aspects*, Wiesbaden: Harrassowitz Verlag.

Friedland, Roger. (2001) 'Religious Nationalism and the Problem of Collective Representation,' *Annual Review of Sociology* 27, pp. 125–152.

——. (2002) 'Money, Sex, and God: The Erotic Logic of Religious Nationalism,' *Sociological Theory* 27 November, pp. 381–425.

Frye, Richard. (1975) *The Golden Age of Persia*, London: Weidenfeld & Nicolson.

——. (1983) 'The Political History of Iran under the Sassanians, in E. Yarshater (ed.) *Cambridge History of Iran*, vols. 3(1), Cambridge: Cambridge University Press.

——. (1962) 'Soviet Historiography on the Islamic Orient,' in B. Lewis, P. M. Holt (eds.) *Historians of the Middle East*, London: Oxford University Press.

Gabrieli, Francesco. (1955) 'Literary Tendencies,' in Gustave E. von Grunebaum (ed.) *Unity and Variety in Muslim Civilization*, Chicago: The University of Chicago Press.

Gafurov, B. G. (1975) 'The Study of Aryan Problems in USSR,' in *Iran Ancièn*. Paris: L'Asiatheque.

Gellner, Ernest. (1983) *Nations and Nationalism*, Ithaca, New York: Cornell University Press.

Ghirshman, Roman. (1976) *L'Iran des Origines à l'Islam*, Paris: Albin Michel.

——. (1972) *L'Iran et la Migration des Indo-Aryens et des Iraniens*, Leiden: E. J. Brill, 1972.

Gibb, H. A. R. (1951) 'Near East Perspective: The Present and the Future,' in T. C. Young (ed.) *Near Eastern Culture and Society*, Princeton: Princeton University Press.

Gignoux, Phillipe. (1983) 'Middle Persian Inscriptions,' in E. Yarshater (ed.) *Cambridge History of Iran,* vol. 3(2), Cambridge: Cambridge University Press.

Gilbert, Felix. (1975) 'Italy,' in Orest Ranum (ed.) *National Consciousness, History and Political Culture in Early Modern Europe,* Baltimore: The Johns Hopkins University Press.

Gnoli, Gherardo. (1989) *The Idea of Iran,* Rome: Instituto Italiano per il Media ed Estremo Oriente.

——. (2006 updated 2012) "Iranian Identity ii: Pre-Islamic Period," *Encyclopaedia Iranica,* Online Edition. http://www.iranicaonline.org/articles/iranian-identity-ii-pre-islamic-period.

Gobineau, Arthur, comte de. (1963) *Introduction à l'Essai sur l'inégalité des races humaines,* Paris: Nouvel Office d'Edition.

——. (1980) *Trois en Asie,* Paris: Edition A. M. Metailie.

Goldziher, Ignaz. (1920) *Le Dogme et la Loi de l'Islam,* Paris.

——. (1971) *Muslim Studies,* vol. I, 1890, translated by C. M. Barber and S. M. Stern. London: Allen & Unwin.

Gökalp Ziya. (1975) *Turkish Nationalism and Western Civilizations,* translated. and edited by Niyazi Berkes. Westport, Connecticut: Greenwood Press.

Goode, James F. (2007) *Negotiating for the Past: Archaeology, Nationalism, and Diplomacy in the Middle East, 1919–1941,* Austin: University of Texas Press.

Gosden, Chris. (2006) 'Race and Racism in Archaeology: Introduction,' *World Archaeology* 38/1 March, Race, Racism, and Archaeology, pp. 1–7.

Greenberg, Joseph H. (1987) 'Languages of the World,' *The New Lexicon Webster's Dictionary of English Language,* New York: Lexicon Publications, Inc.

Greenfield, Jonas. (1975) 'Iranian or Semitic,' *Acta Iranica* 1, pp. 311–316.

Grenet, Franz. (2005) 'An Archaeologist's Approach to Avestan Geography,' in Vesta Sarkhosh Curtis and Sarah Stewart (eds.) *Birth of the Persian Empire,* London: I. B. Tauris.

Grigor, Talinn. (2005) 'Of Aryan Origin(s), Western Canon(s), and Iranian Modernity,' *Repenser les limites: l'architecture à travers l'espace, le temps et les disciplines,* Paris: INHA Actes de Colloques.

Grousset, Rene. (1990) 'L'âme de l'Iran et l'humanisme,' in *L'Âme de l'Iran*, sous la direction de R. Grousset, L. Massignon, H. Massé. Paris: Albin Michel.

Gyselen, Ryka. (2006) 'Note de Glyptique Sassanide. 6. Phénomène des motifs iconographiques communs à l'Iran Sassanide et au bassin Méditerranéen,' in Josef Wiesehöfer and Philip Huyse (eds.)*Ērān und Anērān: Studien zu den Bezeichungen zwischen dem Sasanidenreich und der Mittelmeerwelt*, München: Franz Steiner Verlag.

Hairi, Abdul-Hadi. (1985/1364) *Shi'ism and Constitutionalism in Iran*, Tehran: Amir Kabir.

Halliday, Fred. (1980) *Iran: Dictatorship and Development*, London: Penguin Press.

Hanaway, William. (1991) 'Alexander and the question of Iranian identity,' *Acta Iranica*, XVI, pp.93–103.

Hammer-Purgstall, Joseph von. (1812–1813) *Der Diwan von Mohammed Schamsed-din Hafis: Aus dem Persischen zum erstemal ganz übersetzt* (teils 1–2), Stuttgart: Tubigen.

Hatch Dupree, Nancy. (2002) 'Cultural Heritage and National Identity in Afghanistan,' *Third World Quarterly* 23/5, pp. 977–989.

Hayes, Carlton. (1928) *Essays on Nationalism*, New York: The Macmillan Co.

——. (1931) *The Historical Evolution of Modern Nationalism*, New York: The Macmillan Co.

——. (1931) *The Historical Evolution of Modern Nationalism*, New York: The Macmillan Co.

——. (1933) *A Political and Social History of Modern Europe*, vols. II&III. New York: The Macmillan Co.

Henning, W. B. (1939) 'Soghdian Loan-words in New Persian,' *Bulletin of the School of Oriental Studies* 10/1, pp. 93–106.

Hermann, Denis. (2010) 'La défense de l'enseignement de l'arabe au cours du mouvement constitutionnel iranien (1906–1911),' in Denis Hermann and Fabrizio Speziale (eds.) *Muslim Cultures in Indo-Iranian World During the Early Modern and Modern Periods*, Berlin: Klaus Schwarz Verlag.

Higgins, Patricia and Shoar Ghafari, Pirouz, (1995) 'Changing Perception of Iranian Identity in Elementary Textbooks,' in E. W. Farnea (ed.) *Children of the Muslim Middle East*, Austin, Texas: University of Texas Press.

Hitler, Adolf. (1943) *Mein Kampf,* Boston: Houghton Mifflin Co.

Hobsbawm, E. (1962) *The Age of Revolution, 1789–1848,* Cleveland and New York: The World Publishing Co.

——. (1983) 'Introduction: Inventing Traditions,' in E. Hobsbawm, and T. Ranger (eds.) *The Invention of Tradition,* Cambridge: Cambridge University Press.

——. (1983) 'Mass Producing Traditions: Europe 1870–1914,' in E. Hobsbawm, and T. Ranger (eds.) *The Invention of Tradition,* Cambridge: Cambridge University Press.

——. (1990) *Nations and Nationalism since 1780,* Cambridge: Cambridge University Press.

Holliday, Shabnam J. (2011) *Defining Iran: Politics of Resistance,* Surrey: Ashgate.

Humai, Jalal al-Din. (1930) *Tārīkh-i Adabīyāt-i Iran,* vols. I & II. Tabriz.

Ibn al-Nadim, Muhammad b. Ishaq. (1964) *Kitāb al-Fihrist,* Tehran.

Ibn Bibi. (1902) *Histoire des Seljoucides d'Asie Mineure,* Leiden: E. J. Brill.

Ibn Hisham. (1970) *Sirat al-Nabī,* vol. I. Cairo. ·

Ibn Isfandiyar, Muhammad b. al-Hasan. (1941) *Tārīkh-i Tabaristān,* Abbas Iqbal (ed.) Tehran: Ketabkhaneh Majlis.

Ibn Muqaffaʿ. (1962/1341) Annotated by Abdul-Hadi Ha'iri. Tehran.

Ibn Rusta, Muhammad b. Umar. (1986/1365) *al-ʿAlaq al-Nafisa,* Tehran: Amir Kabir.

Iliffe, A. H. (1968) 'Persia and the Ancient World,' in A. J. Arberry (ed.) *The Legacy of Persia,* London: Oxford University Press.

Imam Shushtari, Seyed Muhammad Ali. (1973) *Davazdah Maghāleh-i Tārīkhī,* Tehran, 1973.

Iranshahr (Journal published in Iran, 1914).

Iranshahr. (1963–1964) vols. I & II, UNESCO, Tehran: Tehran University Press.

Isfahani, Hamza b. Hasan. (1988/1367) *Tārīkh-i Sinī Muluk al-Ard wal Anbīā (Tārīkh-i Payambarān va Shāhān),* Tehran: Amir Kabir.

Isfahani, Sadik. (1832) *A Critical Essay on Various Manuscript Works-Arabic and Persian,* translated by J. C. London.

——. (1832) *The Geographical Works,* translated by J. C. London.

Islam, Nasir. (1981) 'Islam and National Identity: The Case of Pakistan and Bangladesh,' *International Journal of Middle East Studies* 13/1 February, pp. 55–72.

Istakhrī, Abu Ishiq Ibrahim. (1961/1340) *Masālik wa Mamālik*, Tehran: Nashr-i-Kitab.

Jayhani, Abolghasem b. Ahmad. (1989/1368) *Ashkāl ul-ʿAlam*, Tehran: Shirkat bih Nashr.

Joseph, Bernard. (1929) *Nationality: Its Nature and Problems*, London: George Allen & Unwin Ltd.

Kaabi, Mongi. (1983) *Les Tahirides au Ḥurasan et en Iraq*, Thèses Doctorat d'Etat, Université de Paris-Sorbonne. Published in Tunis.

Kammari, M. D. (1951) *The Development of J. V. Stalin of the Marxist-Leninist Theory of the National Question*, Moscow: Foreign Language Publishing House.

Kant, Emmanuel, (1960) 'Idea of a Universal History from a Cosmopolitan Point of View,' in P. Gardiner (ed.) *Theories of History*, Glencoe, Illinois: The Free Press.

Kashani-Sabet, Firoozeh. (1999) *Frontier Fictions: Shaping the Iranian Nation, 1804–1946*, Princeton: Princeton University Press.

———. (1998) 'Picturing the Homeland: Geography and National Identity in Late Nineteenth and Early Twentieth-century Iran,' *Journal of Historical Geography* 24/4, pp. 413–430.

———. (1997) 'The Frontier Phenomenon: Perceptions of the Land in Iranian Nationalism,' *Critique: Critical Middle Eastern Studies* 6/10 Spring, pp. 19–39.

———. (1997) 'Fragile Frontiers: Diminishing Domains of Qajar Iran,' *International Journal of Middle East Studies* 29/2 May, pp. 205–234.

Kashmirshekan, Hamid. (2010) 'The Question of Identity vis-à-vis Exoticism in Contemporary Iranian Art,' *Iranian Studies* 43/4 September, pp. 489–512.

Kasravi, Ahmad. (1977/1357) *Tārīkh-i Mashroteh-i Iran*, vols. I & II. Tehran: Amir Kabir.

Kaveh (Journal published in Berlin, 1916–1922).

Kazemzadeh, Firouz. (1962) 'Iranian Historiography,' in B. Lewis, P. M. Holt (eds.) *Historians of the Middle East*, London: Oxford University Press.

Keddie, Nikki. (1969) 'Pan-Islam as Proto-Nationalism,' *Journal of Modern History* 41/1, pp. 17–28.

———. (1962) 'Religion and Irreligion in Early Iranian Nationalism,' *Comparative Studies in Society and History* 4/3, pp. 265–295.

Kedourie, Ellie. (1960) *Nationalism*, London: Hutchinson.

Kemiläinen, Aira. (1964) *Nationalism: Problems Concerning the Word, the Concept and Classification,* Jayvaskylan, Kasvatusopillinen-Korkea Koulu.

Khanlari, Parviz Natel. (1964/1343) *Zabān Shenāsī va Zabān-i Farsi,* Tehran: Amir Kabir.

Kinneir, John MacDonald. (1813) *A Geographical Memoir of the Persian Empire,* London.

Kirmani, Nazim al-Islam. (1982/1361) *Tārīkh-i Bīdārī Iranian,* vols. I & II. Tehran: Agah.

Klima, Otakar. (1967) 'The Official Name of the Pre-Islamic Iranian State,' *Sir J. J. Zarthoshti Madressa Centenary Volume,* Bombay, pp. 144–146.

Koenigsberger, H. (1975) 'Spain,' in Orest Ranum (ed.) *National Consciousness, History and Political Culture in Early Modern Europe,* Baltimore: The Johns Hopkins University Press.

Kohn, Hans. (1962) *The Age of Nationalism,* New York: Harper & Row Publishers.

——. (1929) *A History of Nationalism in the East,* New York: Harcourt, Brace & Co.

——. (1946) *Prophets and Peoples,* New York: The Macmillan Co.

Koichi, Haneda. (1984) 'The Meaning of Iran: Preliminary Essay on the Emergence of 'Iranian' Consciousness,' *Journal of Asian and African Studies,* 27, pp. 188–193 (in Japanese).

Kohl, Philip L. (1998) 'Nationalism and Archaeology: On the Constructions of Nations and the Reconstructions of the Remote Past,' *Annual Review of Anthropology* 27, pp. 223–246.

Krieger, Leonard. (1975) 'Germany,' in Orest Ranum (ed.) *National Consciousness, History, and Political Culture in Early-Modern Europe,* Baltimore: The Johns Hopkins University Press.

Krifka, Manfred. (1989) "Sprache," *Geo: Wissen,* pp. 288–92.

Krusinski, Judasz Tadeusz. (1973) *History of the Late Revolutions of Persia,* London, 1740; reprinted by New York: Arno Press.

Kurzman, Charles, and Owens, Lynn. (2002) 'The Sociology of the Intellectuals, *Annual Review of Sociology* 28, pp. 63–90.

Lamberg-Karlovsky, C. C. (2002) 'Archaeology and Language: The Indo-Iranians,' *Current Anthropology* 43/1 February, pp. 63–88.

Lambton, Ann K. S. (1987) *Qajar Persia: Eleven Studies,* Austin, Texas: University of Texas Press.

——. (1981) 'Social Change in Persia in the Nineteenth Century,' *Asian and African Studies* 15, pp. 123–148.

——. (1957) 'The Impact of the West on Persia,' *International Affairs* 33/1, pp. 12–25.

Lane-Poole, Stanley. (1876) *The Coins of the Mohammadan Dynasties*, London.

——. (1881) *The Coins of the Mongol*, London.

La Palombara, Joseph. (1974) *Politics Within Nations*, Englewood Cliffs, New Jersey :Prentice-Hall.

Lazard, George. (1971) 'Pahlavi, Parsi, Dari les Langues de l'Iran d'Après Ibn al Muqaffaʻ,' in C. E. Bosworth (ed.) *Iran and Islam*, Edinburgh: Edinburgh University Press.

——. (1975) 'The Rise of the New Persian Language,' in R. Frye (ed.) *Cambridge History of Iran*, vol. 4, Cambridge: Cambridge University Press.

Leopold, Joan. (1974) 'British Applications of the Aryan Theory of Race to India, 1850–1870,' *The English Historical Review* 89/352 July, pp. 578–603.

Levy, L. (1968) 'Persia and the Arabs,' in A. J. Arberry (ed.) *The Legacy of Persia*, London: Oxford University Press.

Lockhart, L. (1968) 'Persia as seen by the West,' in A. J. Arberry (ed.) *The Legacy of Persia*, Oxford: Oxford University Press.

Lorenz, Konrad. (1983) *Der Abbau des Menschlichen*, München: Piper Verlag GmbH.

Low, Alfred. (1958) *Lenin on the Question of Nationality*, New York: Bookman Associates.

M. J. (1984) 'The Textbooks of the Islamic Republic,' *Iran Nameh* III, pp. 1–17 (in Farsi).

Madelung, Wilfred. (1969) 'The Assumption of the Title Shahanshah by the Buyids and the 'Reign of the Dayiam (Dawlat al-Daylam)',' *Journal of Near Eastern Studies* 28, pp. 168–183.

Mahdjoub, Mohammad Djaʻfar. (1990) "The Indian Cultural Heritage and Its Effect on the Enrichment of the Islamic Civilization in Iran," *Iran Nameh* III, 2, pp. 177–195 (in Farsi).

Malcolm, Sir John. (1829) *The History of Persia*, vols. I & II. London: John Murray.

Marʻashi Safavi, Mirza Khalil. (1983/1362) *Madjmal ul-Tawārīkh*, Tehran.

Marsden, William. (1869) *The Plates of the Oriental Coins*, London.

Masʻudī, Ali b. Husayn. (1938) *al-Tanbīh wal Ashrāf*, Baghdad.

——. (1965) *Muruj ul-Dhahab wal Maʻden al-Jawhar*, vol. I. Beirut.

Marashi, Afshin. (2008) *Nationalizing Iran: Culture, Power, and the State, 1870–1940*, Seattle: University of Washington Press.

Massé, Henri. (1935) *Firdousi et l'Epopée Nationale,* Paris: Librairie Academique Perrin.

——. (1952) 'Les Sassanides,' in *La Civilisation Iranienne: Perse, Afghanistan, Iran Extérieure,* Paris: Payot.

Massignon, Louis. (1990) 'Les penseurs Iraniens et l'éssor de la civilisation arabe,' *L'Âme de l'Iran,* sous la direction de R. Grousset, L. Massignon, H. Massé. Paris: Albin Michel.

Matin-Asgari, Afshin. (2012) 'The Academic Debate on Iranian Identity: Nation and Empire Entangled,' in Abbas Amanat and Farzin Vejdani (eds.) *Iran Facing Others: Identity Boundaries in a Historical Perspective*, New York: Palgrave Macmillan.

McDowall, David. (1985) "The Kurds," *The Minority Rights,* Group Report 23, June, pp. 3–31.

Mercer, Jonathan. (1995) 'Anarchy and Identity,' *International Organization* 49/2 Spring, pp. 229–252.

Meskub, Shahrukh. (1988) *Zabān va Mellīat*, 2nd ed. Paris.

Michalak, Laurance. (1974) *An Analysis of Bulletins and Memoirs of the Anthropological Society of Paris,* Berkeley, CA: University of California, (unpublished paper).

——. (1974) *Carlton Coon: The Hemingway of Anthropology,* Berkeley, California: University of California, (unpublished paper).

Miles, George. (1971) 'The Coinage of the Bawanids of Tabaristan,' in C. E. Bosworth (ed.) *Iran and Islam,* Edinburgh: Edinburgh University Press.

Millward, W. (1976) 'Iran,' in R. M. Savory (ed.) *Introduction to Islamic Civilization*, Cambridge: Cambridge University Press.

Minorsky, Vladimir. (1964) 'Geographical Factors in Persian Art,' *Iranica, Twenty Articles,* Tehran: University of Tehran.

——. (1955) 'Iran: Opposition, Martyrdom and Revolt,' in G. E. von Grunebaum (ed.) *Unity and Variety in Muslim Civilization,* Chicago: The University of Chicago Press.

——. (1932) *La Domination des Dailamites*, Paris: Librairie Ernest Leroux.

——. (1964) 'The Older Preface to the Shahnama,' *Iranica, Twenty Articles,* Tehran: University of Tehran.

Mirahmadi, Maryam. (1984/1363) *Dīn va Madhab dar Asr-i Safavī,* Tehran: Amir Kabir.

Mirchondi. (1808) *Historia Samanidarum*, Göttingen.

———. (1838) *Historia Seldschukidarum*, Gissen.

Moʿīn, Muhammad. (1951–63) *Farhang-i Farsi*, 5 vols. Tehran: Ketabkhaneh Zavvar.

Mohl, Jules. (1843) 'Extraits du Modjmel el-Tawarikh relatifs à l'histoire de la Perse,' *Journal Asiatique*, I, pp. 385–432.

Molé, M. (1965) *L'Iran Ancien*, Paris: Bloud & Gay.

Montagu, Ashley. (1965) *The Idea of Race*, Lincoln: University of Nebraska Press.

Morgan, David. (1988) *Medieval Persia, 1040–1797*, London and New York: Longman.

Morony, Michael G. (1984) *Iraq after the Muslim Conquest*, Princeton: Princeton University Press.

Moscati, Sabatino, A. Spilater, E. Ullendor, and W. von Sodor. (1964) *An Introduction to the Comparative Grammar of the Semitic languages*, Weisbaden.

Moscati, Sabatino. (1960) *Ancient Semitic Civilizations*, New York: Capricorn Books.

———. (1955) 'Per una storia dell' antica Siʾa,' *Rivisita degli Studi Orientali* XXX, pp. 251–267.

Mostaufī, Hamdullāh. (1957/1336) *Nodhat ul-Qulub*, Tehran.

———. (1985/1364) *Tārīkh-i Gozīdeh*, Tehran: Amir Kabir.

Mottahedeh, Roy P. (1976) 'The Shuʾubiyah Controversy and the Social History of Early Islamic Iran,' *International Journal of Middle East Studies* 7, pp. 161–182.

———. (2012) 'The Idea of Iran in the Buyid Dominions,' in Edmund Herzig and Sarah Stewart (eds.) *Early Islamic Iran: The Idea of Iran*, vol. V, London: I. B. Tauris.

Muhammad Rahim, Muhammad Reza. (1885) *Makhzan al-Inshā*, Tehran.

Munck, Ronald. (1986) *The Different Dialogue: Marxism and Nationalism*, London: Atlantic Highlands.

Nafīsī, Saʿīd. (1985/1364) *Tārīkh-i Ijtemāʿi va Sīyāsī-i Iran*, vols. I & II. Tehran: Entesharat Boniad.

Najmabadi, Afsaneh. (1997) 'The Erotic Vatan [Homeland] as Beloved and Mother: To Love, to Possess, and to Protect,' *Comparative Studies in Society and History* 39/3 July, pp. 442–467.

Nash, Geoffrey. (2005) *From Empire to Orient: Travellers to the Middle East 1830–1926*, London: I. B. Tauris.

Nateq, Homa. (1988) *Iran dar Rāh Yābī Farhangī, 1834–1848*, London: Payam Publisher.

Nava'i, Abdul-Husayn. (1987/1366) *Iran va Jahān: Az Mughul ta Qājārieh*, Tehran: Nashr-i Homa.

———. (1973/1352) *Shah Abbas*, vol. I. Tehran: Entesharat Boniad Farhangi-i Iran.

———. (1968/1347) *Shah Ismā'īl Safavī*, Tehran: Entesharat Boniad Farhangi-i Iran.

Nima Kitab, (Ketab-e Nima). (1990/1369) *Zabān va Huvīyat-i Mellī*, Los Angeles: Nima Foundation Inc.

Nizam ul-Mulk. (1978) *Sīyāsat Nāmeh (The Book of Government or Rules for Kings)*, London: Routledge & Keagan Paul.

Nock, Arthur Darby. (1949) 'The Problem of Zoroaster,' *American Journal of Archaeology* 53/3 July–September, pp. 272–285.

Nöldeke, Theodor. (1920) *Das Iranische Nationalepos*, Berlin and Leipzig.

———. (1892) *Sketches from Eastern History*, London and Edinburgh: Adam and Charles Black.

Olmstead, Albert. (1966) *History of the Persian Empire*, Chicago: The University of Chicago Press.

Omidsalar, Mahmoud. (2011) *Poetics and Politics of Iran's National Epic, The Shahnameh*, New York: Palgrave Macmillan.

Oppert, Jules. (1883) 'Le Peuple et la langue des Mèdes,' in J. Darmesteter (ed.) *Études Iraniennes*, vol. II, Paris.

Parviz, Abbas. (1972/1351) *Qīyām Iranian dar Rāh-i Tajdīd Mahd va Azemat-i Iran*, Tehran: Entesharat Elmi.

Petruchevsky, I. (1985) *Islam in Iran*, London: Athlone.

Pictet, Adolph. (1877) *Les Origines Indo-Européennes: ou les Aryans Primitif*, Paris.

Pīrnīā, Hasan. (1983/1362) *Iran Bastan*, vols. I–III. Tehran: Doniya-i Ketab.

Pizzi, Italo. (1894) *Storia della Poesia Persiana*, vols. I & II, Torino.

Pocock, John. (1975) 'England,' in Orest Ranum (ed.) *National Consciousness, History, and Political Culture* in *Early-Modern Europe*, Baltimore: The Johns Hopkins University Press.

Poliakov, Leon. (1974) *The Aryan Myth: A History of Racist and Nationalist Ideas in Europe*, Translated by E. Howard. New York: New American Library.

Potts, D. T. (2005) 'Cyrus the Great and the Kingdom of Anshan,' in Vesta Sarkhosh Curtis and Sarah Stewart (eds.) *Birth of the Persian Empire*, London: I. B. Tauris, 2005.

Pourshariati, Parvaneh. (2008) *Decline and Fall of the Sasanian Empire*, New York: I. B. Tauris.

Puech, Henri-Charles. (1952) 'La Situation Religieuse dans l'Iran Occidental à l'avènement des Sassanides,' *La Civilisation Iranienne, Perse, Afghanistan, Iran Extérieure*, Paris: Payot.

Qā'im Maqāmī, Jahāngir. (1969/1348) *Yek sad-u Panjāh Sanad-i Tārīkhī*, Tehran: Chapkhaneh-i Artesh.

Qānun (Journal published by Malkum Khan in London 1890–1891, Numbers: 1–41.

Quatremère, E. M. (1839) 'De l'Ouvrage Persan qui pour titre Moudjmel attawarikh: Sommaire des histoires,' *Journal Asiatique* VII, pp. 246–285.

Rahimi-Laridjani, Fereydoun. (1988) Die *Entwicklung der Bewässerungslandwirtschaft im Iran bis in sasadisch-frühislamische Zeit*, Wiesbaden.

Ram, Haggay. (2000) 'The Immemorial Iranian Nation? School Textbooks and Historical Memory in Post-Revolutionary Iran,' *Nations and Nationalism* 6/1, pp. 67–90.

Ranking, George S. A. (1910) *A History of the Minor Dynasties of Persia* (an extract from the *Habīb us-Siyār* of Khondamir), London: Oxford University Press.

Rawlinson, George. (1876) *The Seventh Great Oriental Monarchy*, London: Longmans, Green & Co.

Renan, Ernest. (1862) *Peuples Sémitiques dans l'Histoire de la Civilisation*, Paris.

Rendal, Gerald H. (1889) *The Cradle of the Aryans*, London: The Macmillan Co.

Renfrew, Colin. (1987) *Archaeology and Language: The Puzzle of Indo-European Origins*, New York: Cambridge University Press.

Richter-Bernburg, Lutz. (1974) "Linguistic Shu'ūbīya and Early Neo-Persian Prose," *Journal of the American Oriental Society* 94/1 January–March, pp. 55–64.

Ringbom, Lars-Ivar. (1967) 'The Seven Keshvars of the Earth,' Sir *J. J. Zarthoshti Madressa Centenary Volume*, Bombay, pp. 9–16.

Ringer, Monica. (2012) 'Iranian Nationalism and Zoroastrian Identity: Between Cyrus and Zoroaster,' in Abbas Amanat and Farzin Vejdani (eds.) *Iran Facing Others: Identity Boundaries in a Historical Perspective*, New York: Palgrave Macmillan.

Risso, Patricia. (1989) 'Muslim Identity in Maritime Trade: General Observation and Some Evidence from the 18th-Century

Persian Gulf/Indian Ocean Region.' *International Journal of Middle East Studies* 21/3 August, pp. 381–392.

Rodinson, Maxime. (1987) *Europe and the Mystique of Islam*, Seattle: University of Washington Press.

Rosenthal, Franz. (1952) *A History of Muslim Historiography*, Leiden: E. J. Brill.

Roskin, Michael. (1977) *Other Governments of Europe*, Englewood Cliffs, New Jersey: Prentice-Hall.

Ruiz, Miguel. (2005) *Les quatre accords toltèques: La voie de la liberté personnelle*, Archamps: Editions Jouvence.

Russell, Bertrand. (1972) *A History of Western Philosophy*, New York: Simon & Shuster.

Sadīq, Isa. (1974) 'Le Role de l'Iran dans la Renaissance,' *Hommage Universel* III, pp. 381–397.

———. (1975/1354) *Tārīkh-i Farhang-i Iran*, Tehran: Entesharat Danishgah-i Tehran.

Sadjadi, Zia-Oddin. (1975) 'Mithra et le Christ dans la Poésie de Khaghani: VIᵉ Siècle de L'Hegire – XIIᵉ Siècle,' in *Iran Ancien*, Paris: L'Asiatheque.

Safā, Zabīhullah. (1956/1335) *Tārīkh-i Adabīyāt dar Iran*, vol. I–IV, Tehran: Amir Kabir & Ferdos.

———. (1968/1347) *Tārīkh-i Ulum va Adabīyāt-i Irani*, Tehran: Ibn Sina Library.

Said, Edward. (1979) *Orientalism*, New York: Vintage Books.

Safran, Janina M. (2001) 'Identity and Differentiation in Ninth-Century al-Andalus,' *Speculum* 76/3 July, pp. 573–598.

Sand, Shlomo. (2009) *The Invention of the Jewish People*, London: Verso.

Sarkhosh Curtis, Vesta. (2007) 'The Iranian Revival in the Parthian Period,' in Vesta Sarkhosh Curtis and Sarah Stewart (eds.) *The Age of the Parthians: The Idea of Iran*, vol. II, London: I. B. Tauris.

Savory, Roger. (1981) 'L'Empire du Lion et du Soleil,' in Bernard Lewis (ed.) *L'Islam d'Hier à Aujourd'hui*, Paris: Elsevier Bordas.

Sayce, A. H. (1885) *The Ancient Empire s of the East*, New York: Charles Scribner's Sons.

Sayyad (al), Muhammad Mahmoud. (1971) *Min Wijhat ul-Jughrāphia*, Beirut.

Schimmel, Annemarie (ed.). (1966) *Friedrich Rückert, 1788–1866: Übersetzungen persischer Poesie*, Wiesbaden: Harrassowitz.

Schlegel, Friedrich von. (1967) 'On the Languages and Wisdom of the Indians,' in W. P. Lehmann (ed.) *A Reader in Nineteenth Century Historical Indo-European Linguists*, Bloomington: Indiana University Press.

Schmitt, R. (1987) 'Aryans,' *Encyclopaedia Iranica*, vol. II (7), E. Yarshater (ed.) London and New York: Routledge & Kegan Paul. pp. 684–687.

Schwab, Raymond. (1950) *La Renaissance Orientale*, Paris: Payot.

Shahrastani, Muhammad b. Abdulkarim. (1979/1358) *al-Milal wal-Nihal*, vols. I–II. Tehran: Offset Co.

Shahbazi, Shahpur. (2005) 'The History of the Idea of Iran,' in Vesta Sarkhosh Curtis and Sarah Stewart (eds.) *Birth of the Persian Empire*, London: I. B. Tauris.

Silvestre de Sacy, A. I. (1793) *Mémoires sur Diverses Antiquités de la Perse*. Paris.

Skjærvø, P. O. (2005) 'The Achaemenids and the Avesta,' in Vesta Sarkhosh Curtis and Sarah Stewart (eds.) *Birth of the Persian Empire*, London: I. B. Tauris.

Smedley, Audrey. (1998) 'Race and the Construction of Human Identity,' *American Anthropologist* 100/3 September, pp. 690–702.

Snyder, Louis L. (1968) *The New Nationalism*, Ithaca, New York: Cornell University Press.

Spegno, Maria Serena. (1982–1989) 'Italia,' 'Italiani,' *Letteratura Italiana*, vol. V. Torino: Giuilo Einaudi Editore.

Spooner, Brian. (1983) 'Who are the Baluch? A Preliminary investigation into the dynamics of an ethnic identity from Qajar Iran,' in *Qajar Iran*, Edinburgh: Edinburgh University Press.

Spuler, Bertold. (1962) 'The Evolution of Persian Historiography,' in B. Lewis, P. M. Holt (eds.) *Historians of the Middle East*, London: Oxford University Press.

——. (1955) 'Iran: The Persistent Heritage,' in G. E. von Grunebaum (ed.) *Unity and Variety in Muslim World*, Chicago: The University of Chicago Press.

——. (1969) *The Muslim World: Part III, The Mongol Period*, translated by F. R. C. Bagley. Leiden: E. J. Brill.

Stern, S. M. (1971) 'Ya'qub the Coppersmith and Persian National Sentiment,' in C. E. Bosworth (ed.) *Iran and Islam*, Edinburgh: Edinburgh University Press.

Sur Isrāfil (Journal published by A. A. Dehkhodā in Iran and Switzerland, 1907–1909), numbers 1–32, 13.

Sykes, Sir Percy. (1969) *A History of Persia*, vols. I & II, London: Routledge & Kegan Paul.

Tabarī, Muhammad Ibn Jarir. (1983–1985) *Tārikh*, I–XVI, Tehran.

Tagore, Rabindranath. (1917) *Nationalism*, New York: The MacMillan Co.

Talbot, Cynthia. (1995) 'Inscribing the Other, Inscribing the Self: Hindu-Muslim Identities in Pre-Colonial India,' *Comparative Studies in Society and History* 37/4 October, pp. 692–722.

Tārīkh-i Naw (1939/1318) (tenth-grade history textbook), Tehran.

Tārīkh-i Naw (1930/1309) (secondary-school history textbook), Tehran.

Tārīkh-i Sistān. (1956/1335) Malik ul-Shuara-i Bahar (ed.) Tehran: Kitabkhaneh Zavvar.

Tashnar, Maqbul Ahmad. (1989/1368) *Tārikhche-i Jughrāphiā dar Tamadon-i Islamī*, Tehran: Boniad Daerot ul-Muʻarif-i Islami.

Tavakoli-Targhi, Mohamad. (2002) 'From Patriotism to Matriotism: A Tropological Study of Iranian Nationalism, 1870–1909,' *International Journal of Middle East Studies* 34/2 May, pp. 217–238.

———. (2001) *Refashioning Iran: Orientalism, Occidentalism, and Historiography*, New York: Palgrave.

———. (1996) 'Contested Memories: Narrative Structures and Allegorical Meanings of Iran's Pre-Islamic History.' *Iranian Studies* vol. 29, No. 1/2 Winter-Spring, pp. 149–175.

Tavernier, Jean Baptiste. (1679) *Voyages en Perse*, Paris; reprinted Paris, 1964.

Thapar, Romila. (2003) *The Penguin History of Early India: from the Origin to AD 1300*, New Delhi: Penguin Books.

Thomas, Lewis V. (1951) 'The National and International Relations of Turkey,' in T. C. Young (ed.) *Near Eastern Culture and Society*, Princeton: Princeton University Press.

Tzoref-Ashkenazi, Chen. (2006) 'India and the Identity of Europe: The Case of Friedrich Schlegel,' *Journal of the History of Ideas* 67/4 October, pp. 713–734.

Ulc, Otto. (1984) 'Czechoslovakia,' in T. Rakowska-Harm-stone (ed.) *Communism in Eastern Europe*, Bloomington: Indiana University Press.

Varheram, Gholamreza. (1987/1366) *Tārīkh-i Sīyāsī va Ijtemā'ī-i Iran dar Asr-i Zand,* Tehran: Moassesseh Entesharat-i Mo'in.

Vaziri, Mostafa. (1990) 'Dogma Islamico e Problemi di Storiografia,' *SYNESIS* (Milano) 2, pp. 29–33.

———. (1992) *The Emergence of Islam: Prophecy, Imamate, and Messianism in Perspective,* New York: Paragon House.

———. (2001) *Quantum Poetry: Verses of Hafiz and Views on Interconnections,* Innsbruck: Dream & Reality and MEPO Publications.

———. (2012) *Buddhism in Iran: An Anthropological Approach to Traces and Influences,* New York: Palgrave Macmillan.

Vesel, Živa. (1986) *Les Encyclopédies Persanes,* Paris: Edition Recherche sur les civilisations.

Voyages de Pietro della Valle, (1745) vol. II–IV, Rouen.

Voyages de Texeira au l'Histoire des Rois des Perse, *(1681) Paris.*

Watson, Robert Grant. (1866) *A History of Persia from the Beginning of the Nineteenth Century to the Year 1858,* London.

Wiesehöfer, Josef. (2006) 'Statt einer Einleitung: 'Randkultur' oder 'Nabel der Welt'? Das Sasanidenreich und der Westen. Anmerkungen eines Althistorikers,' in Josef Wiesehöfer and Philip Huyse (eds.) *Ērān und Anērān: Studien zu den Bezeichungen zwischen dem Sasanidenreich und der Mittelmeerwelt,* München: Franz Steiner Verlag.

Wilson, C. E. (1922) 'The Formation of Modern Persian, the Beginnings and Progress of the Literature, and the So-Called Renaissance,' *Bulletin of the School of Oriental Studies* 2/2, pp. 215–223.

Wyatt, William F. (1970) 'The Indo-Europeanization of Greece,' in G. Cardona, H. M. Hoenigswald, A. Senn (eds.) *Indo-European and Indo-Europeans,* Philadelphia: University of Pennsylvania Press.

Wickens, G. M. (1976) 'Persian literature: an affirmation of identity,' in R. M. Savory (ed.) *Introduction to Islamic Civilization,* Cambridge: Cambridge University Press.

Wilber, Donald. (1981) *Iran Past and Present,* Princeton: Princeton University Press.

———. (1975) *Riza Shah Pahlavi: The Resurrection and Reconstruction of Iran,* New York: Exposition Press.

Wolff, Fritz. (1935) *Glossar zu Firdosis Schahname,* Berlin.

Ya'qubi, Ahmad b. (1960) *Tārīkh al-Ya'qubī,* vol. I, Beirut.

Yapp, M. E. (1962) 'Two British Historians of Persia,' in B. Lewis, P.M. Holt (eds.) *Historians of the Middle East,* London: Oxford University Press, 1962.

Yāqut al-Hamawī. (1968/1347) translated Muhammad P. Gonabadi. Tehran: Ibn Sina Library.

Yarshater, Ehsan. (1985) 'The Absence of Median and Achaemenian Kings in Iran's Traditional History,' *Iran Nameh* III, pp. 2191–213 (in Farsi).

———. (1958/1337) *Dāstānhā-yi Iran Bāstān,* Tehran: Nashri-i Ketab.

———. (1988) 'Iran is 'Persia' in Western World and not 'Iran',' *Rahavard,* vols. V, VI, 20/21, pp. 70–75, (in Farsi).

———. (1983) 'Iranian National History,' in E. Yarshater (ed.) *Cambridge History of Iran,* vol. 3(1), Cambridge: Cambridge University Press.

Young, T. Culyer. (1951) 'Interaction of Islamic and Western Thought in Iran,' in T. C. Young (ed.) *Near Eastern Culture and Society,* Princeton: Princeton University Press.

———. (1951) 'The National and International Relations of Iran,' in T. C. Young (ed.) *Near Eastern Culture and Society,* Princeton: Princeton University Press.

Yule, Henry Colonel. (1871) *The Book of Ser Marco Polo,* London.

Zhao, Gang. (2006) 'Reinventing China: Imperial Qing Ideology and the Rise of Modern Chinese National Identity in the Early Twentieth Century,' *Modern China* 32/1 January, pp. 3–30.

Zarinkub, Abdul Husayn. (1957/1336) *Doo Gharn Soukut,* Tehran: Amir Kabir.

Zeman, Z. A. B. (1961) *The Break-up of the Habsburg Empire, 1914–1918,* London: Oxford University Press.

Zia-Ebrahimi, Reza. (2011) 'Self-Orientalization and Dislocation: The Uses and Abuses of the 'Aryan' Discourse in Iran,' *Iranian Studies* 44/4 July, pp. 445–472.

Zimmern, Alfred. (1918) *Nationality and Government — with Other Wartime Essays,* New York: Robert M. McBridge & Co.

Zubaida, Sami. (2002) 'The Fragments Imagine the Nation: The Case of Iraq,' *International Journal of Middle East Studies* 34/2 May, pp. 205–215.

INDEX

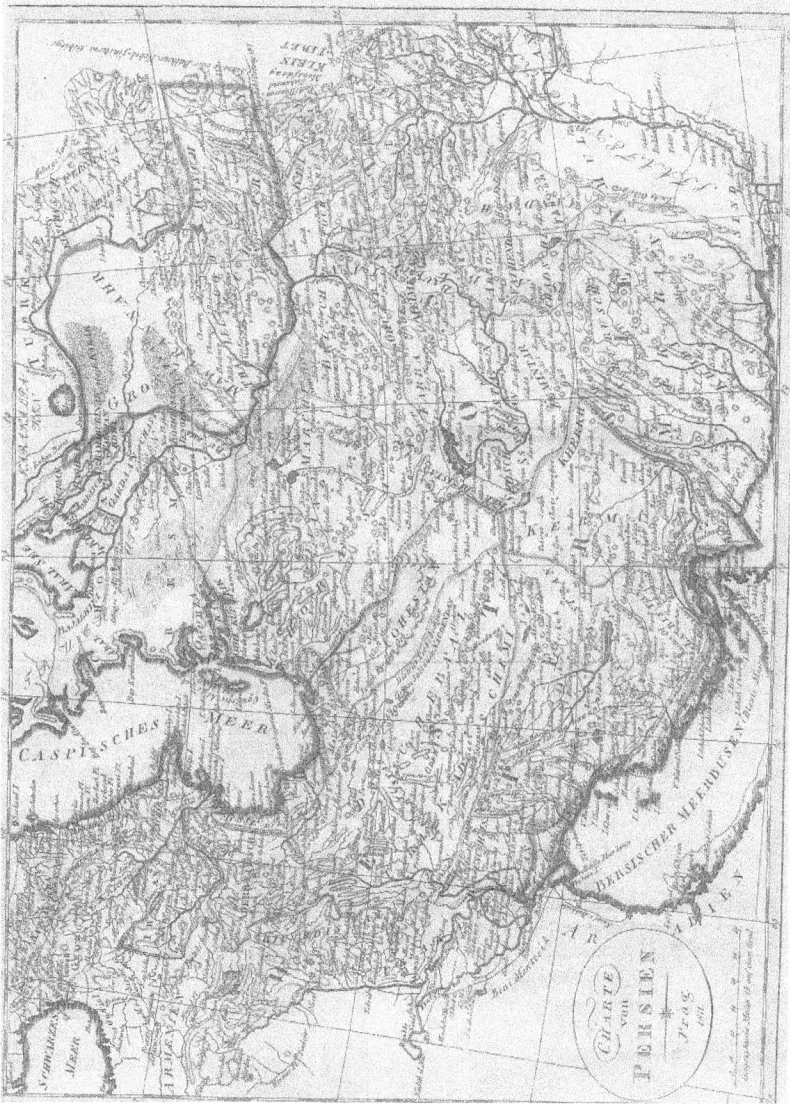

Map of Iran, produced in Prague in 1811
(private collection: courtesy of Pourmand family in Innsbruck)

www.ingramcontent.com/pod-product-compliance
Lightning Source LLC
Chambersburg PA
CBHW071834270326
41929CB00013B/1993